Workshop on Universal Dependencies 2017

Held at NODALIDA 2017

NEALT Proceedings Series Volume 31

Gothenburg, Sweden
22 May 2017

Editors:

Marie-Catherine de Marneffe
Joakim Nivre
Sebastian Schuster

ISBN: 978-1-5108-4169-7

Preface

These proceedings include the program and papers that are presented at the first workshop on Universal Dependencies, held in conjunction with NoDaLiDa in Gothenburg (Sweden) on May 22, 2017.

Universal Dependencies (UD) is a framework for cross-linguistically consistent treebank annotation that has so far been applied to over 50 languages (http://universaldependencies.org/). The framework is aiming to capture similarities as well as idiosyncrasies among typologically different languages (e.g., morphologically rich languages, pro-drop languages, and languages featuring clitic doubling). The goal in developing UD was not only to support comparative evaluation and cross-lingual learning but also to facilitate multilingual natural language processing and enable comparative linguistic studies.

After a period of rapid growth since the release of the first guidelines in October 2014 and the release of the second version of the guidelines in December 2016, we felt it was time to take stock and reflect on the theory and practice of UD, its use in research and development, and its future goals and challenges. We are returning to Gothenburg where UD, in its actual implementation, was born in the spring of 2014.

We received 29 submissions of which 24 were accepted. Submissions covered several topics: the workshop feature papers describing treebank conversion or creation, while others focus on resources useful for annotation; some work targets specific syntactic constructions and which analysis to adopt, sometimes with critiques of the choices made in UD; some papers exploit UD resources for parsing or downstream tasks, often in a cross-lingual setting, and others discuss the relation of UD to different frameworks.

We are honored to have two invited speakers: Mirella Lapata (School of Informatics, University of Edinburgh, Scotland), with a talk on "Universal Semantic Parsing", and William Croft (Department of Linguistics, University of New Mexico, USA), speaking about "Using Typology to Develop Guidelines for Universal Dependencies". Our invited speakers' work target different aspects of UD: Mirella Lapata's talk is an instance of how UD facilitates building downstream applications which can operate multilingually, whereas William Croft will address how UD and typological universals intersect.

We are grateful to the program committee, who worked hard and on a tight schedule to review the submissions and provided authors with valuable feedback. We thank Google, Inc. for its sponsorship which made it possible to feature two invited talks. We also want to thank the organizing committee for their help; in particular Francis Tyers and Sebastian Schuster for their invaluable help with the conference software and these proceedings, as well as Sampo Pyysalo for setting up the website and providing immediate response for updating it.

We tried to set up the program to favor discussions, and we wish all participants a productive workshop!

Marie-Catherine de Marneffe and Joakim Nivre

Workshop Co-Chairs:

Marie-Catherine de Marneffe, The Ohio State University, USA
Joakim Nivre, Uppsala University, Sweden

Organizing Committee:

Filip Ginter, University of Turku, Finland
Yoav Goldberg, Ben Gurion University, Israel
Sampo Pyysalo, University of Cambridge, UK
Sebastian Schuster, Stanford University, USA
Reut Tsarfaty, Open University of Israel, Israel
Francis Tyers, University of Tromsø, Norway

Program Committee:

Çağri Çöltekin, Tübingen, Germany
Kim Gerdes, Paris III, France
Jan Hajič, Charles University in Prague, Czech Republic
Olga Lyashevskaya, National Research University Higher School of Economics, Russia
Ryan McDonald, Google, UK
Teresa Lynn, Dublin City University, Ireland
Lilja Øvrelid, University of Oslo, Norway
Nathan Schneider, Georgetown University, USA
Amir Zeldes, Georgetown University, USA
Dan Zeman, Charles University in Prague, Czech Republic

Invited Speakers:

Mirella Lapata, University of Edinburgh, UK
William Croft, University of New Mexico, USA

Table of Contents

Workshop Program

Monday, May 22, 2017

9:00–10:15   **Opening & Invited Talk**

9:00–9:15   Opening Remarks

9:15–10:15   Invited Talk: *Universal Semantic Parsing*
Mirella Lapata

10:15–10:45   **Coffee Break**

10:45–12:00   **Resources and Applications**

10:45–10:57   *Studying Consistency in UD Treebanks with INESS-Search* (in TLT14)
Koenraad De Smedt, Victoria Rosén and Paul Meurer

10:57–11:09   *Udapi: Universal API for Universal Dependencies*
Martin Popel, Zdeněk Žabokrtský and Martin Vojtek

11:09–11:21   *Universal Dependencies to Logical Forms with Negation Scope* (in SemBEaR 2017)
Federico Fancellu, Siva Reddy, Adam Lopez and Bonnie Webber

11:21–11:33   *Does Syntactic Informativity Predict Word Length? A Cross-Linguistic Study Based on the Universal Dependencies Corpora*
Natalia Levshina

11:33–11:45   *Automatic Morpheme Segmentation and Labeling in Universal Dependencies Resources*
Miikka Silfverberg and Mans Hulden

11:45–11:57   *Towards Universal Morpho-Syntactic Processing: Closing the Morphology Gap*
(non-archival submission)
Amir More and Reut Tsarfaty

12:00–13:30   **Lunch & Treebanks (Posters)**

Increasing Return on Annotation Investment: The Automatic Construction of a Universal Dependency Treebank for Dutch
Gosse Bouma and Gertjan Van Noord

Converting the TüBa-D/Z Treebank of German to Universal Dependencies
Çağrı Çöltekin, Ben Campbell, Erhard Hinrichs and Heike Telljohann

Universal Dependencies for Afrikaans
Peter Dirix, Liesbeth Augustinus, Daniel van Niekerk and Frank Van Eynde

Towards Universal Dependencies for Learner Chinese
John Lee, Herman Leung and Keying Li

Universal Dependencies for Greek
Prokopis Prokopidis and Haris Papageorgiou

Universal Dependencies for Serbian in Comparison with Croatian and Other Slavic Languages (in BSNLP 2017)
Tanja Samardžić, Mirjana Starović, Željko Agić and Nikola Ljubešić

Toward Universal Dependencies for Ainu
Hajime Senuma and Akiko Aizawa

Universal Dependencies for Arabic (in WANLP 2017)
Dima Taji, Nizar Habash and Daniel Zeman

13:30–15:30   Invited Talk & Constructions and Annotation

13:30–14:30   Invited Talk: *Using Typology to Develop Guidelines for Universal Dependencies*
William Croft

14:30–14:36   *Gapping Constructions in Universal Dependencies v2*
Sebastian Schuster, Matthew Lamm and Christopher D. Manning

14:36–14:42   *Elliptic Constructions: Spotting Patterns in UD Treebanks*
Kira Droganova and Daniel Zeman

14:42–14:48   *Swedish Prepositions are not Pure Function Words*
Lars Ahrenberg

14:48–14:54   *Estonian Copular and Existential Constructions as an UD Annotation Problem*
Kadri Muischnek and Kaili Müürisep

14:54–15:30   Panel and Discussion
Lars Ahrenberg, Kira Droganova, Kadri Muischnek and Sebastian Schuster

15:30–16:00   Coffee Break

16:00–17:30   Syntax and Parsing & Closing

16:00–16:12   *Cross-Lingual Parser Selection for Low-Resource Languages*
Željko Agić

16:12–16:24   *Universal Dependency Evaluation*
Joakim Nivre and Chiao-Ting Fang

Invited Talk: Mirella Lapata, University of Edinburgh

Universal Semantic Parsing

The Universal Dependencies (UD) initiative seeks to develop cross-linguistically consistent annotation guidelines as well as a large number of uniformly annotated treebanks for many languages. Such resources could advance multilingual applications of parsing, improve comparability of evaluation results, and enable cross-lingual learning. Seeking to exploit the benefits of UD for natural language understanding, we introduce UDepLambda, a semantic interface for UD that maps natural language to logical forms, representing underlying predicate-argument structures, in an almost language-independent manner.

Our framework is based on DepLambda (Reddy et al., 2016), a recently developed method that converts English Stanford Dependencies to logical forms. DepLambda works only for English, and cannot process dependency graphs, which allow to handle complex phenomena such as control. In contrast, UDepLambda applies to any language for which UD annotations are available and can also process dependency graphs. We evaluate our approach on question answering against Freebase. To facilitate multilingual evaluation, we provide German and Spanish translations of the WebQuestions and GraphQuestions datasets. Results show that UDepLambda outperforms strong baselines across languages and datasets. For English, it achieves the strongest result to date on GraphQuestions, with competitive results on WebQuestions.

References

Siva Reddy, Oscar Täckström, Michael Collins, Tom Kwiatkowski, Dipanjan Das, Mark Steedman, and Mirella Lapata. Transforming dependency structures to logical forms for semantic parsing. *Transactions of the Association for Computational Linguistics*, 4:127–140, 2016.

Invited Talk: William Croft, University of New Mexico

Using Typology to Develop Guidelines for Universal Dependencies

1. Linguistic Typology and Universal Dependencies

Language structures are incredibly diverse. Although typologists have discovered many language universals, a common saying in the field is that the only exceptionless language universal is that all language universals have exceptions. There are two major reasons for this diversity. First, language is a general-purpose communication system, and every subtly different thing we want to communicate has to be put into a (relatively) small number of words and constructions. Speakers of different languages do this in many different ways. Second, language change is gradual: constructions change their morphosyntactic properties one at a time, which increases structural diversity and blurs lines between construction types.

This is what typological theory would tell us. But for practical purposes, we have to carve up this continuum of language phenomena, and at any rate, the continuum is lumpy: the space of possible structures is dense in some regions and sparse in others. Hence there are better and worse ways to carve up the continuum.

Universal Dependencies represents one practical task that requires making such choices. UD aims to develop a syntactic annotation scheme used across languages that, if applied consistently, allows for comparison across languages, including languages not yet possessing UD resources (Nivre, 2015; Nivre et al., 2016).

Another practical task that requires making such choices is teaching a typologically-informed syntax course to undergraduates as their first syntax class. In both UD and teaching syntax, the aim is to develop a small set of annotations that can be applied more or less uniformly across languages, to capture similarities as well as reveal differences. This is how I became involved in UD. My focus has been on the syntactic dependency annotation of UD. There are different and more difficult issues in the POS tagging and morphological feature tagging of the UD enterprise, which I will not go into here.

2. Two basic principles for typological annotation of dependencies

Several basic principles guided my effort, and the two most important principles are described here; for more details, see Croft et al. (2017). The first is based on a distinction between *constructions* and *strategies* in crosslinguistic comparison. Constructions describe the class of grammatical structures in any language that is used to express a particular function. For example, *Ivan is the best dancer* is an instance of the predicate nominal construction, that is, the construction whose function is to predicate an object category of a referent.

Strategies are particular morphosyntactic structures, defined in a cross-linguistically valid fashion, that are used to express a function. For example, English uses an inflecting copula strategy for predicate nominals, that is, a word form distinct from the object word that inflects for at least some of the grammatical categories that ordinary predicates do. Other languages also use the inflecting copula strategy; but still other languages use an uninflected copula, or no copula at all, or inflect the object word. These are all different strategies.

The principle for designing a universal set of dependencies is that the structure of constructions should form the backbone of the dependency structure; strategies are secondary, although they have to be annotated when they are expressed by independent words, such as the English copula. UD's content-word-to-content-word principle basically conforms to this principle.

The second important principle is based on the hypothesis that constructions always involve the information packaging of the semantic content of the sentence, that is, the function of constructions has to be defined in terms of both semantic content and information packaging. For example the predicate nominal construction involves packaging an object concept as a predication.

The principle that emerges from this hypothesis is that universal dependencies are, to a great extent, describing information-packaging relations, not semantic relations. That is, information packaging functions are much more isomorphic to syntactic structures than semantic classes or semantic relations. Information packaging functions are less variable across languages than semantics, especially lexical semantics. UD minimizes reliance on semantics in defining UD dependencies and in applying them to specific languages, so UD basically conforms to this principle as well.

3. UD dependencies: inventory and guidelines

The principles described in the preceding section, and other principles described in Croft et al. (2017), led me to a set of universal dependencies that is quite close but not identical to the set of universal dependencies in UD (version 2). These differences are relatively minor, although I will discuss one of them in this talk. The much bigger issue is the development of guidelines for consistent annotation of the many different constructions and the many different strategies that languages use, both for languages for which there exist UD resources and for new languages which may be added.

What is the best way to do this? Constructions, as defined in the preceding section, are not enough: they are defined by function, whereas we need to carve breaks in the range of strategies used to express function. The basic idea is to find typological universals constraining the distribution of strategies over constructions in such a way that the universals reveal the "cleanest" breaks and the best strategies to use as uniform guidelines across languages.

This will be a "good news, bad news" story. The "good news" is that some current practice, based mainly on Western grammatical tradition and the Western European languages that make up most of the UD treebanks, are justified in a broader typological perspective, and allow for uniform guidelines. The "bad news" is that some current practices, and some distinctions among UD dependencies, are not very well justified typologically. In some of these cases, the dependencies I use in teaching syntax differ from the current version of UD.

I believe that for the most part, the good news exceeds the bad news. The most important conclusion is that detailed guidelines are necessary, and ideally should be typologically justified. An overview of the typological variation and typological universals constraining that variation—and justifying distinctions we need to make—will appear in my forthcoming textbook for the advanced syntax class I teach (Croft, In preparation).

4. Some examples of how typology can be used to develop guidelines for UD

UD distinguishes between core grammatical roles (*subj, dobj, iobj*) from oblique roles (*obl*). In practice, however, this is difficult. We cannot rely on semantic roles (patient, instrument, etc.) because voice, argument structure alternations and applicative constructions change the syntactic roles of participants. Hence we must look elsewhere.

There are three strategies used for encoding core and oblique arguments: case marking (adpositions and affixes), indexation (agreement) and word order. The categories of case markers vary a lot, and there are mismatches across strategies. How safe is it to rely on these strategies for annotating core vs. oblique?

Fortunately, there are two universals that support the identification of core vs oblique arguments:

- *If case marking is zero, then the argument is overwhelmingly likely to be core.*

- *If the predicate indexes the argument, then the argument is overwhelmingly likely to be core.*

There are exceptions, but the point is that they are rare. So we can assume that if the argument phrase has zero-coded case marking and/or is indexed on the verb, it is core, without having to rely on semantic roles. The universals are one-way conditionals: some core arguments have overt case marking, and others are not indexed on the predicate. But it is usually clear which case-marked arguments are core.

An example which represents not so good news is when there are mismatches in strategies for arguments. Two common examples are so-called "dative subjects", common in South Asian languages, and "patient subjects" (passives). There is a diachronic typological universal governing the acquistion of subjecthood (Cole et al., 1980; Croft, 2001):

- *Nonsubject arguments may become subjectlike, first by word order, then indexation, then case marking.*

Unfortunately, this universal implies a gradient of strategies from nonsubject to subject, and does not offer guidelines as to when to decide when an argument is a subject, or still is not a subject. However, it is unlikely that the constructions with mismatches are common. In the case of mismatches, I would suggest that if an argument uses any morphological strategy associated with subject status—that is, case marking or indexation—then it should be annotated as subject. The universal indicates that such mismatches will have subject-like indexation but nonsubject case marking.

Other cases of a gradient of strategies are found in several common paths of grammaticalization (Heine and Kuteva, 2002; Lehmann, 2002). These cases also involve a reversal of headedness in UD, which is problematic in a dependency grammar (heads are in boldface):

- **Verb** + Complement $\rightarrow$ Auxiliary + **Verb**
- **Relational Noun** + Noun $\rightarrow$ Adposition + **Noun**
- **Verb** + Noun $\rightarrow$ Adposition + **Noun**
- **Quantity** + Noun $\rightarrow$ Quantifier + **Noun**

As with the acquisition of subjecthood, it is likely that the intermediate cases are crosslinguistically not that common. I would suggest, as with subject annotation, that once a construction acquires the first typical strategy for the more grammaticalized construction, it should be annotated like the more grammaticalized construction.

Some semantic roles, such as recipient, are sometimes core and sometimes oblique across languages; and they are sometimes both in the same language, in which case they are described as object-oblique alternations: *I showed the policeman my driver's license/I showed my driver's license to the policeman.* In typology, these are called different strategies for encoding the recipient, specifically alignment strategies (Haspelmath, 2011).

If they are simply different strategies, then perhaps they should be annotated the same way in a universal scheme like UD. But in fact a construction should be defined by both semantic content and information packaging (Croft, 2016, In preparation). Encoding a participant role as object or oblique arguably does differ in information packaging. In most languages, only one option exists, object or oblique. But the crosslinguistic variation is due to competing motivations: for example, a recipient is a less central event participant, yet it is almost always human and hence of greater salience. So I conclude that one should follow the language's structure in annotating a semantic role as object or oblique.

In the equivalent German sentence, the recipient role is in the Dative case, whlie the theme role is in the Accusative case: *Ich zeigte dem Polizisten* [Dative] *meinen Führerschein* [accusative]. Many Germanists analyze the Dative as an object, despite the oblique-like case marking. This is justified by the fact that the dative noun phrase occurs without a preposition. Yet there is a language universal that suggests this is the right choice, albeit for a different reason (Siewierska, 1998; Levin, 2008):

- *Constructions with a dative coding of the recipient distinct from the allative or locative coding are crosslinguistically in complementary distribution to constructions with the same coding of recipient and theme.*

Hence, even a language-specific annotation choice may be typologically justified, though in this case the rule should be whether the dative is distinct from allative or locative, not whether the dative noun phrase is accompanied by a preposition.

Modifiers are a more complex case. Modifiers come in many different semantic types: definiteness (articles), deixis (demonstrative), cardinality (cardinal numerals), quantification (quantifiers), properties (adjective), actions (relative clauses, participles) and possession (genitive) and other noun-noun relations. UD distinguishes a subset of those semantic types: *det, nummod, amod, nmod* and *acl*. Modifiers also use a wide range of strategies: gender/number agreement, case marking, classifiers, and linkers (more grammaticalized, invariant markers of a relation). However, all the different strategies are found across almost all modifier types, although there is typological evidence that noun modifiers and relative clauses tend to stand apart. In this case, I have lumped together all modifiers into a single mod dependency, except for *nmod* and *acl*.

Finally, one of the more challenging problems is distinguishing subordinate clauses from nominalizations (or in the case of participles, adjectivalizations). Constructions using all the structure of main clauses— tense-aspect-modality (TAM) inflections, indexation of core arguments, main clause-like case marking of core arguments—such as *I am surprised that he fired Flynn* are clearly subordinate clauses. But there is a wide range of constructions lacking some or all of the typical structure of main clauses, as in *His firing Flynn surprised me* or *Him firing Flynn was surprising*. Also, the terminology in grammatical description here is very confusing: there are special terms such as infinitives, gerunds, masdars, and converbs; but many descriptions use the term "nominalization" for all sorts of non-clause-like constructions.

Fortunately, there is a reliable grammatical criterion that has two significant typological universals associated with it, which allows us to consistently distinguish subordinate clauses from nominalizations. The grammatical criterion is that an event nominalization allows for "reasonably productive" case marking (Comrie, 1976). The two universals are (Cristofaro, 2003):

- *If a verb form can take case affixes or adpositions, then with overwhelming frequency it does not inflect for TAM like a main clause verb (it either has no TAM inflections, or uses special TAM forms).*

- *If a verb form can take case affixes or adpositions, then with overwhleming frequency it does not express person indexation/agreement like a main clause verb (it either has no person indexation, or special person indexation forms different from those in main clauses).*

In other words, external case marking of verb forms coincides with non-clauselike TAM inflection and person indexation. Again,this is a one-way conditional: subordinate clauses may lack the TAM or indexation of main clauses. Case marking of dependent arguments of the verb, however, does not conform to these universals and so cannot be used reliably to distinguish subordinate clauses from nominalizations. But case marking of the verb form can be used reliably and consistently as a guideline to distinguish subordinate clauses from nominalizations (or adjectivalizations, for participial modifiers).

Deciding whether a verb form allows "reasonably productive" case marking is not always easy, since dependent constructions denoting actions do not take the full range of case forms, and infinitives are often historically derived from allative case marking, such as English *I began **to** work*. But case marking of the verb form is a consistent and typologically justified criterion.

Finally, there is an asymmetry in strategies between complement clauses and adverbial subordinate clauses that can be used for guidelines to distinguish complement relations (UD *scomp, ccomp, xcomp*) from adverbial ones (UD *advcl*):

- *If the subordinating conjunction is relational, that is, expresses contrastively a semantic relation between the matrix clause and the subordinate clause, then the subordinate clause is overwhelmingly likely to be an adverbial clause.*

- *If the subordinating conjunction is a linker, so does not express a specific semantic relation, then the subordinate clause is overwhelmingly likely to be a complement (or relative clause).*

If a verb form that semantically looks like a complement appears to take case marking, then it is likely that either it is part of a paradigm of case-marked verb forms and hence is an event nominal, or the putative case marking no longer contrasts meaningfully with another form, as in English infinitival *to*, and so should be analyzed as a linker governing a complement clause.

These examples indicate how typological universals about the relationship between functions of constructions—semantic content and information packaging—and the grammatical strategies used to express those functions can help in constructing guidelines for applying Universal Dependencies across languages in a consistent fashion.

References

Peter Cole, Wayne Harbert, Gabriella Hermon, and S. N. Sridhar. The acquisition of subjecthood. *Language*, 56:719–743, 1980.

Bernard Comrie. The syntax of action nominals: a cross-language study. *Lingua*, 40:177–201, 1976.

Sonia Cristofaro. *Subordination.* Oxford: Oxford University Press, 2003.

William Croft. *Radical Construction Grammar: Syntactic Theory in Typological Perspective.* Oxford University Press, 2001.

William Croft. Comparative concepts and language-specific categories: theory and practice. *Linguistic Typology*, 20:377–393, 2016.

William Croft. *Morphosyntax: constructions of the world's languages.* Cambridge: Cambridge University Press, In preparation.

William Croft, Dawn Nordquist, Katherine Looney, and Michael Regan. Linguistic typology meets universal dependencies. In Markus Dickinson, Jan Hajič, Sandra Kübler, and Adam Przepiórkowski, editors, *Proceedings of the 15th International Workshop on Treebanks and Linguistic Theories (TLT15)*, pages 63–75. CEUR Workshop Proceedings, 2017.

Martin Haspelmath. On S, A, P, T, and R as comparative concepts for alignment typology. *Linguistic Typology*, 15:535–67, 2011.

Bernd Heine and Tania Kuteva. *World lexicon of grammaticalization.* Cambridge: Cambridge University Press, 2002.

Christian Lehmann. *Thoughts on grammaticalization: a programmatic sketch, Vol. I*, volume 9, Arbeitspapiere des Seminars für Sprachwissenschaft der Universität. Erfurt: Seminar für Sprachwissenschaft der Universität, 2002.

Beth Levin. Dative verbs: a crosslinguistic perspective. *Linguisticæ Investigationes*, 31:285–312, 2008.

Joakim Nivre. Towards a universal grammar for natural language processing. In Alexander Gelbukh, editor, *Computational linguistics and intelligent text processing*, pages 3–16. New York: Springer, 2015.

Joakim Nivre, Marie-Catherine de Marneffe, Filip Ginter, Yoav Goldberg, Jan Hajič, Christopher D. Manning, Ryan McDonald, Slav Petrov, Sampo Pyysalo, Natalia Silveira, Reut Tsarfaty, and Daniel Zeman. Universal Dependencies v1: a multilingual treebank collection. In *Proceedings of the 10th International Conference on Language Resources and Evaluation*, pages 1659–1666. European Language Resources Association, 2016.

Anna Siewierska. Languages with and without Objects: the Functional Grammar perspective. *Languages in Contrast*, 1:173–90, 1998.

Cross-lingual parser selection for low-resource languages

Željko Agić

Department of Computer Science
IT University of Copenhagen
Rued Langgaards Vej 7, 2300 Copenhagen S, Denmark
zeag@itu.dk

Abstract

In multilingual dependency parsing, transferring delexicalized models provides unmatched language coverage and competitive scores, with minimal requirements. Still, selecting the single best parser for any target language poses a challenge. Here, we propose a lean method for parser selection. It offers top performance, and it does so without disadvantaging the truly low-resource languages. We consistently select appropriate source parsers for our target languages in a realistic cross-lingual parsing experiment.

1 Introduction

Treebanks are available for only ~1% of the languages spoken in the world today, the resource-rich *sources*. One major goal of cross-lingual transfer learning is to provide robust NLP for all the *targets*, or the remaining ~99%.

If we want to parse *any* language for syntactic dependencies, the only principled method that currently enables it is delexicalized model transfer. By relying on uniform POS tags only, it offers unprecedented language coverage. First introduced by Zeman and Resnik (2008), and consolidated by the seminal works of McDonald et al. (2011; 2013) and Søgaard (2011), delexicalized parsing is nowadays considered to be a simple baseline.

Recent work promises cross-lingual methods that score almost as high as supervised parsers. Unfortunately, it also introduces requirements that a vast majority of languages cannot meet. The systems proposed by, e.g., Ma and Xia (2014) or Rasooli and Collins (2015) require:

- very large parallel corpora, often in excess of 2M parallel sentences for each language pair, coupled with near-perfect tokenization and sentence splitting;

- high-quality sentence and word alignments for all the language pairs, provided by aligners that favor closely related languages;
- accurate POS tagging using fully supervised taggers that score ~95% on held-out data.

Latest work by Johannsen et al. (2016), among a few others, shows that in a real-world scenario, where no such unrealistic assumptions are made, delexicalized transfer still constitutes a very competitive choice for multilingual parsing.

Here, we assert that even simple delexicalized parsing might be in need of a reality check.

Realistic delexicalized parsing? The idea behind delexicalization is very simple: we omit all lexical features from the parsers, both at training and at runtime, so that they operate on POS sequences only. All that is then needed to parse an unknown language is a tagger using a uniform POS representation such as the "universal" POS tagset by Petrov et al. (2011).

Delexicalized parsing itself comes in two distinct basic variants:

i) **multi-source**, where we train a single parser by joining multiple delexicalized source-language treebanks, and

ii) **single-source**, where each source-language treebank contributes a single parser, and then we select the one to use from this pool of parsing models.

Most often, we pick the **single-best** source parser for a given target language. The rankings of the candidate source parsers are determined by evaluation on target language test data.

Single-best parsers generally perform better than multi-source parsers. For example, in their experiment, Agić et al. (2016) show that the single-source variant beats multi-source delexicalization in 23/27 languages and scores +3 points higher in UAS on average. For fairness, their parsers all work with cross-lingual POS taggers.

Proceedings of the NoDaLiDa 2017 Workshop on Universal Dependencies (UDW 2017), pages 1–10,
Gothenburg, Sweden, 22 May 2017.

However, we argue that single-best source parsing is **not realistic**. Only in an evaluation framework do we possess prior knowledge of i) which target language we are parsing, and ii) what the source rankings are for the targets. Single-best parsing thus amounts to an oracle. By contrast, in the real world, we expect to parse by i) **predicting** the target language name from the text input at runtime, and by ii) **selecting** the most appropriate source parser for that language from the parser pool. If the prediction or selection turn out incorrect, we are likely to end up producing a suboptimal parse. Furthermore, while parsing accuracy is measured on test sets of $\sim$1000 sentences on average, the real input can take a much wider size range. This variation in size may challenge the validity of any design choices made on test set-level only.

The cross-lingual parsing community has largely ignored this problem, focusing instead on test set-based evaluation by proxy. This, in addition to a list of methodological biases, has spawned a number of complex models incapable of scaling down to real low-resource languages.

Our contributions. How do we single out the best source parser if the language of the input text has to be predicted at runtime?

To answer this question, our paper makes the following contributions:

i) We propose a set of methods for matching texts to source parsers. Our methods are simple, as they rely on nothing but character-based language identification and typological similarity. They consistently find the best parsers for the target languages.

ii) We set aside the test-set granularity assumption. Instead, we assume that the parser input can vary in size from as little as one sentence. Our methods prove to be remarkably adaptable to this size variation.

iii) By combining our approaches, our best system even manages to exceed the performance of single-best oracle source parsers.

In our submission, we strive to introduce only the minimal requirements, and to maintain a realistic setup. For example, in all the experiments, we apply cross-lingual POS taggers for truly low-resource languages. By controlling for POS sources, we show how an ingrained bias towards direct supervision of taggers may render any parsing results irrelevant in a low-resource context. Our code and data are freely available.[1]

2 Method

Say we had to find a suitable source parser for the following sentence, written in an unknown target language:

Knjiga	*ima*	*12*	*svezaka*	.
NOUN	VERB	NUM	NOUN	PUNCT

Intuitively, and following the language relatedness hypothesis of McDonald et al. (2013), among the source languages, we would single out the one typologically closest to the target sentence, and apply its delexicalized parser. Further, we build our approach on this intuition.

More formally, let $S \in \mathcal{S}$ be a source language treebank, and $T \in \mathcal{T}$ a POS-tagged target text to parse. Further, let $\mathrm{dist} : \mathcal{S} \times \mathcal{T} \rightarrow [0, +\infty)$ be a cross-lingual distance measure.[2] In this framework, finding the single-best parser amounts to minimizing the distance over all sources:

$$\hat{S}_{min} = \arg \min_{S \in \mathcal{S}} \mathrm{dist}(S, T)$$

2.1 Distance measures

In estimating distance, or similarity as its inverse, we consider two basic sources of available information for sources and targets: i) the raw texts and ii) the POS tag sequences.

We proceed to define three distance measures over these information sources. The first measure is based on sequences of POS tags. The other two model character sequences and typological information, and they are novel to our work.

KL-POS. This is the POS trigram-based distance metric of Rosa and Žabokrtský (2015a). Essentially, it expresses the Kullback–Leibler (KL) divergence between distributions of source and target trigrams of POS tags:

$$\mathrm{dist}_{\mathrm{K}}(S, T) = \sum_{t_i \in T} f_T(t_i) \log \frac{f_T(t_i)}{f_S(t_i)}$$

The relative frequencies f_S and f_T of trigrams t_i in source and target data are estimated on the re-

---

[1] `https://bitbucket.org/zeljko_agic/freasy`

[2] Rather than *metric*, we use the term *measure*, as not all conditions for metrics are satisfied by all proposed measures. Namely, KL divergence is not symmetric.

spective POS sequences:

$$f(t_i) = \frac{\text{count}(t_i)}{\sum_{\forall t_j} \text{count}(t_j)}$$

We inherit the properties of the original KL-POS proposal, but we introduce one minor change: while i) special tag values are used to encode sentence beginnings and endings, and ii) the source counts for unseen trigrams are smoothed for the distance to be well-defined, we use linear interpolation smoothing following Brants (2000) rather than set these counts to 1 in the Rosa and Žabokrtský (2015a) implementation.

In plain words, this measure compares the relative frequencies of target POS trigrams $t_i \in T$ to the frequencies of these trigrams in all the sources $S \in \mathcal{S}$, and then we select the one associated with lowest KL divergence. For our example sentence, KL-POS predicts Finnish to be the best source parser. The sentence is, however, in Croatian, for which the Finnish parser ranks as 19/26 in our experiment. In contrast, if we feed KL-POS five sentences at a time, it selects Slovene (1/26).

We expect KL-POS to be sensitive to both the sample size and the POS tagging quality. The latter is of particular importance for low-resource dependency parsing. Incidentally, the POS tags in our Croatian example are all correct. For these reasons, we propose the following two measures. The first one (LANG-ID) is based on character, i.e., byte n-grams, while the other one (WALS) augments the n-grams approach by leveraging typological data.

LANG-ID. The approach is very straightforward: We use Lui and Baldwin's (2012) `langid.py` module to identify the best source language for the given input. They employ a naive Bayes classifier with a multinomial event model, and feed it a mixture of byte n-grams ($1 \leq n \leq 4$).

More specifically, `langid.py` has predefined models for $\sim$100 languages, but we constrain it to predict into the set of source languages $\mathcal{S}$ only. We also use its probability re-normalization feature. Our distance measure then amounts to:[3]

$$\text{dist}_\text{L}(S, T) = 1 - p_S, (S, p_S) \in \texttt{langid.rank}(T)$$

As `langid.py` estimates p_S, the probability of

input T belonging to a source language S, we convert it to a distance $(1 - p_S)$.

For our Croatian sample sentence, LANG-ID predicts Slovene with a confidence of 0.99, and it converges already for the first token.

On the downside, limiting `langid.py` predictions to sources S only might negatively impact parsing. The classifier commits early on to one answer, assigning it a high confidence, and for languages with fewer related source languages in the model, source selection might be significantly off. For example, take this Hungarian sentence:

Ettől	*a*	*győzelemtől*	*magabiztos*	*lettem*	*.*
ADV	VERB	NOUN	NOUN	NOUN	PUNCT

While KL-POS selects Estonian (1/26), our source-constrained LANG-ID predicts Spanish (19/26) as the best source. However, if we allow LANG-ID to predict beyond the list of source languages only, it guesses Hungarian with $p = 1$.

Since Hungarian poses as a target language, we cannot use this correct guess to select a model directly, but we can exploit it downstream. Our next distance measure does so by leveraging typology data on top of LANG-ID.

WALS. Our typology-based approach relies on a simple premise: If we can guess the language of the target text, we can employ a language database to match the input with a similar source language. This language database should encode various linguistic properties across many languages in a principled way. One such resource is WALS (Dryer and Haspelmath, 2013). Currently it contains structured data for 2,679 languages.[4] Each language is described through 202 features: they include various structural properties in several categories, most notably in phonology, morphology, and syntax.

Now we describe the WALS-reliant distance measure. For any target language T, we predict the language name using LANG-ID. For this prediction, we retrieve the corresponding feature vector $\mathbf{v_T}$ from WALS, provided that WALS contains some information on T. Our distance measure then amounts to comparing the target WALS vector $\mathbf{v_T}$ to source WALS vectors $\mathbf{v_S}, \forall S$:

$$\text{dist}_\text{W}(S, T) = d_h(\mathbf{v_S}, \mathbf{v_T}),$$

where d_h is the Hamming distance between WALS source and target vectors $\mathbf{v_S}$ and $\mathbf{v_T}$.

---

[3]Note that `langid.rank(T)` returns pairs of source languages and respective probabilities $(S, p_S), \forall S \in \mathcal{S}$. We apply `langid.py` with the options `-d -l -n`, see https://github.com/saffsd/langid.py.

[4]http://wals.info/download

For each S and T, we only compare the subsets of features for which both $\mathbf{v_S}$ and $\mathbf{v_T}$ are non-empty. If there would be no WALS entries for T, we would fall back to LANG-ID. In our experiments, however, all the languages are already represented in WALS.

For our Croatian example input, WALS predicts Slovene as source (1/26), while it chooses Finnish (6/26) for the Hungarian sentence.

2.2 Combining the measures

Both LANG-ID and WALS suffer a same constraint: in contrast to KL-POS, they do not abstract away from the alphabet. This may cause issues for languages with distinct alphabets. On the other hand, KL-POS needs more data for estimation, and might deteriorate with POS tagging accuracy.

Since the strengths and drawbacks of the three approaches appear to be complementary, here we propose their linear combination.

Normalization. The distances that our measures output are not directly comparable, even if their source language rankings are. We normalize the distances into probability distributions by applying a softmax function:

$$\hat{P}(S|T) = \text{softmax}(\text{dist}^{-1}(S, T), \tau)$$
$$= \frac{\exp \frac{\text{dist}^{-1}(S,T)}{\tau}}{\sum_{X \in \mathcal{S}} \exp \frac{\text{dist}^{-1}(X,T)}{\tau}}$$

Note that we invert the distances (dist^{-1}) as a small distance between S and T translates into a high probability of S lending its parser to T. We use the softmax temperature τ for controlling the contributions of the sources. For very large τ, $\tau \to +\infty$, the probabilities for the individual sources all even out at $p \to 1/|\mathcal{S}|$, while $\tau \to 0^+$ isolates the most probable source at $p \to 1$.

The change from dist to $\hat{P}(S|T)$ changes our objective from minimizing the distance between sources and targets to maximizing the probability of S lending a parser to T:

$$\hat{S}_{max} = \arg \max_{S \in \mathcal{S}} \hat{P}(S|T)$$

COMBINED. With the probability normalization in place, we now introduce the linear combination of the three approaches:

$$\hat{P}(S|T) = \sum_i \lambda_i \hat{P}_i(S|T), \text{with} \sum_i \lambda_i = 1$$

Algorithm 1: Source selection and reparsing.

Data: Target language sample T, source language treebanks S, and parsers h_S

Result: Predicted single-best parses G^t_{max}, reparsed trees $\text{DMST}(G^t), \forall t \in T$

Create the sources distribution.
$\hat{P}(S|T) \leftarrow \text{softmax}(\text{dist}^{-1}(S, T), \tau), \forall S$
Find the best source.
$\hat{S}_{max} \leftarrow \arg \max_{S} \hat{P}(S|T)$
for *each sentence t in T* **do**
    Get all parses, build the graph.
    $G^t = (V, E), E = \{(u_S, v) \in h_S(t), \forall S\}$
    Get the single-best parse.
    $G^t_{max} = (V, E_{max}),$
        where $E_{max} = \{(u_{\hat{S}_{max}}, v)\}$
end
return $G^t_{max}, \text{DMST}(G^t), \forall t \in T$

The values λ_i can be tuned empirically on development data, with i indexing our three distance measures. That way, we can control the amounts of contributions for the individual methods, similar to tuning the contributions of the individual sources through softmax temperature τ.

With the COMBINED approach, we aim specifically at providing "the best of both worlds" in source discovery: an improved robustness to orthographies on one side, and an added stability to varying input sample sizes on the other.

3 Experiments

In our setup, we parse the target texts T with multiple source parsers h_S, and we seek to predict the best source parses for all the targets. We now expose the details of this experiment outline.

Data. We use the Universal Dependencies (UD) treebanks (Nivre et al., 2016) version 1.3.[5] UD currently offers 54 dependency treebanks for 41 different languages.

Since our experiment requires realistic cross-lingual POS taggers, we use the freely available collection of training sets by Agić et al. (2016).[6] It is built through low-resource annotation projection over parallel texts from The Watchtower online library (WTC).[7] Thus, we intersect the lan-

---

[5]`hdl.handle.net/11234/1-1699`
[6]`https://bitbucket.org/lowlands/release/`
[7]`http://wol.jw.org/`

guages with POS tagging support from WTC with the UD treebanks for a total of 26 languages whose training and testing sets that we proceed to use in the experiment. We make use of the English UD development data in hyper-parameter tuning.

Tools. For POS tagging, we use a state-of-the-art CRF-based tagger MarMoT[8] (Müller et al., 2013). We use Bohnet's (2010) `mate-tools` graph-based dependency parser. Both tools are run with their default settings.

In our experiments, we control for the sources of POS tags. We distinguish i) direct in-language supervision, where the taggers are trained on target language UD training data, from ii) cross-lingually predicted POS, where we train the taggers on WTC-projected annotations.

For training the delexicalized source parsers, we use the following standard features, in reference to the CoNLL 2009 file format:[9] ID, POS, HEAD, and DEPREL (Hajič et al., 2009). In specific, we don't leverage the UD morphological features (FEATS) as not all languages support them in the 1.3 release. We subsample the treebanks for parser training with a ceiling of 10k sentences, so as to avoid the bias towards the largest treebanks such as Czech with 68k training set sentences.

Baselines and upper bounds. We set the oracle SINGLE-BEST source parsing results as the main reference point for our evaluation. We compare all systems to these scores, as our benchmarking goals are to i) reach SINGLE-BEST performance through best source prediction and to ii) surpass it by weighted reparsing.

We compare our approach to the standard multi-source delexicalized parser of McDonald et al. (2011) (*multi-dir* in their paper, **MULTI** here). In training, we uniformly sample from the contributing sources up to 10k sentences.

Reparsing. We collect all single-source parses of target sentences $t \in T$ into a dependency graph. The graph $G^t = (V, E)$ has target tokens as vertices V. The edges $(u_S, v) \in E$ originate in the delexicalized source parsers $h_S, \forall S$.

Following Sagae and Lavie (2006), we can apply directed maximum spanning tree decoding $\mathrm{DMST}(G^t)$, resulting in a voted dependency

parse for a target sentence t, where each source contributes a unit vote. Such unit voting presumes that all edges have a weight of 1. We refer to this approach as **UNIFORM** reparsing. We also experiment with weighing the edges in G^t through the distance measures KL-POS, WALS, and COMBINED:

$$\mathrm{weight}(u_S, v) = \hat{P}(S|T), \forall u_S \in G^t, \forall t \in T$$

The weights in turn depend on the granularity, as varying sizes of T influence the similarity estimates coming from KL-POS and WALS.

Parameters. We tune the softmax temperature to $\tau = 0.2$ for both KL-POS and WALS by using the English UD development data. For simplicity, we fix $\lambda_K = \lambda_W = 0.5$, $\lambda_L = 0$ without tuning, i.e., in the COMBINED system we give equal weight to KL-POS and WALS. We exclude LANG-ID from reparsing as it is subsumed by WALS.

Our experiment assumes the variability of input size in sentences. We use the full UD test sets for all 26 languages. However, we vary the sample size or **granularity** g in best source prediction. It is implemented as a moving window over the test sets, with sizes of 1 to 100.

The experiment workflow is condensed in Algorithm 1. It shows how we arrive at best source predictions and reparsed trees for a target sample T. In the algorithm sketch, we assume $g = |T|$, i.e., the granularity is implied by the sample size, but further we provide results for varying g. Any edge weighting in reparsing is made internal to DMST.

4   Results

First, we provide a summary of our experiment results in Table 1. We then proceed to break down the scores by language in Table 2.

Summary. We discern that our COMBINED approach yields the best overall scores in the realistic scenario, both in source selection and in reparsing. The latter score remarkably even surpasses the informed upper bound SINGLE-BEST system by 0.36 points UAS. It reaches the highest UAS over cross-lingual POS in both selection and reparsing, while KL-POS closely beats it in reparsing over fully supervised POS.

We form a general ordering of the four approaches following these summary results: COMBINED>KL-POS≥WALS>LANG-ID.

[8] https://github.com/muelletm/cistern/blob/wiki/marmot.md

[9] https://ufal.mff.cuni.cz/conll2009-st/task-description.html

POS source:	Direct supervision	Cross-lingual	
	95.33±2.42	71.65±5.65	g
Delexicalized			
MULTI	62.04±4.67	49.48±5.37	–
SINGLE-BEST	65.53±2.96	51.96±4.35	–
Source selection			
KL-POS	63.68±3.30	49.84±5.25	100
LANG-ID	60.12±3.83	48.14±5.25	5
WALS	60.37±4.36	48.87±5.45	3
COMBINED	64.18±3.04	50.20±5.20	50
Reparsing			
KL-POS	66.55±3.70	51.55±5.46	4
UNIFORM	64.10±4.68	50.92±5.47	–
WALS	65.17±4.56	51.54±5.52	2
COMBINED	66.50±3.56	52.32±5.30	50

Table 1: Summary UAS parsing scores for all 26 languages, over two underlying sources of POS tags. Gray: highest scores grouped by POS and method. ±: 95% confidence intervals. g: sample size (granularity) associated with the best score.

Looking into the optimal target sample sizes g, the COMBINED system peaks at 50 sentences. KL-POS works best with samples of 100 sentences in source prediction, and only 4 sentences in reparsing. In contrast, WALS needs only 2-3 for both, while LANG-ID peaks at 5 sentences.

Split by languages. The results in Table 2 are provided as differences in UAS to our reference point: the oracle SINGLE-BEST system. In source selection, we aim to match the oracle scores, while we seek to surpass them through reparsing.

The top-performing **source prediction** system is the COMBINED one: it comes closest to the oracle score for 10/26 languages. The other three approaches manage the same feat for 5-7 languages, while the MULTI-source delexicalized parsers still pose a challenge for 8/26 languages.[10]

Notably, KL-POS even beats the SINGLE-BEST oracle by 0.4 UAS for one language (Danish), a score that is made possible by changes in source selection for different portions of the test set due to sample granularity. KL-POS and LANG-ID reach the oracle score for 3 languages, WALS for 5, and COMBINED for 9 languages. In **reparsing**, the COMBINED system once again produces the absolute best scores, here for 15/26 languages. MULTI parsers are unable to match the reparsing systems, as both KL-POS and WALS also come very close to the upper bound on average. Viewed separately,

---

[10]Note that in some cases more than one system records the same score for a language.

these two reparsing systems are evenly split with 13/26 languages for each, and reach almost identical average scores, with KL-POS ahead WALS by only 0.01 point UAS.

5 Discussion

We reflect on the results of our experiment from the viewpoints of i) POS tagging impact, and ii) input size or granularity.

Sources of POS tags. Throughout the paper, we emphasized the importance of using cross-lingual POS tagging in dependency parsing work that features truly low-resource languages.

We conducted triple runs of all our experiments, by changing the underlying POS tags from cross-lingual to i) tags obtained through direct in-language supervision via the UD training data and ii) gold POS tags. The respective average tagging accuracies over the 26 test languages thus changed from 71.65% to 95.33% and 100%. As the observations were virtually unchanged between fully supervised tagging and gold tagging, we reported the former together with cross-lingual tagging.

Table 1 adds insight into the influence of tagging quality. In **source selection**, KL-POS outperforms LANG-ID and WALS by ~2.5 points UAS over monolingual POS, but this advantage drops to less than 1 point with cross-lingual POS.

There is an even more notable turnabout following the underlying POS source change in **reparsing**. With direct supervision, KL-POS beats UNIFORM and WALS by 2.35 and 1.38 points UAS, and even surpasses the COMBINED system by 0.05 points. However, when working with cross-lingually induced POS tags, the COMBINED approach beats the three other systems by 0.77–1.40 points UAS, and KL-POS and WALS even out.

We expected KL-POS to show less resilience to changes in POS tagging quality compared to the other methods. The significant change in the observations highlights the need for more careful treatment of low-resource languages in contributions to cross-lingual parsing.

Granularity. Input size in sentences, or granularity g as a model of input size variation, is an important feature in our experiments. In Table 1 and 2, we only reported the scores with optimal granularities for each method. Here, we add insight by observing the link between g and UAS in

	POS	Delexicalized			Source selection			Reparsing			COMBINED	
		MULTI	SINGLE-BEST		LANG-ID	KL-POS	WALS	UNIFORM	KL-POS	WALS	selection	reparsing
Arabic (ar)	51.48	-2.55	37.02	id	-8.29	-2.51	**-0.24**	-0.25	0.26	**0.40**	-0.90	<u>0.57</u>
Bulgarian (bg)	69.99	-0.42	49.94	cs	-1.79	**-0.45**	-10.00	1.05	**1.50**	1.22	-1.45	1.32
Czech (cs)	78.24	0.38	50.13	sl	-1.14	**-0.17**	-1.79	2.24	2.64	**2.72**	<u>-0.05</u>	<u>2.79</u>
Danish (da)	84.89	0.13	58.74	no	0.00	**0.40**	-0.19	1.29	1.20	**2.00**	0.20	1.87
German (de)	67.54	-1.32	44.64	no	**0.18**	-0.63	-0.11	0.37	0.52	**0.90**	-0.13	<u>1.16</u>
Greek (el)	62.44	2.04	54.98	it	-3.82	**0.00**	-0.82	3.70	**4.00**	3.81	-0.11	3.93
English (en)	79.75	-0.55	56.34	no	-6.17	-1.98	**-1.27**	0.47	0.70	**0.79**	-2.18	<u>0.94</u>
Spanish (es)	86.60	-1.76	69.29	it	-1.34	-1.01	**0.00**	0.36	**1.43**	1.16	<u>0.00</u>	1.27
Estonian (et)	76.11	-7.54	52.34	fi	-0.45	-0.60	**0.00**	-5.75	**-3.88**	-4.68	<u>0.00</u>	<u>0.09</u>
Persian (fa)	28.04	-1.23	25.33	ar	**0.00**	-2.67	-8.88	-0.88	**-0.25**	-0.82	-6.61	<u>-0.13</u>
Finnish (fi)	68.23	-6.03	45.01	et	**0.00**	-0.22	**0.00**	-4.59	**-3.14**	-3.47	<u>0.00</u>	<u>1.00</u>
French (fr)	78.80	-0.64	54.37	es	-2.25	-0.59	**-0.51**	0.02	**0.75**	0.63	<u>-0.51</u>	<u>1.10</u>
Hebrew (he)	62.64	-0.04	44.35	ro	-9.36	**0.00**	-5.12	1.91	1.82	**2.02**	<u>0.00</u>	<u>2.03</u>
Hindi (hi)	51.62	-20.74	37.07	ta	**-0.16**	-21.73	-21.52	-20.20	-20.35	**-19.99**	-19.54	-20.33
Croatian (hr)	75.95	-0.02	49.89	sl	**0.00**	-0.27	**0.00**	2.59	2.52	**2.79**	<u>0.00</u>	<u>2.79</u>
Hungarian (hu)	68.38	-8.08	46.07	et	-10.86	-8.08	**-3.92**	-5.86	-6.02	**-5.48**	<u>0.00</u>	-5.83
Indonesian (id)	77.78	-1.95	56.47	ro	-21.38	**-0.01**	-6.28	1.61	**2.13**	1.87	<u>0.00</u>	2.09
Italian (it)	87.69	-0.21	67.60	es	-0.48	**-0.10**	-0.15	0.69	**2.16**	1.88	-0.36	<u>2.32</u>
Dutch (nl)	71.49	1.08	54.15	es	-1.45	**-0.34**	-0.91	2.70	2.96	**3.29**	-0.91	3.10
Norwegian (no)	86.31	-0.29	63.99	sv	-3.10	**-1.69**	-3.09	0.57	0.86	**1.19**	-1.70	<u>1.29</u>
Polish (pl)	79.07	0.39	62.95	hr	-11.84	-1.70	**-1.41**	1.85	**2.81**	2.59	-1.70	<u>3.15</u>
Portuguese (pt)	85.98	-0.88	67.50	it	-0.38	-0.43	**0.00**	0.10	**1.23**	0.77	<u>0.00</u>	1.09
Romanian (ro)	75.77	-0.10	53.25	es	-4.71	-5.14	**-0.42**	1.96	2.45	**2.50**	<u>-0.24</u>	<u>2.62</u>
Slovene (sl)	76.53	-2.66	53.72	cs	-3.98	**-0.64**	-3.97	-1.67	**-0.81**	-1.07	-4.11	-0.84
Swedish (sv)	88.19	-3.15	66.01	no	**-0.04**	-0.52	-3.50	-2.05	-1.36	**0.30**	-1.54	<u>1.18</u>
Tamil (ta)	43.49	-8.49	29.86	hu	-6.23	**-3.97**	-6.23	-9.45	**-6.73**	-8.39	<u>-3.97</u>	<u>-1.30</u>
Mean	71.65	-2.48	51.96		-3.81	-2.12	-3.09	-1.05	-0.41	-0.42	-1.76	0.36
Best sample size g	–	–	–	–	5	100	3	–	4	2	50	50
Best single #	–	8	–	–	6	5	7	–	–	–	10	–
Absolute best #	–	0	–	–	2	1	0	0	5	3	1	15

Table 2: Parsing target languages using source language weighting. We report changes in UAS over the SINGLE-BEST delexicalized parsers. POS tags are provided by cross-lingual taggers. **Bold**: the best system for a given language, separate for source selection and reparsing, excluding COMBINED. <u>Underlined</u>: COMBINED systems that match or beat the other respective weighting methods. Gray: Best overall average score.

source selection and reparsing, for all the weighting approaches.

Figure 1A shows the changes in UAS for best **source prediction** with varying input sizes. LANG-ID and WALS converge on their predictions early on, so their UAS scores remain nearly constant. Yet, KL-POS largely benefits from more POS data: it starts at around -1.5 UAS from WALS and even below LANG-ID, but steadily rises up to ∼1 point over WALS at its peak UAS for $g = 100$ sentences.

The B part of Figure 1 reveals a different pattern for KL-POS in **reparsing**. While WALS once again stays expectedly constant, KL-POS peaks with +0.01 UAS at $g = 4$, only to decrease with growing input sizes. Since WALS rarely updates its initial predictions, its source distributions $\hat{P}(S|T)$ mostly remain unchanged with g, implying the same invariance for the reparsing scores. However, KL-POS converges much later, which means that its $\hat{P}(S|T)$ decreases in variation as g in-

creases: all but the best source start contributing less weight to the edges in G^t for reparsing. Moreover, while the differences between WALS vectors do not update with g, the KL divergences update towards the predicted best source, and away from the other contributing sources.

The COMBINED method manages to integrate the advantages of KL-POS and WALS. In source selection, it improves its predictions with larger samples, while maintaining the robustness over very small samples (+0.5 UAS over WALS, +1.9 over KL-POS for $g = 1, 2$). In reparsing, the combination significantly outperforms the two systems it integrates. Even more notably, where KL-POS deteriorates and WALS flatlines, the COMBINED reparsing scores steadily improve with g. We suggest that integrating i) the invariance of WALS language vector distances with ii) the variation of KL-POS towards the predicted best source with increasing granularity causes this positive effect.

Source rankings are implicit in the distributions

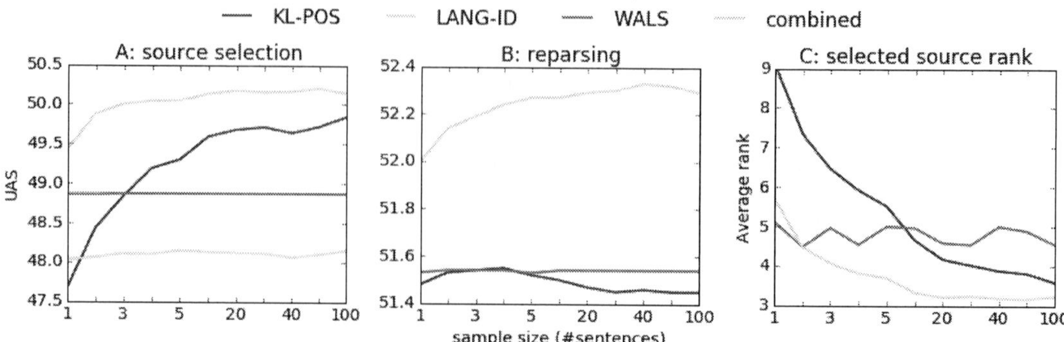

Figure 1: Sample size (granularity) impact on source selection and reparsing. A, B: Changes in UAS over different sample sizes for the four approaches in best single source prediction, and three approaches in reparsing. C: Average true rank of the predicted best source in relation to granularity.

$\hat{P}(S|T)$. Here, we compare them to the gold rankings induced from the SINGLE-BEST scores. In Figure 1C, we observe how the **average true rank** of the selected source changes with granularity. KL-POS significantly improves with larger samples. Working with one-sentence inputs, it assigns the targets to only the 9th best source on average, while with 50-100 sentences, it assigns the 3rd or 4th best source parser. WALS is mostly constant at an average rank of 4.5. COMBINED once again provides the best of both worlds, as it assigns the 5th or 6th best source with $g = 1, 2$, and stably predicts the 3rd best source on average with inputs of +20 sentences.

6 Limitations

Contributions of sources. In our experiments, we used SINGLE-BEST parsers as upper bounds. There, the best source parser was selected for each target language by its overall performance on the respective test set. This system recorded an average UAS of 51.96±4.35. However, if we select the best single source for each *sentence* instead, the oracle score rises significantly: by +13.58 points UAS, to 65.54±4.88.

To substantiate, in Figure 2, we show that for 28.66% of the parsed sentences on average, the best parse does **not** come from the parser that was ranked best in test set-level evaluation. We view this 13-point gap in UAS as a margin for improving our source selection in future work, as it suggests that we have yet to exhaust the search space of predictive features for sentence-level source ranking. For example, we could use the UD development data to learn models that predict the rankings of source parsers from the target sequences of tokens and POS tags, possibly using WALS as an additional feature source.

Scalability. Our contribution is mainly focused on the link between delexicalized parsing and language identification. In that focus, we abstracted away from certain relevant low-level issues in realistic text processing.

Firstly, we used gold-standard tokenization and sentence splits. While accurate splitters exist for many languages, realistic segmentation would still incur a penalty. Secondly, the LANG-ID models we used are readily available for around 100 languages. Scaling up to +1000 languages would require scaling down on the available resources for building identifiers, which would likely result in a minor performance decrease downstream.

Finally, and most importantly, our models depend on the existing cross-lingual POS taggers by Agić et al. (2016), which in turn rely on parallel resources. While their models do scale up, we excluded POS tagging from language identification. A more realistic proposal would assume that taggers, too, have to be selected at runtime before any parsing takes place.

7 Related work

Research in cross-lingual POS tagging and dependency parsing is nowadays plentiful, but only a fraction of it focuses on *truly* low-resource languages and *realistic* proposals.

McDonald et al. (2011) were among the first notable exceptions to use real cross-lingual POS taggers in their multi-source parser transfer experiments. They employed the label propagation-based taggers from Das and Petrov (2011). Agić et al. (2015; 2016) used a simpler approach to projection, but they were the first to propose multilingual projection for building taggers and parsers for 100+ low-resource languages in one pass. Zeman and Resnik (2008) used perplexity per word as a metric to select the source training instances that relate to the target data. Søgaard (2011) extended their approach to sequences of POS tags, and to multiple sources. Their metrics in turn relate to LANG-ID and KL-POS, but their approach is based on test-set granularity and the selection of appropriate data for *training* the parsers, while ours deals with varying input sizes and source parser selection at runtime.

Ammar et al. (2016) noted a -6.3 points decrease in UAS for cross-lingual parsing accuracy when the language identifiers and POS tags are predicted at runtime. Their taggers are fully supervised with 93.3% average accuracy for the seven resource-rich languages from their experiment. They also simulated a low-resource scenario, where they used gold POS and omitted language guessing.

WALS data has been heavily exploited in NLP research. In that line of work, and partly related to our paper, Søgaard and Wulff (2012) proposed adapting delexicalized parsers through distance-based instance weighting over WALS data. Their work in turn relates to Naseem et al. (2012), who also use WALS features in a multilingual parser adaptation model. The research by Naseem et al. (2012) and Täckström et al. (2013) addresses the issues with multi-source delexicalized transfer by selectively sharing model parameters, also with typological motivation through WALS features. This line of work has seen subsequent improvements by Zhang and Barzilay (2015), who introduce a hierarchical tensor-based model for constraining the learned representations based on desired feature interactions. Georgi et al. (2010) and Rama and Kolachina (2012) used WALS to evaluate the concept of language similarity for facilitating cross-lingual NLP. Östling (2015) used WALS to evaluate word order typologies induced through word alignments. O'Horan et al. (2016) provide a comprehensive survey on the usage of typological information in NLP.

Plank and Van Noord (2011) applied similarity measures over cross-domain data for dependency

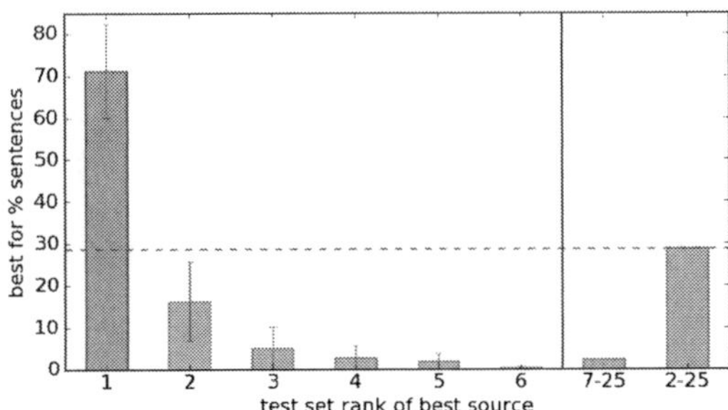

Figure 2: Distribution of per-sentence top-scoring source parsers over their test-set ranks. Blue: Percentage of sentences for which the best parser was ranked #1 in test set-based evaluation. Red: Sentences where the best parser was ranked #2-25, i.e., not ranked #1. The percentages are averaged over 26 languages.

parser adaptation. Prior to our contribution, only Rosa and Žabokrtský (2015a; 2015b) attempted to address source parser selection, by using KL divergence over gold POS tags.

8 Conclusions

We introduced an unbiased approach for cross-lingual transfer of delexicalized parsers. It is a robust and scalable source parser selection and reparsing system for low-resource languages. In a realistic experiment over cross-lingual POS tags and varying quantities of input text, our method remarkably outperformed even the informed upper bound delexicalized system. We emphasize the importance of acknowledging specifics of actual low-resource languages through realistic experiment design when proposing solutions aimed at addressing these languages.

Acknowledgements

We are thankful to Héctor Martínez Alonso, Barbara Plank, and Natalie Schluter for their valuable comments on an earlier version of the paper. We also thank the anonymous reviewers for their feedback. Finally, we acknowledge the NVIDIA Corporation for supporting our research.

References

Željko Agić, Dirk Hovy, and Anders Søgaard. 2015. If all you have is a bit of the Bible: Learning POS taggers for truly low-resource languages. In *ACL*, pages 268–272.

Željko Agić, Anders Johannsen, Barbara Plank, Héctor Martínez Alonso, Natalie Schluter, and Anders Søgaard. 2016. Multilingual Projection for Parsing Truly Low-Resource Languages. *TACL*, 4:301–312.

Waleed Ammar, George Mulcaire, Miguel Ballesteros, Chris Dyer, and Noah A. Smith. 2016. Many Languages, One Parser. *TACL*, pages 431–444.

Bernd Bohnet. 2010. Very High Accuracy and Fast Dependency Parsing is not a Contradiction. In *COLING*, pages 89–97.

Thorsten Brants. 2000. TnT: A Statistical Part-of-Speech Tagger. In *ANLP*, pages 224–231.

Dipanjan Das and Slav Petrov. 2011. Unsupervised Part-of-Speech Tagging with Bilingual Graph-Based Projections. In *ACL*, pages 600–609.

Matthew S. Dryer and Martin Haspelmath, editors. 2013. *The World Atlas of Language Structures Online*. Max Planck Institute for Evolutionary Anthropology, Leipzig.

Ryan Georgi, Fei Xia, and William Lewis. 2010. Comparing Language Similarity Across Genetic and Typologically-Based Groupings. In *COLING*, pages 385–393.

Jan Hajič, Massimiliano Ciaramita, Richard Johansson, Daisuke Kawahara, Maria Antònia Martí, Lluís Màrquez, Adam Meyers, Joakim Nivre, Sebastian Padó, Jan Štěpánek, et al. 2009. The CoNLL-2009 Shared Task: Syntactic and Semantic Dependencies in Multiple Languages. In *CoNLL*, pages 1–18.

Anders Johannsen, Željko Agić, and Anders Søgaard. 2016. Joint Part-of-Speech and Dependency Projection from Multiple Sources. In *ACL*, pages 561–566.

Marco Lui and Timothy Baldwin. 2012. langid.py: An Off-the-Shelf Language Identification Tool. In *ACL*, pages 25–30.

Xuezhe Ma and Fei Xia. 2014. Unsupervised Dependency Parsing with Transferring Distribution via Parallel Guidance and Entropy Regularization. In *ACL*, pages 1337–1348.

Ryan McDonald, Slav Petrov, and Keith Hall. 2011. Multi-Source Transfer of Delexicalized Dependency Parsers. In *EMNLP*, pages 62–72.

Ryan McDonald, Joakim Nivre, Yvonne Quirmbach-Brundage, Yoav Goldberg, Dipanjan Das, Kuzman Ganchev, Keith Hall, Slav Petrov, Hao Zhang, Oscar Täckström, Claudia Bedini, Núria Bertomeu Castelló, and Jungmee Lee. 2013. Universal Dependency Annotation for Multilingual Parsing. In *ACL*, pages 92–97.

Thomas Müller, Helmut Schmid, and Hinrich Schütze. 2013. Efficient Higher-Order CRFs for Morphological Tagging. In *EMNLP*, pages 322–332.

Tahira Naseem, Regina Barzilay, and Amir Globerson. 2012. Selective Sharing for Multilingual Dependency Parsing. In *ACL*, pages 629–637.

Joakim Nivre, Marie-Catherine de Marneffe, Filip Ginter, Yoav Goldberg, Jan Hajič, Christopher D Manning, Ryan McDonald, Slav Petrov, Sampo Pyysalo, Natalia Silveira, et al. 2016. Universal Dependencies v1: A Multilingual Treebank Collection. In *LREC 2016*, pages 1659–1666.

Helen O'Horan, Yevgeni Berzak, Ivan Vulić, Roi Reichart, and Anna Korhonen. 2016. Survey on the Use of Typological Information in Natural Language Processing. *arXiv preprint arXiv:1610.03349*.

Robert Östling. 2015. Word Order Typology Through Multilingual Word Alignment. In *ACL*, pages 205–211.

Slav Petrov, Dipanjan Das, and Ryan McDonald. 2011. A Universal Part-of-Speech Tagset. *arXiv preprint arXiv:1104.2086*.

Barbara Plank and Gertjan Van Noord. 2011. Effective Measures of Domain Similarity for Parsing. In *ACL*, pages 1566–1576.

Taraka Rama and Prasanth Kolachina. 2012. How Good are Typological Distances for Determining Genealogical Relationships among Languages? In *COLING*, pages 975–984.

Mohammad Sadegh Rasooli and Michael Collins. 2015. Density-Driven Cross-Lingual Transfer of Dependency Parsers. In *EMNLP*, pages 328–338.

Rudolf Rosa and Zdeněk Žabokrtský. 2015a. KLcpos3 - a Language Similarity Measure for Delexicalized Parser Transfer. In *ACL*, pages 243–249.

Rudolf Rosa and Zdeněk Žabokrtský. 2015b. MSTParser Model Interpolation for Multi-source Delexicalized Transfer. In *IWPT*, pages 71–75.

Kenji Sagae and Alon Lavie. 2006. Parser Combination by Reparsing. In *NAACL*, pages 129–132.

Anders Søgaard and Julie Wulff. 2012. An Empirical Study of Non-Lexical Extensions to Delexicalized Transfer. In *COLING*, pages 1181–1190.

Anders Søgaard. 2011. Data Point Selection for Cross-Language Adaptation of Dependency Parsers. In *ACL*, pages 682–686.

Oscar Täckström, Ryan McDonald, and Joakim Nivre. 2013. Target Language Adaptation of Discriminative Transfer Parsers. In *NAACL*, pages 1061–1071.

Daniel Zeman and Philip Resnik. 2008. Cross-Language Parser Adaptation between Related Languages. In *IJCNLP*, pages 35–42.

Yuan Zhang and Regina Barzilay. 2015. Hierarchical Low-Rank Tensors for Multilingual Transfer Parsing. In *EMNLP*, pages 1857–1867.

Swedish prepositions are not pure function words

Lars Ahrenberg
Department of Computer and Information Science
Linköping University
lars.ahrenberg@liu.se

Abstract

As for any categorial scheme used for annotation, UD abound with borderline cases. The main instruments to resolve them are the UD design principles and, of course, the linguistic facts of the matter. UD makes a fundamental distinction between content words and function words, and a, perhaps less fundamental, distinction between pure function words and the rest. It has been suggested that adpositions are to be included among the pure function words. In this paper I discuss the case of prepositions in Swedish and related languages in the light of these distinctions. It relates to a more general problem: How should we resolve cases where the linguistic intuitions and UD design principles are in conflict?

1 Introduction

The Universal Dependencies Project, henceforth UD, develops treebanks for a large number of languages with cross-linguistically consistent annotations. To serve this mission UD provides a universal inventory of categories and guidelines to facilitate consistent annotation of similar constructions across languages (Nivre et al., 2016). Automatic tools are also supplied so that annotators can check their annotations.

Important features of the UD framework are linguistic motivation, transparency, and accessibility for non-specialists. This is a delicate balance and it would be hard to claim that they always go hand in hand.

As for any categorial scheme used for annotation, UD abound with borderline cases. The main instruments to resolve them are the guidelines, which in turn rests on the UD design principles. UD makes a basic distinction between con-

tent words and function words and adopts a policy of the primacy of content words. This means that dependencies primarily relate content words while function words as far as possible should have content words as heads. Thus, multiple function words related to the same content word should appear as siblings, not in a nested structure. However, as content words can be elided and (almost) any word can be negated, conjoined or be part of a fixed expression, some exceptions must be allowed.

It is suggested that there is a class of function words, called 'pure function words', with very limited potential for modification. This class 'includes auxiliary verbs, case markers (adpositions), and articles, but needs to be defined explicitly for each language' (UD, 2017c). The choice of candidates is motivated by the fact that some languages can do without them, or express corresponding properties morphologically. In the case of prepositions in Germanic languages the similarity with case suffixes in languages such as Finnish or Russian is pointed out. As noted in (Marneffe et al., 2014) this is a break with the earlier Stanford Dependencies framework, one of the UD forerunners. Thus, a special dependency relation, *case*, is associated with prepositions in their most typical use (see Figures 1 and 2).

It is not clear from the characterization of pure function words if the identification must be made in terms of general categories or in terms of individual words. Given the examples it seems that a combination of part-of-speech categories and features may suffice. We can note that subjunctions are not listed among the pure function words. On the contrary, the UD guidelines include an example, 'just when you thought it was over' where 'just' is analysed as an adverbial modifier, *advmod*, of the subjunction 'when' (UD, 2017c).

The aim of this paper is to discuss how well Swedish prepositions fit the category of pure func-

11

Proceedings of the NoDaLiDa 2017 Workshop on Universal Dependencies (UDW 2017), pages 11–18,
Gothenburg, Sweden, 22 May 2017.

tion words. In the next section I will present data illustrating the range of uses for Swedish prepositions and review the current UD guidelines for their analysis. In section 3, the actual analysis of prepositions in Swedish and other Germanic treebanks will be reviewed. Then, in section 4, the data and the analyses will be discussed with a view to the problems of fuzzy borders in UD, in particular as regards the classification of words. Finally, in section 5, the conclusions are stated.

2   Prepositions in Swedish

Consider the following Swedish sentences, all containing the preposition *på* (on, in):

(1)   Max säljer blommor på torget
      Max sells flowers in the market-square
(2)   Max sätter på kaffet
      Max is making coffee
(3)   Max litar på Linda
      Max trusts Linda

A traditional descriptive account of these sentences goes as follows: In (1) 'på torget' is an adverbial, providing an answer to the question 'Var säljer Max blommor?' (Where does Max sell flowers). It may be moved to the front of the clause as in 'På torget säljer Max blommor'. In (2) 'på kaffet' is not a constituent; it does not answer a question about the location of something, and it cannot be moved to the front. Instead, it is construed with the verb as a verb particle, which means that it will receive stress in speech, and the word 'kaffet' is analysed as an object of the complex *sätta på*. In (3) 'på Linda' is a prepositional (or adverbial) object of the verb. It can be moved to the front but it does not express a location, and the preposition is not stressed.

In UD, the distinction between adverbials and adverbial objects is not made. Thus, for both sentences (1) and (3) the preposition will be assigned the dependency *case* in relation to its head nominal, which in turn will be an oblique dependent (*obl*) of the main verb, as depicted in Figures 1 and 2. The prime motivation is this: *The core-oblique distinction is generally accepted in language typology as being both more relevant and easier to apply cross-linguistically than the argument-adjunct distinction* (UD, 2017a). This position then assumes that we should only have a binary

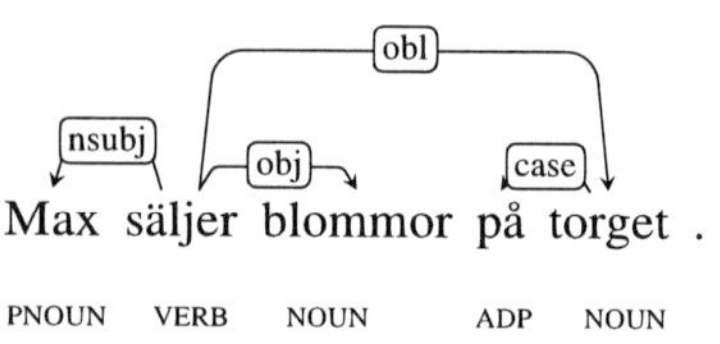

Figure 1: Partial analysis of sentence (1)

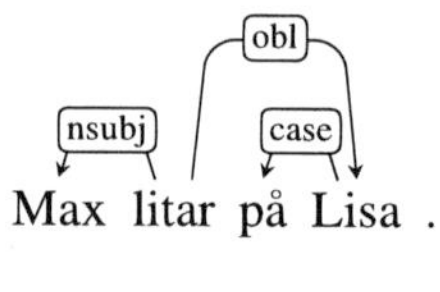

Figure 2: Partial analysis of sentence (3)

division of the nominal dependents of a verb[1].

Although its dependency is different in (2), *på* can be tagged as an ADP there as well. Alternatively, given the possibility of (4), it may be regarded as an adverb (ADV).

(4)   Kaffet är på
      Coffee is on i.e., in the making

Arguably, in (4) 'på' must be analysed as the root as the verb 'är' (*is*) is a copula here, another type of function word in UD. Hence it shouldn't be a function word, specifically not a pure function word. Whatever decision we take on 'på' in these examples they illustrate that the border between content words and function words is not always clear-cut.

Another difference between (1) and (3) is the interpretation of the preposition. In (1) it seems to have more semantic content than in (3). It has a lexical meaning which is independent of the main verb and which can be used in construction with any nominal that refers to an object with a horizontal surface held parallel to the ground. This independence is also shown by the possibility of using a phrase of this type as the title of a story or an image caption. This lexical meaning is not present in (3) where the occurrence and interpretation is wholly dependent on the verb. Thus, (1) can answer a question such as 'Vad händer på torget?' (What's happening in the market square?), whereas (3) cannot answer the question 'Vad händer på Linda?' (What's happen-

---

[1]Formally, further specification could be implemented via the :-technique, but this is reserved for relations assumed to be language-specific

ing on Linda?).

The fact that we can distinguish between (1) and (3) does not necessarily mean that we must do so for any occurrence of a phrase that UD considers to be oblique. In other cases the classification can be much more difficult. UD, however, demands of us to make many other distinctions at the same level of difficulty, including that between pure and non-pure function words and, as we just saw, that between adpositions and adverbs. Other fundamental distinctions concern clauses vs. noun phrases, which have distinct sets of dependencies and largely distinct sets of constituents. For example, adpositions are regarded as different from subjunctions, presumably because typically adpositions are found with noun phrases while subjunctions are found with clauses.

For a scheme such as UD with its 17 part-of-speech categories and some 37 dependency relations there are many borderline cases. The design principles can help us decide, but sometimes they are not informative enough, and may be in conflict with linguistic intuitions. It can also be observed that the design principles are much more developed for syntax than for parts-of-speech.

2.1 Recommended UD analyses

Sentences (1)-(4) showed us different uses of Swedish prepositions. We have seen how UD treats (1) and (3). For (2) the relation *compound:prt* is used, telling us that we are dealing with a specific subtype of multiword expressions. For (4), it was suggested that the preposition is root, although possibly re-categorized as an adverb.

Sentences (5)-(8) illustrates other uses of prepositions in Swedish. They may be stranded as in (5a), or isolated as in (5b) and (5c). They may introduce a VP as in (6a), or a clause as in (6b). They may be modified as in (7) and they may follow after an auxiliary verb, as in (8).

UD has recommendations for all of these cases. For stranded and isolated prepositions the recommendation is *When the natural head of a function word is elided, the function word will be promoted to the function normally assumed by the content word head.* Thus, in (5a) 'på' will relate to 'lita' via the *obl* relation. (5b) and (5c) can be treated in the same way.

Another option used in both the English treebank and Swedish_LinES is to let the moved nom-

(5a)   Vem kan man lita på?
       Who can you trust?
(5b)   Max fick en bild att titta på.
       Max got a picture to look at.
(5c)   Max sitter därborta och Linda
       sitter bredvid.
       Max sits over there and Linda
       sits beside.
(6a)   Max tröttnade på att vänta.
       Max got tired of waiting
(6b)   Max litar på att Linda ringer.
       Max trusts that Linda will call.
(7)   Max blev träffad mitt på näsan.
       Max was hit right on his nose.
(8)   Jag måste i nu.
       I have to get in(to the water) now.

inal be the head of the *case* dependency. An English example (from UD_English item 0029) similar to (5a) is shown in Table 1. This solution can be applied in (5a) and (5b) but not in (5c) except via an enhanced dependency. In (5c), the lack of an NP after the preposition can be attributed to the discourse context.

1 He	PRON	3	nsubj
2 obviously	ADV	3	advmod
3 had	VERB	0	root
4 no	DET	5	det
5 idea	NOUN	3	obj
6 what	PRON	9	obl
7 he	PRON	9	nsubj
8 was	AUX	9	aux
9 talking	VERB	3	ccomp
10 about	ADP	6	case

Table 1: Example analysis from the UD_English treebank.

For (6a) and (6b) the recommendation is to use the *mark* relation, which is otherwise typically used for subjunctions. The issue was discussed in the UD forum (issue #257) with the conclusion that the preposition could keep its POS tag while being assigned the relation *mark*. The main argument was that if the relation would be *case*, it would not be possible to reveal an occurrence of an ADP with the relation *case* to a VERB as an error automatically. This is a good way to promote consistency of annotation, but is quite arbitrary from a linguistic point of view.

For (7) the UD recommendation is that the adverb 'mitt' (right) modifies the head noun 'nä]san' (nose) rather than the preposition. This is in line with the desired constraint that function words should not have dependents, but is contrary to semantic intuitions and the fact that the phrase '*träffad mitt näsan' is ungrammatical. Given that subjunctions are allowed to have adverbs as modifiers, just as predicates, the asymmetry in analyses seems unmotivated. Note that 'på' in 'mitt på' has spatial lexical meaning, in the same way as 'när' (when) has a distinct temporal meaning in a phrase such as 'just när' (just when).

Sentence (8) is similar to (4) involving an auxiliary rather than a copula. The solution can be the same, i.e., analysing the token *i* (in) as root but tagged as adverb rather than as adposition.

3 Adpositions in UD treebanks

As expected, the most common dependency relation assigned to adpositions in Germanic treebanks is *case*. Other alternatives fall far behind. Overall relative frequencies for the treebanks of the Scandinavian languages, English, and German from the v2.0 release (Nivre et al., 2017) are shown in Table 2. The counts are based on the train- and dev-treebanks joined together. Note that Table 2 does not show all alternatives.

Treebank	case	mark	cmp:prt
Danish	0.842	0.110	0.009
English	0.923	0.005	0.041
German	0.952	0.008	0.029
No-Bokmaal	0.801	0.115	0.063
No-Nynorsk	0.795	0.108	0.067
Swedish	0.851	0.059	0.027
Sw-LinES	0.970	0.000	0.009

Table 2: Relative frequencies for some dependency relations of ADP tokens in seven UD v2.0 treebanks.

Of the five Scandinavian treebanks all except Swedish-LinES frequently give an ADP the relation *mark*. Swedish-LinES only has one example; English and German have only a few instances,

The rightmost column of Table 2 shows that there are marked differences in relative frequency for the relation *compound:prt* as applied to ADP tokens in these treebanks. This difference gets its explanation when we look at what parts-of-speech these particles are assigned, shown in Table 3. English and the Norwegian treebanks have a clear dominance for adpositions, German a clear majority, while adverbs are in the majority in the Swedish and Danish treebanks .

Treebank	ADP	ADV	other
Danish	92 (0.25)	269	0
English	802 (0.98)	16	3
German	901 (0.61)	562	3
No-Bokmaal	2308 (1.00)	0	0
No-Nynorsk	2585 (1.00)	0	0
Swedish	236 (0.35)	411	37
Sw-LinES	64 (0.10)	500	62

Table 3: Frequencies for parts-of-speech assigned the relation compound:prt in different treebanks.

Given the close relationship between these languages it is hard to believe that the differences are solely due to language differences. It is more likely that the annotators have followed different principles both as regards parts-of-speech and dependency relations. For instance, the Norwegian treebanks analyse as ADP a number of verb particles that in the Swedish treebanks are analysed as adverbs, such as (from the Norwegian-Bokmaal treebank) *bort* (away), *hjem* (home), *inn* (in), *opp, oppe* (up), *tilbake* (back), *ut* (out).

It is also interesting to look at cases where a preposition has been analysed as the head of a dependency. As expected we find many instances of *fixed* and *conj* in most of the treebanks, but the distributions are not at all similar, as shown in Table 4. The differences are probably due both to differences in treebank-specific guidelines, and to errors in applying them. An interesting fact, however, is that all of them have instances of *advmod*, and just not for negations. Some of these are likely to be errors, but some reasonable examples are the following: *omedelbart efter lunch* (Sw-LinES; immediately after lunch), *langt fra hele* (No-Bokmaal; far from all), *andre ting kan han gå sterkt imot* (No-Nynorsk; other things he may go strongly against), *up to 40 rockets* (English), and *genauso wie in Portugal* (German; just as in Portugal). All of them also have instances of prepositions governing a copula.

Table 5 shows data on part-of-speech assignments for all words that have been analysed as an adposition at least once. Note that the treebanks may have errors so that the figures should not be taken as exact, but the differences in distributions are nevertheless interesting. The first col-

Treebank	fixed	conj	advmod	other
Danish	0.34	0.03	0.03	0.61
English	0.65	0.03	0.03	0.28
German	0.02	0.04	0.06	0.87
No-Bokmaal	0	0.12	0.14	0.74
No-Nynorsk	0	0.10	0.14	0.76
Swedish	0.85	0.02	0.05	0.08
Sw-LinES	0.61	0.08	0.02	0.29

Table 4: Relative frequencies for dependency relations headed by ADP tokens in seven UD v2.0 treebanks.

umn shows the number of words that have ADP as their only part-of-speech tag. We can see that the Norwegian treebanks are markedly different from the others in recognizing a very high number of non-ambiguous adpositional words.

The two Swedish treebanks have different distributions. This may partly be due to differences in genre, but also to differences in the specific guidelines used. In both treebanks, however, we will find tokens that are found in both ADP and ADV, other tokens that are sometimes ADP and sometimes SCONJ and yet others having all three tags.

Treebank	Instances			
	1	2	3	≥ 4
Danish	20	20	13	1
English	34	29	31	35
German	48	48	26	28
No-Bokmaal	116	34	6	3
No-Nynorsk	121	33	13	4
Swedish	44	20	8	2
Sw-LinES	35	39	11	3

Table 5: Number of different POS assignments for words that have been tagged as ADP at least once in different UD v2.0 treebanks.

4 Discussion

The previous section shows with no uncertainty that the UD guidelines and design principles are not followed uniformly by all treebank developers. There are natural explanations for this, such as differences in the original pre-UD guidelines for the different treebanks, and a lack of time for reviewing treebank data. I suspect, however, that there is also a certain conflict between the UD principles and linguistic intuitions of treebank annotators.

4.1 UD part-of-speech categories

The POS tags used in UD are 17. They form an extension of the 12 categories of (Petrov et al., 2012). We note in particular the addition of the category SCONJ for subjunctions.

A treebank is allowed not to use all POS tags. However, the list cannot be extended. Instead, more fine-grained classification of words can be achieved via the use of features (UD, 2017b). In annotations only one tag per word is allowed, and it must be specified.

The basic division of the POS tags is in terms of open class, closed class, and other. The point of dividing them this way is unclear, since most of the syntactic principles referring to POS tags as we have seen use the categories content words and function words[2].

The POS tags that will be of interest here are: ADP(ositions), ADV(erbs), and SCONJ (subordinating conjunctions). These classes are singled out as they are hard to separate consistently and account for a large share of the homonymy found in Table 4. Moreover, many linguists such as (Bolinger, 1971; Emonds, 1985; Aarts, 2007) have questioned the linguistic motivations behind the distinctions. It may also be a problem for users who may find the distinctions less than transparent. The definitions of these parts-of-speech in the UD documentation are not always of help as they focus on the most common and prototypical examples. The categories ADP and SCONJ have partly overlapping definitions. An SCONJ is described as typically incorporating what follows it as a subordinate clause, while an ADP, in addition to NP:s, may have a clause as its complement, when it functions as a noun phrase[3].

4.2 Prepositions and subjunctions

As many other prepositions 'på' can in itself not be used as a subjunction. Removing the infinitive marker from (6a) or the subjunction 'att' from (6b) results in ungrammaticality. There are, however, in Swedish, as in English, many words that can be used both ways, specifically those expressing temporal or causal relations, and comparisons. Common examples are *sedan* (since), *på grund av* (because of), *än* (than), *efter* (after), *innan* (before)

---

[2] A wish for an exact definition was expressed by Dan Zeman in the UD forum issue #122

[3] This description may refer to constructions headed by a gerund, free relatives, and the like, but is fairly non-transparent for a non-linguist.

and *före* (before). The latter two are the subject of a constant debate on grammatical correctness in Swedish where purists would hold that one is a preposition and the other a subjunction, but speakers tend not to follow suit.

For these words the meaning is quite the same whether what follows is a noun phrase or a clause. This fact has been taken as an argument that the prepositions and subjunctions are sufficiently similar to be regarded as one category. The difference can be seen as one of complementation which, in the case of verbs, is not sufficient to distinguish two part-of-speech categories (Emonds, 1976). In UD it may be seen as logical to distinguish the two, given the emphasis on the distinction between noun phrases and clauses. On the other hand, this leads to certain oddities of the kind that allow these words to have dependents when they are subjunctions, but not when they are adpositions.

Sentence (7) illustrated the fact that Swedish prepositions may be modified. There are a number of adverbs that can modify prepositions and some of them can modify prepositions and subjunctions alike. Examples are *alldeles*, (just) *rakt*, *rätt* (both meaning 'right'), *precis* (exactly). Examples are given in (9) and (10)[4]. Spatial and temporal prepositions may actually be modified by noun phrases indicating distance in space and time, as in (11)-(12). Thus, the potential of Swedish prepositions to be modified is quite equal to that of subjunctions.

(9)   Hon kom precis före (oss).
       She came just before us.
(10)   Hon kom precis innan (vi kom).
       She came just before we did.
(11)   Hon kom en timme före (oss).
       She came an hour before us.
(12)   De sitter två rader bakom (oss).
       They're sitting two rows behind (us).

4.3 Adpositions as *mark*

As noted above, the current recommendation for the analysis of (6b) in UD is that the preposition 'på' should be assigned as a dependent of the head of the following clause, in this case the verb 'ringer' (call). This is so because 'på' is not a verb particle in (6b) and it can only attach to the main verb if it functions as a particle. Then there are two

relations to choose from: *case* or *mark*. None of them is ideal; if we choose *case* we add a dependency to clauses which seems to be rare in other languages and which blurs the distinction between clauses and noun phrases; if we choose *mark* we add a property to adpositions that make them more similar to subjunctions.

Another issue is the relation assigned to the clause itself. In the Swedish treebank it is *advcl*. Normally, a clause introduced by the subjunction 'att' would be *ccomp*. However, in the same way as a noun phrase introduced by a preposition would be *obl* it is logical to use *advcl*. Then again, this makes the difference between prepositions and subjunctions fuzzier.

Now, the clause 'att hon ringer' is as independent in (6b) as 'Linda' is in (3). It can be moved to the front ('Att Linda ringer litar Max på'), it can be the target of a question ('Vad litar du på?') and it can be focused: ('Är det något jag litar på är det att Linda ringer'). Thus, there is an NP-like flavour of these verb-headed structures, just as for prepositional objects, suggesting that *ccomp* may be a viable alternative nevertheless.

An interesting observation is the UD recommendation for the analysis of comparative subjunctions such as 'än' (than) and 'som' (as). Since they can virtually combine with phrases of any kind, including clauses, prepositional phrases, and noun phrases, and may use nominative pronouns in the latter case, the question arises as how they should be analysed[5]. In a phrase such as 'än Max' (than Max), 'än' could be an ADP with relation 'case', or it could be an SCONJ with relation 'mark'. However, given the new option why not an ADP with relation 'mark'? We may note that the most detailed analysis of Swedish grammar regards all instances 'än' as subjunctions and allows 'subjunction phrases' (Teleman et al., 2010). We may even regard a phrase such as 'than on Sundays' to have two case markers. The choice seems arbitrary.

The UD decision not to make a distinction between complements and adjuncts serves the interests of transparency and ease of annotation. It means, however, that the UD analyses do not make all the differences that can be made so that what is arguably different phenomena gets identical analyses. When it comes to part-of-speech annota-

---

[4]The brackets indicate material that can be left out without loss of grammaticality.

[5]In the UD_Swedish treebank these two words are actually tagged CCONJ.

tion the situation is a bit different. Extensions are not allowed, but sub-categorization is required (or requested) for some parts-of-speech, specifically pronouns and determiners via features.

We have noted that UD principles are fewer and less developed for part-of-speech categories than for syntax. In particular, there are no principles regulating the degree of homonymy. The current framework suggests that Swedish has three homonyms for the word *innan* (before) although they all have the same meaning. If the framework allowed fewer part-of-speech categories, the degree of homonymy would decrease and annotation would be easier. In particular the degree of homonymity of prepositions could decrease (cf. Table 5).

The idea that prepositions must be pure function words due to their presumed equivalence with case endings can be put into question. The sentences (5)-(8) all illustrate uses that are specific to prepositions. Also, when prepositions have clear semantic content they can be modified in various ways, just as corresponding subjunctions. At the same time there are subjunctions, notably the complementizers such as 'att' (that) and 'som' (that, which) that cannot be modified easily, not even negated. This fact speaks against the view that all adpositions should be put into one basket as pure function words whereas subjunctions should be put into another.

4.4 Prepositions and adverbs

The words that need to be regarded as both prepositions and adverbs are numerous. It includes common prepositions as illustrated in (4) and (8) and a number of prepositions expressing spatial relations such as *utanför* (outside), *innanför* (inside), *nedanför* (down, below), *nerför* (down), and *uppför* (up). For the latter the differences in meaning are minimal, whereas for the more common prepositions such as *på* (on) or *i* (in), the meanings may be varied.

We note that when a sequence of a preposition and a noun is lexicalized into a fixed expression, the result is almost always something adverbial. Some examples are *i kväll* (tonight), *i tid* (in time), *på stört* (at once), *på nytt* (again), *på land* (ashore). In some treebanks, notably UD_Swedish, the preposition keeps its part-of-speech while being assigned the dependency 'advmod'.

We can apply the same arguments and counter-arguments in this case as for the previous case. The difference may be seen just as a difference in complementation, where some prepositions can have both a transitive and an intransitive use and still be prepositions. However, if prepositions are pure function words, and adverbs are not, UD forces a distinction to be made.

5 Conclusions

We have observed that the UD design principles are more elaborated for syntax than for parts-of-speech. This could be interpreted as a recommendation not to take parts-of-speech too seriously; we may assume as much homonymy as the syntactic design principles demands of the data. On the other hand, what the non-expert user would consider to be 'the same word' in a given language should also be given some consideration. I would like to see an attempt to define UD parts-of-speech in more detail, preferably as lists of properties, taking gradience into account. (Aarts, 2007) proposes a simple model for this purpose, which may be taken as an inspiration. In the case of some adpositions and subjunctions such as *before*, however, Aarts sees no difference as it is only a question of complementation possibilities.

To join the categories ADP and SCONJ and include some adverbial uses as well would reduce ambiguity in part-of-speech assignment considerably. If it is desirable to maintain the difference it can be done in the feature column by, say, a type feature (AdpType).

Swedish prepositions, and those of other Scandinavian languages, are more varied in their usage than case suffixes. At the same time, they share important properties with subjunctions and adverbs. Semantically they span the same domains and they share typical positions. The current UD principles allow Swedish prepositions to share the relation *mark* with subjunctions, and the relation *compound:prt* with adverbs. In addition, they share those relations that are common to all parts-of-speech, such as *fixed* and *conj*. Linguistically, at least, Swedish prepositions can be modified adverbially when they have semantic content. Thus, Swedish prepositions are not pure function words.

The possibility to take dependents seems to be more on the level of individual words than a property across the board for any part of speech. In

Swedish it can be found also with subjunctions, in particular complementizers such as *att*, (that), conjunctions such as *och* (and), and adverbs such as *ju* (approx. 'you know'). With this in mind, it can be questioned what benefits are gained from dividing function words further into pure and not-so-pure on the basis of parts-of-speech.

References

Bas Aarts. 2007. *Syntactic Gradience: The Nature of Grammatical Indeterminacy.* Oxford University Press, Oxford.

Dwight L. Bolinger. 1971. *The Phrasal Verb in English.* Harvard University Press, Cambridge, MA.

Joseph E. Emonds. 1976. *A Transformational Approach to English Syntax.* Academic Press, New York.

Joseph E. Emonds. 1985. *A Unified Theory of Syntactic Categories.* Foris, Dordrecht.

Marie-Catherine De Marneffe, Timothy Dozat, Natalia Silveira, Katri Haverinen, Filip Ginter, Joakim Nivre, and Christopher D. Manning. 2014. Universal stanford dependencies: a cross-linguistic typology. In *Proceedings of the Ninth International Conference on Language Resources and Evaluation (LREC'14)*, Reykjavik, Iceland, may.

Joakim Nivre, Marie-Catherine de Marneffe, Filip Ginter, Yoav Goldberg, Jan Hajič, Christopher D. Manning, Ryan McDonald, Slav Petrov, Sampo Pyysalo, Natalia Silveira, Reut Tsarfaty, and Daniel Zeman. 2016. Universal dependencies v1: A multilingual treebank collection. In *Proceedings of the Tenth International Conference on Language Resources and Evaluation (LREC 2016)*.

Joakim Nivre, Željko Agić, Lars Ahrenberg, Maria Jesus Aranzabe, Masayuki Asahara, Aitziber Atutxa, Miguel Ballesteros, John Bauer, Kepa Bengoetxea, Riyaz Ahmad Bhat, Eckhard Bick, Cristina Bosco, Gosse Bouma, Sam Bowman, Marie Candito, Gülşen Cebirolu Eryiit, Giuseppe G. A. Celano, Fabricio Chalub, Jinho Choi, Çar Çöltekin, Miriam Connor, Elizabeth Davidson, Marie-Catherine de Marneffe, Valeria de Paiva, Arantza Diaz de Ilarraza, Kaja Dobrovoljc, Timothy Dozat, Kira Droganova, Puneet Dwivedi, Marhaba Eli, Tomaž Erjavec, Richárd Farkas, Jennifer Foster, Cláudia Freitas, Katarína Gajdošová, Daniel Galbraith, Marcos Garcia, Filip Ginter, Iakes Goenaga, Koldo Gojenola, Memduh Gökrmak, Yoav Goldberg, Xavier Gómez Guinovart, Berta Gonzáles Saavedra, Matias Grioni, Normunds Grūzītis, Bruno Guillaume, Nizar Habash, Jan Hajič, Linh Hà M, Dag Haug, Barbora Hladká, Petter Hohle, Radu Ion, Elena Irimia, Anders Johannsen, Fredrik Jørgensen, Hüner Kaşkara, Hiroshi Kanayama, Jenna Kanerva, Natalia Kotsyba, Simon Krek, Veronika Laippala, Phng Lê Hng, Alessandro Lenci, Nikola Ljubešić, Olga Lyashevskaya, Teresa Lynn, Aibek Makazhanov, Christopher Manning, Cătălina Mărănduc, David Mareček, Héctor Martínez Alonso, André Martins, Jan Mašek, Yuji Matsumoto, Ryan McDonald, Anna Missilä, Verginica Mititelu, Yusuke Miyao, Simonetta Montemagni, Amir More, Shunsuke Mori, Bohdan Moskalevskyi, Kadri Muischnek, Nina Mustafina, Kaili Müürisep, Lng Nguyn Th, Huyn Nguyn Th Minh, Vitaly Nikolaev, Hanna Nurmi, Stina Ojala, Petya Osenova, Lilja Øvrelid, Elena Pascual, Marco Passarotti, Cenel-Augusto Perez, Guy Perrier, Slav Petrov, Jussi Piitulainen, Barbara Plank, Martin Popel, Lauma Pretkalnia, Prokopis Prokopidis, Tiina Puolakainen, Sampo Pyysalo, Alexandre Rademaker, Loganathan Ramasamy, Livy Real, Laura Rituma, Rudolf Rosa, Shadi Saleh, Manuela Sanguinetti, Baiba Saulīte, Sebastian Schuster, Djamé Seddah, Wolfgang Seeker, Mojgan Seraji, Lena Shakurova, Mo Shen, Dmitry Sichinava, Natalia Silveira, Maria Simi, Radu Simionescu, Katalin Simkó, Mária Šimková, Kiril Simov, Aaron Smith, Alane Suhr, Umut Sulubacak, Zsolt Szántó, Dima Taji, Takaaki Tanaka, Reut Tsarfaty, Francis Tyers, Sumire Uematsu, Larraitz Uria, Gertjan van Noord, Viktor Varga, Veronika Vincze, Jonathan North Washington, Zdeněk Žabokrtský, Amir Zeldes, Daniel Zeman, and Hanzhi Zhu. 2017. Universal dependencies 2.0. LINDAT/CLARIN digital library at the Institute of Formal and Applied Linguistics, Charles University.

Slav Petrov, Dipanjan Das, and Ryan McDonald. 2012. A universal part-of-speech tagset. In *Proceedings of the Eigth International Conference on Language Resources and Evaluation (LREC 2016)*, Istanbul, Turkey, may.

Ulf Teleman, Erik Andersson, and Staffan Hellberg. 2010. *Svenska Akademins Grammatik.* Norstedts, Stockholm.

UD. 2017a. Core dependents in ud v2. http://universaldependencies.org/v2/core-dependents.html.

UD. 2017b. Morphology: General principles. http://universaldependencies.org/u/overview/morphology.html.

UD. 2017c. Syntax: General principles. http://universaldependencies.org/u/overview/syntax.html.

Increasing return on annotation investment: the automatic construction of a Universal Dependency treebank for Dutch

Gosse Bouma
Centre for Language and Cognition
University of Groningen
`g.bouma@rug.nl`

Gertjan van Noord
Centre for Language and Cognition
University of Groningen
`g.j.m.van.noord@rug.nl`

Abstract

We present a method for automatically converting the Dutch Lassy Small treebank, a phrasal dependency treebank, to UD. All of the information required to produce accurate UD annotation appears to be available in the underlying annotation. However, we also note that the close connection between POS-tags and dependency labels that is present in UD is missing in the Lassy treebanks. As a consequence, annotation decisions in the Dutch data for such phenomena as nominalization and clausal complements of prepositions seem to differ to some extent from comparable data in English and German.

Because the conversion is automatic, we can now also compare three state-of-the-art dependency parsers trained on UD Lassy Small with Alpino, a hybrid Dutch parser which produces output that is compatible with the original Lassy annotations.

1 Introduction

We present a method for automatically converting Dutch treebanks annotated according to the guidelines of the Lassy project (van Noord et al., 2013) to Universal Dependencies. The Lassy annotation guidelines combine elements from phrase structure treebanks (such as phrasal nodes and use of co-indexed nodes for encoding fronted WH-constituents) with elements from dependency treebanks (such as dependency labels, discontinuous constituents and crossing branches), similar to the Tiger (Brants et al., 2002) and Negra (Skut et al., 1998) corpora for German. The conversion is done by means of an automatic conversion script.[1]

There are two advantages to such a procedure: the original annotation is of high quality as it is the result of careful manual checking and correction of automatically produced parser output. Using this investment as basis for the UD annotation as well means that this investment can also serve as basis for novel annotation projects. Second, an automatic conversion script allows any material that has been annotated according to the guidelines of the Lassy project to be converted to UD, and thus also can be used to convert treebanks outside the UD corpus and to make existing tools compliant with UD.

There are two main challenges for the conversion: the Lassy treebanks contain dependency relations between phrasal nodes, whereas UD uses lexical dependency relations only. Second, the Lassy Treebanks use a more traditional notion of 'head' whereas UD gives precedence to content words over function words. As a consequence, converting from Lassy to UD requires 'head-switching' in a number of cases. In section 2 we outline the main principles of the conversion process.

The conversion has been used to produce UD Dutch Lassy Small (v1.3 and 2.0). Lassy Small is a manually verified 1 million word treebank for Dutch, consisting of mixed sources. For reasons of intellectual property rights, only the Wikipedia part (7.641 sentences, 101.841 tokens) is included in the UD corpus.

One of the goals of the UD enterprise is to ensure similar annotations for similar constructions across languages. While the current state of the general and language specific annotation guidelines suggest that this should be possible for the most common syntactic configurations, it is also true that there still appears to be variation in the way less frequent constructions are annotated. This is particularly true if such constructions challenge the UD annotation principles. We

---

[1] Available at `https://github.com/gossebouma/lassy2ud`

Proceedings of the NoDaLiDa 2017 Workshop on Universal Dependencies (UDW 2017), pages 19–26,
Gothenburg, Sweden, 22 May 2017.

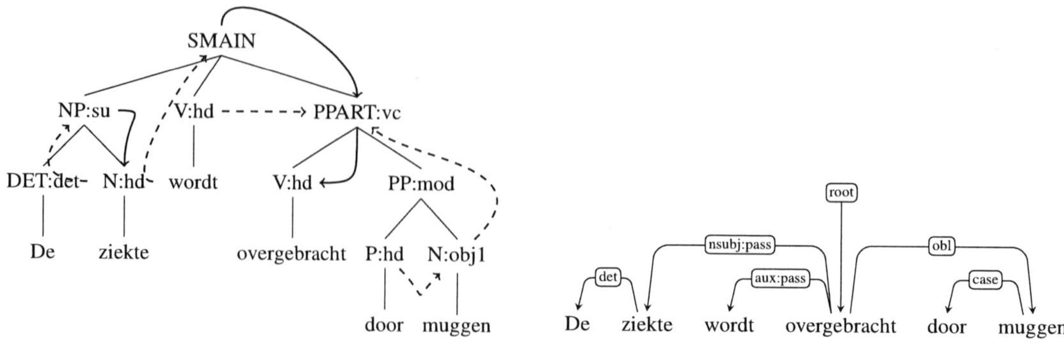

Figure 1: Phrasal annotation and the induced dependency annotation for *de ziekte wordt overgebracht door muggen* (*the disease is transmitted by flies*). External head projection paths are indicated by dashed arrows, and internal heads are indicated by solid arrows.

illustrate this in section 3 by comparing the analysis in Dutch, German, and English, of verbal nominalizations and clausal arguments of prepositions.

In section 4, we compare the performance of three dependency parsers trained on UD Lassy Small with Alpino (van Noord, 2006), a rule-based grammar that produces output compatible with the original Lassy treebank. The comparison crucially relies on the fact that we can use the conversion script to convert Alpino output to UD.

2 Conversion Process

Conversion of a manually verified treebank to UD is possible if the underlying annotation contains the information that is required to do a mapping from the original annotation to POS-tags and bilexical dependencies that is conformant with the annotation guidelines of the UD project. By doing an automatic conversion, we follow a strategy that has been used to create many of the other UD treebanks as well (Zeman et al., 2014; Johannsen et al., 2015; Øvrelid and Hohle, 2016; Ahrenberg, 2015; Lynn and Foster, 2016).

Conversion of Lassy to UD POS-tags can be achieved by means of a simple set of case statements that refer to the original POS-tag and a small set of morphological feature values. The only case that is more involved is the distinction between verbs and auxiliaries. This distinction is missing in the POS-tags and morphological features of the Lassy treebanks, but can be reconstructed using the lemma and valency of the verb (i.e., a limited set of verbs that select for only a subject and a

non-finite verbal complement or predicative complement are considered auxiliaries).

Conversion of the phrasal syntactic annotation to dependency relations is driven by the observation that in a dependency graph each word (except the root) is linked via a labeled arc to exactly one lexical head.[2] Given a sentence annotated according to Lassy guidelines, we can use the phrasal syntactic annotation to predict for each token in the input (except the root) its lexical content head and dependency label. Figure 1 gives an overview of the most important Lassy dependency labels and their UD counterparts.

The rules for finding the content head are defined using two auxiliary notions: the 'external head projection' of a word or phrase is the node that contains the content head for the node. The 'internal head' of a node or phrase is the node that is the content head of the phrase.

In regular configurations, the external head projection of a non-head word (i.e. a word labeled *su, obj1, det, mod, app, etc.*) is its mother node, and the internal head of this mother node is the node with dependency label *hd*. This is shown for example in Figure 1, where the determiner *De* has the NP as its external head projection. The *hd* node within this NP is the content head of this phrase, and thus the content head of the determiner. The external head projection of the *hd* word itself, *ziekte*, is not the parent but the grandparent node, SMAIN. Thus, the content head of *ziekte* is

---

[2]Currently, no secondary edges are used in the UD Lassy Small.

Lassy	UD	Interpretation
su	subj | csubj | nsubj:pass | csubj:pass	various kinds of subjects
obj1	obj | obl | nmod	objects of verbs and prepositions
obj2	iobj	indirect objects
mod	obl | advmod | advcl | nmod | amod	various kinds of modifiers
det	det | nummod	determiners and numbers
app	appos	appositions
cmp	mark	complementizers
crd	cc	conjunctions
sup	expl	expletives
pobj1	expl	expletives
hd		heads of phrases: check label of mother node
...	...	...

Table 1: Overview of re-labeling rules

the internal head of the SMAIN. In this case, as we explain below, this is not the *hd* daughter, but the content head of the daughter labeled with dependency label *vc* (*verbal complement*).

Head-switching cases are exceptions to the general rule. The noun *muggen*, for instance, has a prepositional head as sister. As UD specifies that prepositions are dependent on the noun in these cases, we have to specify that the external head projection of the *obj1* child inside a PP is the parent of the PP. For the same reason, the external head projection of the preposition is not the grandparent, but the sister *obj1* node. The same applies to auxiliaries. As they are dependents of the main verb, their external head projection is the sister node labeled *vc* (or *predc* in copula constructions).

Finally, as the main verb *overgebracht* functions as content head of both the PPART and SMAIN, its external head projection should be the parent of SMAIN. As SMAIN is the root of the phrasal tree, we conclude that *overgebracht* must be the root node.

The analysis of WH-questions and relative clauses in the Lassy treebank uses a co-indexing scheme between the fronted element and an empty node that is comparable to a 'trace' in transformational approaches. The content head for such co-indexed fronted elements can be found by starting the external head projection identification from the co-indexed empty 'trace' node.

The identification of the correct dependency label for a bi-lexical dependency uses a mapping from the original Lassy dependency labels to UD. The most important cases are listed in Table 1.

We have used the conversion script to create UD

Lassy Small (v1.3 and 2.0). This corpus consists of the Wikipedia section of the manually verified part of the Lassy corpus.

One aspect of the corpus that is not according to UD is the annotation of interpunction. As all punctuation marks are attached to the root node in the original treebank, locating the right attachment site according to UD rules is challenging. So far, we have not been able to come up with an error-free solution.

By way of evaluation of the result, we manually verified the annotation for 50 arbitrarily selected sentences from the corpus (v 2.0).[3] We checked whether the annotation was in accordance with the UD guidelines. In cases where we were not sure about the correct annotation (typically attachment decisions), we compared the annotation with the original Lassy treebank annotation. Ignoring punctuation issues, we observed 4 errors: a passive subject labeled as regular subject, an *amod* that has to be *advmod*, a number marked as *det* (should be *nummod*), and an error resulting from head-switching: the auxiliary *bekend staan* (*be known as*) consists of a vebal head and a particle. The head is marked as *cop*, but as a consequence of head-switching, the particle has been reattached to the predicative head. This is clearly wrong, although the right annotation is not obvious: either this verb should not be considered an auxiliary, or else we must allow for particles to be dependents of auxiliaries. In addition to these errors we also found 6 dubious decisions (unclear distinctions between *amod* and *advmod* (4×), labeling a

---

[3]All sentences from the training section containing the adverb *ook* (*also*).

predicative phrase as *xcomp*, and a case of an incomplete word (part of a coordination) marked as X (in accordance with the original annotation but not the best option according to UD),

We also tried to compare Lassy Small with the UD Dutch corpus that has been included in UD since v1.2. The latter corpus is a conversion of the Alpino treebank (van der Beek et al., 2002). It was used in the CONLL X shared task on dependency parsing (Buchholz and Marsi, 2006) and converted at that point to CONLL format. The UD version is based on a conversion to HamleDT to UD (Zeman et al., 2014). The various conversion steps have lead to loss of information,[4] and apparent mistakes,[5] and the quality of this corpus in general seems to be lower than the UD Lassy Small corpus. A more systematic comparison will be possible once we have been able to reconstruct the original sources of the material included in the Alpino treebank fragment used for CONLL. At that point, it will also be possible to create an improved version of the data using the current conversion script.

3   Cross-lingual comparison

The inventory of dependency labels in UD is a mixed functional-structural system, which distinguishes oblique arguments, for instance, on the basis of their part-of-speech, i.e. a PP dependent is labeled *obl*, a dependent clause *advcl*, and an adverbial *advmod*. Also, attachment to predicates is differentiated from attachment to nominals.

The original Lassy Small treebank has both phrasal categories and dependency labels, and seems to make a more clear-cut distinction between structural and dependency information. For instance, a single *mod*-relation is used for adjuncts in the verbal domain (PPs, adverbs and adverbial phrases, as well as clausal adjuncts) as well as in the nominal domain. The relevant structural distinctions are not lost, as phrasal nodes can be differentiated by the category and lexical items by their POS.

The mixed functional-structural approach of UD leads to surprising outcomes in cases where

---

[4]for instance, all heads and dependents of compound relations have been assigned the POS tag X, ignoring the original assignment of POS tags

[5]e.g. in 13.050 sentences, there are 353 cases where a verb or (proper) noun functions as dependent of the *case* relation, and 953 cases where an auxiliary has an *nsubj* dependent

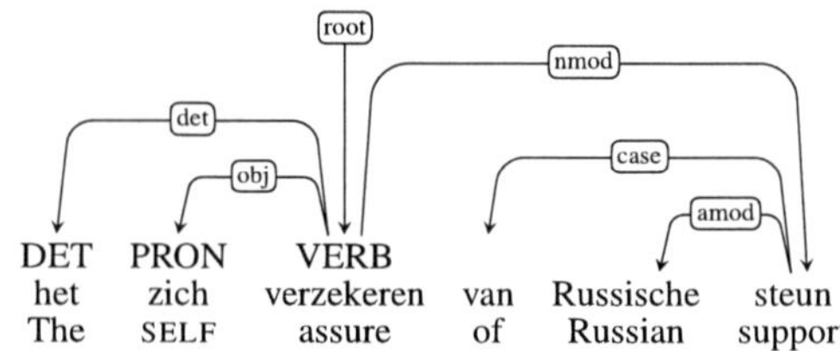

Figure 2: Nominalization in UD-Dutch Lassy Small

structural relations do not align with the predicate/nominal distinction. We discuss two such situations below.

3.1 Nominalizations

Nominalizations are constructions in which a verb functions as a noun. Nominalizations can be formed by means of derivational morphology, but there are also many cases in which there is no (overt) morphological suffix to mark the nominal status of the verb (Chomsky, 1968). Interestingly, in nominalizations we see both dependents typically associated with the verbal domain as well as dependents associated with the nominal domain, as in example (2). Here, a verb clearly heads a nominal phrase, as it is introduced by a determiner. Yet, at the same time, it selects an inherent reflexive pronoun, something that is not possible for nouns. The dependency annotation for this example in Figure 2 also shows that the PP phrase is labeled *nmod*, giving preference to the nominal interpretation of *verzekeren*. Note that the the the parallelism between (1) and (2) suggests that it could perhaps also have been labeled *obl*. In fact, the NomBank corpus (Meyers et al., 2004) adopts the rule that the same semantic role labels should be used as much as possible for verbs and nominalised versions of these verbs.

(1)   Hij verzekert zich   van Russische steun
       He assures   himself of Russian support

(2)   het zich verzekeren van Russische steun
      the self assuring   of Russian support
      was het doel
      was the goal
      'The assuring oneself of Russian support
      was the goal'

The presence of such mixed nominal/verbal configurations differs strongly between treebanks. In Table 2 we give counts for the number of verbs that have a *det* dependent, and for verbs that have an incoming dependency label *nsubj* or *obj* in the Dutch Lassy Small and German and English UD treebanks (v2.0).[6] In all cases, we are dealing with a verb that has clearly nominal properties: it has a determiner as dependent, or functions as subject or object of a predicate. The Dutch treebank has the highest number of nominalizations. It should also be noted that the (14) cases in English where a verb has a *det* dependent include bona fide cases like *the following* and *(please use) the attached*, but also several apparent annotation errors. The low number of nominalizations for English is unexpected, as nominalizations involving gerunds appear to be a common phenomenon in English.

| | NL | DE | EN |
Query	(101K)	(277K)	(229K)
VERB >det _	112.9	22.0	6.1
VERB <nsubj _	62.4	1.4	5.2
VERB <obj _	21.8	2.2	8.3

Table 2: Frequency per 100.000 tokens for verbal heads with nominal properties in three UD treebanks.

3.2 Clausal arguments of prepositions

Another situation where the distinction between the predicative and nominal domain gives surprising results are PPs containing a verbal rather than a nominal content head. Some of these are nominalizations, and were already discussed above. However, there are also genuine clausal cases as in Figure 3.

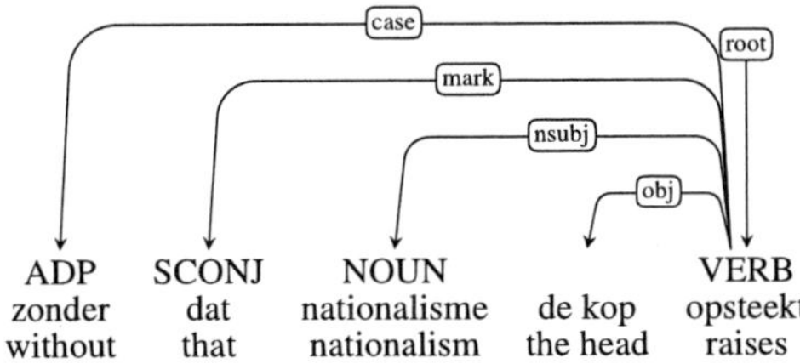

Figure 3: Prepositional phrases containing a clausal argument: *'without nationalism raising its head'*

Again, we compared counts for such phenomena in the Dutch, German, and English UD treebanks. Table 3 shows that verbs with a preposition as dependent or verbs heading a phrase with

label *obl* (i.e., verbs heading an oblique dependent of a predicate) do hardly occur in English, but do occur with some frequency in Dutch and German. However, closer inspection of the German data suggests that these are dominated by annotation errors of the form *nach Dortmund gefahren (driven to Dortmund)*, where a regular *obl* dependent of a verb has been annotated erroneously with a *case* relation between the verb and the preposition. Prepositions are seen as case markers in UD, and for that reason should only have dependents themselves in exceptional cases. Most of these cases are fixed phrases of the form *due to* or *because of*. This is true for the Dutch data and to a large extent also for the English data. The German data, however, has a high number of prepositions with dependents that are not labeled *fixed*. This might be another signal of the same annotation error, in that prepositions in the German data apparently head regular PPs in many cases.

query	NL	DE	EN
VERB >case ADP	102.0	105.8	0.4
VERB <obl _	64.4	0.0	4.8
ADP > _	357.4	253.4	97.8
ADP >fixed _	318.8	6.9	30.6

Table 3: Frequency per 100.000 tokens for verbs with a *case* dependent and prepositions governing a dependent.

We believe that the relatively high number of 'non-canonical' configurations in the Dutch Lassy Small treebank may well be due to the fact that POS-tagging and syntactic annotation were performed as two independent annotation tasks in the original Lassy treebank. As a consequence, in both annotation tasks annotators made the decision that seemed most appropriate for that task (i.e. choosing the correct POS-tag and syntactic annotation, respectively). The English UD treebanks, on the other hand, is a manually verified and corrected version of an automatic conversion of the Web treebank, where POS-tags have been added automatically. The construction of the German treebank was done automatically and is minimally documented.[7] Therefore, we cannot be sure whether the differences observed above reflect genuine typological differences or whether they are a consequence of the decisions made in

---

[6] All counts in this section have been collected using the dep_search facility of `bionlp-www.utu.fi`.

[7] `https://github.com/UniversalDependencies/UD_German`

the underlying annotation and/or of the conversion
method.

4 Parsing Experiments

The inclusion of a large number of languages and
corpora in the UD corpus has led to a growing
number of parsing toolkits that are language independent and that can be trained and evaluated
on any of the UD treebanks. In this section, we
compare state-of-the-art dependency parsers for
UD trained on Lassy Small with Alpino, a parser
based on a hand-written grammar for Dutch.

Andor et al. (2016) introduce SyntaxNet, an
open-source implementation of a novel method
for dependency parsing based on globally normalized neural networks. They also provide a pre-
trained parser for English, Parsey McParseface.
On the Penn Treebank, the released model for English (Parsey McParseface) recovers dependencies
at the word level with over 94% accuracy, beating
previous state-of-the-art results.

SyntaxNet has been used to train a parser for a
large number of corpora in UD (v1.3). 'Parsey's
Cousins'[8] is a collection of syntactic models
trained on UD treebanks, for 40 different languages. Per language, more than 70 models have
been trained, leading to models that are up to 4%
more accurate than models trained without hyper-
parameter tuning.

The easy-first hierarchical LSTM model of
Kiperwasser and Goldberg (2016) introduces a
novel method for applying the LSTM framework
to tree structures that is particularly apt for dependency parsing. Another notable feature is that it
does not use word embeddings. It achieves state-
of-the-art results on dependency parsing for English and Chinese, and can be used to train parsers
for any language for which a UD treebank is available.[9]

'ParseySaurus' (Alberti et al., 2017) is a collection of models for UD version 2.0 corpora. It uses
a variant of SyntaxNet that also includes character
level embeddings. The model has a labeled attachment accuracy score that is on average 3.5% better
than the SyntexNet models of Parsey's cousins.

Alpino (van Noord, 2006) is a wide-coverage
parser for Dutch consisting of a carefully developed hand-written unification-based grammar and

	LAS	UAS
Alpino	84.31	89.22
Parsey's Cousins	78.08	81.63
Easy-first	77.16	81.10
ParseySaurus	80.53	84.02

Table 4: Parse results for UD Dutch Lassy Small
(v1.3), using standard training (6641 sentences)
and test set (350 sentences), using CONLL 2007
evaluation script, not counting punctuation.

a maximum entropy disambiguation model. Its
output is compatible with the original Lassy treebank. Although Alpino is not a dependency parser,
it can be evaluated on UD Dutch data by converting
the parser output into UD compatible annotation
using the same conversion script that was also used
to convert the original Lassy Small treebank to UD.
For the experiment, the disambiguation model for
Alpino was trained only on the training section of
Lassy Small UD treebank (6641 sentences).

We compare the accuracy of the Dutch SyntaxNet models as well as a model trained with
the easy-first LSTM model, with results obtained
using Alpino. Table 4 gives labeled and unlabeled attachment accuracy scores on the test set
of the Lassy Small corpus. The scores for Parsey's
Cousins are the scores reported in the Google blog
post. The scores for easy-LSTM were obtained by
running the code using the default options. The
scores for ParseySaurus are taken from (Alberti et
al., 2017).

Among the dependency parsers trained on the
treebank data, the ParseySaurus model achieves
a 2.5-3.0% LAS improvement over the two other
models. Alpino performs even better, with a 3.8%
LAS improvement over the best dependency parser
model. We can only speculate about the reasons for this difference. The training corpus is
relatively small, and it might be that the purely
data-driven approaches would benefit relatively
strongly from being trained on more data.[10]

On the other hand, results can also be improved
by simply correcting errors in the original data.
As we pointed out in section 3, one difference between the original Lassy dependency annotation
and UD is that UD dependency labels are organized
more strongly in accordance with the POS tag of

---

[8]`research.googleblog.com/2016/08/`
`meet-parseys-cousins-syntax-for-40.html`
[9]https://github.com/elikip/htparser

[10]However, note that if we use the standard Alpino disambiguation component, trained on a larger, news domain corpus, its accuracy slightly decreases (88.21 UAS).

	LAS	UAS
Alpino	84.31	89.22
with corrected treebank	85.95	89.41

Table 5: Parse results for UD Dutch Lassy Small (v1.3 with corrections), using standard training (6641 sentences) and test set (350 sentences), using CONLL 2007 evaluation script, not counting punctuation.

the head and the dependent than the Lassy dependency labels. The relative independence of Lassy POS annotation and syntactic analysis (as well as the fact that these were done by different partners in the Lassy project), has led to a situation where errors in POS annotation have gone largely unnoticed when evaluating parser output. For evaluation on UD treebanks, annotating and predicting the correct POS tag is crucial, as it influences the choice of the dependency label. Thus, correcting POS tags in the original treebank leads to more consistent data in the original treebank as well as in the converted UD treebank. If we evaluate the Alpino parser on a version of the UD treebank based on the corrected underlying Lassy Small treebank, we obtain the accuracy scores given in table 5. These corrections have been included in UD 2.0 release.

5 Conclusions

Automatic conversion of existing treebanks to UD has the advantage that existing annotation efforts can be re-used, that treebanks that for some reason cannot be included in the UD corpus can be converted easily, and that tools developed for the original annotation can be used to produce UD compliant output as well. We have developed a method for converting the Dutch Lassy treebank to UD. It has been used to produce UD Dutch Lassy Small, included in UD v1.3 and v2.0.

Although all information required to do the conversion appears to be present in the underlying annotation (with the exception of punctuation attachment perhaps), we did notice that there are also subtle differences between the Lassy treebank annotation and UD annotation guidelines. This is particularly clear in cases where structural and functional information does not align well, as in nominalizations.

Using our automatic annotation script, we were able to compare parsing accuracies for three de-

pendency parsers and Alpino. Although the results for dependency parsing are encouraging, the Alpino parser, based on a hand-written grammar, still outperforms these approaches.

In future work, we would like to expand the UD Lassy Small corpus by including more of the material of the original Lassy Small corpus (where this is allowed according to IPR). For parser evaluation, it would be interesting to see what the effect is of larger training sets on automatically trained dependency parsers in particular.

References

Lars Ahrenberg. 2015. Converting an English-Swedish parallel treebank to universal dependencies. In *Third International Conference on Dependency Linguistics (DepLing 2015), Uppsala, August 24-26*, pages 10–19. Association for Computational Linguistics.

Chris Alberti, Daniel Andor, Ivan Bogatyy, Michael Collins, Dan Gillick, Lingpeng Kong, Terry Koo, Ji Ma, Mark Omernick, Slav Petrov, Chayut Thanapirom, Zora Tung, and David Weiss. 2017. Syntaxnet models for the CoNLL 2017 shared task.

Daniel Andor, Chris Alberti, David Weiss, Aliaksei Severyn, Alessandro Presta, Kuzman Ganchev, Slav Petrov, and Michael Collins. 2016. Globally normalized transition-based neural networks. In *Proceedings of the ACL*.

Sabine Brants, Stefanie Dipper, Silvia Hansen, Wolfgang Lezius, and George Smith. 2002. The TIGER treebank. In *Proceedings of the workshop on Treebanks and Linguistic Theories*, volume 168.

Sabine Buchholz and Erwin Marsi. 2006. CoNLL-X shared task on multilingual dependency parsing. In *Proceedings of the Tenth Conference on Computational Natural Language Learning*, pages 149–164. Association for Computational Linguistics.

Noam Chomsky. 1968. *Remarks on nominalization*. Linguistics Club, Indiana University.

Anders Johannsen, Héctor Martínez Alonso, and Barbara Plank. 2015. Universal dependencies for Danish. In *International Workshop on Treebanks and Linguistic Theories (TLT14)*, page 157.

Eliyahu Kiperwasser and Yoav Goldberg. 2016. Easy-first dependency parsing with hierarchical tree LSTMs. *Transactions of the ACL*, 4:445–461.

Teresa Lynn and Jennifer Foster. 2016. Universal dependencies for Irish. In *Celtic Language Technology Workshop*, pages 79–92.

Adam Meyers, Ruth Reeves, Catherine Macleod, Rachel Szekely, Veronika Zielinska, Brian Young, and Ralph Grishman. 2004. Annotating noun argument structure for NomBank. In *LREC*, volume 4, pages 803–806.

Lilja Øvrelid and Petter Hohle. 2016. Universal dependencies for Norwegian. In *Proceedings of the Tenth International Conference on Language Resources and Evaluation. Portorož, Slovenia.*

Wojciech Skut, Thorsten Brants, Brigitte Krenn, and Hans Uszkoreit. 1998. A linguistically interpreted corpus of German newspaper text. *arXiv preprint cmp-lg/9807008.*

Leonoor van der Beek, Gosse Bouma, Rob Malouf, and Gertjan van Noord. 2002. The Alpino dependency treebank. In *Computational Linguistics in the Netherlands (CLIN) 2001*, Twente University.

Gertjan van Noord, Gosse Bouma, Frank van Eynde, Daniel de Kok, Jelmer van der Linde, Ineke Schuurman, Erik Tjong Kim Sang, and Vincent Vandeghinste. 2013. Large scale syntactic annotation of written Dutch: Lassy. In Peter Spyns and Jan Odijk, editors, *Essential Speech and Language Technology for Dutch: the STEVIN Programme*, pages 147–164. Springer.

Gertjan van Noord. 2006. At last parsing is now operational. In Piet Mertens, Cedrick Fairon, Anne Dister, and Patrick Watrin, editors, *TALN06. Verbum Ex Machina. Actes de la 13e conference sur le traitement automatique des langues naturelles*, pages 20–42.

Daniel Zeman, Ondřej Dušek, David Mareček, Martin Popel, Loganathan Ramasamy, Jan Štěpánek, Zdeněk Žabokrtský, and Jan Hajič. 2014. HamleDT: Harmonized multi-language dependency treebank. *Language Resources and Evaluation*, 48(4):601–637.

Converting the TüBa-D/Z treebank of German to Universal Dependencies

Çağrı Çöltekin[1]   **Ben Campbell**[2]   **Erhard Hinrichs**[1]   **Heike Telljohann**[1]

Department of Linguistics, University of Tübingen

[1] {cagri.coeltekin, erhard.hinrichs, heike.telljohann}@uni-tuebingen.de

[2] ben.campbell@student.uni-tuebingen.de

Abstract

This paper describes the conversion of TüBa-D/Z, one of the major German constituency treebanks, to Universal Dependencies. Besides the automatic conversion process, we describe manual annotation of a small part of the treebank based on the UD annotation scheme for the purposes of evaluating the automatic conversion. The automatic conversion shows fairly high agreement with the manual annotations.

1 Introduction

During the past decade, dependency annotations have become the primary means of syntactic annotation in treebanks. Compared to more traditional constituency annotations, the increasing popularity of dependency annotations has multiple reasons, including the easy interpretation of dependency annotations by non-experts, more successful applications of the dependency parses to NLP tools, faster parsing methods, and the community formed around successive dependency parsing shared tasks. In recent years, we have seen a surge of interest towards unified tagsets and annotation guidelines for various types of annotations found in (dependency) treebanks (Zeman, 2008; de Marneffe and Manning, 2008; Petrov et al., 2012; Zeman et al., 2012). The Universal Dependencies (UD) project (Nivre et al., 2016) is a large-scale community effort to build unified tagsets and annotation guidelines across many languages.

Despite the growing popularity of UD, and the growing number of new treebanks using the UD annotation scheme, many of the large treebanks with high-quality annotations are still constituency treebanks. Since Collins (1999), a well-known solution for obtaining high-quality dependency annotations is automatically converting the constituency annotations to dependency annotations, which includes some of the present UD treebanks which were converted from constituency treebanks or dependency treebanks with different annotation schemes. In this paper, we describe our efforts of automatically converting one of the major German treebanks, TüBa-D/Z (Hinrichs et al., 2004; Telljohann et al., 2004), to UD annotation scheme version 2.

German is one of the few languages with multiple large hand-annotated treebanks. Apart from the TüBa-D/Z, the TIGER treebank (Brants et al., 2002) is another large constituency treebank of German, as well as the NEGRA treebank (Skut et al., 1997). Another large German treebank is the Hamburg dependency treebank (HDT; Foth (2006), Foth et al. (2014)), which is natively annotated as a dependency treebank. The Universal Dependencies distribution also includes a German dependency treebank (UD German), which is based on the Google Universal Dependencies treebanks (McDonald et al., 2013), and converted to Universal Dependencies annotation scheme by the UD contributors.[1] The dependency and POS tag annotations in the UD German treebank were based on manual annotations, while other annotation layers, e.g., morphological features and lemmas, are automatically annotated. Besides being the smallest of the treebanks listed above, and despite continuous improvements over the previous UD versions, UD German does not yet seem to have the same level of annotation quality as the other German treebanks listed above. An overview of the treebanks with the indication of their sizes is presented in Table 1. In this study we focus only on conversion of TüBa-D/Z, but note that the present effort may be a precursor to obtaining a very large dependency treebank of German annotated uniformly using the UD scheme.

---

[1] http://universaldependencies.org/.

Proceedings of the NoDaLiDa 2017 Workshop on Universal Dependencies (UDW 2017), pages 27–37,
Gothenburg, Sweden, 22 May 2017.

The remainder of this paper is organized as follows: in the next section we provide a brief description of our source treebank, and review the earlier constituency-to-dependency conversion efforts of German treebanks. Section 3 describes the automatic conversion process. Section 4 describes the manual annotation of the evaluation set, and compares the automatic conversion with human annotations. We conclude in Section 5 after a brief discussion.

2   Background

TüBa-D/Z is a large German constituency treebank. We used version 10.00 of the treebank (released in August 2015) which comprises 95 595 sentences and 1 787 801 tokens of 3644 articles from the daily newspaper 'die tageszeitung' (taz). The treebank annotations include lemmas, POS tags, morphological features, syntactic constituency, and grammatical functions. For example, the grammatical function, or edge label, HD indicates the head of a phrase, while OA indicates the accusative object of the head predicate (Telljohann et al., 2015). The grammatical function labels are important for recovering dependencies in German. Since the language exhibits a relatively free word order, one cannot reliably predict the grammatical functions from the word order. The grammatical functions are also annotated in other German constituency treebanks TIGER and NEGRA. Also helpful for recovering dependencies, in TüBa-D/Z (unlike TIGER and NEGRA) phrases are annotated in a more detailed manner, e.g., noun phrases are not annotated as flat structures but with a constituency structure indicating their syntactic makeup (see Figure 1 for an example). Besides the morphosyntactic annotations that we are interested here, TüBa-D/Z also includes a rich set of linguistic annotations such as anaphora and coreference relations (Naumann, 2007), partial annotation of word senses (Henrich and Hinrichs, 2014) and named entity categories. Figure 1 presents an example tree from TüBa-D/Z.

Since its early releases, the TüBa-D/Z distribution also feature an automatically converted dependency version. The dependency conversion is based on Versley (2005), and uses the same dependency tagsets as the HDT annotations (Foth, 2006). However, similar to other automatic conversion efforts, the conversion is based on a set of heuristic 'head-finding rules', and there are some

treebank	type	sentences	tokens
TüBa-D/Z	const	95 595	1 787 801
TIGER	const	50 472	888 238
NEGRA	const	20 602	355 096
HDT	dep	206 794	3 823 762
UD German	dep	14 917	277 089

Table 1: An overview of large-scale (mostly) hand-annotated German treebanks. The number of sentences and tokens are from the latest versions of the treebanks as of this writing, namely, TüBa-D/Z version 10.0, TIGER version 2.2, NEGRA version 2, HDT version 1.0.1 (counting only the hand-annotated parts A and B), and UD German version 2.0.

systematic differences from the HDT, such as default location of attachment of syntactically and semantically ambiguous prepositional phrases and adverbials. These differences are discussed by Versley (2005) in detail. The conversion tool by Versley (2005) was also used for converting TüBa-D/Z to the dependency treebank used in the Parsing German (PaGe) shared task (Kübler, 2008), where both TüBa-D/Z and TIGER treebanks were used in their original form, and as converted dependency treebanks.

There have been other constituency-to-dependency conversion efforts for German treebanks. Bohnet (2003) and Daum et al. (2004) present methods for converting NEGRA to a dependency treebank. Hajič et al. (2009) convert TIGER to a dependency treebank for use in the CoNLL-2009 multi-lingual dependency parsing shared task. The same conversion method is also used in Zeman et al. (2012), again in a multi-lingual setting, but also with an effort to unify the annotation scheme. In a more recent study, Seeker and Kuhn (2012) convert TIGER to a dependency treebank. They focus on representation of empty nodes in resulting dependency annotations.

In all of the earlier studies listed above, with the exception of Zeman et al. (2012), the target dependency treebanks share the tagsets for POS and morphological annotations, and to a large extent the dependency heads already annotated in the source treebank. However, in the present study the morphosyntactic annotations have to diverge, sometimes in non-trivial manner, from the source annotations. We will describe these differences in detail below.

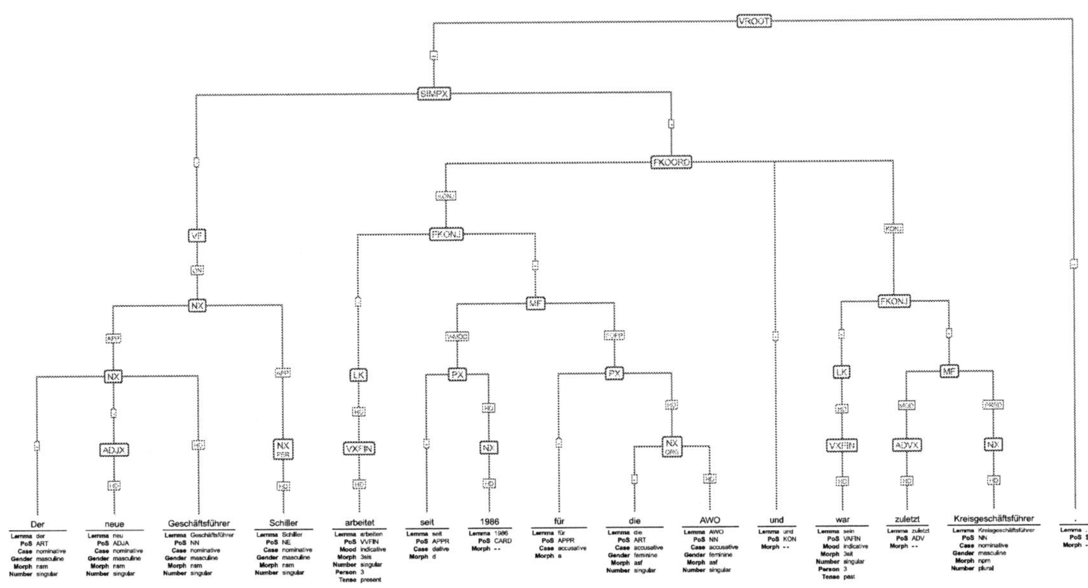

Figure 1: An example sentence from TüBa-D/Z.

3 Conversion process

3.1 POS tag conversion

TüBa-D/Z uses a version of STTS tag set (Schiller et al., 1995) for tagging parts of speech, with slight differences (Telljohann et al., 2015, p.21). We map the POS tags automatically as shown in Table 2. Since TüBa-D/Z POS tagset is more fine-grained than the UD POS tagset, most POS tags can trivially be mapped. However, some of the mappings deserve additional discussion.

In STTS, the tag PWAV covers adverbial interrogatives or relative pronouns, 'wh-words' such as *warum* 'why' or *wobei* 'wherein'. We mapped all words with STTS tag PWAV to UD tag ADV. However, some of these words may function as subordinating conjunctions (SCONJ), as in (1) below where *wobei* is tagged as SCONJ in UD German treebank. This STTS tag also has one of the highest rate of uncertainty with respect to the number of corresponding UD POS tags in the UD German treebank (see Table 5 in Appendix A).

(1) *Ab   1972 spielte er noch 121 mal   für den*
     From 1972 played he yet 121 times for the
     *Würzburger FV **wobei** er 10 Tore   erzielte.*
     Würzburger FV where   he 10 goals scored.

     'From 1972 he played 121 times for the Würzburger FV *where* he scored 10 goals.'

Following the current UD practice, we split the preposition + determiner contractions, such as *zur* *(zu + der)* 'to the', into two syntactic tokens. These closed-class words are marked with STTS tag APPRART in the source treebank. These words are split only if the POS tag is APPRART.

Another interesting case concerns the STTS POS tag TRUNC. This tag is used for split words in coordination constructions, such as *Journalisten mit Fernseh- und Photokameras* 'Journalists with TV and photo cameras'. The well-known complexity and productivity of compounding in German results in quite frequent use of these constructions. In TüBa-D/Z version 10, the number of words with TRUNC tag is 1740. Most of the time, the words marked as TRUNC are nouns or adjectives. However, their forms often include remnants of the compounding process, and does not match with the exact form of the word's usage outside a compound. Since most of these structures contain nouns, we currently mark these words as NOUN, and add a special feature Trunc=Yes in the MISC field.

An alternative approach would be to mark the truncated part with the POS tag of the complete compound, and introduce a syntactic word similar to the tokenization of contracted forms discussed above. In the alternative annotation, the syntactic tokens of the example phrase '*Journalisten mit Fernseh- und Photokameras*' would be '*Journalisten mit Fernsehkameras und Photokameras*'. This can easily be represented in the CoNLL-U file for-

TüBa-D/Z	UD	TüBa-D/Z	UD
ADJA	ADJ	PRF	PRON
ADJD	ADJ	PROP	ADV
ADV	ADV	PTKA	ADV
APPO	ADP	PTKANT	INTJ
APPR	ADP	PTKNEG	PART
APPRART	ADP, DET	PTKVZ	ADP
APZR	ADP	PTKZU	PART
ART	DET	PWAT	DET
CARD	NUM	PWAV	ADV
FM	X	PWS	PRON
ITJ	INTJ	TRUNC	NOUN
KOKOM	ADP	VAFIN	AUX
KON	CCONJ	VAIMP	AUX
KOUI	SCONJ	VAINF	AUX
KOUS	SCONJ	VAPP	AUX
NE	PROPN	VMFIN	AUX
NN	NOUN	VMINF	AUX
PDAT	DET	VMPP	AUX
PDS	PRON	VVFIN	VERB
PIAT	DET	VVIMP	VERB
PIDAT	ADJ	VVINF	VERB
PIS	PRON	VVIZU	VERB
PPER	PRON	VVPP	VERB
PPOSAT	PRON	XY	X
PPOSS	PRON	$,	PUNCT
PRELAT	DET	$.	PUNCT
PRELS	PRON	$(	PUNCT

Table 2: POS conversion table.

```
1  Journalisten     _  NOUN   NN
2  mit              _  ADP    APPR
3-3 Fernseh-        _  _      _
3  Fernsehkameras   _  NOUN   TRUNC
4  und              _  CCONJ  KON
5  Photokameras     _  NOUN   NN
```

Listing 1: An example of the alternative prposal for STTS TRUNC tag (only the relevant columns are included).

mat by utilizing the range records used for multi-word tokens, but specifying a span of only a single surface token. Listing 1 presents an example CoNLL-U fragment demonstrating the alternative coding for TRUNC. This is relatively straightforward to include in TüBa-D/Z conversion since the treebank encodes most of the relevant information in the lemma of the truncated word. Although getting the alternative annotation correct is not as straightforward for automated annotators, e.g., parsers, there are successful tools for German compound splitting (Ma et al., 2016, for example) that can be used for this purpose.

3.2 Morphology

TüBa-D/Z annotates each word with a lemma, and nouns, adjectives, determiners and verbs are also annotated for morphological features. Nouns, adjectives and determiners are marked for *number*, *gender* and *case*, and verbs are marked for *tense* and *mood*. These TüBa-D/Z morphological features map to the UD morphological features in a straightforward manner. We also assign values to the UD features PronType, VerbType, NumType, Poss, Reflex, Foreign, Definite, Voice, and Polarity based on the STTS tags, lemmas (either information coded explicitly, as in sollen%aux, or forms of the closed-class words).

Lemmas are also mapped to the UD version of the treebank with minor modifications. In the current conversion, we strip all the additional information specified on the TüBa-D/Z lemmas, such as grammatical function marking like sollen%aux, the only exception is the separable verb information as in ein#setzen. Reflexive pronouns are always marked as #refl in TüBa-D/Z. Following UD German, we map #refl to the lemma used for the personal pronoun with the same number and person features (e.g., lemma of *mich* 'myself' gets the lemma *ich* 'I') and mark the reflexiveness of the pronoun with the Reflex morphological feature. Finally, we map the ambiguous lemmas as is.

3.3 Extracting dependencies

As in earlier examples in the literature, the dependency extraction uses a set of heuristic 'head-finding rules'. The conversion software first pre-processes constituency trees, since some of the information is easy to extract from the original constituency annotations. Then, the pre-processed trees are converted to UD-like dependencies with a set of head-finding rules. And finally, a post-processing stage, including operations like attaching punctuation to the right parent according to the UD guidelines, makes sure that the dependency trees are UD version 2 compliant. The UD dependency types (including the subtypes) we use, and their counts in the converted treebank are

dep. type	count	percentage
acl	5643	0.328
acl:relcl	14906	0.867
advcl	16495	0.959
advmod	115480	6.715
advmod:neg	12250	0.712
amod	108922	6.334
appos	32246	1.875
aux	42994	2.500
aux:pass	12213	0.710
case	166418	9.677
cc	48115	2.798
ccomp	9174	0.533
compound:prt	9199	0.535
conj	64525	3.752
cop	23109	1.344
csubj	3396	0.197
csubj:pass	326	0.019
dep	37	0.002
det	224248	13.040
det:neg	3418	0.199
discourse	206	0.012
expl	1899	0.110
fixed	326	0.019
flat	20937	1.217
flat:foreign	3677	0.214
iobj	4911	0.286
mark	32575	1.894
nmod	50142	2.916
nmod:poss	55783	3.244
nsubj	126182	7.337
nsubj:pass	10485	0.610
nummod	14330	0.833
obj	74650	4.341
obl	115096	6.693
parataxis	20251	1.178
punct	262109	15.242
xcomp	13029	0.758

Table 3: Number and percentage of dependencies in the converted TüBa-D/Z treebank.

listed in Table 3. In the resulting dependency treebank 4.90 % of the dependencies are crossing dependencies, and analyses of 20.92 % of the sentences contain at least one crossing dependency. The conversion based on Versley (2005) yields 2.33 % crossing dependencies and 20.17 % sentences with crossing dependencies. In this section, we discuss some of the interesting or difficult-to-convert structures, rather than the implementation details. The source code of the conversion software along with detailed documentation is released on GitHub.[2]

TüBa-D/Z (and other German constituency treebanks noted earlier) marks the heads of the phrases explicitly. As a result, finding heads of the words is trivial for most cases. The main difficulty

arises because, unlike the earlier constituency-to-dependency conversion efforts (Versley, 2005, for example), conversion to UD requires changing many of the head choices in the original treebank. This is also apparent in Figure 2, where we present dependency representations of the example tree in Figure 1. For example, the head of the phrase *war zuletzt Kreisgeschäftsführer* is the copula *war* in both the TüBa-D/Z and Versley's conversion. However, in the UD conversion, the head needs to be the subject complement *Kreisgeschäftsführer*. Note that this also interacts with the coordination in this example. The head of the first conjunct, the verbal predicate *arbeitet*, is coordinated with the head of the second conjunct which becomes the noun *Kreisgeschäftsführer* after re-structuring. The other re-assigning requirements include finite auxiliaries and subordination markers which are marked as heads in TüBa-D/Z but should be dependents in UD.

Another difficulty in choosing heads arise because TüBa-D/Z does not mark heads in some grammatical structures, such as in coordinated constituents. In some structures, choice of heads are non-trivial. As noted above, head assignment in coordination also interacts with the change of head direction, for example, between the finite auxiliary verbs and the content verbs (as in 2b).

One more issue that deserves a brief note here is the ambiguities in the conversion process. Although TüBa-D/Z annotations are more detailed than the basic UD annotations in general, for some grammatical relations, a single grammatical function may be mapped to more than one dependency label or structure. For example, TüBa-D/Z functional label APP (apposition) may map to appos, flat or compound. For APP, we use flat if the noun phrase corresponds to a named entity, otherwise we use the UD dependency appos. Another source of head-assignment ambiguity concerns multiply-rooted sentences which are described as side-by-side or run-on sentences in the UD specification. In TüBa-D/Z these sentences are annotated under two separate trees, and connected to a 'virtual root' node without any functional relation assigned. An example constituency tree of multiply-rooted sentence is given in Figure 3. We connect these sentences using parataxis relation during the UD conversion, always marking the first one as the head. However, the UD specification allows marking the 'more prominent' sentence as

---

[2]The source code of the converter is available at https://github.com/bencampbell30/TuebaUdConverter.

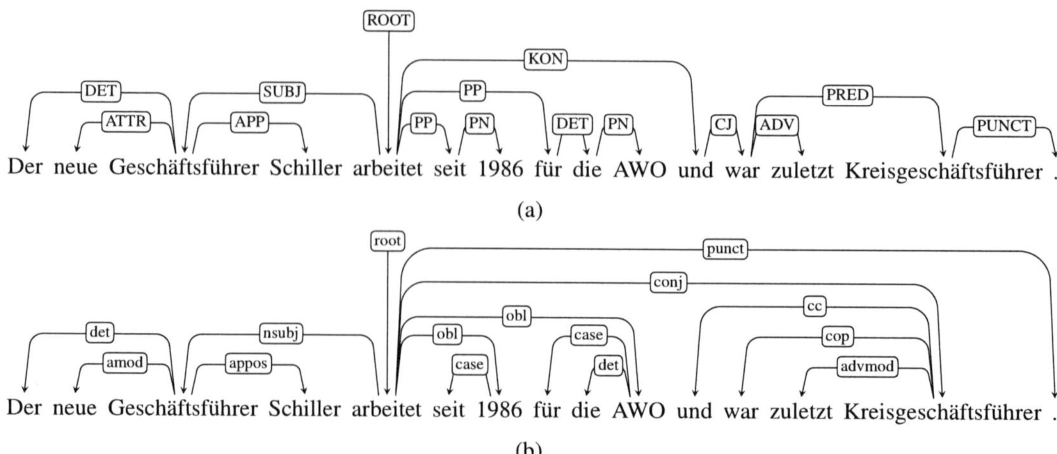

Figure 2: The dependency trees for the sentence in Figure 1, automatically converted using tools from (a) Versley (2005) and (b) this study.

the head of a parataxis relation. Since this information is not available in the TüBa-D/Z annotations, the head of the parataxis relation is expected to be wrong in some cases.

The head-finding rules fail to assign the head and the dependency relation for 37 dependencies in 35 sentences (out of 95 595) in the TüBa-D/Z. In these cases, we attach the token to the highest node that preserves projectivity, and use the dependency label dep. A close examination of the sentences show that most of these cases (22 of 35 sentences) involve either errors in the TüBa-D/Z annotation, or in the original sentence (such as an unintelligible sequence of letters within the sentence). The remaining 13 cases are unusual constructions that the heuristic head-finding rules do not address currently.

3.4 Topological fields

As noted in Section 2, TüBa-D/Z includes some annotations along with the morphosyntactic structure. Among these is the topological field information. Traditionally, topological field information is used to account for word order of different clause types (Höhle, 1986). All clauses in TüBa-D/Z contain nodes that are labeled LK (left bracket), RK (right bracket), MF (middle field), and optionally VF (initial field) and NF (final field). Besides being instrumental in linguistic description, the topological field annotation has been shown to improve the accuracy of both constituency (Kübler et al., 2008) and dependency (de Kok and Hinrichs, 2016) parsers.

Similar to de Kok and Hinrichs (2016), we mark the topological field information at the token level. We include a special feature label TopoField in the MISC field of the CoNLL-U file with a variable length sequence of topological field labels listed above. Unlike de Kok and Hinrichs (2016) who marked tokens only with a single (most specific) topological field label, this representation allows recovering the topological field of the token within all parent clauses. For example, TopoField=VF-NF-MF indicates that the token is within the middle field (MF) of the most-specific clause, which is within the final field (NF) of another sub-clause which, in turn, is within the initial field (VF) of the main clause. The maximum depth of the recursion goes up to 9 clauses, but most (62.31 %) of the tokens are direct descendants of the main clause, and the tokens within a hierarchy of clauses up to depth three cover more than 95 % of the tokens in TüBa-D/Z.[3]

4 Evaluation

To evaluate the accuracy of the automatic conversion, we annotated a selection of 200 sentences from TüBa-D/Z. About half of the sentences (116) were selected manually to cover a wide range of syntactic constructions, while the remaining sentences are randomly sampled. In total, the selection includes 3134 tokens. The overall average tokens per sentence is 15.67. However, the hand-

---

[3]Following TüBa-D/Z style book (Telljohann et al., 2015, p. 25), we also include nodes corresponding to coordinated phrases, e.g., FKOORD, FKONJ, as TopoField labels.

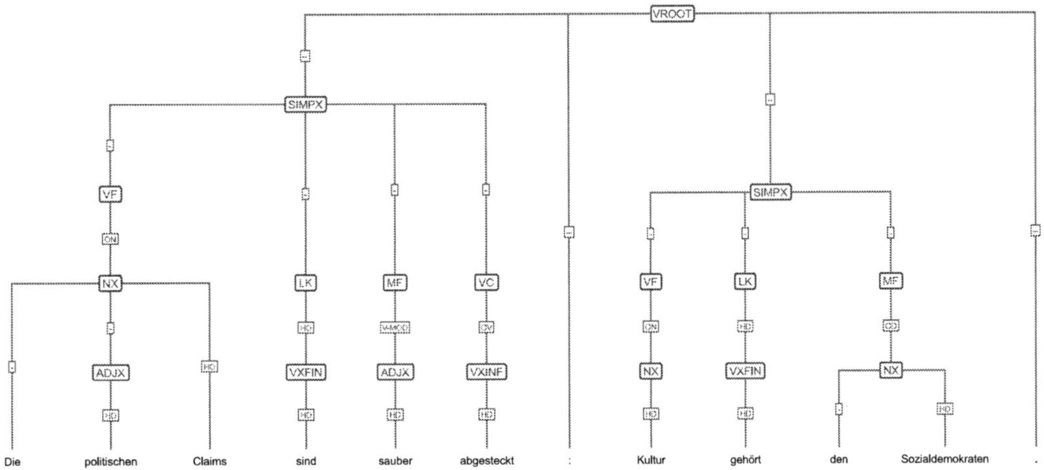

Figure 3: An example multiply-rooted sentence from TüBa-D/Z.

picked sentences are shorter on average (12.05) than the randomly sampled sentences (20.67). We used WebAnno (Eckart de Castilho et al., 2014) for the annotation process.

Only the dependency relations were annotated manually. In manual annotations, we did not use sub-types of the UD relations. The additional information required for all sub-types we use (Table 3) is unambiguously available in the original TüBa-D/Z annotations.

We compare the gold-standard annotations from the human annotators with the automatic conversion on the 200 sentences described above. The labeled and unlabeled attachment agreements on 3134 tokens are 83.55 % and 87.13 % respectively. The agreement values are slightly better for hand-picked linguistic examples, which are also shorter.

A closer look at the disagreements reveal only a few general tendencies. For the attachment disagreements, the annotators seem to be less consistent in attaching punctuation. All cases of punctuation disagreements are annotator mistakes. If we disregard punctuation, the agreement values increase by about three percent. Other head-assignment errors do not follow a clear pattern. The ones we inspected manually correspond to either ambiguous cases like prepositional phrase or adverbial attachment, or annotator errors.

As noted in Section 3, the head of parataxis relation is ambiguous. As a result, the direction of parataxis relation often disagrees between the automatic conversion and the manual annotations. For example, for the sentence in Figure 3, the human annotator marked the head of the second sentence as the head of the dependency tree, while automatic annotation picks the first one. This is also visible in Table 4, where parataxis and root labels seem to be confused rather frequently.

The confusions between dependency types are presented in Table 4. The most common mismatch in label assignment occurs with the appos dependency. As noted earlier, the automatic conversion assigns the label appos in all non-head-marked dependencies between two noun phrases. A large number of dependencies that are labeled as appos by the automatic conversion are labeled flat or nmod by the human annotators. Besides the attachment ambiguity discussed above, parataxis is another frequently confused label, which is often marked as list by the human annotators. This is one of the cases where TüBa-D/Z annotations do allow distinguishing between two dependency relations (in this case, UD parataxis and list dependencies). Other notable label confusions in Table 4 include nmod and obl which is often an annotator error, and expl and nsubj which is often a difficult annotation decision.

In general, we found the cross-tabulation in Table 4 useful. Besides revealing some of the inherent ambiguities for the conversion process, we discovered some of the converter errors, and some of the errors in the original TüBa-D/Z annotations. The remaining items indicate annotation errors, some of which are indications of difficult annotation decisions (such as punctuation attachment) for manual annotation with the UD scheme.

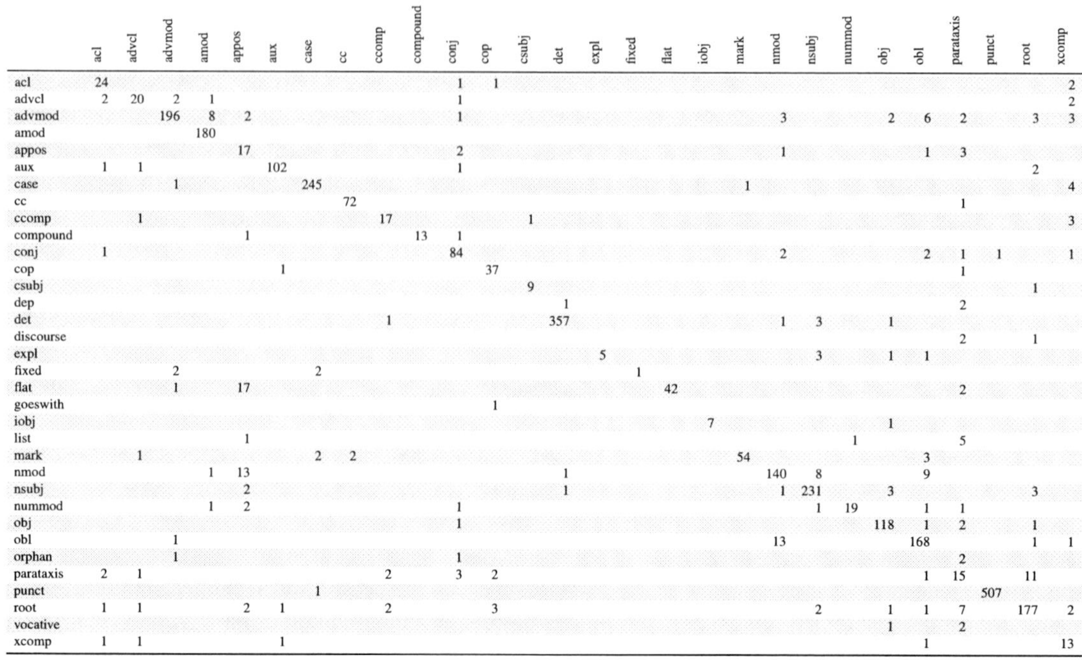

	acl	advcl	advmod	amod	appos	aux	case	cc	ccomp	compound	conj	cop	csubj	det	expl	fixed	flat	iobj	mark	nmod	nsubj	nummod	obj	obl	parataxis	punct	root	xcomp
acl	24										1	1																2
advcl	2	20	2	1							1																	2
advmod			196	8	2						1									3			2	6	2		3	3
amod				180																								
appos					17						2									1				1	3			
aux	1	1				102					1																2	
case			1				245												1									4
cc								72																	1			
ccomp		1							17				1															3
compound					1					13	1																	
conj	1										84									2				2	1	1		1
cop						1						37													1			
csubj													9														1	
dep														1									2					
det									1					357						1	3		1					
discourse																							2				1	
expl													5										3	1	1			
fixed		2					2									1												
flat		1		17													42								2			
goeswith												1																
iobj																			7				1					
list					1																	1			5			
mark		1						2	2										54					3				
nmod				1	13									1						140	8			9				
nsubj					2									1						1	231		3				3	
nummod				1	2						1										1	19		1	1			
obj											1												118	1	2		1	
obl			1																	13				168			1	1
orphan			1								1														2			
parataxis	2	1							2				3	2										1	15		11	
punct								1																		507		
root	1	1		2	1				2				3								2		1	1	7		177	2
vocative																							1		2			
xcomp	1	1				1																		1				13

Table 4: Label agreement between automatic conversion and manual annotation. The row labels are the labels assigned by the human annotator. The columns correspond to the labels assigned by the automatic conversion. The automatic conversion does not use vocative, list, and goeswith relations, it did not find any discourse relation according to its head-finding rules, dep relation was not used since the head-finding heuristics did not fail in this set.

5 Summary and outlook

Automatic conversion of high-quality constituency treebanks to dependency treebanks allow us to make use of earlier high-quality treebanks with new tools and techniques that require dependency annotations. In this paper we describe our efforts of automatic conversion of TüBa-D/Z to Universal Dependencies. We also describe a small-scale annotation project, where we manually annotated 200 sentences from TüBa-D/Z using UD dependency relations. The automatic conversion is based on traditional head-finding heuristics, and agrees well with the manual annotations. The unlabeled and labeled attachment scores are 88.55 % and 87.13 % respectively. Considering that some of these errors are manual annotation errors, the agreement indicates that the result is a high-quality treebank.

The detailed analysis of disagreements between the manual annotations and automatic conversion were primarily motivated for pinpointing the mistakes in automatic conversion in order to refine the heuristic conversion rules. However, the analysis and documentation of the disagreements are also important for a number of other reasons. First, it provides the users of the converted treebank an indication of quality of the annotations for their particular purpose. Second, knowing the disagreements may also improve the accuracy and speed of a manual correction after the automatic conversion. Third, the disagreements also reveal common annotator errors, informing the designers of the target annotation scheme and future annotation project about the difficult cases of annotation. Finally, some cases where conversion heuristics fail and/or disagreements occur indicate annotation errors in the source treebank, which is a valuable feedback for improving the source treebank.

In this study, we used a one-to-one 'best-effort' mapping of the POS tags. In future work, we plan to improve the POS conversion by utilizing syntactic structure. Furthermore, our focus in this study was only on TüBa-D/Z, however, the work can be extended to cover other German treebanks. The result would be a very large, high-quality, uniformly-annotated dependency treebank of approximately 400 000 sentences.

References

Bernd Bohnet. 2003. Mapping phrase structures to dependency structures in the case of (partially) free word order languages. In *Proceedings of the first international conference on Meaning-Text Theory*, pages 217–216.

Sabine Brants, Stefanie Dipper, Silvia Hansen, Wolfgang Lezius, and George Smith. 2002. The tiger treebank. In *Proceedings of The First Workshop on Treebanks and Linguistic Theories (TLT2002)*, pages 24–41.

Michael Collins. 1999. *Head-Driven Statistical Models for Natural Language Parsing*. Ph.D. thesis, University of Pennsylvania.

Michael Daum, Kilian A Foth, and Wolfgang Menzel. 2004. Automatic transformation of phrase treebanks to dependency trees. In *Proceedings of the Fourth International Conference on Language Resources and Evaluation (LREC'02)*, Lisbon, Portugal.

Daniël de Kok and Erhard Hinrichs. 2016. Transition-based dependency parsing with topological fields. In *Proceedings of the 54th Annual Meeting of the Association for Computational Linguistics (Volume 2: Short Papers)*, pages 1–7, Berlin, Germany, August. Association for Computational Linguistics.

Marie-Catherine de Marneffe and Christopher D. Manning. 2008. The Stanford typed dependencies representation. In *Coling 2008: Proceedings of the workshop on Cross-Framework and Cross-Domain Parser Evaluation*, pages 1–8, Manchester, UK.

Richard Eckart de Castilho, Chris Biemann, Iryna Gurevych, and Seid Muhie Yimam. 2014. Webanno: a flexible, web-based annotation tool for clarin. In *Proceedings of the CLARIN Annual Conference (CAC) 2014*, page online, Utrecht, Netherlands. CLARIN ERIC. Extended abstract.

Kilian A. Foth, Arne Köhn, Niels Beuck, and Wolfgang Menzel. 2014. Because size does matter: The hamburg dependency treebank. In *Proceedings of the Ninth International Conference on Language Resources and Evaluation (LREC'14)*, Reykjavik, Iceland, may. European Language Resources Association (ELRA).

Kilian A. Foth. 2006. Eine umfassende constraint-dependenz-grammatik des deutschen. Technical Report 54.75, University of Hamburg.

Jan Hajič, Massimiliano Ciaramita, Richard Johansson, Daisuke Kawahara, Maria Antònia Martí, Lluís Màrquez, Adam Meyers, Joakim Nivre, Sebastian Padó, Jan Štěpánek, Pavel Straňák, Mihai Surdeanu, Nianwen Xue, and Yi Zhang. 2009. The conll-2009 shared task: Syntactic and semantic dependencies in multiple languages. In *Proceedings of the Thirteenth Conference on Computational Natural Language Learning (CoNLL 2009): Shared Task*, pages 1–18, Boulder, Colorado. Association for Computational Linguistics.

Verena Henrich and Erhard Hinrichs. 2014. Consistency of manual sense annotation and integration into the tüba-d/z treebank. In *Proceedings of The 13th Workshop on Treebanks and Linguistic Theories (TLT13)*, pages 62–74.

Erhard Hinrichs, Sandra Kübler, Karin Naumann, Heike Telljohann, and Julia Trushkina. 2004. Recent developments in linguistic annotations of the TüBa-D/Z treebank. In *Proceedings of the Third Workshop on Treebanks and Linguistic Theories*, pages 51–62.

Tilman Höhle. 1986. Der begriff "mittelfeld", anmerkungen über die theorie der topologischen felder. pages 329–340.

Sandra Kübler. 2008. The page 2008 shared task on parsing german. In *Proceedings of the Workshop on Parsing German*, PaGe '08, pages 55–63, Stroudsburg, PA, USA. Association for Computational Linguistics.

Sandra Kübler, Wolfgang Maier, Ines Rehbein, and Yannick Versley. 2008. How to compare treebanks. In *Proceedings of the Sixth International Conference on Language Resources and Evaluation (LREC'08)*, pages 2322–2329, Marrakech, Morocco.

Jianqiang Ma, Verena Henrich, and Erhard Hinrichs. 2016. Letter sequence labeling for compound splitting. In *Proceedings of the 14th SIGMORPHON Workshop on Computational Research in Phonetics, Phonology, and Morphology*, pages 76–81.

Ryan McDonald, Joakim Nivre, Yvonne Quirmbach-Brundage, Yoav Goldberg, Dipanjan Das, Kuzman Ganchev, Keith Hall, Slav Petrov, Hao Zhang, Oscar Täckström, Claudia Bedini, Núria Bertomeu Castelló, and Jungmee Lee. 2013. Universal dependency annotation for multilingual parsing. In *Proceedings of the 51st Annual Meeting of the Association for Computational Linguistics (Volume 2: Short Papers)*, pages 92–97, Sofia, Bulgaria, August. Association for Computational Linguistics.

Karin Naumann. 2007. Manual for the annotation of in-document referential relations. Technical report, University of Tübingen.

Joakim Nivre, Marie-Catherine de Marneffe, Filip Ginter, Yoav Goldberg, Jan Hajič, Christopher Manning, Ryan McDonald, Slav Petrov, Sampo Pyysalo, Natalia Silveira, Reut Tsarfaty, and Daniel Zeman. 2016. Universal dependencies v1: A multilingual treebank collection. In *Proceedings of the Tenth International Conference on Language Resources and Evaluation (LREC'16)*, pages 23–28.

Slav Petrov, Dipanjan Das, and Ryan McDonald. 2012. A universal part-of-speech tagset. In *Proceedings of the Eight International Conference on Language Resources and Evaluation (LREC'12)*, Istanbul, Turkey.

Anne Schiller, Simone Teufel, and Christine Thielen. 1995. Guidelines für das tagging deutscher textcorpora mit STTS. Technical report, Universities of Stuttgart and Tübingen.

Helmut Schmid. 1994. "probabilistic part-of-speech tagging using decision trees. In *Proceedings of International Conference on New Methods in Language Processing*, page 154.

Wolfgang Seeker and Jonas Kuhn. 2012. Making ellipses explicit in dependency conversion for a german treebank. In *Proceedings of the Eight International Conference on Language Resources and Evaluation (LREC'12)*, Istanbul, Turkey, may. European Language Resources Association (ELRA).

Wojciech Skut, Thorsten Brants, Brigitte Krenn, and Hans Uszkoreit. 1997. Annotating unrestricted german text. In *Fachtagung der Sektion Computerlinguistik der Deutschen Gesellschaft fr Sprachwissenschaft.*

Heike Telljohann, Erhard Hinrichs, and Sandra Kübler. 2004. The TüBa-D/Z treebank: Annotating German with a context-free backbone. In *In Proceedings of the Fourth International Conference on Language Resources and Evaluation (LREC 2004)*, pages 2229–2232.

Heike Telljohann, Erhard Hinrichs, Heike Zinsmeister, and Kathrin Beck. 2015. Stylebook for the tübingen treebank of written German (TüBa-D/Z). Technical report, University of Tübingen, Seminar für Sprachwissenschaft.

Julia Trushkina and Erhard Hinrichs. 2004. A hybrid model for morpho-syntactic annotation of german with a large tagset. In Dekang Lin and Dekai Wu, editors, *Proceedings of EMNLP 2004*, pages 238–245, Barcelona, Spain, July. Association for Computational Linguistics.

Yannick Versley. 2005. Parser evaluation across text types. In *Proceedings of the Fourth Workshop on Treebanks and Linguistic Theories.*

Daniel Zeman, David Mareček, Martin Popel, Loganathan Ramasamy, Jan Štěpánek, Zdeněk Žabokrtský, and Jan Hajič. 2012. Hamledt: To parse or not to parse? In *Proceedings of the Eight International Conference on Language Resources and Evaluation (LREC'12)*, Istanbul, Turkey. European Language Resources Association (ELRA).

Daniel Zeman. 2008. Reusable tagset conversion using tagset drivers. In *Proceedings of the Sixth International Conference on Language Resources and Evaluation (LREC'08)*, Marrakech, Morocco. European Language Resources Association (ELRA).

A   STTS to UD POS tag mapping in UD German version 2.0 treebank

	ADJ	ADP	ADV	AUX	CCONJ	DET	NOUN	NUM	PART	PRON	PROPN	PUNCT	SCONJ	VERB	X
XY	0	2	0	0	0	0	39	5	0	0	5	5	0	0	21
VVIMP	1	0	1	0	1	0	16	0	0	0	19	0	0	27	1
APPRART	0	10	0	0	0	0	1	0	0	0	2	0	0	0	7
APZR	0	19	13	0	0	0	0	0	8	0	0	0	0	0	0
ITJ	0	0	1	0	0	0	0	0	1	0	6	0	0	0	1
PTKANT	0	0	1	0	0	0	2	0	4	0	0	0	0	0	0
PTKA	1	12	34	0	0	0	0	0	4	0	0	0	0	0	0
PWAV	0	0	190	0	4	0	0	0	0	26	0	0	60	0	0
APPO	1	29	7	0	0	0	2	0	0	0	0	0	0	1	0
ADJD	4898	12	1161	0	2	0	100	19	3	0	283	3	0	132	16
PTKVZ	28	912	623	0	0	0	4	0	17	0	5	0	0	4	0
TRUNC	2	0	0	0	0	0	5	0	0	0	19	0	0	0	0
VAFIN	0	0	0	4241	1	0	7	0	0	0	14	1	0	4645	9
VAPP	0	0	0	115	0	0	0	0	0	0	0	0	0	68	0
PIAT	265	0	20	0	0	19	5	0	1	1315	10	0	0	4	0
KOUS	0	139	55	0	56	0	0	0	0	0	3	0	1441	0	2
PPOSAT	3	0	0	0	0	1841	2	0	0	468	13	0	0	3	0
VAINF	0	0	0	462	0	0	0	0	0	0	0	0	0	151	0
KOKOM	0	1511	42	0	187	0	0	0	2	0	1	0	36	0	0
NN	264	19	31	8	2	0	48880	24	2	0	11891	27	1	34	84
PDAT	44	0	0	0	0	113	0	0	0	991	1	0	0	0	0
ADJA	13597	8	21	0	0	0	276	23	2	0	1431	5	3	107	22
PRELAT	0	0	0	0	0	67	0	0	0	12	0	0	0	0	0
PAV	3	5	1136	1	5	0	0	0	0	133	0	0	3	0	0
VVPP	715	1	23	0	0	0	4	0	0	0	3	0	0	4936	0
VAIMP	0	0	0	6	0	0	0	0	0	0	0	0	0	1	0
PDS	0	0	0	0	0	53	1	0	0	470	1	0	5	0	0
PIS	28	0	19	0	0	0	30	3	0	1103	7	0	0	1	0
KON	0	546	73	0	8079	0	2	0	0	0	89	0	36	0	3
PWS	0	0	4	0	0	0	1	0	0	79	2	0	0	0	0
FM	1	4	0	0	3	0	7	1	0	0	420	0	0	0	13
KOUI	0	216	1	0	3	0	1	0	0	0	1	0	8	0	0
ADV	237	36	10075	0	119	0	44	0	8	1	31	0	33	10	49
PRELS	0	0	0	0	0	112	1	0	0	1779	3	0	6	2	1
VVFIN	110	4	14	9	7	0	62	1	4	0	243	0	9	10702	31
NE	56	14	21	2	1	0	622	19	2	0	15721	0	0	12	55
CARD	3	0	0	0	0	0	23	7204	0	0	363	0	0	0	0
VMFIN	0	0	0	1445	0	0	4	0	0	0	3	0	0	41	0
APPR	30	27264	118	0	3	0	16	0	22	0	400	0	12	1	7
VMINF	0	0	0	82	0	0	0	0	0	0	0	0	0	2	0
ART	0	0	1	1	0	33063	3	68	0	252	256	0	5	0	1
VVINF	10	0	3	1	0	0	10	0	0	0	7	0	0	2439	0
PPER	0	0	0	1	1	0	6	0	4	5655	57	1	0	0	4
PTKZU	0	5	0	1	0	0	0	0	927	0	1	0	0	0	0
PTKNEG	0	0	2	0	0	0	1	0	978	0	2	0	0	0	0
$(	0	4	0	0	0	0	10	0	0	0	2	10160	0	0	28
VVIZU	0	0	0	0	0	0	0	0	0	0	1	0	0	240	0
PRF	0	0	1	0	0	0	0	0	0	1648	1	0	0	0	0
$.	0	0	0	0	0	0	1	0	0	0	4	15389	0	0	1
PWAT	0	0	0	0	0	0	0	0	0	6	0	0	0	0	0
$,	0	0	0	0	0	0	0	0	0	0	0	11126	0	0	0

Table 5: The cross-tabulation of STTS and UD POS tag sets in UD version 2.0 treebank. The rows are sorted by entropy. The UD POS tags converted from the manual annotations of Google Universal dependencies treebanks. The (language-specific) STTS tags are automatically added using TreeTagger (Schmid, 1994). The table shows that, despite the fact that UD POS tags are more coarse in comparison to STTS, mapping from STTS tags to UD is not always straightforward. Correct conversion of the POS tags often require paying attention to syntactic structure, which has been successful in earlier similar studies (Trushkina and Hinrichs, 2004).

Universal Dependencies for Afrikaans

Peter Dirix[1], Liesbeth Augustinus[1,2], Daniel van Niekerk[3], and Frank Van Eynde[1]

[1] University of Leuven, Centre for Computational Linguistics, `fname.lname@kuleuven.be`
[2] FWO-Vlaanderen
[3] North West University, Centre for Text Technology, `fname.lname@nwu.ac.za`

Abstract

The Universal Dependencies (UD) project aims to develop a consistent annotation framework for treebanks across many languages. In this paper we present the UD scheme for Afrikaans and we describe the conversion of the AfriBooms treebank to this new format. We will compare the conversion to UD to the conversion of related syntactic structures in typologically similar languages.

1 Introduction

Afrikaans is a West Germanic language spoken by about 7 million people in South Africa, Namibia and a worldwide diaspora, mainly in English-speaking countries. It is one of the eleven official languages in South Africa and a main lingua franca in both South Africa and neighbouring Namibia.

Until recently, not many NLP tools were available for Afrikaans. Pilon (2005) developed a fine-grained morpho-syntactic tag set and trained a version of the TnT tagger (Brants, 2000) on a manually corrected set of ca 20K words. This tagger was used to annotate the 58M-word Taalkommissie corpus.[1] The annotated corpus was subsequently put into a search tool (Augustinus and Dirix, 2013). The first small Afrikaans treebank was only created in 2015 in the context of the the AfriBooms project (Augustinus et al., 2016).

We will discuss the setup of the AfriBooms treebank in Section 2 and continue with a short overview of Universal Dependencies in Section 3. The UD language-specific description for Afrikaans as well as the conversion to the UD scheme will be given in Section 4. Section 5 concludes and discusses some plans for future work.

2 AfriBooms treebank

The basis for the development of the AfriBooms treebank is a filtered subset of the Afrikaans part of the NCHLT Annotated Text Corpora.[2] It contains ca 49K tokens of PoS tagged government domain documents.

The original PoS annotation of the NCHLT corpus was based on a fine-grained tag set (Pilon, 2005). As some of the information in that tag set turned out to be superfluous for determining the sentence dependency structure, the PoS tag set was simplified to a largely universal set of PoS tags (Petrov et al., 2012). This was done in order to facilitate the syntactic annotation process for the human annotators. For example, 17 classes of verb PoS tags, distinguishing present and past tense; main verbs and auxiliaries; copular verbs, transitive verbs, intransitive verbs and verbs requiring a prepositional phrase for main verbs; separable and inseparable verbs; and finally for auxiliaries the type (modal, auxiliary of tense, auxiliary of aspect, auxiliary of mode) were all mapped to one tag VERB. Table 1 presents the resulting tag set.

The simplified corpus was syntactically annotated with the first version of an Afrikaans parser.[3] In a next step, the annotations were manually checked by one primary annotator while a subset containing 943 words was double-checked by a second annotator. The inter-annotator agreement (IAA) is calculated in terms of labelled attachment score (LAS) and unlabelled attachment score (UAS) averaged over words (Nivre et al., 2007). The LAS is 82.5%, while the UAS is 88.9%.

---

[1]Taalkommissiekorpus, version 1.1 (2011), published by CText, North-West University, Potchefstroom.

[2]Afrikaans NCHLT Annotated Text Corpora, edition 1.0, created by M. Puttkammer, M. Schlemmer and R. Bekker and available through the South African Language Resource Management Agency, Potchefstroom, ISRLN 139-586-400-050-9.

[3]The parser was retrained afterwards on the resulting treebank.

Proceedings of the NoDaLiDa 2017 Workshop on Universal Dependencies (UDW 2017), pages 38–47,
Gothenburg, Sweden, 22 May 2017.

AB PoS tag	FREQUENCY	DESCRIPTION
ADJ	2781	Adjectives
ADP	5561	Adpositions
ADV	1481	Adverbs
CONJ	2616	Conjunctions
DET	4113	Determiners
NOUN	9964	Nouns (including proper nouns)
NUM	635	Numerals
PRON	3561	Pronouns
PRT	1677	Particles
PUNCT	4028	Punctuation
VERB	6720	Verbs (including auxiliary verbs)
X	758	Catch-all class (including abbreviations and interjections amongst others)

Table 1: The PoS tag set and its frequencies in the AfriBooms treebank

AB DEPENDENCY TAG	FREQ.	DESCRIPTION
dep	1009	dependent
dep:**punct**	4497	punctuation
dep:**root**	1870	root
dep:**aux**	2534	auxiliary (verb)
dep:**conj**	2359	conjunct
dep:**cc**	1886	coordination (e.g. to conjunctions)
dep:**arg**	1130	argument
dep:arg:**subj**	2605	subject
dep:arg:**comp**	3	complement
dep:arg:comp:**obj**	3763	object
dep:arg:comp:obj:**dobj**	111	direct object
dep:arg:comp:obj:**iobj**	0	indirect object
dep:arg:comp:obj:**pobj**	6106	object of preposition
dep:arg:comp:**compl**	0	complementiser
dep:arg:comp:**mark**	5	marker (introducing adverbial clause)
dep:arg:comp:**rel**	0	relative (introducing relative clause)
dep:arg:comp:**acomp**	0	adjectival complement
dep:**mod**	11120	modifier
dep:mod:**advcl**	0	adverbial clause modifier
dep:mod:**tmod**	0	temporal modifier
dep:mod:**amod**	2447	adjectival modifier
dep:mod:**num**	462	numeric modifier
dep:mod:**number**	0	element of compound number
dep:mod:**appos**	0	appositional modifier
dep:mod:**abbrev**	63	abbreviation modifier
dep:mod:**adv**	0	adverbial modifier
dep:mod:**adv:neg**	0	negation modifier
dep:mod:**poss**	830	possession modifier
dep:mod:**prt**	1375	phrasal verb particle
dep:mod:**det**	5101	determiner
dep:mod:**prep**	0	prepositional modifier

Table 2: The Stanford dependency tag set and its frequencies in the AfriBooms treebank

For the dependency relations, a subset of the Stanford tag set was adopted, applying the conventions of De Marneffe (2006; 2008). An overview of the dependency tags together with their frequencies is given in Table 2.

The figures in Table 2 show that the annotators often fell back onto more generic tags such as dep, dep:arg and dep:mod, resulting in a large amount of syntactic relations that could have been further specified.

All sentences in the treebank are validated according to the following principles:

- *Graph completeness*: Each sentence must form a single complete graph, i.e. all words must be reachable from the root node.

- *Dependence restriction*: Words may have multiple dependents and each phrase has at most one head.

- *Projectivity*: Connection lines between words should not cross each other.

The treebank was delivered in the Folia-XML format (van den Bosch et al., 2007). An example of a sentence from the AfriBooms treebank is given in Figure 1. It visualizes the PoS tag and dependency annotation for the sentence *Die webtuiste sal 'n nuwe deurblaai-venster oopmaak.* 'The website will open a new browser window'.

The different phases of the bootstrapping of the parsing process, as well as the details of the manual annotation and verification process are described in Augustinus et al. (2016).

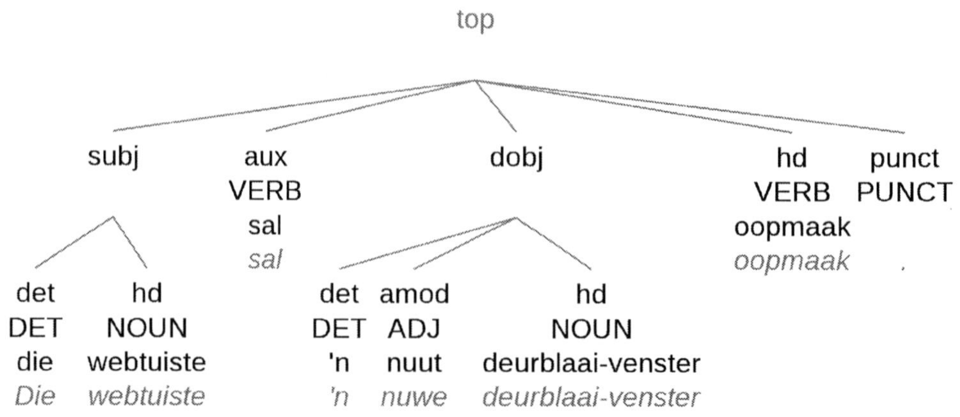

top

subj | aux | dobj | hd | punct
VERB | | VERB | PUNCT
sal | | oopmaak
sal | | *oopmaak* | .

det | hd | det | amod | hd
DET | NOUN | DET | ADJ | NOUN
die | webtuiste | 'n | nuut | deurblaai-venster
Die | *webtuiste* | *'n* | *nuwe* | *deurblaai-venster*

Figure 1: An example sentence taken from the AfriBooms treebank

3   Universal Dependencies

Universal Dependencies (UD) is a project developing cross-language consistent treebank annotation for as many languages as possible, aiming to facilitate multilingual or language-independent parser development, cross-lingual learning, and linguistic research from a language typology perspective (Nivre et al., 2016). The annotation scheme is based on a combination of adapted (universal) Stanford dependencies (de Marneffe et al., 2006; de Marneffe and Manning, 2008), Google universal PoS tags (Petrov et al., 2012), and the Interset interlingua for morphosyntactic tag sets (Zeman, 2008). The general philosophy is to provide a universal inventory of categories and guidelines to facilitate consistent annotation of similar constructions across languages, and allowing language-specific extensions when necessary to encode specific features. Guidelines for version 2.0 as well as the treebanks released in this version are published on the project's website.[4]

Universal dependencies describe dependency relations between words. For most languages, white space determines what a token is. Apart from contractions and clitics, words are not segmented. The use of multi-word tokens is limited to a few fixed expressions that function as adverbs or adpositions.

UD treebanks are represented in the CoNLL-U format, which is an adaptation of the older CoNLL-X format. This format is a tab-separated text file with ten columns. The first three columns respectively contain the position of the token in the sentence, the token and its lemma. Lemmas are defined as the dictionary form of the token, which depends on the language. For example verb lemmas are typically represented by the infinitive, but in Greek the indicative present first person singular is employed. Column 4 contains the universal PoS tag. The morphosyntactic annotation of the pre-converted treebank, if any, can be put in column 5. The universal and language-specific morphological features describing number, case, person, gender, mood, tense etc. in the column 6. Column 7 indicates the head of the current token in reference to its position in the sentence (column 1). Column 8 contains the universal dependency relation, while column 9 (optionally) contains an enhanced dependency graph in the form of head-dependency relation pairs. Any other type of annotation can be placed in column 10. Fields should never be empty and may have an underscore as place-holder if necessary. Figure 2 presents the sentence in Figure 1 in the UD format.

4   Converting AfriBooms to the UDT format

4.1   Language-specific definitions for Afrikaans

In general, the structural conversion for the Afrikaans treebank aims to be in line with what was done for Dutch and German UDs, as they are the two languages closest to Afrikaans. For those languages, UD treebanks are already available. Despite the fact that Afrikaans has a simplified morphology compared to Dutch, the languages share a lot of features, which include gen-

---

[4]https://universaldependencies.org

1	Die	die	DET	LB	Definite=Def|PronType=Art	2	det	_	_
2	webtuiste	webtuiste	NOUN	NSE	Number=Sing	7	nsubj	_	_
3	sal	sal	AUX	VTUOM	Tense=Pres|VerbForm=Fin,Infl|VerbType=Mod	7	aux	_	_
4	'n	'n	DET	LO	Definite=Ind|PronType=Art	6	det	_	_
5	nuwe	nuut	ADJ	ASA	AdjType=Attr|Case=Nom|Degree=Pos	6	amod	_	_
6	deurblaai-venster	deurblaai-venster	NOUN	NSE	Number=Sing	7	obj	_	_
7	oopmaak	oopmaak	VERB	VTHSG	Subcat=Tran|Tense=Pres|VerbForm=Fin,Inf	0	root	_	_
8	.	.	PUNCT	ZE	_	7	punct	_	_

Figure 2: Example for an Afrikaans sentence in the UDT format

eral Indo-European ones, but also very specific (West) Germanic characteristics such as extensive nominal compounding, separability of compound verbs, and extensive diminutive formation.

4.1.1 PoS tags and morphological features

The Afrikaans Universal PoS tags and features are listed in Table 3.

Nouns For nouns (NOUN) and proper names (PROPN), we introduce a feature Degree next to number. As in in Dutch, this is in order to cover the extensive possibilities of diminutive formation, e.g. *huis* 'house' gets *huisie* 'little house' and *Jan* ('John') has *Jantjie* 'little John'. Besides this language-specific feature, we need the Num feature, but not Case as Afrikaans has hardly any remainders of the old Germanic case system. The genitive is expressed by the particle *se*, which is covered by the feature PartType=Gen for particles. There are still a few fixed expressions inherited from Dutch, like *ter ere van* 'in honour of', which will be considered as multi-word adverbials or prepositions. We will treat fixed Latin expressions such as *ex aequo* similarly. We do not include the difference between common nouns, measurement nouns, collectives and abstract nouns, which was present in the original tag set, as most of those tags did not occur in the training set of the tagger anyway. Pluralia tanta will be represented as 'plural' nouns.

Adjectives Adjectives (ADJ) have degrees of comparison like most other Indo-European languages. We introduce the Case feature to cover for the formal, archaic genitive forms like *iets interessants* 'something interesting' (Donaldson, 1993). Other archaic accusative or dative forms might occur in fixed expressions (e.g. *te geleëner tyd* 'at the proper time'), but as there are very few, these expressions are also considered multi-word adverbials. In addition to these features we need to introduce a new language-specific feature AdjType

to account for the fact that most adjectives have a different form depending on whether they are used attributively or predicatively, e.g. *'n eerlike kêrel* ('an honest guy') vs. *dié kêrel is eerlik* ('this guy is honest'). This is only relevant for the nominative case. The forms are indistinguishable in the comparative and superlative, but as our original tag set does make the distinction, we propose to keep it. As prescribed in the UD guidelines, ordinal numbers form part of adjectives.

Adverbs For adverbs (ADV), we only keep the differences in degree and we will not introduce features to describe the type of adverb (temporal, modal, etc.) at this point.

Verbs Verbs (VERB) have a very simple morphology in Afrikaans. Apart from a few auxiliaries and modals, verbs only have one present form, which also serves as infinitive, and a past participle, which is used in the formation of the past tense. The verb *wees* 'to be' has a separate infinitive next to the present form *is* 'is', while it also has an old preterite form to express the past (*was* 'was'), just like some modals. Present and past participles are considered as adjectives when they behave as such. An indication of the distinction native speakers make between past participles and their (declinable) adjectival forms, is the fact that the old Dutch strong forms can only be used in adjectival positions and not to form the past tense (Donaldson, 1993). For example, one cannot say *die kind word aangenome*, only *die kind word aangeneem* 'the child is adopted'. However, one can say *die kind is aangenome*, in which case this is analysed as a combination of the copula and a predicative complement, next to *die kind is aangeneem*, which means 'The child has been adopted'. The strong form often has a more figurative or abstract meaning, as in *'n gebroke hart* ('a broken heart') vs. *'n gebreekte bord* ('a broken plate') (Conradie, 2017).

For the category of auxiliaries (AUX) we intro-

UD PoS TAG	DESCRIPTION	MORPHOLOGICAL FEATURES
ADJ	Adjectives	AdjType=Attr,Pred; Case=Nom,Gen; Degree=Cmp,Pos,Sup
ADP	Adpositions	AdpType=Circ,Post,Prep
ADV	Determiners	Degree=Cmp,Pos,Sup
AUX	Auxiliaries	Tense=Past,Pres; VerbForm=Fin,Inf; VerbType=Aux,Cop,Mod,Pas
CCONJ	Coordinating conjunctions	
DET	Determiners	Definite=Def,Ind; PronType=Art,Dem,Ind;
INTJ	Interjections	
NOUN	Nouns	Degree=Dim; Num=Plur,Sing
NUM	Numerals	
PART	Particles	PartType=Inf,Neg,Gen
PRON	Pronouns	Case=Nom,Acc; Number=Plur,Sing; Person=1,2,3; Poss=Yes; PronType=Ind,Int,Prs,Rcp,Rel; Reflex=Yes
PROPN	Proper names	Degree=Dim; Num=Plur,Sing
PUNCT	Punctuation	
SCONJ	Subordinating conjunctions	
SYM	Symbols	
VERB	Non-auxiliary verbs	Tense=Pres,Past; VerbForm=Fin,Inf,Part; Subcat=Intr,Prep,Tran
X	Other	

Table 3: Afrikaans Universal PoS tags and their potential morphosyntactic feature values

duce the `VerbType` feature to distinguish between copular verbs, modal verbs, the passive auxiliaries *word* 'be' (present) and *wees* (past), and other auxiliaries. This is similar to the Dutch treatment, apart from the introduction of the passive voice category. Like Dutch and German, Afrikaans has separable verbs, i.e. verbs that are actually compounds of a particle (or sometimes an adjective or a noun) and another verb. In verb-initial clauses, the two parts get separated and the particle moves to the end of the clause. An example is *Ek gaan die huis binne* 'I enter the house' with the separable verb *binnegaan* 'to enter' (literally 'inside go').[5]

Pronouns and determiners Pronouns are treated in a similar way as in Dutch. Possessive and reflexive pronouns are considered a subset of the personal pronouns and have person and number features. We do not indicate the gender of third person pronouns. On top of this, we distinguish relative, interrogative, indefinite, and reciprocal pronouns as a part of the `PRON` class. Demonstrative pronouns are put in the `DET` class together with indefinite determiners and articles, as required by the UD guidelines. For articles, the distinction between definite and indefinite articles is indicated by the `Definite` feature.

Adpositions We also follow the Dutch annotations in defining three types of adpositions (`ADP`): prepositions, postpositions and circumpositions, encoded with the `AdpType`.

Particles We introduce three types of particles (`PART`): *te* 'to' introducing the infinitive (denoted by `Inf`), the genitive particle *se* 'his/her/their' (similarly used as *'s* in English and denoted by `Gen`, and the negative particle *nie* 'not' which is used in most negative sentences in addition to a negative adverb or determiner (Huddlestone, 2010).

Remaining PoS tags The other PoS tags for numerals (`NUM`), coordinating conjunctions (`CCONJ`), subordinating conjunction (`SSCONJ`), interjections (`INTJ`), punctuation (`PUNCT`), symbols (`SYM`), and the remainder class (`X`) do not have any additional features.

Contracted forms One common contraction is the colloquial *dis* for *dit is* (the expletive 'it is'), which needs to be split. Note that this construction does not appear in AfriBooms treebank.

4.1.2 Dependency relations

UD represents dependency relations between words in the form of a tree. Only one word, dependent on the ROOT, can be the head of the sentence. All other words are dependent on another word in the tree. The main driving principle of the UD formalism is the primacy of content words.

---

[5]In verb-final clauses, the verb is placed at the end of the clause after the particle, and the two are (usually) treated as a single orthographic unit. Compare the verb-initial construction to a construction with a subordinate clause: *Hy sien dat ek die huis binnegaan* 'He sees that I enter the house'.

UD PoS tag	Morphological features	Freq.	Example
ADJ	AdjType=Attr|Case=Nom|Degree=Cmp	34	*minder*
ADJ	AdjType=Attr|Case=Nom|Degree=Pos	2321	*tweede*
ADJ	AdjType=Attr|Case=Nom|Degree=Sup	41	*doeltreffendste*
ADJ	AdjType=Pred|Case=Nom|Degree=Cmp	20	*vinniger*
ADJ	AdjType=Pred|Case=Nom|Degree=Pos	419	*nuttig*
ADJ	AdjType=Pred|Case=Nom|Degree=Sup	5	*hoogste*
ADP	AdpType=Prep	5604	*in*
ADV	Degree=Cmp	54	*beter*
ADV	Degree=Pos	1728	*vandag*
ADV	Degree=Sup	11	*mees*
AUX	Tense=Past|VerbForm=Fin|VerbType=Cop	54	*was*
AUX	Tense=Past|VerbForm=Fin|VerbType=Mod	20	*wou*
AUX	Tense=Past|VerbForm=Fin|VerbType=Pas	266	*is*
AUX	Tense=Pres|VerbForm=Fin,Infl|VerbType=Aux	384	*het*
AUX	Tense=Pres|VerbForm=Fin,Infl|VerbType=Cop	608	*is*
AUX	Tense=Pres|VerbForm=Fin,Infl|VerbType=Mod	1049	*sal*
AUX	Tense=Pres|VerbForm=Fin,Infl|VerbType=Pas	543	*word*
CCONJ	_	1768	*en*
DET	Definite=Def|PronType=Art	3237	*die*
DET	Definite=Ind|PronType=Art	876	*'n*
DET	PronType=Dem	396	*hierdie*
DET	PronType=Ind	315	*baie*
NOUN	Degree=Dim|Number=Plur	5	*koekies*
NOUN	Degree=Dim|Number=Sing	9	*koekie*
NOUN	Number=Plur	2610	*blaaiers*
NOUN	Number=Sing	6784	*toegang*
NUM	_	197	*twee*
PART	PartType=Gen	152	*se*
PART	PartType=Inf	836	*te*
PART	PartType=Neg	244	*nie*
PRON	Case=Acc,Nom|Number=Plur|Person=1|PronType=Prs	470	*ons*
PRON	Case=Acc,Nom|Number=Plur|Person=2|PronType=Prs	4	*julle*
PRON	Case=Acc,Nom|Number=Plur|Person=3|PronType=Prs	96	*hulle*
PRON	Case=Acc|Number=Sing|Person=1|PronType=Prs	8	*my*
PRON	Case=Acc|Number=Sing|Person=2|PronType=Prs	19	*jou*
PRON	Case=Acc|Number=Sing|Person=3|PronType=Prs	13	*haar*
PRON	Case=Nom|Number=Sing|Person=1|PronType=Prs	66	*ek*
PRON	Case=Nom|Number=Sing|Person=2|PronType=Prs	186	*u*
PRON	Case=Nom|Number=Sing|Person=3|PronType=Prs	350	*dit*
PRON	Number=Plur|Person=1|Poss=Yes|PronType=Prs	308	*ons*
PRON	Number=Plur|Person=1|PronType=Prs|Reflex=Yes	13	*ons*
PRON	Number=Plur|Person=3|Poss=Yes|PronType=Prs	89	*hul*
PRON	Number=Plur|Person=3|PronType=Prs|Reflex=Yes	3	*hulself*
PRON	Number=Sing|Person=1|Poss=Yes|PronType=Prs	10	*my*
PRON	Number=Sing|Person=2|Poss=Yes|PronType=Prs	90	*jou*
PRON	Number=Sing|Person=2|PronType=Prs|Reflex=Yes	1	*jouself*
PRON	Number=Sing|Person=3|Poss=Yes|PronType=Prs	56	*sy*
PRON	Number=Sing|Person=3|PronType=Prs|Reflex=Yes	12	*homself*
PRON	PronType=Ind	307	*enige*
PRON	PronType=Int	20	*wat*
PRON	PronType=Rcp	6	*mekaar*
PRON	PronType=Rel	1116	*wat*
PROPN	Number=Sing	463	*Suid-Afrika*
PUNCT	_	4027	.
SCONJ	_	946	*as*
SYM	_	435	*R5*
VERB	Subcat=Intr|Tense=Past|VerbForm=Part	64	*gedemonstreer*
VERB	Subcat=Intr|Tense=Pres|VerbForm=Fin,Inf	547	*werk*
VERB	Subcat=Prep|Tense=Pres|VerbForm=Fin,Inf	25	*voldoen*
VERB	Subcat=Tran|Tense=Past|VerbForm=Part	725	*gemeet*
VERB	Subcat=Tran|Tense=Pres|VerbForm=Fin,Inf	2445	*ontdek*
X	_	385	*DRK*

Table 4: Frequency of the UD PoS tags and the morphological features in the Afrikaans UD treebank

This means that in general content words are the head instead of function words, e.g. nouns are the head of prepositional phrases. The aim of this principle is to allow for maximal comparability across languages. In addition to the obligatory dependency relations, it is possible to add an enhanced dependency graph to this scheme with a more complete basis for semantic interpretation.[6]

For instance, the regular dependency relations lack a dependency relation between raised subjects and an embedded verb. It is possible to encode this kind of information in the enhanced dependency graph.

The UD scheme defines 37 types of relations, of which 24 are actual dependency relations. The taxonomy for the latter is organized along two dimensions, which can be represented in the form of a matrix.[7] The first dimension corresponds to functional categories in relation to the head (core arguments of clausal predicates, non-core dependents of clausal predicates, and dependents of nominals) whereas the second dimension corresponds to the structural categories of the dependent (nominals, clauses, modifiers, and function words).

Additionally, there are 13 relations that are not dependency relations in the narrow sense. It concerns relations for analyzing coordination, multiword expressions, ellipsis, and special relations for concepts such as root, punctuation and multi-word expressions.

Afrikaans shares many syntactic features with Dutch and German. It has, for instance, verb-second in main clauses but verb-final in (most) subordinate clauses (Biberauer, 2003); and there is the occurrence of substitute infinitives, also known as *Infinitivus Pro Participio* or IPP (Augustinus and Dirix, 2013). Afrikaans also has particular features such as double negation (Huddlestone, 2010).

In principle, all types of Universal Dependency relations can be applied to Afrikaans. The only exception is the classifier relation (`clf`), as Afrikaans has no grammaticalized classifier system. As in Dutch and German, we introduce the `compound:prt` relation for compounds of which a part has been elided, e.g. *in- en uitvoer* 'import and export', as well as for the particle of separable verbs. We also introduce `nsubj:pass` and

`csubj:pass` for the subjects of passive verbs, using *word* (present) or *is* (past) as auxiliary.

4.2 Conversion and issues

As described in section 2 the original NCHLT corpus was available with original more fine-grained tags of the NCHLT corpus. We reintroduced those features in the AfriBooms treebank in order to prepare for conversion to UD, as they contain morphological information which is required by the UD guidelines. In general, we kept the morphological features used in UD releases for other languages. Most of the original morphological tags have been converted to UD features, but we did not do this for the types of adverbs or the type of nouns, and as well as the types of symbols and punctuation marks, as these were semantic in stead of morphosyntactic features. The XML format of AfriBooms treebank was converted into a tab-separated format, which facilitates the conversion to the CoNLL-U format considerably. The actual conversion was done using a Perl script.

4.2.1 PoS tags and morphological features

At the level of PoS tags and features there were hardly any disambiguation issues. Pronouns that have the same form in their base and oblique forms have a `Case=Nom,Acc` feature which could be disambiguated manually. We have not done this yet. This is also the case for the feature `VerbForm=Fin,Inf` which is assigned to most verbs including auxiliaries, as the form of the present tense is identical to the infinitive.

The counts for the PoS tags and their morphological features in the automatically converted version of AfriBooms can be found in Table 4.

As the AfriBooms treebank is relatively small, not all possible morphological forms occur in the treebank, e.g. the genitive form of articles and their comparatives. This will obviously inhibit automated parser training.

4.2.2 Dependency relations

Table 5 lists the initial mapping of the dependency relations. Compared to the conversion of the PoS tags and morphological features, the conversion of the dependency relations was less straightforward, as some structural conversion was needed.

The first problem is due to the small size of the AfriBooms treebank, as a about one third of the Stanford dependencies tags was not used in the

---

treebank and we can only provide mappings for dependencies occurring in that treebank.

AB DEP. TAG	UD DEP. TAG	UD DESCRIPTION
root	root	root
aux	aux	auxiliary
conj	conj	conjunct
cc	cc	coordinating conjunction
subj	nsubj	nominal subject
dobj	obj	object
iobj	iobj	indirect object
pobj	case	case-marking element
obj	obj	object
amod	amod	adjectival modifier
mod	amod	adjectival modifier
num	nummod	numeric modifier
appos	appos	appositional modifier
poss	det	determiner
det	det	determiner
prt	mark	marker
dep	dep	unspecified dependency
arg	dep	unspecified dependency
comp	dep	unspecified dependency
mark	dep	unspecified dependency
abbrev	appos	appositional modifier
punct	punct	punctuation

Table 5: Initial mapping between the AfriBooms and UDT dependency relations

The second problem with respect to the automated conversion is the underspecification of dependency relations in the AfriBooms treebank. The UD relations only have one generic tag (dep), while the dependencies used in the AfriBooms treebank have several levels of underspecification, e.g. mod, arg, obj (see Table 2). Those relations need to be either specified automatically or manually. In Dutch, there were actually similar issues with underspecification; when possible they were resolved in an automated way (Bouma and van Noord, 2017).

The third issue is that the human annotators of the AfriBooms treebank did not consistently follow the content word primacy principle. For instance in the case of prepositional phrases they assigned the head status to the preposition, which means we had to flip the dependency relation between them and have the noun point to the governor of the phrase. The dependency relation was set to nmod or obl, depending on the PoS of the governor. A similar issue exists for copular constructions: the verb is assigned the head of the relation, while the predicative complement is identified as an object. Again, we changed the dependency relation, making the nonverbal predicate the

head (mostly the root of the sentence), introducing the cop relation and switching the governor of the subject to the nonverbal predicate. Similarly, we had to fix possessive constructions like *leerders se vermoë* ('learners' ability'), to make sure the possessive particle had the case relation, and swapping the relation between the two nouns, making the second one the governor and giving it the dependency relation of the former one, while giving the former one the nmod relation. Another dependency relation that had to swap its head, are the cc types for conjunctions, which need to point to the following noun (phrase) and not to the preceding one.

The fourth problem is that some relations are not distinguished in the original AfriBooms annotation. A number of them could be (semi-)automatically introduced. For instance, as the original treebank annotations do not make a distinction between nsubj (nominal subject) and csubj (clausal subject), we converted them all to nsubj and replaced them afterwards to csubj if the governor of the subject is either a verb or an auxiliary. Furthermore, we introduced compound:prt for compounds with partial elision, as mentioned in the previous section. In order to do this, we again had to swap the dependency relation and change the governors of all the tokens depending on the partially elided compound, as the first part of the expression was treated as the head in the AfriBooms treebank. The result needs to be reviewed manually, as there are also phrases consisting of more than one compound with partial elision (e.g. *klein-, medium- en mikro-ondernemings* – 'small, medium and micro-enterprises'), and phrases of the type *besigheids- en ander sektore* ('business and other sectors'), which stands for *besigheidsektor en ander sektore*. In the latter example the first item is a partially elided compound, but the second part consists of an adjective followed by a noun, which is also the elided part of the first compound.

In addition, we introduced aux:pass for passive auxiliaries based on their morphological features, and specified nsubj:pass for the nominal subject of those verbs. We also introduced iobj for a list of ca 30 verbs for which the indirect object is introduced with the preposition *aan*. Finally, we also specified the flat relation in multiword named entities.

We replaced amod with advmod for all adverbs and negative particles that had this dependency re-

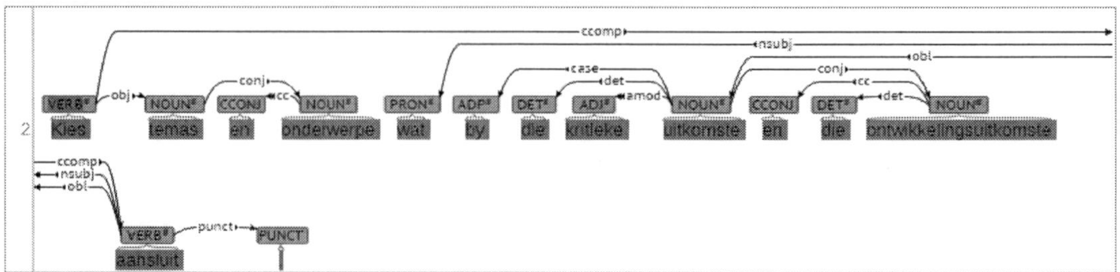

Figure 3: Example for an Afrikaans sentence after automated conversion in the UDT format: 'Choose themes and subjects that link with the critical outcomes and the developmental outcomes.'

lation in the original treebank.

We also fixed the dependency relation of verbs following the particle *te* to xcomp, as the original treebank did not distinguish between nominal and clausal constituents. Furthermore, we also had to flip the dependency relation between relative pronouns and the content verb of the relative sentence, and made sure the verb has the xcomp dependency relation.

All of this patching work was done using an additional Perl script which we ran after the initial conversion. As mentioned in section 2 the Afri-Booms treebank contains many generic dep relations, which need to be further specified. Even though the patching work greatly reduced the number of generic items, many of them should be manually reviewed. This is currently in progress. An example of a converted sentence is given in Figure 3.

As a final step, the converted treebank was validated using the UDT tools available on GitHub.[8] Table 6 presents the final figures of each dependency relation category after conversion and patching.

5 Conclusion and future work

We created a UD treebank for Afrikaans using an automated conversion scheme from the existing AfriBooms treebank. It is a small treebank of about 49K words consisting of governments documents. Due to its small size and the specific genre, it does not contain all possible dependency relations and morphological feature values.

As many of the dependency relations were underspecified in the original treebank, the next step consists of a manual check. We furthermore plan to train parsers for the annotation of both the dependency relations and the morphological information. Those parsers will be used to create more annotated data, for starters from Wikipedia, but possibly also for other text types, such as the Taalkommissie corpus. A (small) part of those data could be verified manually in order to improve parsing accuracy.

UD DEP. TAG	FREQ.	DESCRIPTION
advmod	1780	adverbial modifier
amod	5080	adjectival modifier
appos	63	appositional modifier
aux	1663	auxiliary
aux:pass	854	passive auxiliary
case	5890	case-marking element
cc	1886	coordinating conjunction
ccomp	905	clausal complement
compound:prt	408	separable verb particle / elided part of a compound
conj	2001	conjunct
cop	149	copula
csubj	3	clausal subject
csubj:pass	0	clausal subject of passive verb
dep	1668	unspecified dependency
det	5775	determiner
flat	231	flat multiword expression
iobj	53	indirect object
mark	1051	marker
nmod	2948	nominal modifier
nsubj	3010	nominal subject
nsubj:pass	500	nominal subject of passive verb
nummod	461	numeric modifier
obj	2804	object
obl	2728	oblique nominal
punct	4497	punctuation
root	1903	root
xcomp	965	open clausal complement

Table 6: The UD tag set with number of occurrences in the AfriBooms treebank

---

[8]https://github.com/UniversalDependencies/tools

References

Liesbeth Augustinus and Peter Dirix. 2013. The IPP effect in Afrikaans: a corpus analysis. In *Proceedings of the 19th Nordic Conference of Computational Linguistics (NODALIDA 2013) - NEALT Proceedings Series 16*, pages 213–225, Oslo.

Liesbeth Augustinus, Peter Dirix, Daniel Van Niekerk, Ineke Schuurman, Vincent Vandeghinste, Frank Van Eynde, and Gerhard Van Huyssteen. 2016. AfriBooms: An Online Treebank for Afrikaans. In *Proceedings of the Tenth International Conference on Language Resources and Evaluation (LREC 2016)*, pages 677–682, Portorož. European Language Resources Association (ELRA).

Theresa Biberauer. 2003. *Verb Second (V2) in Afrikaans: a Minimalist investigation of word-order variation*. Ph.D. thesis, University of Cambridge, Cambridge.

Gosse Bouma and Gertjan van Noord. 2017. Increasing return on annotation investment: the automatic construction of a Universal Dependency Treebank for Dutch. In *Proceedings of the Universal Dependencies Workshop at the 21st Nordic Conference of Computational Linguistics (NODALIDA 2017)*, Gothenburg.

Thorsten Brants. 2000. TnT – A Statistical Part-of-Speech Tagger. In *Proceedings of the Sixth Applied Natural Language Processing Conference (ANLP-2000)*, pages 224–231, Seattle.

Jac Conradie. 2017. The re-inflecting of Afrikaans. Paper given at the Germanic Sandwich 2017, Münster.

Marie-Catherine de Marneffe and Christopher D. Manning. 2008. The Stanford typed dependencies representation. In *Proceedings of the Workshop on Cross-Framework and Cross-Domain Parser Evaluation at COLING 2008*, pages 1–8, Manchester, UK.

Marie-Catherine de Marneffe, Bill MacCartney, and Christopher D. Manning. 2006. Generating Typed Dependency Parses from Phrase Structure Parses. In *Proceedings of the 6th International Conference on Language Resources and Evaluation (LREC 2006)*, pages 449–454, Genoa. European Language Resources Association (ELRA).

Bruce C. Donaldson. 1993. *A Grammar of Afrikaans*. Mouton de Gruyter, Berlin/New York.

Kate Huddlestone. 2010. *Negative Indefinites in Afrikaans*. Ph.D. thesis, Utrecht University.

Joakim Nivre, Johan Hall, Sandra Kübler, Ryan McDonald, Jens Nilsson, Sebastian Riedel, and Deniz Yuret. 2007. The CoNLL 2007 shared task on dependency parsing. In *Proceedings of the CoNLL shared task session of EMNLP-CoNLL*, pages 915–932.

Joakim Nivre, Marie-Catherine de Marneffe, Filip Ginter, Yoav Goldberg, Jan Hajič, Christopher D. Manning, Ryan McDonald, Slav Petrov, Sampo Pyysalo, Natalia Silveira, Reut Tsarfaty, and Daniel Zeman. 2016. Universal Dependencies v1: A Multilingual Treebank Collection. In *Proceedings of the Tenth International Conference on Language Resources and Evaluation (LREC 2016)*, pages 1659–1666, Portorož. European Language Resources Association (ELRA).

Slav Petrov, Dipanjan Das, and Ryan McDonald. 2012. A Universal Part-of-Speech Tagset. In *Proceedings of the 8th International Conference on Language Resources and Evaluation (LREC 2012)*, pages 2089–2096, Istanbul. European Language Resources Association (ELRA).

Suléne Pilon. 2005. *Outomatiese Afrikaanse woordsoortetikettering*. Master's thesis, North-West University, Potchefstroom.

Antal van den Bosch, Bertjan Busser, Sander Canisius, and Walter Daelemans. 2007. An efficient memory-based morphosyntactic tagger and parser for Dutch. In *Computational Linguistics in the Netherlands: Selected papers from the Seventeenth CLIN Meeting*, pages 191–206, LOT, Utrecht.

Daniel Zeman. 2008. Reusable Tagset Conversion Using Tagset Drivers. In *Proceedings of the 6th International Conference on Language Resources and Evaluation (LREC 2008)*, pages 213–218, Marrakesh. European Language Resources Association (ELRA).

Elliptic Constructions: Spotting Patterns in UD Treebanks

Kira Droganova and **Daniel Zeman**
ÚFAL, Faculty of Mathematics and Physics, Charles University
Malostranské náměstí 25, CZ-11800 Praha, Czechia
`{droganova|zeman}@ufal.mff.cuni.cz`

Abstract

The goal of this paper is to survey annotation of ellipsis in Universal Dependencies (UD) 2.0 treebanks. In the long term, knowing the types and frequencies of elliptical constructions is important for parsing experiments focused on ellipsis, which was also our original motivation. However, the current state of annotation is still far from perfect, and thus the main outcome of the present study is a description of errors and inconsistencies; we hope that it will help improve the future releases.

1 Introduction

Elliptic constructions (ellipsis) are linguistic phenomena which refer to the omission of a word or several words from a sentence. The meaning of the omitted words, however, can be understood in the context of the remaining elements. For instance, in the sentence "John gave a flower to Mary and [he gave] a book to his son" (an example from (Hajič et al., 2015)) the second predicate and its subject are omitted because of ellipsis. From the syntactic point of view, this significantly alters the sentence structure.

Ellipsis exists in the majority of languages (Merchant, 2001a) and thus deserves careful attention in theoretical and empirical studies, and with regard to NLP applications. The most difficult types of ellipsis (which are the focus of this paper) tend to be rare in comparison to other grammatical patterns, which makes them hard to learn and recognize by parsers. The parsers' ability to recognize elliptic constructions also heavily depends on the annotation scheme used in a particular corpus: some annotation schemes make ellipsis more visible and identifiable than others.

There is a number of previous dependency analyses of ellipsis. (Mel'čuk, 1988) proposed to use a node labeled as elided, for instance, in the sentence "Alan went to Paris and Leo to Coruña" (an example from (Polguère and others, 2009)), the second verb is marked as elided and thus is invisible. (Lombardo and Lesmo, 1998) used non-lexical nodes and so called non-primitive dependency rules to express gapped coordination. (Osborne et al., 2012) introduced the catena concept and described the elided material of ellipsis mechanisms in terms of catena. (Kahane, 1997) proposed "bubble trees" for gapped coordination.

In this paper we will focus on the *basic representation* of Universal Dependencies (UD) (Nivre et al., 2016), in which most types of ellipsis are solved by dependent promotion and thus are invisible, i.e., not explicitly annotated as ellipsis; the only exception is missing predicate with multiple overt dependents (orphans). Section 2 gives a brief overview of common ellipsis types and their analysis in UD.

2 Classification

According to (Testelets, 2011), a single rule that motivates elliptical constructions cannot be defined even within one language. The UD guidelines define the following set of rules that proposes a solution for the representation of elliptic constructions:

- *If the elided element has no overt dependents, no special relation is required;*

- *If the elided element has overt dependents, one of those dependents is promoted to take the role of the head;*

Following are examples of constructions solved this way:

2.1 Ellipsis in Nominals

When the head noun of a noun phrase is elided (Corver and van Koppen, 2009), according to the

Proceedings of the NoDaLiDa 2017 Workshop on Universal Dependencies (UDW 2017), pages 48–57,
Gothenburg, Sweden, 22 May 2017.

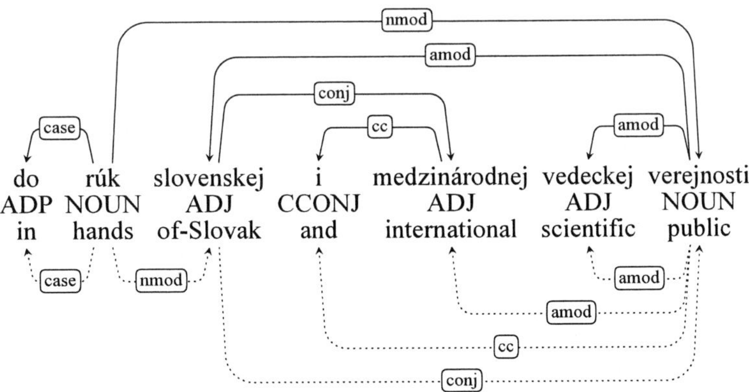

Figure 1: Slovak: An example of adjective coordination, which semantically corresponds to coordination of two full nominals *(slovenskej [vedeckej verejnosti] i medzinárodnej vedeckej verejnosti)*, but the UD approach is to analyze it just as coordinate modifiers. While we consider this approach correct, note that promoting the adjective *slovenskej* to the head position of the first nominal phrase would lead to a different result: the noun *verejnosti* would be connected to *slovenskej* as a conjunct, as shown by the dotted relations below the text.

UD guidelines, one of the orphaned dependents should be promoted to the head position and the other dependents (if any) are attached via the same relations that would be used with the elided head. As a result, there are no means to detect this type of ellipsis in the data (except for unusual POS tag-dependency combinations, such as an adjective serving as a subject).

Coordination of adjectival modifiers can be seen as a special case of an elided noun; however, in this case the usual approach in UD is to just coordinate the adjectives (Figure 1).

2.2 Comparative Deletion

Ellipsis occurs commonly in the complement clause of comparative constructions: in "He plays better drunk than sober," the full meaning is actually "He plays better [when he is] drunk than [how he plays when he is] sober."

Here, too, "sober" is promoted all the way up to the head of the adverbial clause that modifies "better". The relation between the two adjectives is still clausal (advcl); together with the missing subject and copula, these are indirect signs that betray the ellipsis. However, there is no explicit annotation of it.

2.3 Sluicing

Sluicing refers to reduced interrogative clauses, often to a bare interrogative word (Merchant, 2001b). In the following example from UD English, the content in brackets is understandable

from the previous sentence: "It's easy to understand why [the cats refused to eat it]."

Following the UD promotion rules, "why" should be promoted to the head position of the elided complement clause and attached to "understand" via the ccomp relation. (As a matter of fact, it is currently attached as advmod, which we think is an error.)

2.4 VP Ellipsis and Pseudogapping

If a non-finite verb phrase has been elided but a finite auxiliary verb has not, the auxiliary is promoted. Such constructions are called *VP-ellipsis* (Johnson, 2001) and *pseudogapping* (Lasnik, 1999). Like with elided nominals, promoting the auxiliary makes these types difficult to identify in the treebank (but see Figure 6 for a counterexample.) Note that the same applies to clauses with non-verbal predicates where the predicate is elided and only copula remains (and is promoted): "John is not smart but Mary is."

2.5 Gapping and Stripping

Gapping means that the entire predicate is elided, including auxiliary verbs; however, two or more arguments or adjuncts ("orphans") are overtly expressed[1] (Johnson, 2001; Johnson, 2009; Sag, 1976).

---

[1]Note that the v2 guidelines mistakenly required the orphans to be core dependents. We argue and demonstrate that the same situation can be caused also by oblique arguments or adjuncts.

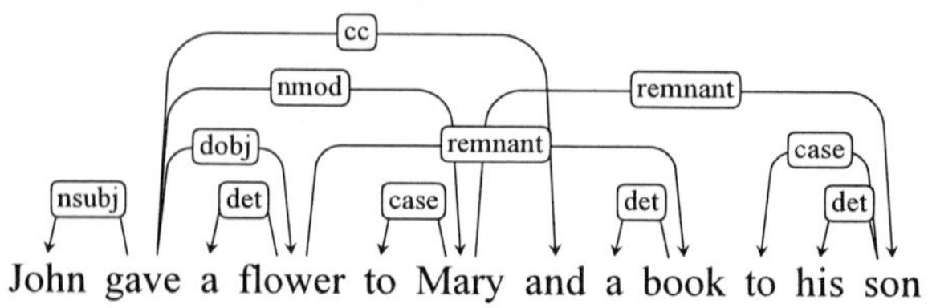

Figure 2: UD v1 annotation of ellipsis used the `remnant` relation to link orphaned dependents to the corresponding dependents of the first predicate.

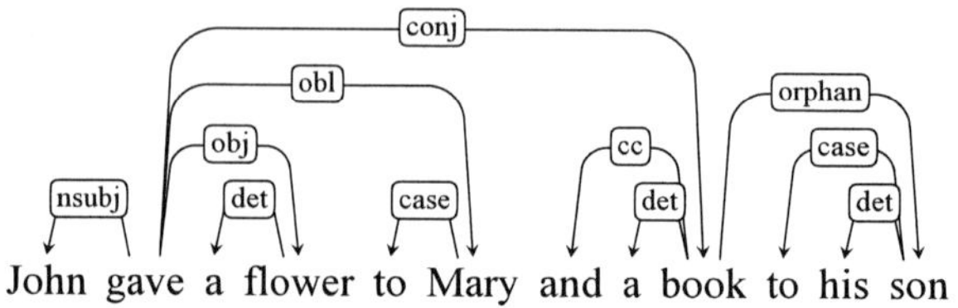

Figure 3: UD v2 annotation uses the `orphan` relation to attach unpromoted dependents of a predicate to the promoted dependent.

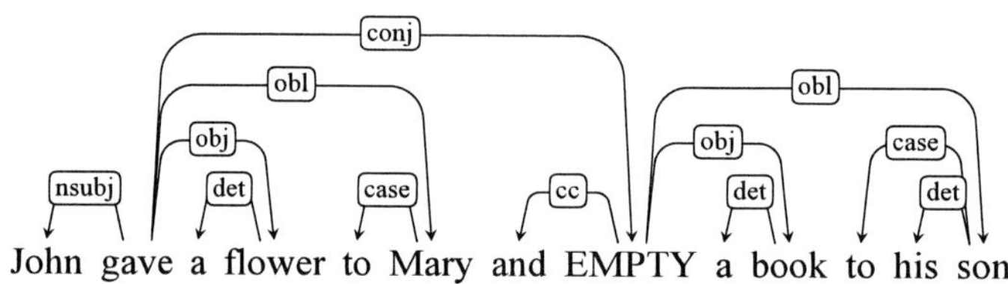

Figure 4: The enhanced UD v2 annotation, currently available only for English, Finnish and Russian, uses reconstructed "empty nodes" to represent the elided predicate *(gave)*.

In the UD v1 guidelines, the `remnant` relation was used "to reconstruct predicational or verbal material in the case of gapping or stripping" (de Marneffe et al., 2014); see Figure 2. Practical application showed that such treatment of elliptic constructions has several disadvantages:

- The `remnant` relation does not produce a clear representation if the second clause contains additional modifiers of the elided predicate;

- The antecedent of the remnant may not exist in the same sentence;

- The annotation style generates many non-projective and parallel structures, thus reducing parsing quality (Nivre and Nilsson, 2005).

The orphan relation is introduced to specify ellipsis more transparently[2] in the UD guidelines v2 (Figure 3). One of the orphaned dependents is promoted and the others are attached to it via the orphan relation. An obliqueness hierarchy is defined, inspired by (Pollard and Sag, 1994);[3] the dependent higher in the hierarchy is promoted. The orphan relation is the only explicit annotation of ellipsis in the basic representation of UD, i.e. only constructions of this type can be easily identified in the data.

UD v2 also defines an *enhanced representation* where the elided material can be reconstructed using empty nodes (Figure 4). Such representation is currently available only in three treebanks and we do not investigate it further in the present work. Therefore we will focus on the orphan relation in the rest of the paper.

Even more radical reduction is stripping (Hankamer and Sag, 1976) where only one argument remains, assuming that the rest would be identical to

---

[2] http://universaldependencies.org/u/ overview/specific-syntax.html#ellipsis

[3] nsubj > obj > iobj > obl > advmod > csubj > xcomp > ccomp > advcl

the previous clause. However, the orphaned argument is usually accompanied at least by an adverb like "too" or "not". This puts stripping in a gray zone that is not clearly delimited in the UD guidelines. Either we treat the adverb as just a connecting function word, and we attach it to the promoted argument as `cc` or `advmod`. Or we treat it as gapping, i.e. the relation is `orphan` (Figure 9). We cannot quantify the two approaches but both have been observed in the treebanks.

3 Ellipsis in Numbers

Table 1 summarizes the statistics of elliptical constructions in the UD 2.0 treebanks (Nivre et al., 2017). The treebanks are sorted by the last column, which shows the ratio of `orphan` relations to the total number of nodes in the treebank. 41 treebanks have at least 1 `orphan` relation in the data, but only 12 treebanks have more than 100 sentences with orphans. Most treebanks have less than 1 `orphan` per 10,000 nodes, but several treebanks are significantly higher, peaking with the PROIEL treebank of Ancient Greek, which has an `orphan` in every 500 nodes (Figure 5 shows an example from that treebank).

The number of treebanks which mark elliptic constructions explicitly has doubled since UD release 1.4 (Table 2). However, 29 treebanks from UD 2.0 do not use the `orphan` relation at all. Some of them are large enough to assume that the studied type of ellipsis actually occurs there but is not annotated properly (we try to address this problem in Section 4.2). Most UD treebanks are conversions of older data annotated under different annotation schemes. If the original scheme does not mark missing predicates somehow, it may not be possible to identify the `orphan` relations within an automatic conversion procedure.

4 Typical Patterns

Based on the UD guidelines for the `orphan` relation, one would expect that the most frequent pattern with `orphan` is coordination of clauses where only the first clause has an overt verbal predicate, while it has been elided from the subsequent conjuncts (clauses). The trees in Figure 3 and Figure 7 are examples of such pattern. However, coordination is not the only possible configuration— Figures 5 and 6 show subordination in a comparative construction. The latter is somewhat less typical in that a copula is promoted but one dependent

UD Treebank	Orphans	%
Ancient Greek PROIEL	701/417	0.205%
Czech	3714/2264	0.036%
Finnish	276/175	0.033%
Czech CAC	1784/1066	0.025%
Russian SynTagRus	2405/838	0.02%
Latin ITTB	836/607	0.014%
Romanian	66/47	0.01%
Greek	220/137	0.01%
Croatian	143/103	0.008%
Norwegian Bokmaal	189/173	0.008%
Norwegian Nynorsk	207/179	0.007%
Latin PROIEL	571/295	0.007%
Gothic	169/96	0.005%
Old Church Slavonic	182/105	0.003%
Arabic	217/72	0.003%
Slovenian SST	28/19	0.002%
Hungarian	64/43	0.002%
Russian	81/66	0.002%
Catalan	12/7	0.001%
English	24/22	0.001%
Dutch	33/12	0.001%
Swedish	44/31	0.001%
French Sequoia	38/29	0.001%
Slovak	110/75	0.001%
Chinese	2/1	0.0%
Estonian	2/2	0.0%
Portuguese	7/6	0.0%
Italian ParTUT	7/7	0.0%
Czech CLTT	14/11	0.0%
Lithuanian	3/3	0.0%
Coptic	2/1	0.0%
Belarusian	14/7	0.0%
Bulgarian	3/2	0.0%
English ParTUT	10/10	0.0%
French ParTUT	3/3	0.0%
Latvian	9/8	0.0%
Galician TreeGal	1/1	0.0%
Spanish AnCora	29/19	0.0%
French	3/3	0.0%
Swedish LinES	4/4	0.0%
Italian	49/44	0.0%

Table 1: Statistics on UD v.2.0 treebanks. Orphans: number of orphan nodes/number of sentences. %: the ratio of orphan nodes to all nodes in the treebank.

is still attached as `orphan` because it complements the elided adjective rather than the whole clause.

The range of dependents that can qualify as or-

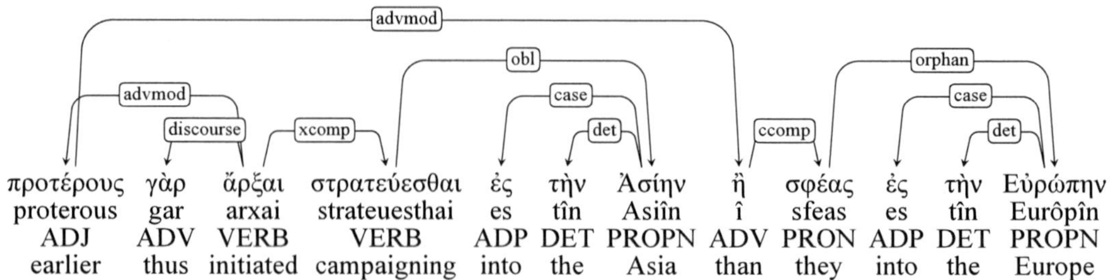

Figure 5: Ancient Greek (PROIEL), Herodotos, Histories Book 1: "for they set the first example of war, making an expedition into Asia before the Barbarians made any into Europe."

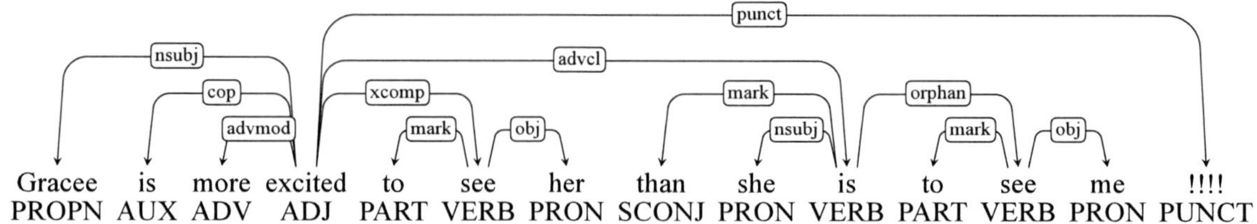

Figure 6: English: The copula *is* is promoted to the position of the elided non-verbal predicate *excited*.

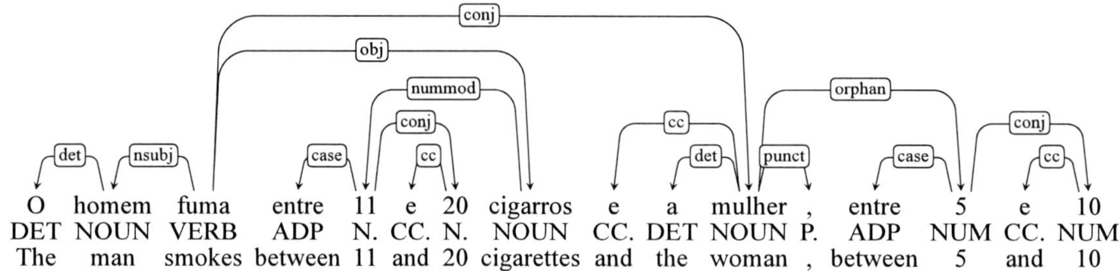

Figure 7: Portuguese: "O homem fuma entre 11 e 20 cigarros por dia e a mulher, entre 5 e 10." ("The man smokes between 11 and 20 cigarettes per day, and the woman between 5 and 10.") The subject of the second clause is promoted and the object is attached to it as `orphan`. Note that there are other instances of ellipsis, too: *entre 5 e 10 [cigarros]* (solved by simple promotion of *5*), and even the first range, *entre 11 e 20 cigarros*, in fact stands for *entre 11 [cigarros] e 20 cigarros*.

phans is rather wide. Core arguments (subjects and objects) are the prototypical cases but oblique arguments or adjuncts (including adverbial modifiers) cannot be excluded (see Figure 8). A special case is the yes-no opposition, rendered in some languages as coordination of a full affirmative verb, and a negative element (without repeating the main verb). Figure 9 demonstrates this on Czech. Note that a similar English sentence would not need the `orphan` relation: in *"they got a meal and I didn't"*, there is an obligatory auxiliary verb in the second part, which gets promoted to the head position.

4.1 Annotation Errors

Ellipsis is a difficult phenomenon, and annotation of ellipsis is a difficult task. Since we are dealing with material missing from the sentence, various annotation styles also miss various bits of information; automatic conversion between annotation styles may have to employ heuristics, and sometimes the correct analysis cannot be obtained without a human in the loop. It is thus not surprising that some of the most common "patterns" we observed in the data are annotation errors. We do not present a complete quantitative evaluation though—we were not able to check all orphans in

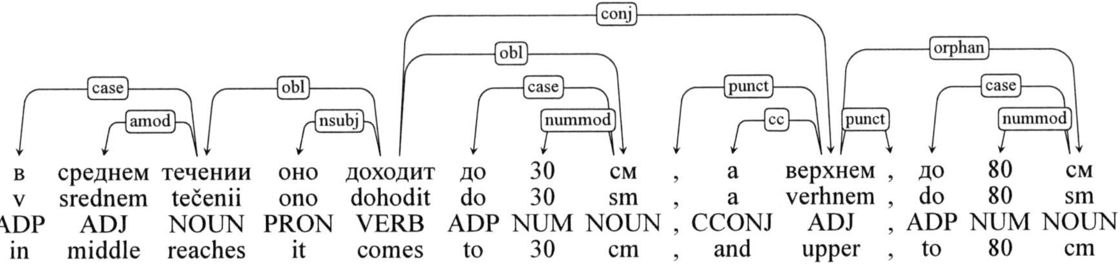

Figure 8: Russian: "In the middle reaches it comes to 30 cm and in the upper [reaches it comes to] 80 cm." One orphaned adjunct is promoted, the other is attached as `orphan`.

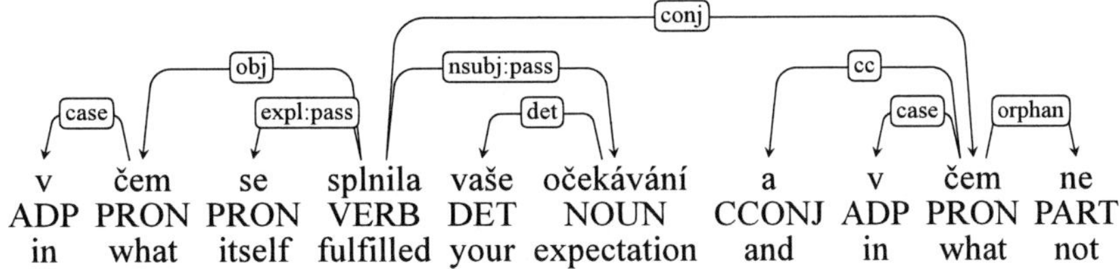

Figure 9: Czech: "where was your expectation met and where not?" The negative particle is not considered an auxiliary and is not selected for promotion. Note that if the verb was present, its polarity would be marked by a bound morpheme.

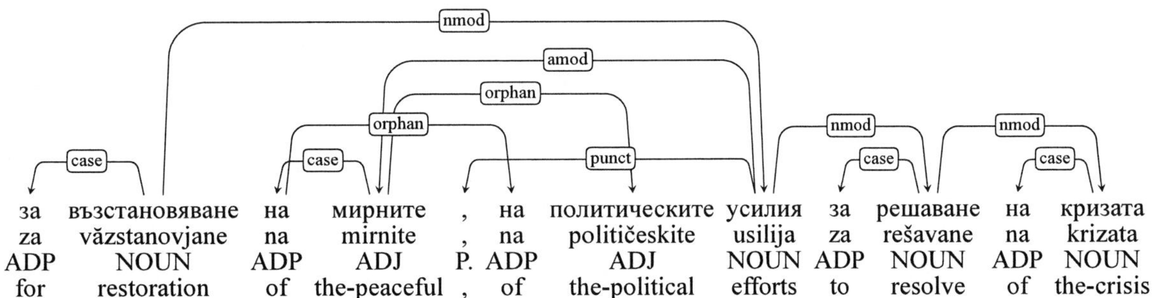

Figure 10: Bulgarian: "for restoration of peaceful, political efforts to resolve the crisis." The two `orphan` relations are used in the `v1-remnant` style, as if the relations were just relabeled instead of conversion. Moreover, the `orphan` relation should not be used in this situation at all. It is simple coordination of two adjectives, *мирните* and *политическите*.

all treebanks. However, Table 3 shows some figures for a small number of treebanks. We think that these figures could help contributors to improve their data, but they do not provide a complete overview of the phenomena that are misrepresented in UD treebanks, e.g., the 100% error rate in Spanish AnCora is caused exclusively by erroneous assignment of orphan relation instead of conj relation; the figures for Belarusian and Portuguese cannot be interpreted in a statistically significant way due to small number of sentences containing the orphan relation.

The typical error classes are the following:

1. The `orphan` relation is used instead of `conj` (Figure 10);

2. Relations are correct, structure is wrong (Figures 11, 12 and 13);

3. The priority of promotion violates the obliqueness hierarchy (Figures 11 and 13);

4. There are two (or more) orphans instead of one, and both are attached to their common ancestor (Figure 14).

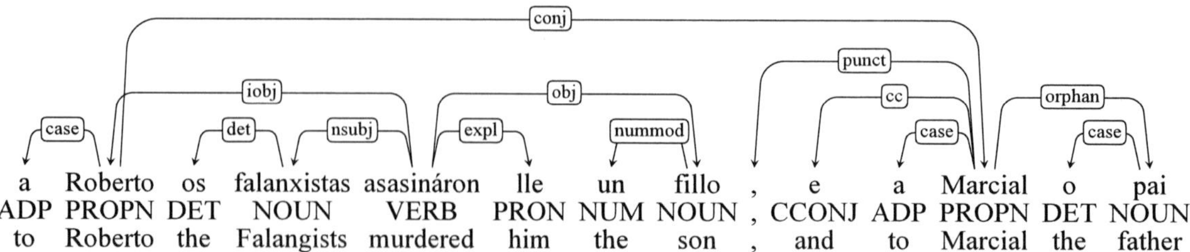

Figure 11: Galician (TreeGal): "The Falangists murdered Roberto's son and Marcial's father." According to the obliqueness hierarchy, the direct object *(pai)* should be promoted, not the indirect object *(Marcial)*. Moreover, the promoted dependent takes the position of the missing verb, hence it should be connected via `conj` to *asasináron*, not to *Roberto*.

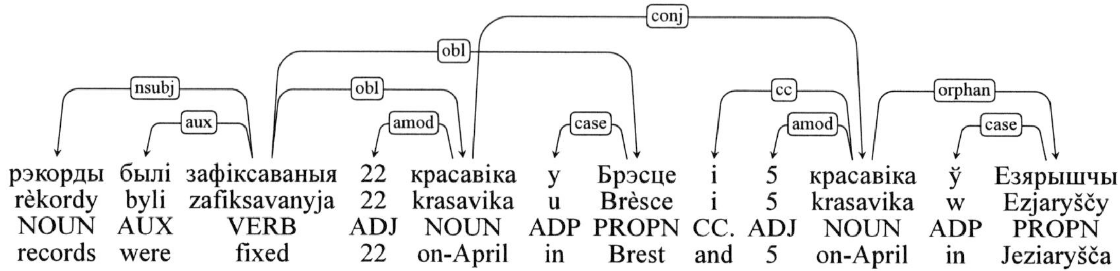

Figure 12: Belarusian: "Records were fixed on April 22 in Brest and on April 5 in Jeziaryšča." Two pairs of time-location adjuncts (`obl`). They have equal rank in the obliqueness hierarchy, thus the first one is promoted. However, it should be connected via `conj` to the verb and not to the corresponding adjunct in the first pair.

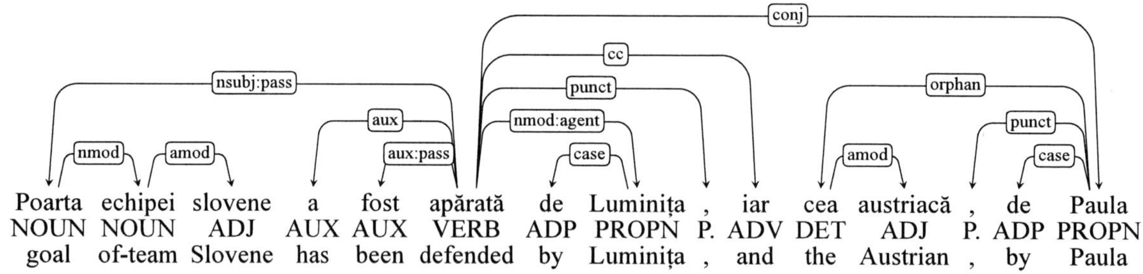

Figure 13: Romanian: "Poarta echipei slovene a fost apărată de românca Luminița Huțupan, iar cea austriacă, de Paula Rădulescu." ("The goal of the Slovenian team was defended by Luminița Huțupan from Romania, and the Austrian by Paula Rădulescu.") Following the obliqueness hierarchy, the subject *(austriacă)* should be promoted and the oblique agent *(Paula)* attached as `orphan`. Moreover, `nmod:agent` should be `obl:agent` in UD v2, and `punct` + `cc` should be attached to the right.

5. The structure is correct but relations are wrong. In particular, some of the treebanks that completely lack orphans fall into this category (Figure 15).

Although we can show examples only from a few treebanks, similar errors can be found in other treebanks, too.

4.2 Search for Missing Orphans

While it is difficult to automatically check whether existing orphan relations are correct, it is even more difficult to identify sentences where an orphan is missing. To prove our hypothesis that the studied type of ellipsis occurs also in treebanks not mentioned in Table 1, we search for the most

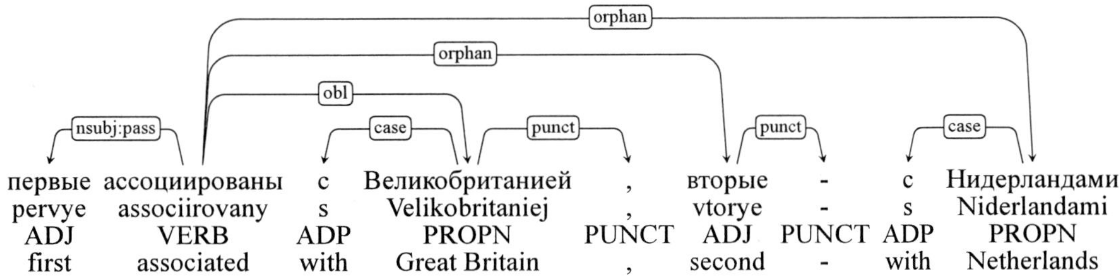

Figure 14: Russian (SynTagRus): "The former were associated with Great Britain, the latter with the Netherlands." Instead of promoting one orphaned dependent and attaching the other to it as orphan, both dependents are attached to the parent of the elided predicate, via the orphan relation.

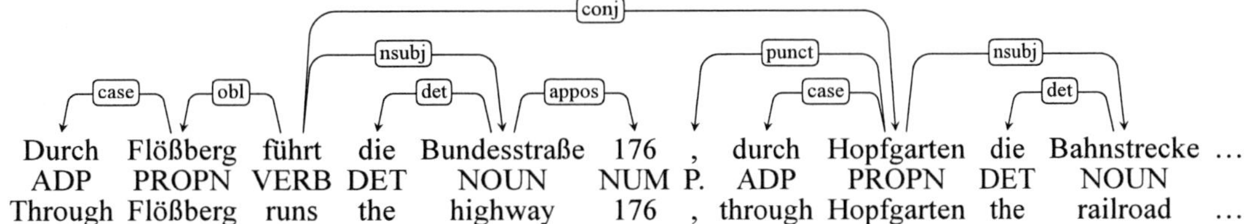

Figure 15: German: "The Highway 176 runs through Flößberg and the railroad [runs] through Hopfgarten." The relation between *Hopfgarten* and *Bahnstrecke* is labeled nsubj because *Bahnstrecke* is the subject of the missing copy of the verb *führt*. The orphan relation should be used instead.

typical pattern: a noun is attached to a verb via the conj relation, and the noun has another noun as dependent. The latter noun must be attached via a relation that is not typically used to connect two nouns (i.e. we specifically exclude nmod, appos and some other relations). We also try to exclude arguments of non-verbal predicates by checking whether there is a copula; but obviously this does not work well in languages like Russian, where the copula may be omitted. Also note that such a search pattern does not guarantee that we get all instances of gapping. It assumes that the annotation follows the tree structure required by UD v2, except it does not know the orphan label. Obviously there is a range of other approaches that the treebanks could take. Still, there are 19 treebanks with 10 or more instances. Some of them may be false positives but manual verification of Spanish and German has revealed that there are indeed true positives, too (Figure 15 presents an example). To give at least a limited picture of the precision of the heuristic (we cannot assess recall), we examined all 30 instances in UD Spanish. Only 5 of them (17%) were true orphans in the UD v2 sense. However, all the remaining cases deserve attention as well because they were only found due to an-

notation errors (such as a verb tagged NOUN). (In addition, two of these errors occur next to orphans that were not detected by the heuristic.)

5 Conclusion

We have presented the elliptic constructions within the UD 2.0 treebanks. We showed some typical patterns occurring in the data as well as rarely occurring constructions.

The differences in ratio of orphans to treebank size (Table 1) can be explained both by unannotated orphans in some treebanks and by annotation errors ("orphan" instead of "conj") in others.

It turned out that the number of annotation errors is rather high which surely reflects the complexity of this linguistic phenomenon.

The current state of the UD annotation w.r.t. ellipsis is insufficient and supports neither parser learning nor (cross-)linguistic studies. While human revisiting of the data is desirable, it is obviously not possible for all the treebanks, and automatic tests/corrections would be highly desirable. We have shown that such tests can at least partially help, and we collected a number of examples, which will hopefully help to improve future heuristics for identifying ellipsis in UD.

UD Treebank	Remnants	%
Ancient Greek PROIEL	1117/458	0.403%
Finnish	352/175	0.047%
Romanian	128/56	0.022%
Croatian	259/166	0.016%
Greek	230/149	0.011%
Latin PROIEL	780/344	0.011%
Gothic	297/120	0.009%
Norwegian	256/230	0.008%
Hungarian	169/68	0.007%
Old Church Slavonic	325/145	0.007%
English	92/54	0.004 %
Russian	177/89	0.004%
Chinese	4/1	0.0%
Coptic	6/2	0.0%
English ESL	5/4	0.0%
Bulgarian	4/3	0.0%
Kazakh	22/9	0.0%
Galician TreeGal	15/10	0.0%
French	1/1	0.0%
Portuguese Bosque	24/11	0.0%
Ukrainian	6/2	0.0%

Table 2: Statistics on UD v.1.4 treebanks. Remnants: number of remnant nodes/number of sentences. %: the ratio of remnant nodes to all nodes in the treebank.

UD Treebank	Err/Sent	%
English	1/22	4.55%
Italian	3/44	6.82%
Belarusian	2/7	28.6%
Portuguese	2/6	33.3%
Russian	48/66	72.73%
Spanish AnCora	19/19	100.00%

Table 3: Manually assessed error rate in selected treebanks. Err/Sent: number of erroneous sentences/number of sentences with orphans. %: error rate.

Acknowledgments

The work was partially supported by the grant 15-10472S of the Czech Science Foundation, and by the GA UK grant 794417.

References

Norbert Corver and Marjo van Koppen. 2009. Let's focus on noun phrase ellipsis. In *Groninger Arbeiten zur germanistischen Linguistik*, volume 48, pages 3–26.

Marie-Catherine de Marneffe, Timothy Dozat, Natalia Silveira, Katri Haverinen, Filip Ginter, Joakim Nivre, and Christopher Manning. 2014. Universal Stanford Dependencies: a cross-linguistic typology. In *Proceedings of the 9th International Conference on Language Resources and Evaluation (LREC 2014)*, Reykjavík, Iceland.

Jan Hajič, Eva Hajičová, Marie Mikulová, Jiří Mírovský, Jarmila Panevová, and Daniel Zeman. 2015. Deletions and node reconstructions in a dependency-based multilevel annotation scheme. In *16th International Conference on Computational Linguistics and Intelligent Text Processing, Lecture Notes in Computer Science, ISSN 0302-9743, 9041*, pages 17–31, Berlin / Heidelberg. Springer.

Jorge Hankamer and Ivan Sag. 1976. Deep and surface anaphora. *Linguistic inquiry*, 7(3):391–428.

Kyle Johnson. 2001. *What VP ellipsis can do, and what it can't, but not why.* Blackwell Publishers, Oxford.

Kyle Johnson. 2009. Gapping is not (VP) ellipsis. *Linguistic Inquiry*, 40(2):289–328.

Sylvain Kahane. 1997. Bubble trees and syntactic representations. In *Proceedings of mathematics of language (mol5) meeting*, pages 70–76. Citeseer.

Howard Lasnik, 1999. *Pseudogapping puzzles.*, pages 141–174. Oxford University Press, Oxford.

Vincenzo Lombardo and Leonardo Lesmo. 1998. Unit coordination and gapping in dependency theory. In *Proceedings of the Workshop on Processing of Dependency-Based Grammars*, pages 11–20.

Igor Mel'čuk. 1988. Dependency syntax: Theory and practice, state university of new york press. *Arabic Generation in the Framework of the Universal Networking Language*, 209.

Jason Merchant. 2001a. *The syntax of silence: Sluicing, islands, and the theory of ellipsis.* Oxford University Press on Demand.

Jason Merchant. 2001b. *The syntax of silence: Sluicing, islands, and the theory of ellipsis.* Oxford University Press on Demand.

Joakim Nivre and Jens Nilsson. 2005. Pseudo-projective dependency parsing. In *Proceedings of the 43rd Annual Meeting on Association for Computational Linguistics*, ACL '05, pages 99–106, Stroudsburg, PA, USA. Association for Computational Linguistics.

Joakim Nivre, Marie-Catherine de Marneffe, Filip Ginter, Yoav Goldberg, Jan Hajič, Christopher Manning, Ryan McDonald, Slav Petrov, Sampo Pyysalo, Natalia Silveira, Reut Tsarfaty, and Daniel Zeman. 2016. Universal Dependencies v1: A multilingual treebank collection. In *Proceedings of the 10th International Conference on Language Resources and Evaluation (LREC 2016)*, pages 1659–1666, Portorož, Slovenia.

Joakim Nivre, Željko Agić, Lars Ahrenberg, and
.... 2017. Universal dependencies 2.0. LIN-
DAT/CLARIN digital library at the Institute of
Formal and Applied Linguistics, Charles University, Prague, `http://hdl.handle.net/11234/`
`1-1983`.

Timothy Osborne, Michael Putnam, and Thomas Groß.
2012. Catenae: Introducing a novel unit of syntactic
analysis. *Syntax*, 15(4):354–396.

Alain Polguère et al. 2009. *Dependency in linguistic
description*, volume 111. John Benjamins Publishing.

Carl Pollard and Ivan A. Sag. 1994. *Head-Driven
Phrase Structure Grammar*. Studies in Contempo-
rary Linguistics. University of Chicago Press.

Ivan Sag. 1976. *Deletion and Logical Form*. MIT.
PhD dissertation.

Yakov Testelets. 2011. Ellipsis in Russian: Theory
versus description. In *Typology of Morphosyntactic
Parameters*, pages 1–6, Moscow, Russia. MSUH.

Dependency Schema Transformation with Tree Transducers

Felix Hennig and **Arne Köhn**
Department of Informatics
Universität Hamburg
{3hennig, koehn}@informatik.uni-hamburg.de

Abstract

The problem of (semi-)automatic treebank conversion arises when converting between different schemas, such as from a language specific schema to Universal Dependencies, or when converting from one Universal Dependencies version to the next. We propose a formalism based on top-down tree transducers to convert dependency trees. Building on a well-defined mechanism yields a robust transformation system with clear semantics for rules and which guarantees that every transformation step results in a well formed tree, in contrast to previously proposed solutions. The rules only depend on the local context of the node to convert and rely on the dependency labels as well as the PoS tags. To exemplify the efficiency of our approach, we created a rule set based on only 45 manually transformed sentences from the Hamburg Dependency Treebank. These rules can already transform annotations with both coverage and precision of more than 90%.

1   Introduction

Since the inception of the Universal Dependencies project (McDonald et al., 2013), a number of treebanks were converted from language specific schemas to UD, in an effort to create a large multi-lingual corpus. More recently, the whole UD corpus was converted to a revised annotation schema. As treebanks and their syntax annotation guidelines are not static but are evolving constantly, converting between different schemas or modifying some parts of an existing one is a recurring problem and as such needs a reliable and systematic solution. Annotating a whole treebank again manually for a different schema is neither viable due to the sheer amount of work needed, nor necessary, since the new annotation can mostly be deduced from the syntactic information in the existing schema. Therefore, usually semi-automatic conversion is used. However, most of the time only the resulting treebank is of interest and small throwaway scripts are created just for this one conversion at hand which can not be easily used for other conversions.

We introduce a conversion system which makes it easy to specify conversion rules based on the local context of a node (i. e. word) in a dependency tree. It is based on tree transducers, a well-defined formalism already used with phrase structure trees.

Because the syntactic information is only transformed into a different representation, a rule-based approach based on local information works particularly well, as reappearing structures in the source schema correspond to reappearing structures in the generated schema. By using tree transducers, it is easy to extract rules from a small initial set of manually transformed annotations which can then be applied to the whole corpus. The rule applications can be manually observed and verified, and the ruleset can be refined based on these observations.

2   Related Work

While tree transducers have been around for a while, they have not been used with dependency trees so far. Treebank conversion itself is a topic which has gained attention only recently in association with the Universal Dependencies project.

2.1   Treebank Conversion

The UD project included six languages initially (McDonald et al., 2013) and since its inception, a number of treebanks with native annotation schemas have been converted to Universal Dependencies (e.g. Danish (Johannsen et al., 2015), Norwegian (Øvrelid and Hohle, 2016), Swedish (Nivre, 2014; Ahrenberg, 2015) and Hindi (Tandon et al., 2016)). By establishing a new annotation scheme which is also still evolving, (semi-)automatic con-

Proceedings of the NoDaLiDa 2017 Workshop on Universal Dependencies (UDW 2017), pages 58–66,
Gothenburg, Sweden, 22 May 2017.

version is gaining importance, yet no common system or supporting framework was established.

However, a common pattern can be observed across conversion techniques: Usually, conversion starts with the treatment of language specific oddities such as splitting tokens into multiple syntactic words followed by conversion of PoS tags which can mostly be done on a simple word for word basis, and conversion of dependency labels combined with restructuring of the tree.

For tree restructuring and dependency label conversion, rules matching and converting parts of the tree have been proposed in different approaches. The Finnish Turku Dependency Treebank was converted with dep2dep[1], a tool based on constraint rules which are converted to Prolog (Pyysalo et al., 2015). Tyers and Sheyanova (2017) convert North Sámi to UD with a rule pipeline implemented as XSLT rules. Both approaches match edges based on node features and local tree context, matching is done anywhere in the tree, in contrast to top-down conversion in a tree transducer approach.

Ribeyre et al. (2012) outline a two step process where the rules to be applied are determined in the first step and are then iteratively applied in the second with meta-rules handling conflicting rule applications. Neither of these approaches can inherently guarantee well-formed tree output.

For the transition from UD version 1 to version 2 a script has been published based on the udapi framework, which simplifies working with CoNLL-U data.[2] All transformations in the transition script are encoded directly into the source code, making adaptations difficult and error-prone.

2.2 Applications of Tree Transducers

Thatcher (1970) extended the concept of sequential transducers to trees and already mentioned its potential usefulness for the analysis of natural language. Transducers in general can often be found in natural language processing tasks, such as grapheme to phoneme conversion, automatic speech recognition (Mohri et al., 2002) or machine translation (Maletti, 2010), however a finite state transducer is limited to reading its input left-to-right, in a sequential manner.

In machine translation tree transducers can be used, where they operate on constituency trees. The tree is traversed top to bottom and thus subtrees in the sentence can be reordered to accommodate for differences in the grammatical structure of source and target language. In a similar manner, tree transducers can be used for semantic parsing (Jones et al., 2011), converting a syntax input tree to a tree structure representing the semantic information contained in the input.

A constituency tree consists of internal nodes which represent the syntactical structure of the sentence, and leaf nodes, which are the actual words of the sentence. For dependency trees however, the internal nodes as well as the leaves are already the words of the sentence and syntactical structure is represented using the edges in the tree, which carry labels. To our knowledge, tree transducers were not used with dependency trees so far. The model has to be adapted in some ways to accommodate for the differences between dependency trees and constituency trees (see Section 3.2).

3 Tree Transducers for Dependency Conversion

Tree transducers, or more specifically top-down tree transducers, are automata which convert tree structures from the root to the leaves using rules. A rule matches parts of the tree and is therefore ideal in applications where the conversion of the whole tree can be decomposed into smaller conversion steps that rely only on local context. In constituency trees as well as dependency trees, parts of a sentence are grouped together to form a single syntactic unit, such as the subject of a sentence consisting of a noun with a determiner and an adjective or even a relative clause. When converting the tree, the size and structure of the subtree attached as subject is irrelevant, just like the rest of the tree becomes irrelevant when looking at the subtree.

3.1 Formal Definition of a Tree Transducer

A tree transducer is a five-tuple $M = (Q, \Sigma, \Delta, I, R)$.[3] Tree transducers operate on trees. A tree consists of elements from the *input alphabet* Σ, which is a set of symbols. The *rank* of a symbol is the number of child elements it needs to have in the tree. A *ranked alphabet* is a tuple (Σ, rk) where rk is a mapping of symbols to their rank. For simplicity, the ranked alphabet is called Σ, like the set of symbols it contains. The set of

---

[1] https://github.com/TurkuNLP/dep2dep

[2] https://github.com/udapi/; the Java implementation is also used in our tree transducer implementation.

[3] Our notation follows (Maletti, 2010), which also offers an expanded discussion on the formal aspects of top-down tree transducers.

possible trees that can be created from the alphabet is denoted by T_Σ.

In addition to the input alphabet, a transducer also has an *output alphabet* Δ with $\Sigma \cap \Delta = \emptyset$. The translation frontier is marked using *state nodes*, which are part of the set of state nodes Q, Q is disjoint with both Σ and Δ. The state nodes are also ranked symbols. Initially, the tree to be converted consists only of input symbols. A state node from the set of *initial states* $I \subseteq Q$ is added at the root, to mark the position in the tree that needs to be converted next. With each step the frontier of state nodes is pushed further down the tree. The state nodes separate the output symbols from the input symbols which still need to be converted (see Figure 1 for an example of a tree being converted top down with multiple local conversions).

The local conversion steps are performed using rules. Each top-down tree transducer has a *rule-set* $R \subseteq Q(T_\Sigma(X)) \times T_\Delta(Q(X))$, i.e. a rule is a tuple containing two tree structures: one to match parts of the tree to be converted, one to replace the matched parts. On the left-hand side, the root of each tree is a state node. The other nodes are from the input alphabet Σ. Leaf nodes may also be from the set of *variables* X. The state node is used as the anchor point to determine if a rule matches the current tree structure. The subtree of input nodes below the state node given on the left side of the rule needs to be identical to the subtree of input nodes in the tree to be converted. While the subtree of an extended tree transducer can be of arbitrary depth, a basic tree transducer can only contain subtrees of depth one. The variables on the left-hand side of the rule can match any node in the tree if they are in the correct relation to the rest of the tree. Subtrees below the one to be converted in this rule are matched to these variables, marking the end of the local context the rule seeks to convert.

If the left hand-side of the rule matches, the rule can be applied to the tree and the right-hand side of the rule is used to replace the matched subtree in the tree to be converted. The right-hand side of the rule consists of a tree of output symbols T_Δ. Again, leaves may be variables. Each variable needs to have a state node from the set Q as parent. Here, the same variables which were used on the left-hand side of the rule can be used again, to attach the unconverted subtrees below the new converted subtree. The newly introduced state nodes mark the subtrees described by the variables for further

conversion. In this way, the frontier of state nodes is pushed down the tree.

A rule is linear and nondeleting if the variables $x_i \in X$ used on the left-hand side of the rule are neither duplicated nor deleted on the right-hand side of the rule and each variable is used only once on the left-hand side. If all the rules in R are linear and nondeleting, the transducer is linear and nondeleting.[4] For machine translations tasks, these properties ensure that no part of the sentence is deleted or duplicated.

3.2 Adaptations for Dependency Conversion

When defining an extended top-down tree transducer for dependency trees, we treat the labels of the edges as properties of the dependent, as tree transducers have no notion of labeled edges. We then use the set of input and output dependency labels for Σ and Δ, respectively. In contrast to the previously discussed formalism, the vertices in the dependency tree are not simply dependency labels, but also contain the word and its index in the sentence, among other information that needs to remain unchanged. We therefore define the input alphabet Σ not just as the set of input labels L_{in} but rather as $\Sigma \subseteq L_{in} \times \mathbb{N}$, which means that each node is a tuple of the dependency relation and a natural number serving as a node identifier (i.e. the index of the word in the current sentence). We will write n^σ as a shorthand for $(\sigma, n) \in \Sigma$.

The need for this becomes apparent when looking at the example in Figure 2. In the second conversion step, the tree is converted with a rule like this: $q(PP(PN(x_1))) \rightarrow obl(case(), q(x_1))$ which we will use as a running example throughout this section. The new structure of the dependency relations is clearly defined, but which node should receive which label cannot be inferred. The node previously attached with the *PP* relation could either receive the label *obl* and not change its position in the tree, or it could be attached below the node with the *obl* label with a *case* relation. This is why the nodes need to be identified, which is done via their respective index. The rules do not contain explicit indices, only the correspondence between the left and right-hand side of the rule is relevant. The concrete indices are substituted during the rule matching. In the following rule, n_1 and n_2 stand for abstract indices that are to be replaced with a concrete

---

[4]A more elaborate definition of these properties can be found in (Maletti, 2010)

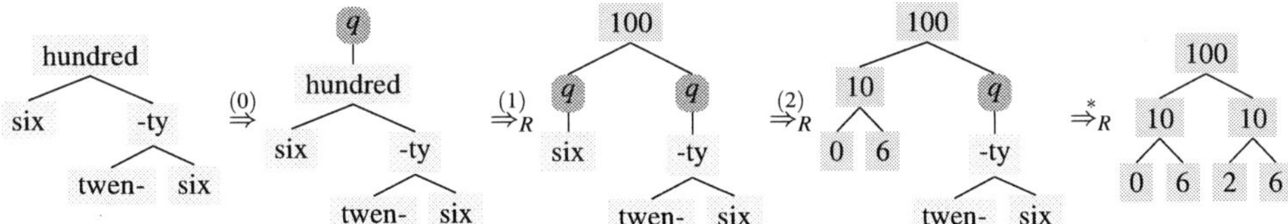

Figure 1: An example of a tree transformation of the numeric expression "six hundred twenty six" to its digit form 626, using a top-down tree transducer. The yellow nodes are nodes from the input alphabet, the green nodes are from the output alphabet and the orange nodes are state nodes. Example based on Maletti (2010), the last step includes multiple transformation steps.

index: $q(n_1^{PP}(n_2^{PN}(x_1))) \rightarrow n_2^{obl}(n_1^{case}(),q(x_1))$ It can be seen that n_1 and n_2 switch their position in the tree, so the node previously attached as *PP* got moved below the *obl* node and received the *case* relation.

After defining $\Sigma \subseteq L_{in} \times \mathbb{N}$ and $\Delta \subseteq L_{out} \times \mathbb{N}$ as described above, we can define a new property of transducers. A rule $r = (T_l, T_r)$ is *word-preserving* if it meets the following conditions: First, r is linear and nondeleting. Second, the left-hand side of r cannot contain the same node index twice: $n \neq m \; \forall (\cdot, n), (\cdot, m) \in T_l, (\cdot, n), (\cdot, m) \in \Sigma$. Third, r neither deletes nor duplicates a matched word. This means that for $N_{in} := \{n \in \mathbb{N} | (\cdot, n) \in T_l\}$ each $n \in N_{in}$ appears exactly once in T_r. A ruleset is word-preserving if all its rules are word-preserving. This property ensures that word attachments and dependency relations of the sentence can change but no word is removed or duplicated.

The input symbols of a tree transducer are ranked. A node in a dependency tree can have any number of children, therefore the alphabet in the tree can be assumed to contain each symbol with multiple different ranks to adhere to the formalism. To accommodate for the varying number of dependents in the rules, without requiring a rule for each possible number of dependents, the variable mechanism to match subtrees is extended to match multiple subtrees into one *catch-all* variable. As an example, the dependency tree in Figure 2 could have additional dependents below the "Transducer" node, such as adjectives or a relative clause. Our running example rule used in step two of the conversion process does not account for additional dependents. To account for them, the rule can be adapted as follows: $q(n_1^{PP}(n_2^{PN}(xs_1))) \rightarrow n_2^{obl}(n_1^{case}(),q(xs_1))$. Here, xs_1 can match a variable amount of nodes, hence formally it could be represented by $x_1, x_2, ..., x_n \in X$. In this way, one rule represents multiple rules with symbols of dif-

$$n_0(q(n_1^{NEB}(n_2^{KONJ}()), n_3^{OBJA})) \rightarrow$$
$$n_0(n_1^{advcl}(q(n_2())), q(n_3())) \quad (1)$$

$$n_0(q(n_1^{NEB}(n_2^{KONJ}()))) \rightarrow$$
$$n_0(n_1^{ccomp}(q(n_2()))) \quad (2)$$

$$q(n_1^{KONJ}()) \rightarrow n_1^{mark}() \quad (3)$$

Figure 3: Formal representation of tree transducer rules for transforming subordinate clauses.

ferent rank, which means that the transducer can still be seen as ranked, just with a compact representation. Also in contrast to the conventional formalism, the child elements in the tree structures of the rules are not ordered and can therefore be matched to the annotation nodes in any order.

We only use one type of state node. Information about the already converted part of the tree can be accessed by matching nodes above the frontier. This way, different rules can be executed based on, for example, the dependency relation of the parent node, without the requirement to pass this information down encoded in a state node. Only direct ancestors can be matched, as these are guaranteed to have been translated already. Matching dependents of parents would introduce ordering effects based on the order in which the children of a node are converted. Because the information in the parent nodes could be encoded in a state node, accessing it by matching the parent is not a violation of the transducer formalism.

3.3 Look-ahead Extension

Similarly to this look-back mechanism, a look-ahead mechanism is required to inspect context

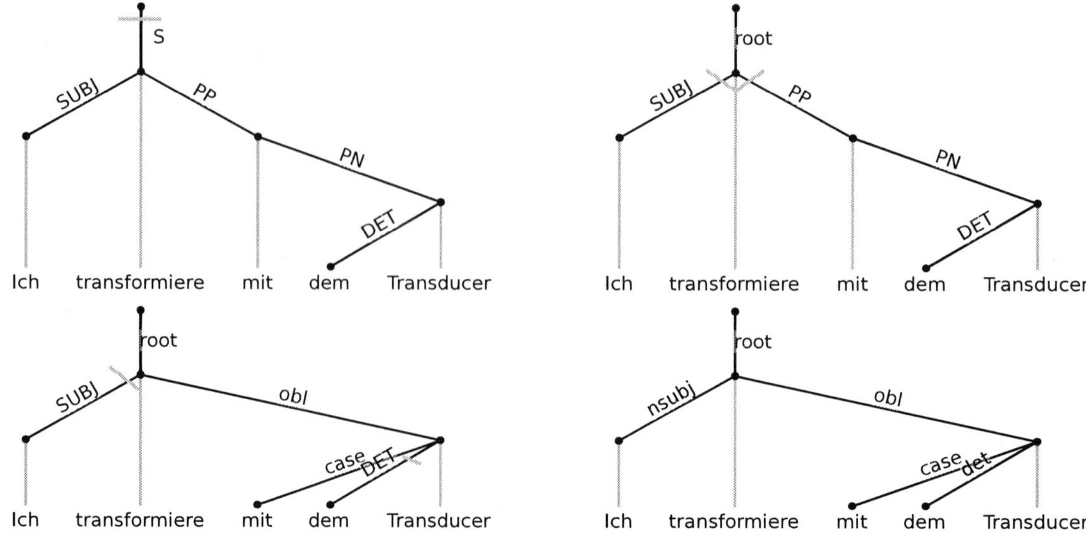

Figure 2: Conversion of "Ich transformiere mit dem Transducer" (*i transform with the transducer*); yellow lines indicate the state nodes, HDT labels are uppercase, UD are lowercase.

below the current node without converting it immediately. Figure 3 contains an example for this. A *NEB* dependent, a subordinate clause, is converted differently based on its context. The subordinate clause can either be a core dependent as a *ccomp* (rule 2), or it can have an adverbial function and would be attached as *advcl* (rule 1). In this case a simple heuristic based on the presence of an object is used to distinguish core and non-core subordinate clauses. *KONJ* and *OBJA* in the first two rules are matched to constrain rule application by requiring a certain context, but the conversion of these nodes is left to be treated in additional rules. The *KONJ* dependent, a subordinate conjunction, is transformed in an additional rule (rule 3) to clearly separate the conversion of different labels into different rules and to avoid duplicating conversion logic.

The *OBJA* dependent is attached with different labels based on its context, just like the *NEB* dependent in this case. Converting *NEB* and *OBJA* together in the same rule would result in a combinatorial explosion of rules, as not only would multiple rules be required to convert the *NEB* to different output symbols, but also multiple variants of the *NEB* rules for the different conversions of the *OBJA* dependent. While this separation of concerns into different rules results in a more structured and systematic ruleset, it requires rules to be tested in a specific order, as the *NEB* conversion now relies on the *OBJA* to be converted afterwards.

3.4   Cross-frontier Modifications

When converting a function-head treebank to a content-head scheme like Univeral Dependencies, edges are inverted a lot and in some cases the function and content word appear in the same pattern all the time, like the *case nmod* combination, but sometimes the structure varies more. Verb modality and tense is often expressed with auxiliary verbs or modality verbs in addition to the content bearing verb. In a function-head treebank this means there can be long chains of auxiliary verbs with the actual main verb at the bottom of the chain. The varying depths would require multiple rules for different depths of the chain, as all the function words and the content word at the end need to be converted at once, to allow for the inversion of the head. For these cases it is practical to make modifications to already converted parts of the tree.

An example of such a use case is shown in Figure 4. The *S* and *SUBJ* node are converted just like they would be if there were no auxiliary verbs. When the first auxiliary relation is converted, the already transformed root node is matched above the frontier and repositioned below the node previously attached as *AUX*, thereby inverting the relation between head and auxiliary verb. For the next auxiliary relation, the same rule is used. On the left-hand side of the rule the dependency relation of the parent is assigned to a variable x, to reassign this relation to the previous auxiliary verb. Using a

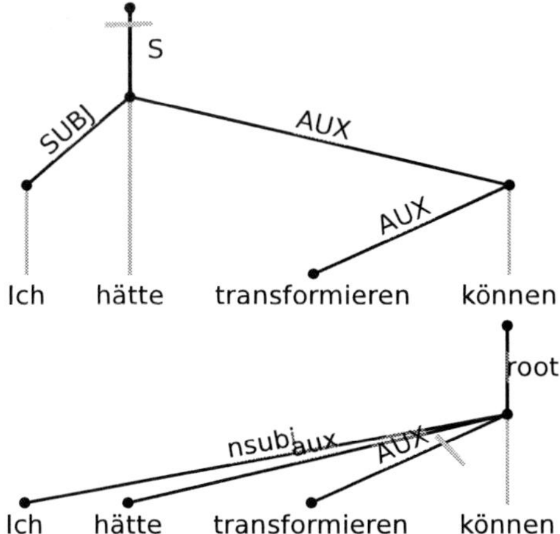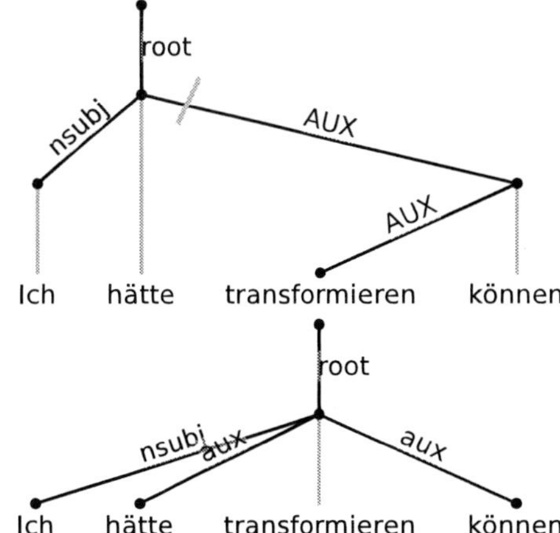

Figure 4: Conversion of a dependency tree from a function-head to a content-head scheme. The *AUX* edges are inverted when they are converted. The rule used in step 2 and 3 is $p^{\$x}(q(n^{AUX}(xs_n),xs_q),xs_p) \rightarrow n^{\$x}(p^{aux}(),q(xs_n,xs_q),xs_p)$

variable eliminates the need to have an additional rule for each possible parent relation.

The rule also contains catch-all variables below each individual node in the tree to cover all possible dependent attachments. Specifying a transformation strategy for each possible dependent makes this rule adaptable to different structures. While the first application of the rule matches "ich" in the xs_p variable and "transformieren" in the xs_n variable, the second application matches both "ich" and "hätte" in xs_p.

4 Implementation

The implementation of the transducer incorporates all properties discussed in Section 3. A transducer is specified through a single file containing the rules. The input and output alphabet are specified implicitly, by the labels used in these rules.

Figure 5 demonstrates the syntax, which is similar to the rule notation introduced in Section 3. A node is specified by an identifier and optionally its dependency relation, connected with a colon. Catch-all variables consist of an identifier prefixed by a question mark. A state node is denoted by curly braces, it does not have an identifier as there is only a single type of state node. A basic label translation is shown in (a), (b) shows the rule example discussed throughout Section 3.2 and (c) shows the rule mentioned in Figure 4.

Not all left-hand sides of the rules contain state nodes, and the right-hand sides never contain them. If a rule does not contain a state node on the left-

```
(a) n:SUBJ() -> n:nsubj();

(b) n1:PP(n2:PN(?r2), ?r1)
    -> n2:nmod(n1:case(), ?r1, ?r2);

(c) parent:$x({n:AUX(?auxr), ?fr}, ?r)
    -> n:$x(parent:aux(), ?auxr, ?r, ?fr);

(d) p({n:SUBJ(?r), ?fr}, ?pr)
    -> p(n:nsubj({?r}), {?fr}, ?pr)

(e) p({n1:OBJA(), n2:OBJD()})
    -> p(n1:obj(), n2:iobj());
    n:OBJA() -> n:obj();
    n:OBJD() -> n:obj();

(f) p.NE({n.NN:APP()}) -> p(n:appos());
    p.NN({n.NN:APP()}) -> p(n:compound());

(g) p({n:APP()}) -> p(n:compound()) :-
    {n.getOrd() < p.getOrd()};
```

Figure 5: Rule (a) to (c) show rule syntax examples and (d) is a verbose version of (a). Rule (e) and (f) show rule combinations and (g) shows the use of groovy code to further constrain rule applicability.

hand side, it is assumed to be above the root node. As state nodes on the right-hand side of rules are always above non-converted nodes, these state nodes are inferred as well.

The n node in (a) does not have a variable node as a dependent like the n1 and n2 node in (b). Whenever a node does not have a catch-all dependent, it is assumed that potential dependents should remain attached the way they are, not that the node should not have dependents at all. Therefore, it is only necessary to use catch-all variables if the words matched by the variable should be reattached somewhere else. For example, the `?r1` catch-all variable in (b) is necessary, whereas `?r2` could be omitted – it is only stated explicitly to avoid confusion about the location of the n2 dependents. Rule (a) as used in the transducer after inference of all additional parts mentioned is shown in (d): Above the n node, a frontier and a parent node are inferred. In addition, the n node as well as the frontier and parent node each receive a catch-all variable.

The rules are tested in the order in which they are written in the file. Each rule is tested at each frontier node, and if it cannot be applied anywhere, the next rule is tested. Rules which only apply within a narrow context and describe exceptions to a general rule appear above these generic fall-back rules. This is exemplified in (e), where the first rule covers the specific case of ditransitive verbs, attaching one object as `obj` and the other as `iobj`, based on their grammatical case. The other two rules cover the common case of simple transitive verbs with a single object only.

The Part-of-Speech tags are important to distinguish structures with otherwise identical dependency relations. They can be accessed directly via a period after the node identifier, as illustrated in (f). The PoS tags are only used to constrain rule applicability and cannot be set on the right-hand side of a rule.

Lastly, arbitrary groovy[5] code can added to the rules to further constrain matching or even to modify the resulting tree. Rule (g) shows an example where linear order in the sentence is checked using groovy. In the groovy code the tree before and after the transformation can be accessed and modified, allowing to formulate additional constraints or modify the resulting tree, to for example add feats to the nodes.

5 Experiments and Results

To evaluate the feasibility of the tree transducer approach to treebank conversion, a ruleset for the conversion of the Hamburg Dependency Treebank (Foth et al., 2014) to Universal Dependencies was created and applied to the treebank. Due to its size of more than 200k manually annotated sentences, a conversion needs to be streamlined as much as possible.

5.1 Ruleset

To get familiar with both the HDT and UD tagset, a sample subset of 45 sentences was chosen based on the requirement that each dependency relation from the HDT tagset appears at least three times in the selected dependency trees. Each sentence was converted manually to UD and notes of reappearing patterns or difficult and unusual relation structures were taken. The notes and knowledge of both schemas was then used to create an initial ruleset, which was tested on the previously annotated trees. In an iterative manner the ruleset was refined by comparing the generated results against the previously manually converted trees.

It took about a week of work to annotate the trees, take notes and create the ruleset. This was largely due to being unfamiliar with the HDT as well as the UD tagset and not knowing which features the software should even have. The software was also adapted in this time to incorporate new features which were deemed necessary while the rules were created. The resulting ruleset contains 58 rules, each with a complexity similar to the ones shown in Figure 5. Having the conversion software already, as well as previous knowledge about the source and target annotation schema, a ruleset with similar effectiveness can be created in one or two days.

As the HDT annotation guidelines do not include punctuation, it is always attached to the root and no information about the potential attachment in the tree using the UD schema can be inferred from the local context. Therefore, punctuation was ignored in the experiment.

5.2 Evaluation

We used the ruleset to convert part B of the treebank, containing about 100k sentences. 91.5% of the words were converted successfully.

To evaluate the correctness of the conversions, we used 50 sentences manually converted to UD. These sentences were chosen randomly from the treebank, excluding the sentences used to create the ruleset. The sentence annotations were converted with the ruleset and compared to the manually annotated ones. Out of 698 words in total, 36 words were not converted and 51 words were converted incorrectly, yielding a precision of 92% and a recall of 94%.

The transducer also uncovered a few annotation errors in the manually annotated trees. For example, nmod relations on words which should have

---

been attached as `obl`. These errors in the target data were corrected before calculating the values mentioned above, as they would distort the actual evaluation results of the transducer.

6 Analysis

Converting a node requires that the node and its context can be matched by a rule in the ruleset. This means that adding rules with a narrow context – and therefore wide applicability – as fall-back rules to more specific transformations will increase the coverage of the ruleset, an effect that is amplified by the fact that the descendants of an unconvertible node cannot be converted as well, as the frontier cannot move beyond a node for which no conversion rule exists. About half of the unconverted nodes were descendants of an unconvertible node and not necessarily unconvertible themselves. The ruleset contains rules which make strict assumptions about the PoS tags of the nodes, specifically in the rules concerning the conversion of appositions, as well as assuming that certain dependency relations always appear together, such as a conjunct and a coordinating conjunction. In both cases, adding fall-back rules with less context will increase coverage.

On the other hand, to increase precision, some rules need to be more constrained by including more context. This is especially the case where distinctions need to be made in the target schema which are not encoded in the source schema. For example, the UD schema makes a distinction between `appos`, `compound`, and `flat`. These syntactic relations are all grouped under the APP label in the HDT annotation schema. Also, the distinction between `obl` and `nmod` as well as between `advcl` and `ccomp` has no correspondence in the HDT schema. While these distinctions are difficult to make, it is most of the time possible to distinguish between the cases by looking at the PoS tags of the nodes and their parents or inspecting the dependents through look-ahead.

Some conversions are exceptions to the rule and cannot be converted automatically. This is the case with multiword expressions, a concept not used in the HDT. Different multiword expressions consist of different types of words, each German multiword expression would require a specific rule based on the word forms. Also, reflexive pronouns attached to inherently reflexive verbs should not be attached as objects in UD, but as `expl`. This is not the case in the HDT, and as it cannot be inferred from the structural context if a verb is inherently reflexive or not, it is impossible to convert these relations correctly in an automated transformation process. These cases can be decided by a human annotator, prompting to the implementation of an interactive conversion system (see Section 7).

Large parts of the conversion worked very well, such as the conversion of different types of objects to `obj` and `iobj`, distinguishing `nmod` and `obl`, and `amod` and `nummod`. Distinguishing `advcl` and `ccomp` worked in most cases, but some cases are also hard to decide for a human. The inversion of function and content head worked well, such as switching `case` and `nmod` nodes or inverting `aux` relations. A relevant portion of the HDT labels had a correct correspondence to a UD label and could therefore be converted easily.

7 Conclusion and Outlook

We introduced a framework which makes it possible to write a useful tree transducer for dependency schema transformation based on a very small amount of manually transformed annotations in little time. An approach relying on converting groups of words in a local context fits the structure of natural language, where functional units in a sentence often consist of multiple sub groups of words. By relying on the tree transducer framework, the rule writer can focus on the conversion itself and does not need to worry about termination or preserving the tree structure. In addition, no programming skills are needed for writing transformation rules.

The experiments performed indicate the need of an interactive transformation mode: While detecting ambiguous structures is possible, deciding them automatically is hard. As such, semi-interactive conversion is the next step, showing the intermediate conversion results of rules that are not fully reliable to a human annotator and allowing her to chose whether to perform this step or even to restructure the tree manually before continuing with automatic conversion.

For the conversion of the HDT into UD, more time needs to be invested to refine the rules, and the final conversion should be done interactively.

Code and data is available under:
`http://nats.gitlab.io/truducer`

Acknowledgements   We would like to thank the anonymous reviewers for helpful comments.

References

Lars Ahrenberg. 2015. Converting an english-swedish parallel treebank to universal dependencies. In *Proceedings of the Third International Conference on Dependency Linguistics (Depling 2015)*, pages 10–19, Uppsala, Sweden, August. Uppsala University, Uppsala, Sweden.

Kilian A. Foth, Arne Köhn, Niels Beuck, and Wolfgang Menzel. 2014. Because size does matter: The Hamburg Dependency Treebank. In *Proceedings of the Language Resources and Evaluation Conference 2014*. LREC, European Language Resources Association (ELRA).

Anders Johannsen, Héctor Martínez Alonso, and Barbara Plank. 2015. Universal dependencies for danish. In Markus Dickinson, Erhard Hinrichs, Agnieszka Patejuk, and Adam Przepiórkowski, editors, *Proceedings of the Fourteenth International Workshop on Treebanks and Linguistic Theories (TLT14)*, pages 157–167, Warsaw, Poland.

Bevan Jones, Mark Johnson, and Sharon Goldwater. 2011. Formalizing semantic parsing with tree transducers. In *Proceedings of the Australasian Language Technology Association Workshop 2011*, pages 19–28, Canberra, Australia, December.

Andreas Maletti. 2010. Survey: Tree transducers in machine translation. In Henning Bordihn, Rudolf Freund, Thomas Hinze, Markus Holzer, Martin Kutrib, and Friedrich Otto, editors, *Proc. 2nd Int. Workshop Non-Classical Models of Automata and Applications*, volume 263 of *books@ocg.at*, pages 11–32. Österreichische Computer Gesellschaft.

Ryan McDonald, Joakim Nivre, Yvonne Quirmbach-Brundage, Yoav Goldberg, Dipanjan Das, Kuzman Ganchev, Keith Hall, Slav Petrov, Hao Zhang, Oscar Täckström, Claudia Bedini, Núria Bertomeu Castelló, and Jungmee Lee. 2013. Universal dependency annotation for multilingual parsing. In *Proceedings of the 51st Annual Meeting of the Association for Computational Linguistics (Volume 2: Short Papers)*, pages 92–97, Sofia, Bulgaria, August. Association for Computational Linguistics.

Mehryar Mohri, Fernando Pereira, and Michael Riley. 2002. Weighted finite-state transducers in speech recognition. *Computer Speech & Language*, 16(1):69 – 88.

Joakim Nivre. 2014. Universal dependencies for swedish. In *Proceedings of the Swedish Language Technology Conference (SLTC)*, Uppsala, Sweden, November. Uppsala University, Uppsala, Sweden.

Lilja Øvrelid and Petter Hohle. 2016. Universal dependencies for norwegian. In Nicoletta Calzolari, Khalid Choukri, Thierry Declerck, Sara Goggi, Marko Grobelnik, Bente Maegaard, Joseph Mariani, Hélène Mazo, Asunción Moreno, Jan Odijk, and Stelios Piperidis, editors, *Proceedings of the Tenth International Conference on Language Resources and Evaluation LREC 2016, Portorož, Slovenia, May 23-28, 2016*. European Language Resources Association (ELRA).

Sampo Pyysalo, Jenna Kanerva, Anna Missilä, Veronika Laippala, and Filip Ginter. 2015. Universal dependencies for finnish. In *Proceedings of the 20th Nordic Conference of Computational Linguistics (NODALIDA 2015)*, pages 163–172, Vilnius, Lithuania, May. Linköping University Electronic Press, Sweden.

Corentin Ribeyre, Djamé Seddah, and Éric Villemonte de la Clergerie. 2012. A linguistically-motivated 2-stage tree to graph transformation. In *Proceedings of the 11th International Workshop on Tree Adjoining Grammars and Related Formalisms (TAG+11)*, pages 214–222, Paris, France, September.

Juhi Tandon, Himani Chaudhry, Riyaz Ahmad Bhat, and Dipti Misra Sharma. 2016. Conversion from paninian karakas to universal dependencies for hindi dependency treebank. In Katrin Tomanek and Annemarie Friedrich, editors, *Proceedings of the 10th Linguistic Annotation Workshop held in conjunction with ACL 2016, LAW@ACL 2016, August 11, 2016, Berlin, Germany*. The Association for Computer Linguistics.

James W. Thatcher. 1970. Generalized sequential machine maps. *Journal of Computer and System Sciences*, 4(4):339–367.

Francis M. Tyers and Mariya Sheyanova. 2017. Annotation schemes in north sámi dependency parsing. In *Proceedings of the Third Workshop on Computational Linguistics for Uralic Languages*, pages 66–75, St. Petersburg, Russia, January. Association for Computational Linguistics.

Towards Universal Dependencies for Learner Chinese

John Lee, Herman Leung, Keying Li
Department of Linguistics and Translation
City University of Hong Kong
jsylee@cityu.edu.hk, leung.hm@gmail.com, keyingli3-c@my.cityu.edu.hk

Abstract

We propose an annotation scheme for learner Chinese in the Universal Dependencies (UD) framework. The scheme was adapted from a UD scheme for Mandarin Chinese to take interlanguage characteristics into account. We applied the scheme to a set of 100 sentences written by learners of Chinese as a foreign language, and we report inter-annotator agreement on syntactic annotation.

1 Introduction

A learner corpus consists of texts written by non-native speakers. Recent years have seen a rising number of learner corpora, many of which are error-tagged to support analysis of grammatical mistakes made by learners (Yannakoudakis et al., 2011; Dahlmeier et al., 2013; Lee et al., 2016b). In order to derive overuse and underuse statistics on syntactic structures, some corpus have also been part-of-speech (POS) tagged (Díaz-Negrillo et al., 2010; Reznicek et al., 2013), and syntactically analyzed (Ragheb and Dickinson, 2014; Berzak et al., 2016). These corpora are valuable as training data for robust parsing of learner texts (Geertzen et al., 2013; Rehbein et al., 2012; Napoles et al., 2016), and can also benefit a variety of downstream tasks, including grammatical error correction, learner proficiency identification, and language learning exercise generation.

While most annotation efforts have focused on learner English, a number of large learner Chinese corpora have also been compiled (Zhang, 2009; Wang et al., 2015; Lee et al., 2016a). However, POS analysis in these corpora has been limited to the erroneous words, and there has not yet been any attempt to annotate syntactic structures. This study presents the first attempt to annotate Chinese learner text in the Universal Dependencies (UD) framework. One advantage of UD is the potential for contrastive analysis, e.g., comparisons between a UD treebank of standard Chinese, a UD treebank of language X and portions of a UD treebank of learner Chinese produced by native speakers of X.

The rest of the paper is organized as follows. Section 2 reviews existing treebanks for learner texts. Section 3 describes the adaptation of a Mandarin Chinese UD scheme to account for non-canonical characteristics in learner text. Section 4 reports inter-annotator agreement.

2 Previous work

Two major treebanks for learner language — the Treebank of Learner English (TLE) (Berzak et al., 2016) and the project on Syntactically Annotating Learner Language of English (SALLE) (Ragheb and Dickinson, 2014) — contain English texts written by non-native speakers. TLE annotates a subset of sentences from the Cambridge FCE corpus (Yannakoudakis et al., 2011), while SALLE has been applied on essays written by university students. They both adapt annotation guidelines for standard English: TLE is based on the UD guidelines for standard English; SALLE is based on the POS tagset in the SUSANNE Corpus (Sampson, 1995) and dependency relations in CHILDES (Sagae et al., 2010).

Both treebanks adopt the principle of "literal annotation", i.e., to annotate according to a literal reading of the sentence, and to avoid considering its "intended" meaning or target hypothesis.

2.1 Lemma

SALLE allows an exception to "literal annotation" when dealing with lexical violations. When there is a spelling error (e.g., "*ballence"), the annotator puts the intended, or corrected form of the word ("balance") as lemma. For real-word spelling errors, the distinction between a word selection error and spelling error can be blurred. SALLE requires

Proceedings of the NoDaLiDa 2017 Workshop on Universal Dependencies (UDW 2017), pages 67–71,
Gothenburg, Sweden, 22 May 2017.

a spelling error to be "reasonable orthographic or phonetic changes" (Ragheb and Dickinson, 2013). For a sentence such as "... *loss its ballence", the lemma of the word "loss" would be considered to be "lose". The lemma forms the basis for further analysis in POS and dependencies.

To identify spelling errors, TLE follows the decision in the underlying error-annotated corpus (Nicholls, 2003). Further, when a word is mistakenly segmented into two (e.g., "*be cause"), it uses the UD relation goeswith to connect them.

2.2 POS tagging

For each word, SALLE annotates two POS tags, a "morphological tag" and a "distributional tag". The former takes into account "morphological evidence", i.e., the linguistic form of the word; the latter reflects its "distributional evidence", i.e., its syntactic use in the sentence. In a well-formed sentence, these two tags should agree; in learner text, however, there may be conflicts between the morphological evidence and the distributional evidence. Consider the word "see" in the sentence "*I have see the movie." The spelling of "see" provides morphological evidence to interpret it as base form (VV0). However, its word position, following the auxiliary "have", points towards a past participle (VVN). It is thus assigned the morphological tag VV0 and the distributional tag VVN.

These two kinds of POS tags are similarly incorporated into a constituent treebank of learner English (Nagata et al., 2011; Nagata and Sakaguchi, 2016). They are also implicitly encoded in a POS tagset designed for Classical Chinese poems (Wang, 2003). This tagset includes, for example, "adjective used as verb", which can be understood as a morphological tag for adjective doubling as a distributional tag for verb. Consider the sentence 春風又綠江南岸 *chūnfēng yòu lù jiāngnán àn* "Spring wind again greens Yangtze's southern shore"[1]. The word *lù* 'green', normally an adjective, serves as a causative verb in this sentence. It is therefore tagged as "adjective used as a verb".

TLE also supplies similar information for spelling and word formation errors, but in a different format. Consider the phrase "a *disappoint unknown actor". On the one hand, the POS tag reflects the "intended" usage, and so "disappoint" is tagged as an adjective on the basis of its target hypothesis "disappointing". On the other hand, the

"most common usage" of the original word, if different from the POS tag, is indicated in the TYPO field of the metadata; there, "disappoint" is marked as a verb.

2.3 Dependency annotation

In both treebanks, "literal annotation" requires dependencies to describe the way the two words are apparently related, rather than the intended usage. For example, in the verb phrase "*ask you the money" (with "ask you *for* the money" as the target hypothesis), the word "money" is considered the direct object of "ask".

SALLE adds two new relations to handle non-canonical structures. First, when the morphological POS of two words do not usually participate in any relation, the special label '-' is used. Second, the relation INCROOT is used when an extraneous word apparently serves as a second root. In addition, SALLE also gives subcategorization information, indicating what the word can select for. This information complements distributional POS tags, enabling a comparison between the expected relations and those that are realized.

3 Proposed annotation scheme

Our proposed scheme for learner Chinese is based on a UD scheme for Mandarin Chinese (Leung et al., 2016). We adapt this scheme in terms of word segmentation (Section 3.1), POS tagging (Section 3.2) and dependency annotation (Section 3.3). We follow SALLE and TLE in adhering to the principle of "literal annotation", with some exceptions to be discussed below.

3.1 Word segmentation

There are no word boundaries in written Chinese; the first step of analysis is thus to perform word segmentation. "Literal annotation" demands an analysis "as if the sentence were as syntactically well-formed as it can be, possibly ignoring meaning" (Ragheb and Dickinson, 2014). As a rule of thumb, we avoid segmentations that yield non-existing words.

A rigid application of this rule, however, may result in difficult and unhelpful interpretations in the face of "spelling" errors. Consider the two possible segmentations for the string 不關 *bù guān* 'not concern' in Table 1. Literal segmentation should in principle be preferred, since *bù guān* are two words, not one. Given the context, however,

[1]English translation taken from (Kao and Mei, 1971).

	Literal segmentation		Segmentation w/ spelling error
Text	不 *bù* 'not'	關 *guān* 'concern'	不關 *bùguān* 'not-concern'
Lemma	不 *bù* 'not'	關 *guān* 'concern'	不管 *bùguǎn* 'no matter'
POS	ADV	VERB	SCONJ

Table 1: Word segmentation of the string 不關 *bù guān* into two words (left) or one word (right), and the consequences on the lemma and POS tag.

the learner likely confused the character *guān* with the homophonous *guǎn*; the latter combines with *bù* to form one word, namely the subordinating conjunction 不管 *bùguǎn* 'no matter'. If so, the literal segmentation would misrepresent the semantic intention of the learner and yield an unhelpful syntactic analysis. We thus opt for the segmentation that assumes the spelling error; this interpretation, in turn, leads to *bùguǎn* as the lemma and SCONJ as the POS tag.

We follow SALLE in limiting spelling errors to orthographic or phonetic confusions. Specifically, for Chinese, the surface form and the lemma must have similar pronunciation[2] or appearance.[3]

3.2 POS tagging

Similar to SALLE, we consider both morphological and distributional evidence (Section 2.2). When non-native errors create conflicts between them, the former drives our decision on the POS tag, while the latter is acknowledged in a separate, "distributional" POS tag (henceforth, "POS_d tag"). In Figure 1, the POS tag for *kěpà* 'scary' is ADJ, reflecting its normal usage as an adjective; but its POS_d tag is VERB, since the pronoun *tā* 'him' suggests its use as a verb with a direct object.

The POS_d tag is useful for highlighting specific word selection errors involving misused POS (e.g., *kěpà* as a verb). It can also derive more general statistics, such as the use of adjectives where verbs are expected. In some cases, it suggests a target hypothesis (e.g., in Figure 1, to replace *kěpà* with

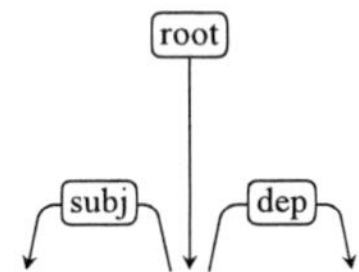

REL:
POS tag: PRON ADJ PRON

Text: 我 可怕 他
wǒ *kěpà* *tā*
'I' 'scary' 'him'

POS_d tag: PRON VERB PRON
REL_d:

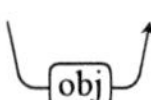

Figure 1: Parse tree for the sentence *wǒ kěpà ta* 'I scary him', likely intended as 'I scare him'. The POS tags and REL relations reflect the morphological evidence. Additionally, the POS_d tags (Section 3.2) and REL_d relations (Section 3.3) consider the distributional evidence.

a verb); but in others, a word insertion or deletion elsewhere might be preferred.

3.3 Dependency annotation

We now discuss how typical learner errors — word selection errors, extraneous words and missing words — may affect dependency annotation.

3.3.1 Word selection error

Dependency relation (henceforth, "REL") is determined on the basis of the POS tags rather than the POS_d tags. As long as these two agree, word selection errors should have no effect on dependency annotation. If a word's POS tag differs from POS_d, however, it can be difficult to characterize its grammatical relation with the rest of the sentence. In this case, we also annotate its "distributional relation" (henceforth, "REL_d") on the basis of its POS_d tag.[4]

Consider the sentence in Figure 1. From the point of view of POS tags, the relation between the adjective *kěpà* 'scary' and the pronoun *tā* 'him' is unclear. We thus assign the unspecified dependency, dep, as their REL.[5] From the point of view of POS_d tags, however, *kěpà* functions as a verb

---

[2]We allow different tones, such as {*guān, guǎn*}; and easily confusable pairs such as {j, zh} and {x, sh}.

[3]E.g., confusion between the characters 了 *le* and 子 *zǐ*.

[4]Similarly, Nagata and Sakaguchi (2016) use error nodes (e.g., VP-ERR) to annotate ungrammatical phrases (e.g., "*I busy").

[5]Similar to the underspecified tag '-' in SALLE, dep is used in English UD "when the system is unable to determine a more precise dependency relation", for example due to a "weird grammatical construction."

Agreement	Overall	Error span only
POS	94.0	91.0
POS_d	93.7	89.7
REL	82.8	75.1
REL_d	82.1	73.8

Table 2: The percentage of POS tags and labelled attachment on which the two annotators agree, measured overall and within text spans marked as erroneous.

and takes *tā* as a direct object, with the relation obj as their REL_d.

3.3.2 Extraneous words

When a word seems extraneous, we choose its head based on syntactic distribution. For example, the aspect marker 了 *le* must modify the verb that immediately precedes it with the relation 'auxiliary' (aux). Even when *le* is extraneous — i.e., when the verb should not take an aspect marker — we would annotate it in the same way.

A more difficult situation arises when there is no verb before the extraneous *le*, e.g., in the sentence * 我被了他打 *wǒ bèi le tā dǎ* 'I PASS ASP he hit' ("I was hit by him"). In this case, we choose *bèi* as head of *le* on account of word order, but the relation is dep rather than aux.

3.3.3 Missing words

When a word seems missing, we annotate according to UD guidelines on promotion by head elision. For example, in the sentence fragment 在中國最近幾年 *zài zhōngguó zuìjìn jǐ nian* 'in China recent few years', we promote *nian* 'year' to be the root. Although both *zhōngguó* 'China' and *nian* would be obl dependents if a verb was present, *nian* is promoted because it is closer to the expected location of the verb.

4 Evaluation

We harvested a 100-sentence evaluation dataset from the training data of the most recent shared task on Chinese grammatical diagnosis (Lee et al., 2016b). The dataset included 20 sentences with extraneous words, 20 with missing words, 20 with word-order errors, and 40 with word selection errors. In order to include challenging cases of word selection errors, i.e., those involving misuse of POS (Section 3.3.1), we examined the target hypothesis in the corpus. We selected 20 sentences where the replacement word has a different POS, and 20 sentences where it is the same. Two annotators, one of whom had access to the target hypothesis, independently annotated these sentences.

Word segmentation achieved 97.0% precision and 98.9% recall when one of the annotators was taken as gold. After reconciling their segmentation, each independently annotated POS tags and dependency relations. The inter-annotator agreement is reported in Table 2. Overall agreement is 94.0% for POS tags and 82.8% for REL (labeled attachment). The agreement levels are comparable to those reported in (Ragheb and Dickinson, 2013), where agreement on labeled attachment ranges from 73.6% to 88.7% depending on the text and annotator. One must bear in mind, however, that annotation agreement for standard Chinese is also generally lower than English.

Annotation agreement based on distributional evidence — i.e., POS_d and REL_d — is slightly lower. This is not unexpected, since it requires a higher degree of subjective interpretation. The most frequent discrepancies between morphological and distributional tags are ADJ vs. VERB, i.e., an adjective used as a verb (as in Figure 1); and VERB vs. NOUN, i.e. a verb used as a noun.

Annotation agreement is also lower within text spans marked as erroneous in the corpus, with agreement dropping to 91.0% for POS tags and 75.1% for labeled attachment. Further analysis revealed that agreement is especially challenging for word selection errors whose target hypothesis has a different POS. A post-hoc discussion among the annotators suggests that multiple plausible interpretations of an ungrammatical sentence was the main source of disagreement. For these cases, more specific guidelines are needed on which interpretation — e.g., considering a word as extraneous, as missing, or misused in terms of POS — entails the most literal reading.

5 Conclusions and Future Work

We have adapted existing UD guidelines for Mandarin Chinese to annotate learner Chinese texts. Our scheme characterizes the POS and dependency relations with respect to both morphological and distributional evidence. While the scheme adheres to the principle of "literal annotation", it also recognizes spelling errors when determining the lemma. Evaluation results suggest a reasonable level of annotator agreement.

Acknowledgments

This work is partially supported by a Strategic Research Grant (Project no. 7004494) from City University of Hong Kong.

References

Yevgeni Berzak, Jessica Kenney, Carolyn Spadine, Jing Xian Wang, Lucia Lam, Keiko Sophie Mori, Sebastian Garza, and Boris Katz. 2016. Universal Dependencies for Learner English. In *Proc. ACL*.

Daniel Dahlmeier, Hwee Tou Ng, and Siew Mei Wu. 2013. Building a Large Annotated Corpus of Learner English: The NUS Corpus of Learner English. In *Proc. 8th Workshop on Innovative Use of NLP for Building Educational Applications*.

Ana Díaz-Negrillo, Detmar Meurers, Salvador Valera, and Holger Wunsch. 2010. Towards Interlanguage POS Annotation for Effective Learner Corpora in SLA and FLT. *Language Forum*, 36(1-2):139–154.

Jeroen Geertzen, Theodora Alexopoulou, and Anna Korhonen. 2013. Automatic Linguistic Annotation of Large Scale L2 Databases: The EF-Cambridge Open Language Database (EFCAMDAT). In *Proc. 31st Second Language Research Forum (SLRF)*.

Yu-Kung Kao and Tsu-Lin Mei. 1971. Syntax, Diction, and Imagery in T'ang Poetry. *Harvard Journal of Asiatic Studies*, 31:49–136.

Lung-Hao Lee, Li-Ping Chang, and Yuen-Hsien Tseng. 2016a. Developing Learner Corpus Annotation for Chinese Grammatical Errors. In *Proc. International Conference on Asian Language Processing (IALP)*.

Lung-Hao Lee, Gaoqi Rao, Liang-Chih Yu, Endong Xun, Baolin Zhang, and Li-Ping Chang. 2016b. Overview of NLP-TEA 2016 Shared Task for Chinese Grammatical Error Diagnosis. In *Proc. 3rd Workshop on Natural Language Processing Techniques for Educational Applications*.

Herman Leung, Rafaël Poiret, Tak sum Wong, Xinying Chen, Kim Gerdes, and John Lee. 2016. Developing Universal Dependencies for Mandarin Chinese. In *Proc. Workshop on Asian Language Resources*.

Ryo Nagata and Keisuke Sakaguchi. 2016. Phrase Structure Annotation and Parsing for Learner English. In *Proc. ACL*.

Ryo Nagata, Edward Whittaker, and Vera Sheinman. 2011. Creating a Manually Error-tagged and Shallow-parsed Learner Corpus. In *Proc. ACL*.

Courtney Napoles, Aoife Cahill, and Nitin Madnani. 2016. The Effect of Multiple Grammatical Errors on Processing Non-Native Writing. In *Proc. 11th Workshop on Innovative Use of NLP for Building Educational Applications*.

Diane Nicholls. 2003. The Cambridge Learner Corpus - error coding and analysis for lexicography and ELT. In *Proc. Computational Linguistics Conference*.

Marwa Ragheb and Markus Dickinson. 2013. Inter-annotator Agreement for Dependency Annotation of Learner Language. In *Proc. 8th Workshop on Innovative Use of NLP for Building Educational Applications*.

Marwa Ragheb and Markus Dickinson. 2014. Developing a Corpus of Syntactically-Annotated Learner Language for English. In *Proc. 13th International Workshop on Treebanks and Linguistic Theories (TLT)*.

Ines Rehbein, Hagen Hirschmann, Anke Lüdeling, and Marc Reznicek. 2012. Better tags give better trees — or do they? *LiLT*, 7(10):1–18.

Marc Reznicek, Anke Lüdeling, and Hagen Hirschmann. 2013. Competing Target Hypotheses in the Falko Corpus: A Flexible Multi-Layer Corpus Architecture. In Ana Díaz-Negrillo, editor, *Automatic Treatment and Analysis of Learner Corpus Data*, pages 101–123, Amsterdam. John Benjamins.

Kenji Sagae, Eric Davis, Alon Lavie, Brian MacWhinney, and Shuly Wintner. 2010. Morphosyntactic Annotation of CHILDES Transcripts. *Journal of Child Language*, 37(3):705–729.

Geoffrey Sampson. 1995. *English for the Computer: The SUSANNE Corpus and Analytic Scheme*. Clarendon Press, Oxford, UK.

Maolin Wang, Shervin Malmasi, and Mingxuan Huang. 2015. The Jinan Chinese Learner Corpus. In *Proc. 10th Workshop on Innovative Use of NLP for Building Educational Applications*.

Li Wang. 2003. *The metric of Chinese poems (Hanyu shiluxue 漢語詩律學)*. Zhonghua shuju, Hong Kong.

Helen Yannakoudakis, Ted Briscoe, and Ben Medlock. 2011. A New Dataset and Method for Automatically Grading ESOL Texts. In *Proc. ACL*.

Baolin Zhang. 2009. The Characteristics and Functions of the HSK Dynamic Composition Corpus. *International Chinese Language Education*, 4(11).

Communicative efficiency and syntactic predictability: A cross-linguistic study based on the Universal Dependencies corpora

Natalia Levshina
Leipzig University
Nikolaistraße 6–10
04109 Leipzig
natalia.levshina@uni-leipzig.de

Abstract

There is ample evidence that human communication is organized efficiently: more predictable information is usually encoded by shorter linguistic forms and less predictable information is represented by longer forms. The present study, which is based on the Universal Dependencies corpora, investigates if the length of words can be predicted from the average syntactic information content, which is defined as the average information content of a word given its counterpart in a dyadic syntactic relationship. The effect of this variable is tested on the data from nine typologically diverse languages while controlling for a number of other well-known parameters: word frequency and average word predictability based on the preceding and following words. Poisson generalized linear models and conditional random forests show that the words with higher average syntactic informativity are usually longer in most languages, although this effect is often found in interactions with average information content based on the neighbouring words. The results of this study demonstrate that syntactic predictability should be considered as a separate factor in future work on communicative efficiency.

1   Research hypothesis

It is well known that more predictable information tends to be presented by shorter forms and less coding material, whereas less predictable information is expressed by longer forms and more coding material. This form-function mapping allows for efficient communication. A famous example is the inverse correlation between the frequency of a linguistic unit and its length discovered by Zipf (1935[1968]). The main cause is an underlying law of economy, saving time and effort (*Ibid*: 38).

In the domain of grammar, Greenberg (1966) provided substantial cross-linguistic evidence that relative frequencies of unmarked members of grammatical categories (e.g. singular number or present tense) are more frequent than their marked counterparts (e.g. dual/plural or future/past, respectively). This idea has been developed further by Haspelmath (2008), who provides numerous examples of coding asymmetries in which the more frequent morphosyntactic forms are shorter than the functionally comparable less frequent ones. These asymmetries can be explained by the tendency of language users to make communication efficient: "The overall number of formal units that speakers need to produce in communication is reduced when the more frequent and expected property values are assigned zero" (Hawkins, 2014: 16).

While the accounts mentioned above are based on context-free probability of linguistic units, some other approaches, which go back to Shannon's (1948) information theory, take into consideration the conditional probability of a unit given its context. The measures computed from these conditional probabilities are often called information content, surprisal, or informativity. There is ample evidence of 'online' word reduction in speech production based on contextual predictability (e.g. Aylett and Turk, 2004; Bell et al., 2009). In addition, one has found 'offline' effects of average informativity on formal length in written corpora: the more predictable a word is on average, the shorter it is (Piatandosi et al., 2011). One of the explanations of such correlations is known as the hypothesis of Uniform Information Density (Levy and Jaeger, 2007), which says that information tends to be distributed uniformly across the speech

Proceedings of the NoDaLiDa 2017 Workshop on Universal Dependencies (UDW 2017), pages 72–78,
Gothenburg, Sweden, 22 May 2017.

signal, so that less predictable elements, which carry more information, get more formal coding, and more predictable elements, which carry less information, get less coding.

In information-theoretic studies, informativity is usually computed from the co-occurrence frequency of a word with the immediately preceding or following word(s) and the frequency of the neighbouring word(s). Corpora of n-grams, such as the Google Books Ngrams, are often used for this purpose. The present study goes beyond the n-gram approach and investigates if formal length can be predicted from the syntactic dependencies between words, regardless of the order in which the latter occur. A more specific hypothesis, which is tested in the present paper, is that the length of a word can be predicted from its average syntactic informativity. This hypothesis is based on the following intuition. Consider, for example, the English article *the*, which is shorter than most nouns it accompanies. At the same time, it is also more predictable from the specific nouns than vice versa. If one hears the noun *table*, there is a relatively high probability that it will be used with the definite article. In contrast, when one hears the article *the*, one is less likely to expect that it defines the specific noun *table*, simply because there are very many other nouns that can be used with the article. This asymmetry is shown in (1):

(1) $P(the|table) > P(table|the)$

From these contextual predictabilities one can compute syntactic informativity scores. Syntactic informativity is defined here as the negative log-transformed conditional probability of x given y:

(2) $I = -\log_2 P(x|y)$

In our example, the noun *table* is less predictable and therefore more informative than the article *the*. One can expect the words that are more syntactically informative in general to be longer than the less surprising ones. For the purposes of our study, one can define average syntactic informativity as shown in (3). This measure is computed as the sum of all syntactic information content scores of the word in a corpus divided by the number of syntactic dependencies n where it occurs:

(3) $\bar{I} = -1/n \sum \log_2 P(x|y)$

In the present study, average syntactic information content, which is referred to as ASIC in the remaining part of the paper, is computed on the basis of the data from nine typologically diverse languages represented by the Universal Dependencies corpora. The UD corpora provide an advantage of having the same or highly similar syntactic annotation in different languages, which makes the statistical models directly comparable.

2 Data

For this case study, I selected nine languages, which are represented by relatively large Universal Dependencies 2.0 corpora (Nivre et al., 2017): Arabic, Chinese, English, Finnish, German, Hindi, Persian, Russian and Spanish. These languages correspond to different points on the synthetic–analytic continuum and have different writing systems.

The procedure of data extraction was as follows. As a first step, I used a Python script to extract all triples that included a dependent, its head and the syntactic dependency that connects them, such as NSUBJ or AUX. The heads and dependents were represented as wordforms associated with a certain part of speech, e.g. *the*/DET, *table*/NOUN or *goes*/VERB. For the sake of simplicity, these expressions will be referred to as 'words' in the remaining part of the paper, with exception of 'word length', when the tags are disregarded. Punctuation marks and special symbols were not taken into account. The frequencies of all unique triples were summarized. I also extracted the frequency of every word in a corpus. From these measures, I computed the ASIC score of every word using the formula in (3).

Word length (without the POS tags) was measured in characters, as the UTF-8 string length. Needless to say, this is only a rough approximation of the effort required by speakers to produce the words.

Finally, the data were cleaned up: the words with token frequency less than five were removed, in order to mitigate problems with data sparseness, which arise in small-size corpora. I also removed numeric expressions because they represent a separate semiotic system. Table 1 displays the number of unique words in each corpus after this procedure, as well the source UD subcorpora. One can see that the Chinese data set is the smallest and the Russian one is the largest.

Language	UD Corpora	Number of unique wordforms
Arabic	UD_Arabic	4,708
Chinese	UD_Chinese	2,246
English	UD_English	3,851
Finnish	UD_Finnish, UD_Finnish-FTB	6,511
German	UD_German	4,269
Hindi	UD_Hindi	4,760
Persian	UD_Persian	3,075
Russian	UD_Russian-SynTagRus	17,811
Spanish	UD_Spanish, UD_Spanish-AnCora	12,832

Table 1. UD corpora and number of unique lemmas for each language.

In addition, I computed the average information content of every word in the data based on its predictability from the word on the left and the word on the right, using the standard procedure described in the literature (e.g. Piatandosi et al., 2011). More exactly, I used the frequencies of the bigrams, which constituted a) the word on the left from the target word and the target word itself, and b) the target word followed by the next word. To compute the average information content, the frequencies of these bigrams were divided by the frequency of the neighbouring word on the left/right, and these proportions were averaged across all occurrences of the target word in the given corpus. Due to the small size of the corpora, it did not make sense to compute the probabilities based on longer n-grams.

The next section presents the results of statistical analyses, which were carried out with the help of R (R Core Team, 2016), including add-on packages *car* (Fox & Weisberg, 2011), *party* (Strobl et al., 2007) and *visreg* (Breheny & Burchett, 2016).

3 Statistical analyses

3.1 ASIC across parts of speech and bivariate correlations

As a first step, I performed a descriptive analysis and compared the informativity of different parts of speech in order to test the original intuition. As an illustration, box-and-whisker plots for the English data are displayed in Figure 1. The plot shows that the English determiners are on average less informative than the English nouns, in accordance with the expectations. The analyses reveal that content words tend to be more informative than functional ones across the languages. In particular, adpositions are less informative than nouns, and auxiliaries are less informative than verbs. These observations support the original intuition behind the present study.

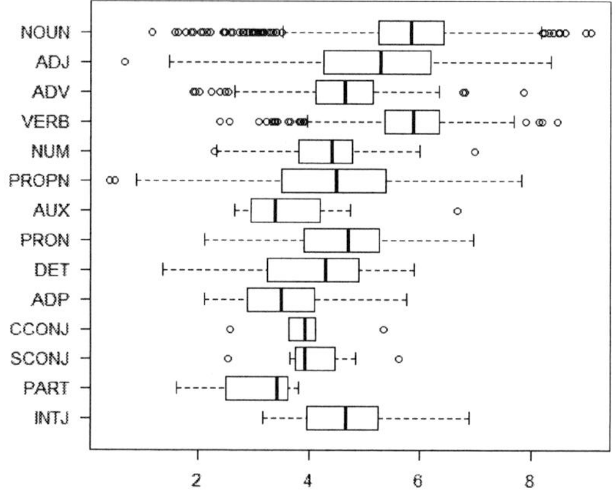

Figure 1. Distribution of average syntactic informativity scores across parts of speech in English.

In addition, I computed Spearman correlation coefficients between ASIC and word length. There are positive highly significant correlations in seven languages: Chinese (Spearman coefficient rho $\rho = 0.29$, $p < 0.0001$), English ($\rho = 0.106$, $p < 0.0001$), German ($\rho = 0.179$, $p < 0.0001$), Hindi ($\rho = 0.24$, $p < 0.0001$), Persian ($\rho = 0.114$, $p < 0.0001$), Russian ($\rho = 0.105$, $p < 0.0001$) and Spanish ($\rho = 0.144$, $p < 0.0001$). In two languages, one finds significant negative correlations: Arabic ($\rho = -0.073$, $p < 0.0001$) and Finnish ($\rho = -0.045$, $p = 0.0002$).

3.2 Poisson generalized linear regression models

The next step was to investigate the relationship between ASIC and word length when taking into account the other frequency-related measures.

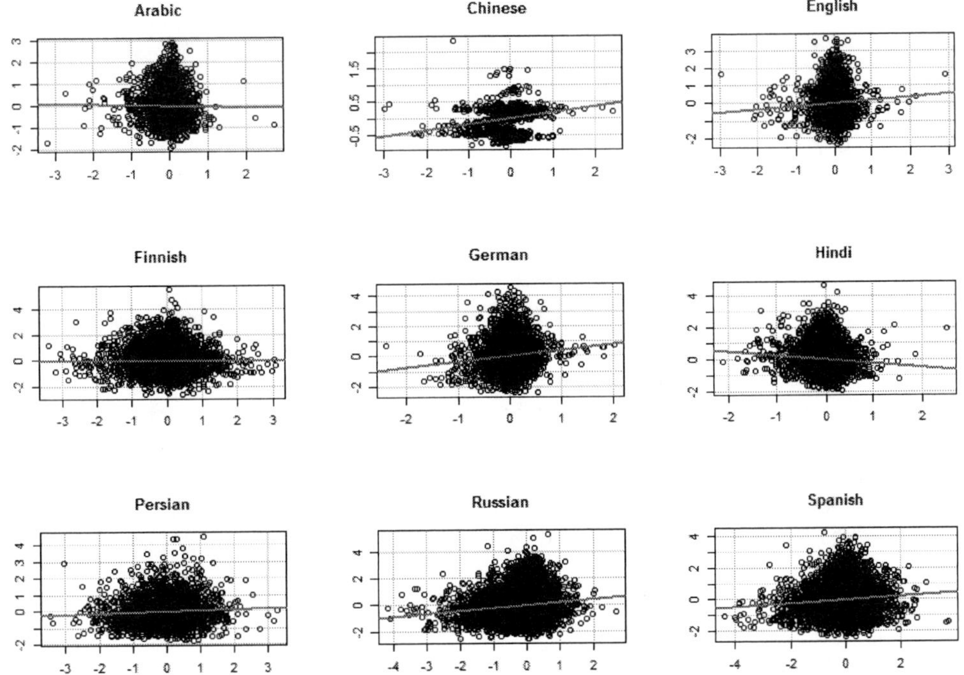

Figure 2. Partial regression plots, which show the direction of the effect of ASIC in nine languages, other variables being controlled for. The axes represent the partial residuals.

For this purpose, I fitted generalized linear regression models for each of the languages with word length (POS tags disregards) as the response and ASIC, as well as average information content based on the preceding word, average information content based on the following word and log-transformed frequency of the target word as predictors. Previous studies have shown that these scores have a substantial effect on word length cross-linguistically (Zipf, 1935[1968]; Piatandosi et al., 2011; Bentz and Ferrer-i-Cancho, 2016). Multiple regression is used here in order to control for the effect of these variables. If ASIC has a separate effect on word length, its estimate will be statistically significant in the presence of all other variables. Poisson models were fitted because the response variable (word length) is always positive, and has a rather skewed distribution.

Figure 2 demonstrates the general effects of ASIC on word length when the effect of other variables is taken into account (so-called added variable, or partial regression plots). The effect is mildly positive in most languages. Exceptions are Arabic and Hindi, where the effect is in fact negative, and there is virtually no effect in Finnish.

However, these results should be taken with caution because of a large number of significant interactions between the variables. To identify interactions, I fitted models with all possible pairwise interactions between the predictors, and then removed those with the p-values above the conventional significance level ($\alpha = 0.05$). The remaining interactions were interpreted visually with the help of interaction plots (e.g. see Figure 3). The conclusions based on these plots are presented below.

In Chinese, English, German and Russian, there was a significant interaction between ASIC and average information content based on the preceding word. The interaction is shown in Figure 2. ASIC correlates positively with word length when the interacting variable has smaller values (panels on the left and in the centre), and negatively when it has higher values (see the panel on the right).

In Arabic, German and Spanish, similar interactions are also found with information content based on the following words. There is a significant interaction in German with log-transformed frequency, as well, which follows the same pattern. In Arabic, however, one finds a negative effect of ASIC on the length for most

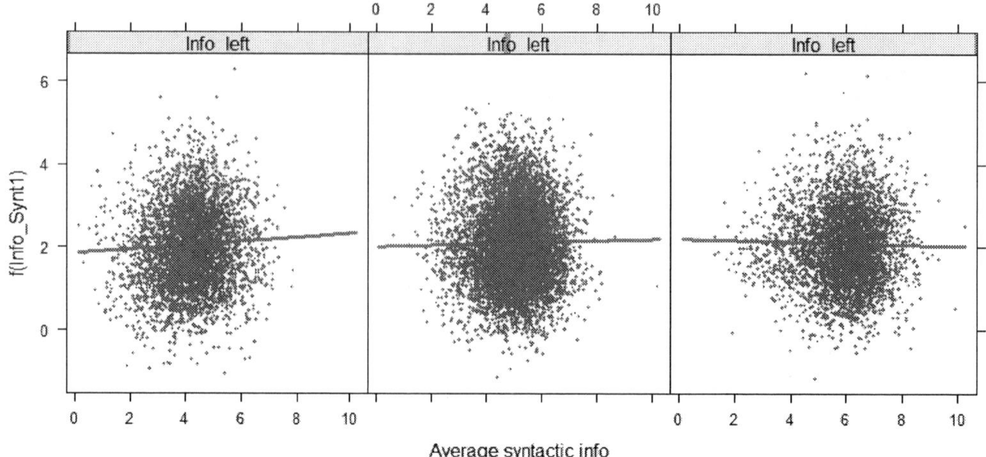

Figure 3. Interaction between ASIC and informative content based on the preceding word in Russian.

values of informative content based on the previous word.

In Hindi, one can find a reverse pattern, when the effect of ASIC becomes stronger and positive as both *n*-gram measures increase. Again, the effect of ASIC is positive in almost all situations. This result is at odds with the negative effect shown in the partial regression plot in Figure 2.

In Finnish, there is a very mild interaction between ASIC and information content based on the following word. The negative effect is observed only for higher values of the interacting variable.

In English, the positive effect of ASIC is only observed for the words which are highly predictable from the left and right context (i.e. have low informativity based on *n*-grams. The positive effect of ASIC is also stronger in highly frequent words.

3.3. Random forests and conditional variable importance

This subsection investigates whether the effect of syntactic informativity is greater or smaller than that of the well-known variables. It is difficult to estimate the importance in the presence of numerous interactions. This is why I used conditional random forests to compute the variable importance scores for each of the variables. This method for regression and classification based on binary recursive partitioning of data allows one to compare strongly intercorrelated and interacting variables

(Strobl et al., 2007). Table 3 displays the results. Note that the scores are not comparable between the languages, and the sign does not mean a negative direction of the correlation. These results are based on random samples of 500 words without replacement drawn for every language because the calculation of conditional variable importance is computationally intensive. The random forests were grown from 1,000 trees. Several samples with different random number seeds were tried in order to make sure that the results are stable.

Lang.	log freq.	Synt. info	Info given previous	Info given next
Arabic	0.147	0.004	0.022	0.019
Chinese	0.019	0.006	0.016	0.003
English	0.399	0.066	0.032	0.165
Finnish	0.612	-0.007	0.051	0.03
German	0.86	0.192	0.09	0.04
Hindi	0.062	0.206	-0.003	0.114
Persian	0.35	0.026	-0.001	0.007
Russian	0.565	0.028	0.06	0.29
Spanish	0.268	0.021	-0.002	0.308

Table 2. Conditional variable importance scores based on random forests.

The results indicate that average syntactic information is more important than one of the information measures based on the preceding (English, German, Hindi, Persian, Spanish) and/or following words (Chinese, German, Hindi, Persian). There is no effect of ASIC in Finnish, as was already shown in Section 3.2, and it is very close to zero in Arabic, but this variable shows up as the most important one in Hindi.

4 Conclusions

The present study has investigated whether the average predictability of a word given the syntactic dependencies where it occurs can be useful for predicting word length. The analyses of data from nine typologically diverse languages based on bivariate correlations and multivariate Poisson regression reveal that words with higher syntactic informativity (or lower syntactic predictability) tend to be longer in most languages, in accordance with the theoretical predictions. These conclusions also mostly hold when the traditional frequency-based measures, which do not take into account the syntactic information, are controlled for. However, we observed negative or absent correlations in Finnish and Arabic. For Hindi, the evidence based on different methods is somewhat discordant, which requires further investigation.

With the exception of Persian, where syntactic predictability serves as an independent factor, the relationships between the frequency-based measures are usually quite complex. In particular, ASIC often plays a role in the contexts where the other information-theoretical measures have low values. The results of conditional random forest modelling reveal that syntactic predictability often outperforms other frequency-based measures in determining word length.

Although the exact nature of the relationships between different types of lexical and syntactic, context-independent and context-dependent information needs to be further investigated, the results of the present study demonstrate that dependency-based syntactic predictability should be taken into account in future investigations of 'offline' communicative efficiency in different languages. Whether it helps to explain formal reduction in 'online' language production is a question for future research. Another question the impact of corpus size. One may wonder whether the effects will become stronger and less dependent on the other variables if the measures are computed from the data with higher and therefore more reliable co-occurrence frequencies. Hopefully, the future growth and development of the Universal Dependencies corpora will provide researchers with new opportunities of measuring the effects of syntactic informativity with the help of increasingly large and diverse linguistic data.

Acknowledgments

The author is grateful to the anonymous reviewers, whose constructive comments have helped to improve the paper significantly. The support of the European Research Council (ERC Advanced Grant 670985, Grammatical Universals) is gratefully acknowledged.

References

Matthew Aylett and Alice Turk. 2004. The smooth signal redundancy hypothesis: A functional explanation for relationships between redundancy, prosodic prominence, and duration in spontaneous speech. *Language and Speech*, 47(1):31-56.

Alan Bell, Jason Brenier, Michelle Gregory, Cynthia Girand and Dan Jurafsky. 2009. Predictability Effects on Durations of Content and Function Words in Conversational English. *Journal of Memory and Language,* 60(1): 92-111.

Christian Bentz and Ramon Ferrer-i-Cancho. 2016. Zipf's law of abbreviation as a language universal. In Bentz, Christian, Gerhard Jäger and Igor Yanovich (eds.), *Proceedings of the Leiden Workshop on Capturing Phylogenetic Algorithms for Linguistics*. University of Tubingen, online publication system: https://publikationen.uni-tuebingen.de/xmlui/handle/10900/68558.

Patrick Breheny and Woodrow Burchett. 2016. visreg: Visualization of Regression Models. R package version 2.3-0. https://CRAN.R-project.org/package=visreg.

John Fox and Sanford Weisberg. 2011. *An R Companion to Applied Regression*. 2nd ed. Thousand Oaks, CA: Sage, http://socserv.socsci.mcmaster.ca/jfox/Books/Companion.

Joseph Greenberg. 1966. *Language universals, with special reference to feature hierarchies*. The Hague: Mouton.

Martin Haspelmath. 2008. Frequencies vs. iconicity in explaining grammatical asymmetries. *Cognitive Linguistics*, 19(1): 1–33.

John A. Hawkins. 2014. *Cross-linguistic Variation and Efficiency*. Oxford: OUP.

Roger Levy and T. Florian Jaeger. 2007. Speakers optimize information density through syntactic reduction. In Bernhard Schlökopf, John Platt & Thomas Hoffman (eds.), *Advances in neural information processing systems (NIPS)* Vol. 19, 849–856. Cambridge, MA: MIT Press.

Joakim Nivre, Željko Agić, Lars Ahrenberg et al. 2017. Universal Dependencies 2.0, LINDAT/CLARIN digital library at the Institute of Formal and Applied Linguistics, Charles

University in Prague, http://hdl.handle.net/11234/1-1983.

Steven T. Piantadosi, Harry Tily and Edward Gibson. 2011. Word lengths are optimized for efficient communication. *PNAS,* 108(9). www.pnas.org/cgi/doi/10.1073/pnas.1012551108

R Core Team. 2016. R: A language and environment for statistical computing. R Foundation for Statistical Computing, Vienna, Austria, https://www.R-project.org/.

Claude E. Shannon. 1948. A Mathematical Theory of Communication, *Bell System Technical Journal,* 27: 379–423 & 623–656.

Carolin Strobl, Anne-Laure Boulesteix, Achim Zeileis & Torsten Hothorn. 2007. Bias in Random Forest Variable Importance Measures: Illustrations, Sources and a Solution. *BMC Bioinformatics,* 8, 25, http://www.biomedcentral.com/1471-2105/8/25.

George K. Zipf. 1935 [1968]. *The Psycho-Biology of Language: An Introduction to Dynamic Philology.* Cambridge, MA: MIT Press.

Estonian copular and existential constructions as an UD annotation problem

Kadri Muischnek
University of Tartu
Estonia
kadri.muischnek@ut.ee

Kaili Müürisep
University of Tartu
Estonia
kaili.muurisep@ut.ee

Abstract

This article is about annotating clauses with nonverbal predication in version 2 of Estonian UD treebank. Three possible annotation schemas are discussed, among which separating existential clauses from copular clauses would be theoretically most sound but would need too much manual labor and could possibly yield inconcistent annotation. Therefore, a solution has been adapted which separates existential clauses consisting only of subject and (copular) verb *olema* be from all other *olema*-clauses.

1   Introduction

This paper discusses the annotation problems and research questions that came up during the annotation of Estonian copular sentences while developing Estonian Universal Dependencies treebank, especially while converting it from version 1 of UD annotation guidelines to version 2.

Copular clauses are a sentence type in which the contentful predicate is not a verb, but falls into some other category. In some languages there is no verbal element at all in these clauses; in other languages there is a verbal copula joining the subject and the non-verbal element (Mikkelsen, 2011, p. 1805).

In Estonian, there is mainly one verb, namely *olema* 'be', that functions as copula in copular clauses. Estonian descriptive grammar (Erelt et al., 1993) uses the term copular verb (Est 'köide') only for describing sentences with subject complements, stating that in such sentences the verb *olema* has only grammatical features of a predicate (time, mode, person). Also, the copula *olema* is semantically empty if used alone and it can not have any other dependents than non-verbal predicate. At the same time, verb *olema* is the most

frequent verb of Estonian language which can also function as auxiliary verb in compound tenses, be part of phrasal verbs, and may occur in existential, possessor or cognizer sentences.

As the descriptive grammar of Estonian (Erelt et al., 1993) lacks more detailed treatment of copular sentences, the label "copula" has not been introduced into original Estonian Dependency Treebank (EDT) (Muischnek et al., 2014). In copular clauses *olema* is annotated as the root of the clause and other components of the sentence depend on it; that is also the case if the sentence contains a subject complement. As subject complements have a special label PRD (predicative) in EDT, such sentences can be easily searched.

Estonian treebank for UD v1.3 has been generated automatically from EDT using transfer rules. The guidelines for UD v1 implied that subject complements serve as roots in copular clauses. This analysis of copula constructions, according to UD v1 guidelines, extended to adpositional phrases and oblique nominals as long as they have a predicative function. By contrast, temporal and locative modifiers were treated as dependents on the existential verb 'be'.

Therefore, while converting EDT to UD v1, sentences with subject complements were relatively easily transferred to sentences with copular tree structure (Muischnek et al., 2016). However, oblique nominals and adpositional phrases were not annotated as instances of nonverbal predication.

Since UD v 2.0 assumes a more general annotation scheme for copular sentences, we faced several conversion problems and also linguistic questions. This paper provides insights into these research questions, gives an overview how copular clauses are annotated in some UD v2 treebanks for some other languages (Finnish, German, English) and describes what are the options for annotating Estonian sentences.

Proceedings of the NoDaLiDa 2017 Workshop on Universal Dependencies (UDW 2017), pages 79–85,
Gothenburg, Sweden, 22 May 2017.

In the remainder of this paper, Section 2 we give a short account of UD v2 guidelines for annotating copular clauses and show how these constructions are annotated in some UD v2 treebanks for Finnish, German and English. Section 3 is dedicated to copular constructions in Estonian language and Estonian UD versions 1 and 2. Some conclusions are drawn in Section 4.

2 UD annotation guidelines for nonverbal predication

According to the UD annotation scheme version 1, copular constructions are to be annotated differently from other clause types, analysing the predicative element as root and if there is an overt linking verb present, it should be attached to this nonverbal predicate as copula. The copula relation is restricted to function words whose sole function is to link a non-verbal predicate to its subject and which does not add any meaning other than grammaticalised TAME categories. Such an analysis is motivated by the fact that many languages often or always lack an overt copula, so annotation would be cross-linguistically consistent[1].

Version 2 of UD annotation guidelines extend the set of constructions that should be annotated as instances of nonverbal predication, defining six categories of nonverbal predication, namely those of equation, attribution, location, possession, benefaction and existence[2].

In order to get better overview of practical annotation of copular constructions cross-linguistically, we studied the v2 versions of UD treebanks of Finnish, which is the most closely related language to Estonian present in UD, and also German and English. As the language-independent annotation guidelines for UD version 2 were published in the very end of last year, there are no language-specific guidelines published yet. So we had to rely on treebank queries in order to gain information about annotating copular and related constructions in the afforementioned languages. We queried UD v2 treebanks using the SETS treebank search maintained by the University of Turku[3].

There are two UD treebanks for Finnish: the Finnish UD treebank, based on Turku Dependency Treebank, and Finnish-FTB (FinnTreeBank). In

Finnish UD v2 treebank, clauses with *olla* 'be' are mostly regarded as instances of nonverbal predication, annotating *olla* as copula (1), among them also possessive clauses (2). However, if the clause contains only subject besides some form of *olla*, *olla* is annotated as root (3).

In Finnish FTB v2 treebank more clause types are annotated with *olla* as root, e.g. possessive clause (4) and clause containing predicative adverbial (5). It seems that annotation of copular constructions in Finnish FTB resembles that in version 1 of Estonian UD only subject complements are annotated as roots in copular constructions.

In the UD v2 treebank of German, sentences with subject complement are annotated as instances of nonverbal predication (6) and other instances of *sein* and *werden* 'be' seem to be annotated as main verbs, not copulas (7).

(1) Hyllyllä   oli H&M
    shelf-ADE was H&M
    ROOT   cop nmod
    Home-tuotteita
    Home-product-PL.PRT
    nsubj:cop
    'There were some H&M products on the shelf'

(2) Kuvia   minulla ei   ole
    picture-PL.PRT I-ADE   not be
    nsubj:cop   ROOT   aux cop:own
    'I have no pictures'

(3) Kun rahaa   ei ole   ...
    If   money-PRT not is
    mark nsubj   aux ROOT
    'If there is no money'

(4) Meillä   ei   ole   rahaa
    we-ADE   not is   money-PRT
    nmod:own aux ROOT nsubj
    tuhlata.
    waste-INF
    acl
    'We have no money to waste'

(5) Talonmies on   juovuksissa.
    Caretaker is   drunkenness-INE
    nsubj   ROOT   advmod
    'The caretaker is drunk'

(6) Das Personal ist freundlich.
    DET staff   is   friendly
    det nsubj:cop cop ROOT

[1] http://universaldependencies.org/v2/copula.html

[2] http://universaldependencies.org/u/overview/simple-syntax.html#nonverbal-clauses

[3] http://bionlp-www.utu.fi/dep_search/

'The staff is friendly.'

(7) Ich war in dem Dezember bei
    I   was in DET December at
    nsubj ROOT case obl case   det
    Küchen Walther.
    Küchen Walther
    obl   flat
    'I was in December at Küchen Walther.'

There are four English UD treebanks, but we queried only the largest of them, the English Web Treebank. It seems that predicative (e.g. Fig. 1) and locative (Fig. 2) constructions are analysed as instances of non-verbal predication, whereas existential clauses (Fig. 3) are not.

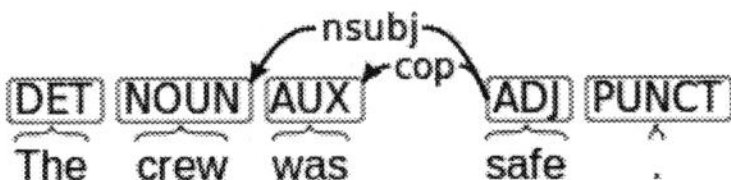

Figure 1: Predicative construction in the English UD treebank.

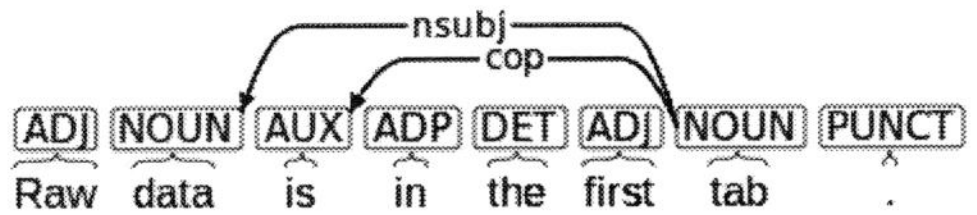

Figure 2: Locative construction in the English UD treebank.

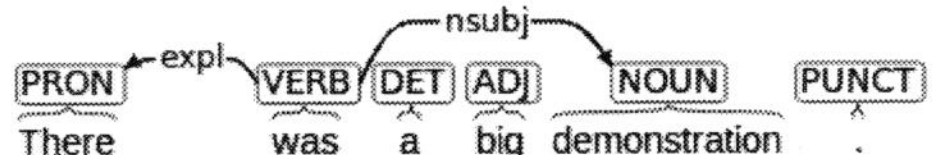

Figure 3: Existential clause in the English UD treebank.

As the above discussion illustrates, annotation of copular constructions varies across different languages and also across different treebanks. Having better documentation for v2 treebanks would facilitate better understanding of these differences. It would also be helpful for those teams which are still working on v2 of their treebanks to make more informed decisions.

3 Copular and existential constructions in Estonian

In Estonian, copular verb can not be omitted in normal writing or speech. However, there are some exceptions. First, copula is often omitted in headlines like (8).

(8) Valitsus   otsustusvõimetu
    Government indecisive
    'Government is indecisive.'

And due to time pressure, copula, but also other verbs, can be omitted in online communication (9).

(9) Ma nii kurb
    I so sad
    'I am so sad.'

As a sidenote, although ellipsis of verb *olema* is rare in Estonian, it is still more frequent than in Finnish (Kehayov, 2008).

The annotation guidelines for version 2 of Universal Dependencies define six categories of nonverbal predication that can be found cross-linguistically (with or without a copula), namely equation (aka identification), attribution, location, possession, benefaction and existence.

As for Estonian, constructions expressing equation (10a), attribution (10b), location (10c), possession (10d), benefaction (10e) or existence (10f) are all coded using verb *olema*. In addition to the afforementioned clause types, there are also cognizer clauses (10g) that can be viewed as a subtype or metaphorical extension of the possessive clause type. Perhaps also quantification clause (10h) should be mentioned as a separate type.

(10) a. Mari on õpetaja.
         Mari is teacher
         'Mari is a teacher.'
      b. Laps on väike.
         Child is small
         'Child is small.'
      c. Laps on koolis.
         Child is school-INE
         'Child is at school.'
      d. Lapsel   on raamat.
         Child-ADE is book
         'Child has a book.'
      e. See raamat on lapsele.
         This book   is child-ALL
         'This book is for child.'
      f. Oli tore kontsert.
         was nice concert
         'This was a nice concert.'

    g. Lapsel   on igav.
       Child-ADE is boring.
       'Child is bored.'

    h. Lund   on palju.
       Snow-PRT is lot
       'There is a lot of snow.'

Further in this section we will discuss three possible ways to annotate Estonian clauses containing the (copular) verb *olema*.

Among the constructions (10 a-h), existential clauses (f) are exceptional as they can consist also only of subject and some form of verb *olema*. In our opinion, such construction can not be annotated as an instance of nonverbal predication as there is no possible predicate except the verb *olema*. As for the sake of consistency, all existential clauses should be annotated in the same way, i.e. as instances of verbal predication, not nonverbal, we would have to distinguish existential constructions from all other *olema*-clauses.

In what follows in this Section, we will study if this solution can be applied while annotating real corpus sentences. For that we have to find out, if and how existential clauses can be identified. We start with investigating the linguistic features of the existential clause type on the background of main clause types in Estonian. Subsection 3.1 presents the linguistic features of Estonian existential constructions. Subsection 3.2 gives overview of constructions annotated as instances of nonverbal predication in version 1 of Estonian UD treebank. In subsection 3.3 we discuss three possibilities for annotating *olema*-clauses in Estonian UD v2 and conclude the section with adopting a compromise solution.

3.1 Existential clauses in Estonian

Characteristic features of Estonian existential clauses include the possibility of partitive subject (the default case of Estonian subject is nominative) and inverted word order (subject comes after verb), but existential clauses share these features with possessive clauses and also some other minor clause types. In order to understand the problem, we start with a small overview of main clause types in Estonian, explain how *olema*-clauses are distributed among those clause types, paying special attention to the existential clause type.

Descriptive grammars of Estonian (Erelt et al., 1993, pp. 14–15) and (Erelt, 2003, pp. 43–46)

distinguish between three main clause types, depending on whether syntactic subject, semantic macrorole of actor and clause topic (theme) overlap, i.e. are coded by the same nominal. In so-called normal clauses, the same nominal functions as subject, actor and topic; in possessor-cognizer clauses, the possessed or cognized entity is both subject and topic, but not actor, which in turn denotes the possessor or cognizer. Subject noun denotes actor in existential clauses, but is rhematic.

Possessor-cognizer and existential clauses are regarded as marked clause types, also termed inverted clauses (Erelt, 2003, pp. 93–55), as they have inverted word order in pragmatically neutral sentences - XVS instead of SVX, otherwise typical for "ordinary" Estonian sentences. Subjects of these marked clause types can be in partitive case form, while nominative is the unmarked and statistically dominant subject case.

A few remarks about the possible case forms of subject in Estonian are in place here. Estonian descriptive grammars (Erelt et al., 1993, p. 15) and (Erelt, 2013, p. 36) state that existential and possessive clauses differ from other clause types in the possibility of subject case alternation: the subject is mostly in partitive case form in negative sentences (12), (14) and can be in partitive case form also in affirmative sentences (11),(13) if the referent of the subject noun is quantitatively unbounded.

(11) Selles   klassis   on targad   lapsed /
     this-INE class-INE are smart-PL kid-PL /
     tarku   lapsi.
     smart-PL.PRT kid-PL.PRT
     'There are smart kids in this class. / There are some smart kids in this class.'

(12) Selles   klassis   ei ole tarku
     this-INE class-INE not are smart-PL.PRT
     lapsi.
     kid-PL.PRT
     'There are no smart kids in this class.'

(13) Tal   on head   sõbrad   /
     (S)he-ADE are good-PL friend-PL /
     häid   sõpru.
     good-PL.PRT friend-PL.PRT
     '(S)he has good friends. / (S)he has some good friends.'

(14) Tal   ei ole häid
     (S)he-ADE not are good-PL.PRT

sõpru.
friend-PL.PRT

'(S)he has no good friends.'

Statistically, negation is the most powerful predictor of partitive subject (Miestamo, 2014). Of the clause types defined in UD documentation, existential clauses share the property of case-alternating subject with possessive clauses, but partitive subject is much less frequent in cognizer clauses, which can otherwise be seen as a constructional extension of the possessive clause. Partitive subject is the only option in quantification clause, regardless of its polarity, and in negative possessive clause.

Existential clauses differ from other marked clause types as they can consist also of subject only, besides the verb *olema*; in this case the clause merely states or negates the existence of an entity denoted by subject (15). There is also a special periphrastic verb form *olema olemas* (be be-INE) used for stating that something exists (16).

(15) On kontserte,   kus   loetakse
      Are concert-PL.PRT where read-IMPS
      ka   luuletusi.
      also poem-PL.PRT
      'There are concerts where poems are also chanted.'

(16) Nõiad   on olemas.
      Witches are be-INE
      'Witches exist.'

3.2 Nonverbal predication in version 1 of Estonian UD treebank

According to the first version of Universal Dependencies' guidelines, copular clauses consisting of a noun or an adjective, which takes a single argument with the subject relation were to be analysed as instances of nonverbal predication. The copula verb (if present) was attached to the predicate with the "cop" relation. This analysis of copula constructions was extended to adpositional phrases and oblique nominals as long as they had a predicative function. By contrast, temporal and locative modifiers were to be treated as dependents on the existential verb 'be'. So clauses containing some copular verb were to be divided between categories of verbal and nonverbal predication. In version 1 of Estonian UD treebank, only sentences containing verb *olema* and subject complement in nominative or partitive case form

were annotated as instances of nonverbal predication (17). This was partly motivated by the fact that subject complements were already annotated using a special dependency relation (PRD) in our original treebank, the Estonian Dependency Treebank. All other copular clauses were annotated as instances of verbal predication, annotating form of verb *olema* as root (18).

(17) Mina olen Merlin.
      I   am   Merlin
      'I am Merlin'

(18) Ta   on praegu kodus.
      (s)he is now   home-INE
      '(S)he is at home now.'

3.3 Nonverbal predication in Estonian UD version 2: three possible solutions

As already mentioned in Section 2, version 2 of the Universal Dependencies' guidelines extends the number of constructions that fall into the category of nonverbal predication.

Among the Estonian copular constructions listed in the beginning of Section 3, existential constructions only stating or negating the existence of an entity expressed by subject and consisting only of verb *olema* and its subject (15) pose a problem for UD v2 annotation scheme. We are on the opinion that they can not be analysed as examples of nonverbal predication as one can not label subject as a predicate, so in these sentences verb form of *olema* 'be' has to be annotated as root, not as copula.

Thus we have three basic options for annotating copular constructions in Estonian UD v2: always annotate *olema* as copula; separate clauses consisting of verb *olema* and its subject from all other *olema*-clauses and, as third option, try to separate existential clauses from other *olema*-clauses. The fourth possible solution would be to stick to the solution we had in version 1 of Estonian UD, namely annotate only subject complements, i.e. nouns and adjectives in nominative or partitive case form as non-verbal predicates, but as this solution would violate the guidelines for UD version 2, we will not discuss it further.

We will take a closer look at the first three afforementioned options one by one.

Annotate all *olema*-clauses as instances of nonverbal predication

This would be the most straightforward solution from the point of view of UD v1 to v2 conversion process. The main drawback would be having to annotate subjects as predicates in clauses consisting only of verb *olema* and its subject (Fig. 4).

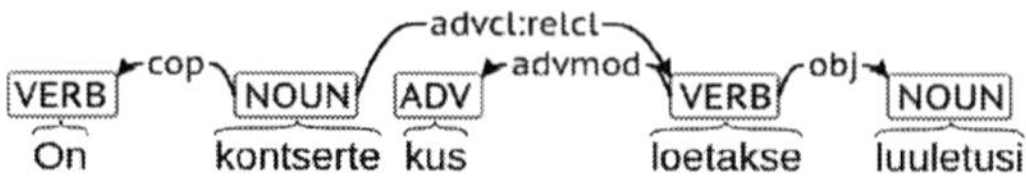

Figure 4: A subject as a root, annotation of the sentence (15).

Distinguishing subject-only clauses and other *olema*-clauses

Second possible option would be to distinguish two separate classes of *olema*-clauses basing on simple syntactic criterion: if the sentence consists only of some form of *olema* or periphrastic verb *olemas olema* and its subject, then *(olemas) olema* is annotated as root. All other sentences are annotated as instances of nonverbal predication. The distinction would be easy to make and the main drawback would be that existential sentences like (15) and (19) get different syntactic structures, which can be regarded as an inconsistent solution.

(19)   Eile   oli kontsert, kus
     Yesterday was concert-PL where
     loeti   ka luuletusi.
     read-IMPS also poem-PL.PRT
     'There was a concert yesterday where poems were also chanted.'

Separate existentials and other *olema*-clauses

For the sake of consistency, all existential constructions should be annotated the same way, irrelevant whether they consist only of subject and verb or do they have more syntactic participants. This approach, although theoretically correct in our opinion, is not easy to apply in annotation practice.

As already described in subsection 3.1, Estonian existential clauses are defined as those, which subject is in partitive case in negative clauses and can be in partitive case also in affirmative clauses. In a pragmatically neutral affirmative clause, word order distinguishes between locative (20) and existential clauses (21). Negative variants of these

clauses show the distinction - subject is in nominative case form in locative clause (22) and in partitive case form in existential clause (23). The example sentences are of course simplifications, especially with regard to word order; in the corpus sentences the word order does not distinguish existential clauses as it is determined mostly by information structure and depends heavily on larger textual context.

(20)   Koer on aias.
     Dog is garden-INE
     'Dog is in the garden.'

(21)   Aias   on koer.
     garden-INE is dog
     'There is a dog in the garden.'

(22)   Koer ei ole aias.
     Dog not is   garden-INE
     'Dog is not in the garden.'

(23)   Aias   ei ole koera.
     garden-INE not is dog-PRT
     'There is no dog in the garden.'

So, if we would like to apply this solution, it would mean that human annotators have to go over all affirmative clauses that could possibly be existential clauses and make the distinction basing on their intuitions about the probable subject case in the negative counterpant of the affirmative clause under consideration - which means that there has to be more than one annotator for every clause. But Peep Nemvalts (2000), who has analysed Estonian existential sentences, comparing them with the same phenomenon in other languages, has concluded that it is impossible to distinguish Estonian existential sentences basing on formal criteria.

Therefore, after considering all possible solutions for distinguishing copular and non-copular usages of *olema* 'be', we had to make a compromise and adopt the second possible solution, i.e. distinguish subject-only clauses and other *olema*-clauses. In resulting annotated treebank, existential clauses are divided between instances of verbal and non-verbal predication, which can be regarded as a drawback. On the other hand, the resulting annotation is consistent, which is a clear advantage.

4   Conclusion

Universal Dependencies is planned to offer language-typologically relevant and cross-linguistically consistent annotation guidelines for building dependency treebanks (Nivre et al., 2016). Its version 2, published only a few months ago, introduced a major change concerning annotating nonverbal predication: the repertoire of clauses that should be treated as examples of nonverbal predication was considerably broadened. Often real corpus data is a challenge even for well-premeditated theoretical constructs; even more so if this corpus data comes in more than 50 languages. So it should not be a surprise that there are still some open issues or inconsistencies.

This article tackled the problems concerning defining and annotating copular constructions in Estonian, with some brief cross-linguistic comparison.

We came forward with three possible annotation schemas, among which separating existential clauses from copular clauses would be theoretically most sound but would need too much manual labor and would possibly result in inconcistent annotation. So we will adapt the solution that, somewhat artificially, separates existential clauses consisting only of subject and (copular) verb *olema* from all other *olema*-clauses.

It seems that delimiting and annotating nonverbal predication and related phenomena is not entirely consistent cross-linguistically. In this article we had a look at a very small set of languages, but the analysis of nonverbal predication and copular constructions from a cross-linguistic (or cross-treebank) perspective deserves in-depth study. For the sake of better understanding the exact annotation of linguistic phenomena in different languages, thorough documentation of principles and decisions underlying the annotation would be beneficial.

As for Estonian UD treebank, the solution that at the first glance seemed most correct from the linguistic point of view, is (almost) impossible to achieve even by manual annotation.

Acknowledgements

This study was supported by the Estonian Ministry of Education and Research (IUT20-56), and by the European Union through the European Regional Development Fund (Centre of Excellence in Estonian Studies).

References

Mati Erelt, Reet Kasik, Helle Metslang, Henno Rajandi, Kristiina Ross, Henn Saari, Kaja Tael, and Silvi Vare. 1993. *Eesti keele grammatika II. Süntaks*. Eesti TA Keele ja Kirjanduse instituut.

Mati Erelt, editor. 2003. *Estonian Language. Linguistica Uralica Supplementary series*, volume 1. Estonian Academy Publishers, Tallinn.

Mati Erelt. 2013. *Eesti keele lausepetus. Sissejuhatus. Öeldis*. Tartu likool.

Petar Kehayov. 2008. Olema-verbi ellipsist eesti kirjakeeles. In *Emakeele Seltsi aastaraamat*, volume 54, pages 107–152. Eesti Teaduste Akadeemia Kirjastus.

Matti Miestamo. 2014. Partitives and negation: A cross-linguistic survey . In *Partitive cases and related categories*, volume 54 of *Empirical Approaches to Language Typology*, pages 63–86. De Gruyter Mouton.

Line Mikkelsen. 2011. Copular clauses. In Klaus von Heusinger Claudia Maienborn and Paul Portner, editors, *Semantics: An International Handbook of Natural Language Meaning*, volume 2, pages 1805–1829. Berlin: Mouton de Gruyter.

Kadri Muischnek, Kaili Müürisep, Tiina Puolakainen, Eleri Aedmaa, Riin Kirt, and Dage Särg. 2014. Estonian Dependency Treebank and its annotation scheme. In Verena Henrich et al., editors, *Proceedings of the Thirteenth International Workshop on Treebanks and Linguistic Theories (TLT13)*, pages 285–291. University of Tübingen.

Kadri Muischnek, Kaili Müürisep, and Tiina Puolakainen. 2016. Estonian Dependency Treebank: from Constraint Grammar Tagset to Universal Dependencies. In *Proc. of LREC 2016*.

Peep Nemvalts. 2000. *Aluse sisu ja vorm*. Eesti Keele Sihtasutus.

Joakim Nivre, Marie-Catherine de Marneffe, Filip Ginter, Yoav Goldberg, Jan Hajic, Christopher D. Manning, Ryan T. McDonald, Slav Petrov, Sampo Pyysalo, Natalia Silveira, Reut Tsarfaty, and Daniel Zeman. 2016. Universal Dependencies v1: A Multilingual Treebank Collection. In *LREC*. European Language Resources Association (ELRA).

Universal Dependency Evaluation

Joakim Nivre
Dept. of Linguistics and Philology
Uppsala University
joakim.nivre@lingfil.uu.se

Chiao-Ting Fang
Dept. of Linguistics and Philology
Uppsala University
chfa4190@student.uu.se

Abstract

Multilingual parser evaluation has for a long time been hampered by the lack of cross-linguistically consistent annotation. While initiatives like Universal Dependencies have greatly improved the situation, they have also raised questions about the adequacy of existing parser evaluation metrics when applied across typologically different languages. This paper argues that the usual attachment score metrics used to evaluate dependency parsers are biased in favor of analytic languages, where grammatical structure tends to be encoded in free morphemes (function words) rather than in bound morphemes (inflection). We therefore propose an alternative evaluation metric that excludes functional relations from the attachment score. We explore the effect of this change in experiments using a subset of treebanks from release v2.0 of Universal Dependencies.

1 Introduction

The last decade has seen a steadily growing interest in multilingual parsing research, inspired by such events as the CoNLL shared tasks on multilingual dependency parsing (Buchholz and Marsi, 2006; Nivre et al., 2007) and the SPMRL shared tasks on parsing morphologically rich languages (Seddah et al., 2013; Seddah et al., 2014). This has led to a number of conjectures about the suitability of different parsing models for languages with different structural characteristics, but it has been surprisingly hard to study the interplay of parsing technology and language typology in a systematic way. To some extent, this is due to data-related factors such as text genre and training set size, which are hard to control for, but even more important has been the fact that syntactic annotation is not standardized across languages. This

has made it almost impossible to isolate the influence of typological variables, such as word order or morphosyntactic alignment, from the effect of more or less arbitrary choices in linguistic representations. The absence of cross-linguistically consistent annotation has also been a constant source of noise in the evaluation of cross-lingual learning of syntax (Hwa et al., 2002; Zeman and Resnik, 2008; McDonald et al., 2011).

Fortunately, there is now also a growing interest in developing cross-linguistically consistent syntactic annotation, which has led to a number of initiatives and proposals (Zeman et al., 2012; McDonald et al., 2013; Tsarfaty, 2013; de Marneffe et al., 2014). Many of these initiatives have now converged into Universal Dependencies (UD), an open community effort that aims to develop cross-linguistically consistent treebank annotation for many languages and that has so far released 70 treebanks representing 50 languages (Nivre, 2015; Nivre et al., 2016). The basic idea behind the UD scheme is to maximize parallelism across languages by focusing on dependency relations between content words, which are more likely to be similar across languages, and to use cross-linguistically valid categories for morphological and syntactic analysis. The UD scheme is illustrated in Figure 1 for two translationally equivalent sentences in English and Finnish. For readability, we display only a subset of the full annotation, in particular suppressing all morphological features except case.

The example shows that English and Finnish have rather different structural characteristics. What is expressed by eight words in English is expressed by four words in Finnish, and whereas word order and function words like *from* are crucial in English for understanding who does what to whom, the same information is encoded in Finnish mainly by nominal case inflection (nominative for the subject, accusative for the object, and ela-

Proceedings of the NoDaLiDa 2017 Workshop on Universal Dependencies (UDW 2017), pages 86–95,
Gothenburg, Sweden, 22 May 2017.

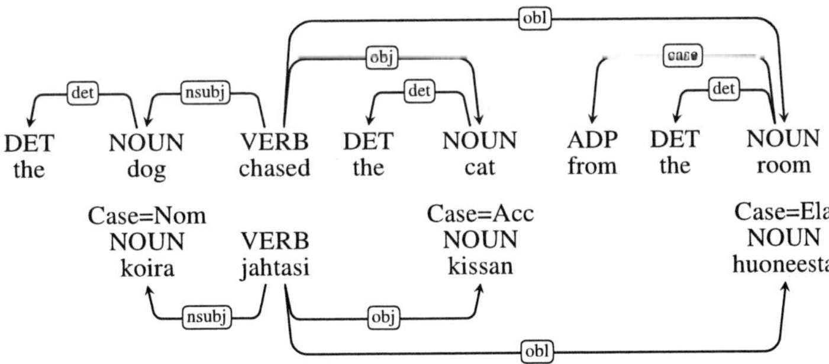

Figure 1: Simplified UD annotation for equivalent sentences from English (top) and Finnish (bottom).

tive for the locative modifier). Moreover, Finnish has no explicit encoding of the information expressed by the definite article *the* in English. Nevertheless, the main grammatical relations are exactly parallel in the two sentences, with the main verb *chased/jahtasi* having three direct nominal dependents, which can be categorized in both languages as (nominal) subject (*nsubj*), object (*obj*), and oblique modifier (*obl*). This illustrates how UD maximizes parallelism by giving priority to dependency relations between content words.

It is tempting to assume that cross-linguistically consistent annotation automatically guarantees cross-linguistically valid parser evaluation. Unfortunately, this is not the case, because our old established evaluation metrics may not be adequate for the new harmonized representations. The most commonly used metric in dependency parsing is the (labeled or unlabeled) attachment score, which measures the percentage of words that have been assigned the correct head (with or without taking the dependency label into account). Suppose now that a parser makes a single mistake on each of the sentences in Figure 1, say, by attaching the locative modifier to the object instead of to the verb. It seems intuitively correct to say that the parser has done an equally good job in both cases. However, for simple arithmetical reasons, the English parser will be credited with an attachment score of 87.5%, while the Finnish parser only gets 75%. In other words, the impact of a single error is doubled in Finnish because of the smaller denominator. Using the attachment score for cross-linguistic comparisons can therefore be quite misleading even if the annotation has been harmonized across languages.

What should we do about this? A drastic proposal would be to give up intrinsic evaluation altogether, on the grounds that it will always be bi-

ased one way or the other, and instead put all our hope on extrinsic evaluation. In doing so, however, we would run the risk of just moving the problem elsewhere. For example, if we decide to evaluate parsers through their impact on machine translation quality, how do we guarantee that the latter evaluation is comparable across languages? Furthermore, intrinsic evaluation metrics will always be useful for internal testing purposes, so we might as well do our best to develop new metrics that are better suited for cross-linguistic comparisons. This is the purpose of this paper.

More precisely, we want to find an alternative evaluation metric for parsing with UD representations, a metric that puts more emphasis on dependency relations between content words in order to maximize comparability across languages, following the same principle as in the design of the annotation itself. We will begin by dividing the syntactic relations used in UD representations into a number of different groups and study their impact on evaluation scores. We will then propose a new metric called CLAS, for Content-Word Labeled Attachment Score, and analyze in more depth how different languages are affected by excluding different functional relations from the evaluation.

2 Syntactic Relations in UD

Annotation in UD consists of a morphological and a syntactic layer. The morphological layer assigns to each word a lemma, a part-of-speech tag and a set of morphological features. The part-of-speech tag comes from a fixed inventory of 17 tags, which is a revised and extended version of the Google universal tagset (Petrov et al., 2012), and the features come from a standardized but extendable inventory based on Interset (Zeman, 2008). The syntactic layer is essentially a dependency tree with labels taken from a set of 37 syntactic relations, which is a revised version of the universal Stanford dependencies (de Marneffe et al., 2014).

As explained in the introduction, the syntactic tree gives priority to grammatical relations between content words, while function words are attached to the content word they specify using special relations such as *case* (for adpositions), *mark* (for subordinating conjunctions) and *aux* (for auxiliary verbs). Although these functional relations are formally indistinguishable from other relations in the tree, they can be seen as encoding features of the content word rather than representing real dependency relations.

When applying the standard attachment score metrics to UD, functional relations are scored just like any other relation encoded in the dependency tree (except the special *punct* relation for punctuation, which is often excluded from evaluation). If a language makes frequent use of function words to encode grammatical information, these relations will therefore make a large contribution to the overall score. Since these relations tend to be local and involve highly frequent words, they also tend to have higher than average accuracy, which means that the overall score comes out higher if they are included. For a language that instead uses morphology to encode grammatical information of a similar kind, there will be no corresponding boost to the evaluation score, because morphological features are not included in the parsing score. Moreover, as illustrated earlier, errors on content word dependencies will be more severely penalized in such a language, because the error rate is normalized by the number of words. In this way, languages with a lower ratio of function words are in effect doubly penalized.

One strategy for dealing with this problem could be to come up with a more comprehensive metric that considers the full grammatical representation and abstracts over different realization patterns and puts morphological features and function words on a more equal footing. Such a metric has been proposed in the context of grammar-based parsing by Dridan and Oepen (2011). In the context of UD, however, this would require a substantial research effort in order to establish correspondences between many languages. And while this is precisely the type of research that UD is meant to enable, it would be premature to assume that we already have the required knowledge. For the time being, we will therefore propose a new metric for syntactic dependencies that is limited to those dependencies that we can expect to find in all or most languages. Besides being less biased from a cross-linguistic perspective, such a metric may also be more relevant for downstream language understanding tasks, where errors on functional relations often matter less than errors on argument and modifier relations. And by comparing results for this metric to those obtained with standard attachment scores, we can estimate the degree of bias inherent in the older metric.

As a preliminary to defining the new metric, we first divide the 37 syntactic UD relations into five disjoint subsets, listed in Table 1. FUN is the subset of relations that relate a function word to a content word, including determiners (*det*), classifiers (*clf*), adpositions (*case*), auxiliaries (*aux*, *cop*), and conjunctions (*cc*, *mark*). The first three can be grouped together as *nominal* functional relations, because they are associated with noun phrases (in the extended sense that includes adpositional phrases), while *aux* and *cop* are connected to clausal predicates, and *mark* and *cc* link clauses (or other phrases) in relations of subordination or coordination.

The set MWE contains relations used to analyze (restricted classes) of multiword expressions. The *fixed* relation is used for completely fixed, grammaticized expressions like *in spite of* and *by and large*; the *flat* relation is used for semi-fixed expressions without a clear syntactic head, and the *compound* relation is used for all kinds of compounding. These relations are clearly different from the functional relations, but their distribution can also be expected to vary across languages, sometimes because of typological factors and sometimes simply because of orthographical conventions. For example, noun-noun compounds like *orange juice* are most commonly written as two space-separated tokens in English, which according to the UD guidelines require that they are analyzed as a syntactic combination using the *compound* relation. Exactly parallel expressions in other Germanic languages like German and Swedish are normally written as a single token (for example, *apelsinjuice* in Swedish), which has as a consequence that the compounding relation is not included in the syntactic evaluation for the latter languages. The relation *goeswith*, finally, is different from the (other) MWE relations in that it is primarily intended for annotation of orthographic

FUN	MWE	CORE	NON-CORE			PUNCT
aux	compound	ccomp	acl	discourse	orphan	punct
case	fixed	csubj	advcl	dislocated	parataxis	
cc	flat	iobj	advmod	expl	reparandum	
clf	goeswith	nsubj	amod	list	root	
cop		obj	appos	nmod	vocative	
det		xcomp	conj	nummod		
mark			dep	obl		

Table 1: Subsets of UD relations: core, non-core, functional, multiword and punctuation.

errors, where a single word has accidentally been split into two, but it is similar in that it does not denote a proper syntactic relation.

The remaining UD relations are divided into CORE, NON-CORE and PUNCT. CORE includes relations for core arguments of predicates, which play a central role in the UD taxonomy and arguably in all syntactic representations. NON-CORE includes all other syntactic relations, including modifier relations at various syntactic levels as well as relations for analyzing coordination and special phenomena like ellipsis and disfluencies. PUNCT, finally, contains the single relation *punct*, which has an unclear status as a syntactic relation and is often excluded in evaluation metrics.

3 Labeled Attachment Score

The labeled attachment score (LAS) evaluates the output of a parser by considering how many words have been assigned both the correct syntactic head and the correct label. If parse trees and gold standard trees can be assumed to have the same yield, and if no syntactic relations are excluded, then it reduces to a simple accuracy score, but in general it can be defined as the labeled F_1-score of syntactic relations.

To get a better view of the impact of different relation types on the overall LAS, we performed a simple experiment where we trained and evaluated MaltParser (Nivre et al., 2006) on treebanks from the latest UD release (v2.0). The parser used an arc-standard transition system with online re-ordering and a lazy oracle (Nivre et al., 2009) and an extended feature model that takes all morphological features into account. We selected one treebank per language[1] but only included treebanks containing morphological features and at

least 30,000 words. We used the dedicated training sets for training and the development sets for evaluation. To make evaluation scores comparable across languages, we replaced all language-specific subtypes of syntactic relations by their universal supertypes.

Table 2 shows the results for the 42 treebanks included in the experiment. The LAS column reports the standard LAS score over all relations (including punctuation). The next four columns report the LAS for CORE, NON-CORE, FUN and MWE separately. The last three columns report the difference in LAS score when excluding relations in PUNCT, FUN and MWE, respectively.

The first thing to note is that there is a very large variation in LAS scores, ranging from a high of 88.29 for Slovenian to a low of 56.35 for Lithuanian. Some of this variation can be explained by data set specific properties like text genre and training set size, and it is undeniable that the parsing model used works better for some languages than others. However, the results in Table 2 also show that the exact difference between two languages is sensitive to which syntactic relations are included.

Examining the LAS scores for different subsets of relations, we find that FUN relations on average are parsed with almost 90% accuracy, to be compared with CORE and NON-CORE relations at about 75% and MWE at about 80%. This means that including FUN relations in the LAS score generally leads to higher scores and that languages with a high share of function words receive a boost. It is also worth noting that, even if CORE and NON-CORE relations are on average parsed with the same accuracy, there is considerable variation across languages. Most languages have a higher LAS score for CORE than

---

[1] For languages with more than one treebank, we selected the treebank without a suffix except in the case of Ancient Greek and Latin, where we selected the PROIEL treebanks to avoid including poetry.

Language	LAS	LAS				LAS Diff		
		CORE	NON-CORE	FUN	MWE	PUNCT	FUN	MWE
Ancient Greek	73.21	67.20	65.76	86.71	66.67	0.00	−6.98	0.01
Arabic	77.00	70.30	73.56	89.49	79.70	0.39	−4.01	−0.02
Basque	73.82	66.61	73.12	86.00	84.95	1.33	−2.79	−0.37
Bulgarian	85.85	76.80	81.68	97.02	83.40	−0.39	−3.94	0.04
Catalan	85.22	79.61	75.43	96.71	89.66	0.87	−7.23	−0.27
Chinese	73.66	63.03	71.09	87.61	91.30	0.86	−5.01	−0.03
Croatian	78.42	78.61	75.16	87.82	54.14	0.14	−2.87	0.49
Czech	84.67	83.35	81.26	94.14	89.15	0.10	−2.37	−0.07
Danish	79.82	81.96	72.82	89.74	82.14	0.49	−3.99	−0.05
Dutch	79.22	68.18	73.21	92.15	89.14	0.43	−5.47	−0.53
English	83.92	86.40	78.04	94.59	79.20	0.96	−4.08	0.28
Estonian	75.58	77.20	71.14	84.86	77.74	−0.31	−1.73	−0.06
Finnish	79.71	80.50	76.22	86.59	78.95	−0.72	−1.28	0.02
French	86.37	87.67	80.35	97.57	81.62	1.99	−6.57	0.15
German	82.58	85.94	75.79	93.52	81.13	1.38	−4.88	0.04
Gothic	76.00	73.27	71.79	86.19	78.79	0.00	−3.70	−0.00
Greek	83.06	82.12	76.82	94.41	86.67	1.28	−6.08	−0.01
Hebrew	80.79	68.04	71.42	96.48	92.78	1.54	−7.93	−1.01
Hindi	85.94	66.94	79.13	96.33	91.46	−0.52	−5.49	−0.66
Hungarian	77.34	77.20	74.74	87.61	91.85	1.67	−2.76	−0.60
Indonesian	75.89	78.67	67.80	90.04	83.65	1.71	−3.14	−1.62
Italian	86.65	80.46	80.49	98.10	91.86	1.70	−7.03	−0.11
Japanese	87.21	47.71	75.23	99.43	96.15	−1.30	−8.98	−0.96
Korean	58.94	49.95	58.19	51.93	56.62	−3.20	0.35	0.54
Latin	70.82	67.58	66.36	82.68	76.43	0.00	−3.97	−0.04
Latvian	73.37	73.18	67.91	84.09	80.44	−1.28	−1.69	−0.10
Lithuanian	56.35	52.84	53.09	72.86	61.54	1.32	−3.70	−0.09
Norwegian (bokmaal)	86.95	86.60	81.93	95.11	85.71	0.33	−3.37	0.03
Norwegian (nynorsk)	86.04	85.79	80.83	94.14	87.72	0.45	−3.51	−0.05
Old Church Slavonic	80.77	78.81	77.99	88.50	80.00	0.00	−2.50	0.00
Persian	81.25	66.63	79.29	90.96	79.16	−0.01	−3.55	0.17
Polish	87.94	85.69	84.72	95.05	80.00	−0.70	−1.63	0.01
Portuguese	87.46	87.10	80.81	97.34	95.00	1.61	−5.72	−0.23
Romanian	79.76	74.24	73.64	92.93	76.78	0.06	−4.83	0.12
Russian	79.79	81.72	76.03	93.56	89.01	1.04	−2.64	−0.38
Slovak	84.61	80.94	82.55	92.82	53.33	−0.34	−1.85	0.19
Slovenian	88.29	85.88	84.75	95.98	83.68	−0.14	−2.59	0.04
Spanish	84.51	79.88	76.74	96.02	81.87	1.04	−7.21	0.07
Swedish	80.08	82.98	75.34	90.54	69.11	1.00	−3.95	0.38
Turkish	60.02	51.84	58.76	75.14	45.43	−1.20	−1.86	0.87
Urdu	78.35	52.88	66.28	93.67	87.24	−0.78	−8.18	−1.27
Vietnamese	64.51	61.93	62.87	74.09	69.33	0.63	−1.77	−0.38
Average	79.09	74.15	74.05	89.77	80.01	0.32	−4.11	−0.13

Table 2: Evaluation scores for 42 UD treebanks (development sets). LAS = Labeled Attachment Score (overall and subsets). LAS Diff = Difference in LAS when excluding a subset of relations. Language families/branches with at least 2 members: Slavonic, Germanic, Romance, Finno-Ugric, Baltic, Greek, Indian, Semitic.

for NON-CORE, including most Germanic and Romance languages. But there are also languages that have a considerably lower score for CORE than for NON-CORE. The most extreme example is Japanese, where the difference is almost 30 percentage points, but large discrepancies can also be found for Basque, Chinese, Korean, Hindi and Persian. It seems that the parsing model used in the experiment fails to learn how core arguments are encoded in these languages, which is an interesting observation but not directly related to the topic of this paper.

Next we examine how the LAS score is affected when different subsets are excluded. Starting with PUNCT, we see that LAS sometimes increases and sometimes decreases. This may be due to inconsistent annotation of punctuation across treebanks, but it could also be due to differences in syntactic complexity, as short and simple sentences increase the frequency of easily predictable punctuation relations while long and complex sentences have the opposite effect. For most languages, the difference is less than a percentage point, but in a few cases it is quite substantial. For Korean, for example, excluding PUNCT from the LAS score decreases the score by over 3 percentage points. We also see that some of the classical languages (Ancient Greek, Gothic, Latin and Old Church Slavonic) lack punctuation completely, and the same would have been true if we had included treebanks of spoken language. This casts additional doubt on the inclusion of PUNCT in an evaluation score for syntactic analysis, and we will propose to exclude it in the new score.

As expected, the relations in FUN have a more significant and differential impact on the score. On average, LAS scores decrease by 4.11 points when these relations are not included, which is consistent with their being parsed more accurately than other relations, but the cross-linguistic variation is considerable. The largest drop is almost 9 points, for Japanese, and 12 languages have a drop of over 5 points. In this group, Romance languages like Catalan, Italian and Spanish and Greek (both ancient and modern) are prominent. At the opposite of the scale, Korean in fact sees a small improvement (0.35) when excluding FUN, and 7 languages have a drop smaller than 2 points. Finno-Ugric language like Estonian and Finnish are in this group, together with Turkish, Vietnamese and a few Baltic and Slavonic languages. This is mostly in line with our expectations based on linguistic typology (although the result for Japanese is unexpected) and consistent with the view that focusing on relations between content words will give a more balanced picture of parsing accuracy. Our new metric will therefore exclude all relations in FUN.

Omitting MWE has a more marginal effect on the evaluation scores. On average, LAS scores decrease by 0.13 points, and for most languages the difference (whether positive or negative) is less than 0.5 points, with a small number of outliers like Indonesian (-1.62), Urdu (-1.27), Hebrew (-1.01) and Turkish ($+0.87$). Based on these results, it is hard to draw any clear conclusions about the status of these relations in a cross-linguistically valid evaluation metric. For the time being, we will therefore simply leave them intact.

4   Content Labeled Attachment Score

Based on the theoretical discussion in the introduction and with further support from the empirical results in the previous section, we propose an alternative evaluation metric for UD parsing called Content-Word Labeled Attachment Score, abbreviated CLAS. CLAS is defined as the labeled F_1-score over all relations except relations in FUN and PUNCT. To make this precise, let S and G be the set of labeled dependencies in the system output and in the gold standard, respectively, and let $C(X)$ denote the subset of labeled dependencies in the set X that are not in FUN or PUNCT. Then we define precision (P), recall (R) and CLAS in the obvious way:

$$P(S, G) = \frac{|C(S) \cap C(G)|}{|C(S)|}$$

$$R(S, G) = \frac{|C(S) \cap C(G)|}{|C(G)|}$$

$$\text{CLAS}(S, G) = \frac{2 \cdot P(S, G) \cdot R(S, G)}{P(S, G) + R(S, G)}$$

The main idea behind this metric is that, by excluding function words, we are left with a set of relations that can be expected to occur with similar frequency across languages, although their structural realization may vary considerably. In this way, we can at least avoid the simple arithmetic biasing effects observed in the introduction and obtain scores that make more sense to compare across languages.

Language	LAS	CLAS	Diff	LAS Diff						
				DET	CLF	CASE	AUX	COP	MARK	CC
Ancient Greek	73.21	66.23	−6.98	−4.05	0.00	−1.67	0.01	0.07	−0.28	0.56
Arabic	77.00	72.95	−4.05	−0.09	0.00	−3.25	−0.08	0.05	−0.24	0.12
Basque	73.82	72.04	−1.79	−0.26	0.00	−0.35	−2.20	0.10	0.03	0.22
Bulgarian	85.85	80.42	−5.43	−0.35	0.00	−2.03	−0.52	0.02	−0.10	−0.26
Catalan	85.22	78.14	−7.08	−2.27	0.00	−2.11	−0.43	−0.02	−0.15	−0.11
Chinese	73.66	68.71	−4.95	−0.51	−0.18	−2.07	−0.06	−0.24	−0.85	−0.10
Croatian	78.42	75.25	−3.17	−0.22	0.00	−1.75	−0.44	0.18	−0.13	−0.05
Czech	84.67	81.91	−2.75	−0.25	0.00	−1.42	−0.14	−0.02	−0.17	−0.05
Danish	79.82	75.64	−4.18	−0.86	0.00	−1.22	−0.39	−0.11	−0.49	0.02
Dutch	79.22	73.28	−5.94	−2.09	0.00	−1.85	−0.16	0.05	−0.17	−0.06
English	83.92	80.42	−3.50	−1.09	0.00	−0.79	−0.52	−0.23	−0.36	−0.15
Estonian	75.58	73.02	−2.55	−0.17	0.00	−0.44	−0.48	0.17	−0.21	−0.36
Finnish	79.71	77.28	−2.42	−0.04	0.00	−0.20	−0.45	−0.05	−0.22	−0.14
French	86.37	81.86	−4.51	−2.18	0.00	−1.95	−0.27	−0.10	−0.08	−0.19
German	82.58	78.69	−3.89	−1.99	0.00	−1.10	−0.46	0.00	−0.07	−0.10
Gothic	76.00	72.31	−3.70	−0.73	0.00	−2.05	−0.04	0.00	−0.54	0.45
Greek	83.06	77.93	−5.13	−2.95	0.00	−1.29	−0.39	0.03	−0.01	0.00
Hebrew	80.79	73.67	−7.11	−2.12	0.00	−3.37	0.02	−0.03	−0.34	−0.21
Hindi	85.94	78.99	−6.95	−0.23	0.00	−2.72	−0.93	−0.08	−0.32	0.10
Hungarian	77.34	76.26	−1.08	−2.21	0.00	−0.32	−0.00	0.01	−0.31	0.38
Indonesian	75.89	74.19	−1.70	−0.20	0.00	−2.10	0.00	−0.18	−0.02	−0.30
Italian	86.65	80.94	−5.71	−2.45	0.00	−2.00	−0.31	−0.04	−0.17	−0.08
Japanese	87.21	74.03	−13.18	−0.03	0.00	−3.53	−1.73	−0.17	−0.71	−0.04
Korean	58.94	55.95	−2.98	0.62	0.00	−0.12	0.00	0.00	−0.10	−0.04
Latin	70.82	66.85	−3.97	−0.48	0.00	−2.11	−0.25	0.14	−0.48	0.03
Latvian	73.37	69.54	−3.84	−0.41	0.00	−0.77	−0.16	0.07	−0.13	−0.11
Lithuanian	56.35	53.26	−3.10	−1.32	0.00	−0.93	−0.12	−0.07	−0.37	−0.34
Norwegian (bokmaal)	86.95	83.40	−3.56	−0.50	0.00	−0.99	−0.38	−0.07	−0.37	−0.23
Norwegian (nynorsk)	86.04	82.56	−3.48	−0.63	0.00	−0.96	−0.33	−0.07	−0.48	−0.16
Old Church Slavonic	80.77	78.28	−2.50	−0.19	0.00	−1.56	−0.43	0.00	−0.33	0.52
Persian	81.25	77.22	−4.03	−0.33	0.00	−2.01	−0.21	0.16	−0.13	−0.37
Polish	87.94	85.01	−2.93	−0.15	0.00	−0.91	−0.13	−0.00	−0.07	−0.17
Portuguese	87.46	83.04	−4.42	−1.98	0.00	−1.95	−0.17	−0.10	−0.05	0.04
Romanian	79.76	73.96	−5.80	−1.00	0.00	−1.86	−0.49	−0.03	−0.26	−0.20
Russian	79.79	77.70	−2.09	−0.19	0.00	−1.80	−0.09	−0.01	−0.08	−0.23
Slovak	84.61	81.94	−2.67	−0.33	0.00	−1.33	0.07	0.05	−0.06	−0.04
Slovenian	88.29	84.96	−3.33	−0.19	0.00	−1.13	−0.38	0.05	−0.22	−0.20
Spanish	84.51	77.58	−6.93	−2.38	0.00	−2.31	−0.16	−0.02	−0.16	−0.13
Swedish	80.08	76.95	−3.13	−0.89	0.00	−1.10	−0.42	−0.04	−0.28	−0.32
Turkish	60.02	56.32	−3.70	−0.70	0.00	−0.90	−0.03	−0.40	0.05	0.26
Urdu	78.35	68.28	−10.07	−0.36	0.00	−3.78	−1.53	−0.13	−0.42	0.03
Vietnamese	64.51	63.15	−1.36	−0.63	0.00	−0.90	−0.07	−0.20	0.26	−0.03
Average	79.09	74.76	−4.32	−0.94	−0.00	−1.59	−0.36	−0.03	−0.23	−0.05

Table 3: Evaluation scores for 42 UD treebanks (development sets). LAS = Labeled Attachment Score. CLAS = Content-Word Labeled Attachment Score. LAS Diff = Difference in LAS when excluding a relation. Language families/branches with at least 2 members: Slavonic, Germanic, Romance, Finno-Ugric, Baltic, Greek, Indian, Semitic.

In order to explore the properties of the new metric, we present additional evaluation scores for the same parsing experiment in Table 3. The first three columns show LAS, CLAS and difference CLAS − LAS. The final seven columns show the difference in LAS when excluding the relations in FUN, one at a time.[2] Comparing CLAS to LAS, we see essentially the same picture as when excluding FUN from LAS in Table 2, although there is sometimes a combined effect when also excluding PUNCT. The average difference is −4.32 points, and the language-specific differences range from −1.08 for Hungarian to −13.18 for Japanese.

Among the languages that exhibit the smallest decrease, we find the Finno-Ugric languages (Estonian, Finnish, Hungarian) together with Basque and Indonesian, which are all agglutinating languages. More surprisingly, the low-decrease group also includes Vietnamese, which is usually described as an analytic language. The explanation seems to be a low LAS for FUN relations in Vietnamese, only 74.09 as shown in Table 2.

Slavonic languages, which are morphologically rich but not agglutinating, mostly have a relatively low decrease in the 2–3 point range, with the exception of Bulgarian (−5.43), which has developed in a typologically different direction from the other Slavonic languages in the sample. The closely related Baltic languages (Latvian, Lithuanian) behave similarly to Slavonic languages, but with a slightly higher decrease, and Germanic languages, which in general are less morphologically rich, are a little higher still with an average decrease of 3–4 points, although Dutch deviates from the general pattern by having an unexpectedly large decrease (−5.94).

Among the languages with the highest decrease we find Japanese, which is again somewhat unexpected and may have to do with particular annotation choices when applying the UD guidelines to Japanese. A high decrease is also observed for Indian languages (Hindi and Urdu), most of the Romance languages (especially Catalan, Italian and Spanish), Greek (both ancient and modern) and the Semitic languages (especially Hebrew).

Zooming in on the individual relations in FUN, we see that most of the difference can be attributed to functional relations in noun phrases, in particular *det* and *case*. (The third relation *clf* is cur-

rently only used in Chinese.) The *det* relation has the largest impact on Ancient Greek, followed by modern Greek, a group of Romance languages (French, Italian, Spanish), Hungarian and Hebrew. The *case* relation instead shows the largest effect for Urdu, Japanese, Hebrew and Arabic.

The remaining four FUN relations *aux*, *cop*, *mark* and *cc* have a less significant effect than the nominal relations. The *cc* relation is different from the rest in that scores sometimes go up when it is excluded. This effect is noticeable for two of the classical languages, Ancient Greek and Gothic, and for Hungarian. More research will be needed to find out why this is the case.

5 Conclusion

Proving that one evaluation metric is superior to another is very difficult in general. Ideally, we should show that it correlates better with independent quality criteria, but such criteria are often not available. This is especially tricky for a component task like syntactic parsing, where there are no real end users and where human assessments are notoriously unreliable. In this paper, we have instead relied primarily on rational argumentation. Since UD has been explicitly designed to capture cross-linguistic similarities in grammatical relations between content words, we argue that multilingual evaluation should focus primarily on these relations. The main metric should therefore exclude both function words and morphological features, to prevent bias towards either analytical or synthetic languages. (In addition, the main metric should exclude punctuation, which is completely absent in some of the treebanks and arguably not part of the syntactic structure.) To back up these rational arguments, we have presented empirical results from a parsing experiment, studying the effect of excluding different relations and showing that the new metric behaves, by and large, as we can expect based on typological considerations.

A common objection against only scoring dependencies between content words is that we will lose important information about parsing quality for languages where functional relations are important. If, in addition, we start tuning parsers on the new metric, we risk favoring systems that score well on a subset of relations at the expense of much lower accuracy on functional relations. We think these risks are exaggerated. First of all, the old LAS score is still available and might even

---

[2] All scores are F_1-scores, which explains why the differences under LAS Diff do not add up to the difference CLAS − LAS. In addition, CLAS also excludes PUNCT.

be the metric of choice for monolingual evaluation, where structural differences across languages are not relevant. Secondly, we are convinced that, in order to achieve high accuracy on argument and modifier relations, a parser must be able to recover other structures that provide information about these relations. For analytical languages, parsers will therefore be forced to pay attention to functional relations, even if they are not scored in the evaluation metric. For more synthetic languages, parsers will instead have to focus more on morphological information. Hence, by *directly* favoring accuracy on major grammatical relations, we are *indirectly* encouraging parsers to pay attention to grammatically relevant information, be it encoded in morphology, function words, or word order patterns. Therefore, we think the risk for an unwanted bias is in fact less of a problem than with the traditional LAS metric, where parsers can score well (for some languages) by being accurate mainly on functional relations, which are highly frequent and easy to parse.

At this point, it is still an empirical question which metric will give the right or wrong kind of bias, although some of the results reviewed in previous sections at least illustrate that the traditional LAS score can be severely inflated for some languages. More research will definitely be needed to better understand the effects of using different metrics, in particular experiments with different parsers and perhaps also different variants of the new metric, but we hope that the proposal made in this paper can be a first step towards more sound metrics for multilingual parser evaluation.

References

Sabine Buchholz and Erwin Marsi. 2006. CoNLL-X shared task on multilingual dependency parsing. In *Proceedings of the 10th Conference on Computational Natural Language Learning (CoNLL)*, pages 149–164.

Marie-Catherine de Marneffe, Timothy Dozat, Natalia Silveira, Katri Haverinen, Filip Ginter, Joakim Nivre, and Christopher D. Manning. 2014. Universal Stanford Dependencies: A cross-linguistic typology. In *Proceedings of the 9th International Conference on Language Resources and Evaluation (LREC)*, pages 4585–4592.

Rebecca Dridan and Stephan Oepen. 2011. Parser evaluation using elementary dependency matching. In *Proceedings of the 12th International Conference on Parsing Technologies (IWPT)*, pages 225–230.

Rebecca Hwa, Philip Resnik, Amy Weinberg, and Okan Kolak. 2002. Evaluating translational correspondence using annotation projection. In *Proceedings of the 40th Annual Meeting of the Association for Computational Linguistics (ACL)*, pages 392–399.

Ryan McDonald, Slav Petrov, and Keith Hall. 2011. Multi-source transfer of delexicalized dependency parsers. In *Proceedings of the Conference on Empirical Methods in Natural Language Processing (EMNLP)*, pages 62–72.

Ryan McDonald, Joakim Nivre, Yvonne Quirmbach-Brundage, Yoav Goldberg, Dipanjan Das, Kuzman Ganchev, Keith Hall, Slav Petrov, Hao Zhang, Oscar Täckström, Claudia Bedini, Núria Bertomeu Castelló, and Jungmee Lee. 2013. Universal dependency annotation for multilingual parsing. In *Proceedings of the 51st Annual Meeting of the Association for Computational Linguistics (Volume 2: Short Papers)*, pages 92–97.

Joakim Nivre, Johan Hall, and Jens Nilsson. 2006. Maltparser: A data-driven parser-generator for dependency parsing. In *Proceedings of the 5th International Conference on Language Resources and Evaluation (LREC)*, pages 2216–2219.

Joakim Nivre, Johan Hall, Sandra Kübler, Ryan McDonald, Jens Nilsson, Sebastian Riedel, and Deniz Yuret. 2007. The CoNLL 2007 shared task on dependency parsing. In *Proceedings of the CoNLL Shared Task of EMNLP-CoNLL 2007*, pages 915–932.

Joakim Nivre, Marco Kuhlmann, and Johan Hall. 2009. An improved oracle for dependency parsing with online reordering. In *Proceedings of the 11th International Conference on Parsing Technologies (IWPT'09)*, pages 73–76.

Joakim Nivre, Marie-Catherine de Marneffe, Filip Ginter, Yoav Goldberg, Jan Hajič, Christopher D. Manning, Ryan McDonald, Slav Petrov, Sampo Pyysalo, Natalia Silveira, Reut Tsarfaty, and Dan Zeman. 2016. Universal Dependencies v1: A multilingual treebank collection. In *Proceedings of the 10th International Conference on Language Resources and Evaluation (LREC)*.

Joakim Nivre. 2015. Towards a universal grammar for natural language processing. In Alexander Gelbukh, editor, *Computational Linguistics and Intelligent Text Processing*, pages 3–16. Springer.

Slav Petrov, Dipanjan Das, and Ryan McDonald. 2012. A universal part-of-speech tagset. In *Proceedings of the 8th International Conference on Language Resources and Evaluation (LREC)*.

Djamé Seddah, Reut Tsarfaty, Sandra Kübler, Marie Candito, Jinho D. Choi, Richárd Farkas, Jennifer Foster, Iakes Goenaga, Koldo Gojenola Galletebeitia, Yoav Goldberg, Spence Green, Nizar

Habash, Marco Kuhlmann, Wolfgang Maier, Joakim Nivre, Adam Przepiórkowski, Ryan Roth, Wolfgang Seeker, Yannick Versley, Veronika Vincze, Marcin Woliński, Alina Wróblewska, and Eric Villemonte de la Clergerie. 2013. Overview of the SPMRL 2013 shared task: A cross-framework evaluation of parsing morphologically rich languages. In *Proceedings of the Fourth Workshop on Statistical Parsing of Morphologically Rich Languages*, pages 146–182.

Djamé Seddah, Sandra Kübler, and Reut Tsarfaty. 2014. Introducing the SPMRL 2014 shared task on parsing morphologically-rich languages. In *Proceedings of the First Joint Workshop on Statistical Parsing of Morphologically Rich Languages and Syntactic Analysis of Non-Canonical Languages*, pages 103–109.

Reut Tsarfaty. 2013. A unified morpho-syntactic scheme of Stanford dependencies. In *Proceedings of the 51st Annual Meeting of the Association for Computational Linguistics (Volume 2: Short Papers)*, pages 578–584.

Daniel Zeman and Philip Resnik. 2008. Cross-language parser adaptation between related languages. In *Proceedings of the IJCNLP-08 Workshop on NLP for Less Privileged Languages*, pages 35–42.

Daniel Zeman, David Mareček, Martin Popel, Loganathan Ramasamy, Jan Štěpánek, Zdeněk Žabokrtský, and Jan Hajič. 2012. HamleDT: To parse or not to parse? In *Proceedings of the 8th International Conference on Language Resources and Evaluation (LREC)*, pages 2735–2741.

Daniel Zeman. 2008. Reusable tagset conversion using tagset drivers. In *Proceedings of the 6th International Conference on Language Resources and Evaluation (LREC)*, pages 213–218.

Udapi: Universal API for Universal Dependencies

Martin Popel, Zdeněk Žabokrtský, Martin Vojtek
Charles University, Faculty of Mathematics and Physics
Malostranské náměstí 25, Prague
`{popel,zabokrtsky}@ufal.mff.cuni.cz, martin.vojtek@hotmail.com`

Abstract

Udapi is an open-source framework providing an application programming interface (API) for processing Universal Dependencies data. Udapi is available in Python, Perl and Java. It is suitable both for full-fledged applications and fast prototyping: visualization of dependency trees, format conversions, querying, editing and transformations, validity tests, dependency parsing, evaluation etc.

1 Introduction

Universal Dependencies (UD)[1] is a project that seeks to develop cross-linguistically consistent treebank annotation, by both providing annotation guidelines and releasing freely available treebanks. Two years after the first release, UD version 2 (UDv2) of the guidelines was published, accompanied by the UDv2.0 release of the data: 70 treebanks for 50 languages, with 12M words in total, contributed by 145 treebank developers.[2]

The steady growth of the UD popularity results in an increased need for tools compatible with UD and its native data format CoNLL-U. Such tools are needed by both the treebank developers and users of the treebanks. Thanks to the simplicity of CoNLL-U, simple tasks can be performed with ad-hoc scripts or even standard Unix tools (`sed`, `cut`, `grep` etc.). However, there are several disadvantages of these ad-hoc solutions:

- They tend to be suboptimal regarding speed and memory, thus discouraging more frequent large-scale experiments.

- The code is less readable because the main logic is mixed with boilerplate.

- It is easy to forget handling edge cases.[3]

- Ad-hoc solutions are difficult to maintain once they outgrow the original simple task.

We present Udapi – a framework providing an API for processing UD, which should solve the above-mentioned problems. Udapi implementation is available in Python, Perl and Java. In this paper, we focus on the Python implementation because it currently has the best support and largest user community. The Perl and Java implementations are kept harmonized with the Python implementation as much as the differences between these programming languages allow.

The API is object-oriented and covers both processing units (§3.1) and data representation (§3.2). The development of Udapi is hosted at GitHub.[4] Anyone is welcome to contribute.

2 Example use cases

Udapi can be used both as Python library and via the command-line interface `udapy`. This section gives examples of the latter.

2.1 Parsing

```
echo "John loves Mary." | udapy \
  read.Sentences  tokenize.Simple \
  udpipe.En tokenize=0 write.Conllu
```

In this example, `udapy` executes a pipeline (called *scenario* in Udapi) with four processing units (called *blocks*): `read.Sentences` reads plain text from the standard input, one sentence per line; `tokenize.Simple` does a naïve tokenization; `udpipe.En` applies a UDPipe (Straka et al., 2016) model for English tagging (filling

---

[3] For example, when deleting a node in a middle of a sentence, we must reindex the ID, HEAD and DEPS columns, delete enhanced dependencies referring to the node, re-attach or delete possible dependents of the node and if it was part of a multi-word token, make sure the token is still valid.

[4] See `http://udapi.github.io` for further info, documentation and a hands-on tutorial.

[1] `http://universaldependencies.org`
[2] `http://hdl.handle.net/11234/1-1983`

Proceedings of the NoDaLiDa 2017 Workshop on Universal Dependencies (UDW 2017), pages 96–101,
Gothenburg, Sweden, 22 May 2017.

attributes *upos*, *lemma* and *feats*) and parsing (*deprel* and *head*). The parameter `tokenize=0` instructs UDPipe to skip tokenization. Finally, `write.Conllu` writes the parsed sentences to the standard output in the CoNLL-U format.

In practice, we recommend to use UDPipe's internal tokenization and `udapy -s` as a shortcut for appending `write.Conllu` to the scenario:

```
echo "John loves Mary." | udapy -s \
   read.Sentences  udpipe.En
```

2.2 Visualization

```
cat latin-sample.conllu | udapy \
  write.TextModeTrees attributes=form,upos
```

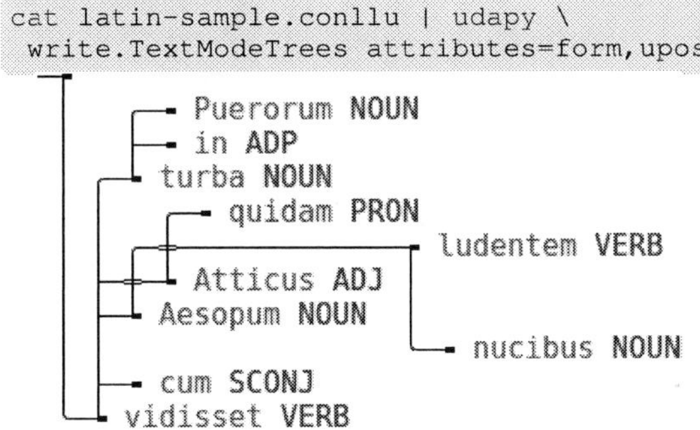

If no reader block is provided, `read.Conllu` is used by default. Block `write.TextMode Trees` is very useful for fast visualization of dependency trees in terminal and tracking changes in `vimdiff`. As the example above shows, it can render non-projectivities, it has a parameter for specifying the node attributes to be printed and it uses color highlighting in the terminal.

For longer documents, it is handy to use a pager (`less -R`)[5] so one can search attributes of all nodes with regular expressions. The shortcut `udapy -T` stands for `write.TextMode Trees color=1` and printing the default set of attributes *form*, *upos* and *deprel*:

```
udapy -T < latin-sample.conllu | less -R
```

Similarly, `udapy -H` is a shortcut for a (static) HTML version of this writer (see Figure 1) and `-A` is a shortcut for printing all attributes. Run `udapy --help` to learn more shortcuts.

Block `write.Html` also generates a HTML file, but it uses JavaScript for traditional-style tree rendering, tooltips, SVG export button, highlighting alignments between the sentence and nodes and possibly also between nodes of word-aligned parallel sentences, see Figure 2.

Block `write.Tikz` generates a LaTeX code, suitable for inclusion in papers, see Figure 3.

---

[5] The `-R` flag ensures the ANSI colors are displayed.

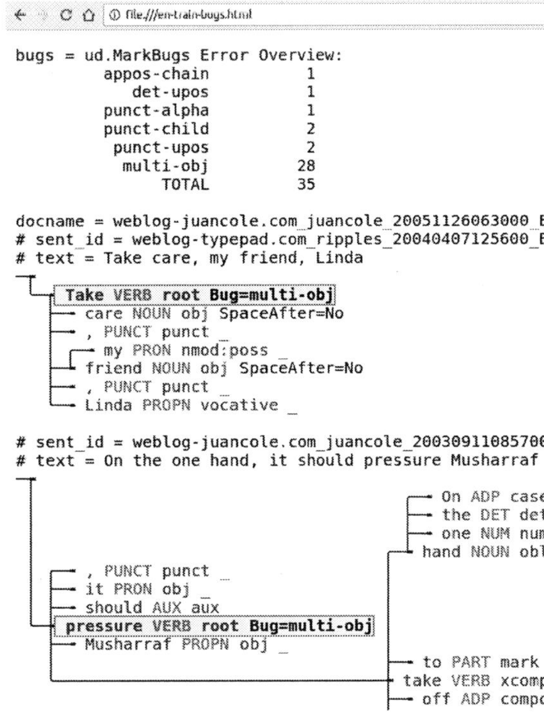

Figure 1: `write.TextModeTreesHtml` example output with a sample of annotation errors (and overall statistics) found by `ud.MarkBugs`.

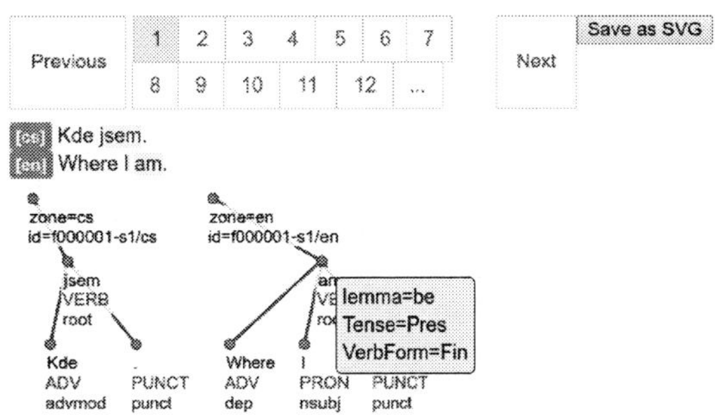

Figure 2: `write.Html` example output with a sample of Czech-English parallel treebank CzEng (Bojar et al., 2016) converted to the UD style.

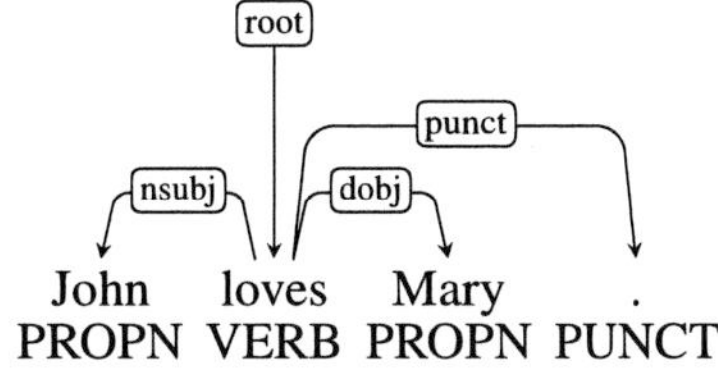

Figure 3: `write.Tikz` example output.

2.3 Format conversions

Udapi can be used for converting between various data formats. In addition to the native CoNLL-U format and to the visualization layouts mentioned in Section 2, Udapi currently supports SDParse (popularized by Stanford dependencies and Brat)[6] and VISL-cg[7] formats as illustrated below:

```
udapy write.Vislcg < x.conllu > x.vislcg
udapy read.Vislcg write.Sdparse \
      < x.vislcg > x.sdparse
```

2.4 Querying and simple edits

There are two online services for querying the released UD treebanks: SETS by the University of Turku[8] and PML-TQ by the Charles University.[9] The SETS querying language is easier to learn, but less expressive than the PML-TQ language.

Udapi offers an alternative where queries are specified in Python and may use all the methods defined in the API, thus being suitable even for complex queries. For example, using the method `is_nonprojective()`, we can find all non-projective trees in a CoNLL-U file, and mark the non-projective edges with a label "nonproj" stored in the MISC column (so the dependent node will be highlighted by `udapy -T`):

```
cat in.conllu | udapy -T \
util.Filter mark=nonproj \
keep_tree_if_node='node.is_nonprojective()'
```

The same can be achieved using `util.Mark` and the `-M` shortcut, which instructs the writer to print only trees that are "marked":

```
cat in.conllu | udapy -TM util.Mark \
node='node.is_nonprojective()'
```

Block `util.Eval` can execute arbitrary Python code, so it can be used not only for querying, but also for simple (ad-hoc) editing. For example, we can delete the subtypes of dependency relations and keep only the universal part:[10]

```
cat in.conllu | udapy -s util.Eval \
node='node.deprel = node.udeprel' \
> out.conllu
```

For better reusability and maintainability, we recommend to store more complex edits in separate Python modules. For instance, module `udapi.block.my.edit` with class `Edit` will be available via `udapy` as `my.Edit`.

2.5 Validation

UD treebanks are distributed with an official `validate.py` script, which checks the CoNLL-U validity and also treebank-specific restrictions (e.g. a set of allowed deprel subtypes). Udapi currently does not attempt to duplicate this *format validation* because it tries to keep CoNLL-U loading as fast as possible, checking only the most critical properties, such as absence of cycles in dependencies. Udapi can also be used for non-UD treebanks,[11] which use a different set of values for UPOS, DEPREL etc., so a strict non-optional validation is not desired.

UD website features also *content validation* available as an online service.[12] It is basically a special case of querying, with a set of tests formalized as queries. For example, the `multi-obj` test searches for nodes with two or more (direct) objects or clausal complements. This can be implemented in Udapi as follows: `len([n for n in node.children if n.deprel in {'obj', 'ccomp'}]) > 1`.

Although some tests may occasionally bring false alarms (finding a construction which is not forbidden by the UD guidelines), it is worth checking the results of tests with most hits for a given treebank as these often signal real errors or inconsistencies. For example, the two `multi-obj` hits highlighted in Figure 1 are both annotation (or conversion) errors: In the first sentence, *friend* should have deprel *vocative* and *Linda* should depend on it as *appos*. In the second sentence, *it* should be a subject (*nsubj*) instead of object. The tree visualization also sets off the erroneous non-projectivity, where *On the one hand* should depend on *pressure*.

Block `ud.MarkBugs` is an improved version of the online content validation with higher precision and coverage. Treebank developers can apply `ud.MarkBugs` on their data offline (before pushing a new version on GitHub, or on secret test data), so it complements the online validation. It is possible to apply only some tests using parameters `tests` and `skip`:

```
udapy -HAM ud.MarkBugs skip='no-NumType' \
    < in.conllu > bugs.html
```

---

[6] http://brat.nlplab.org/

[7] http://visl.sdu.dk/visl/vislcg-doc.html

[8] http://bionlp-www.utu.fi/dep_search/

[9] http://lindat.cz

[10] So e.g. *acl:relcl* is changed to *acl*.

[11] The reader block `read.Conllu` can load even CoNLL-X and CoNLL-2007 formats, using the optional parameter `attributes` listing the column names.

[12] http://universaldependencies.org/svalidation.html

2.6 UDv2 conversion

When the UDv2 guidelines were released, there were many treebanks annotated in the UDv1 style. Luckily, most of the changes could be at least partially automatized. Some of the changes were simple renaming of labels, e.g. CONJ $\rightarrow$ CCONJ, which is easy to implement in any tool. Some of the changes were more difficult to implement correctly, e.g. conversion of ellipsis from the old *remnant* style to the new *orphan* style.

Block `ud.Convert1to2` has been successfully used for converting five UDv2 treebanks: Bulgarian, Romanian, Galician, Russian and Irish. Block `ud.Google2ud` converts data for 15 languages from a pre-UDv1 style used by Google.

2.7 Other use cases

Block `ud.SetSpaceAfter` uses heuristic rules to add the attribute SpaceAfter=No, while `ud.SetSpaceAfterFromText` does the same based on the raw text. Even more advanced is `ud.ComplyWithText`, which can also adapt the annotation so it matches the raw text, e.g. by reverting the normalization of word forms.[13]

Block `ud.AddMwt` splits multi-word tokens into words based on language-specific rules — there are subclasses for several languages, e.g. `ud.cs.AddMwt` for Czech.

Overall statistics (number of words, empty words, multi-word tokens, sentences) can be printed with `util.Wc`. Advanced statistics about nodes matching a given condition (relative to other nodes) can be printed with `util.See`.

For evaluation, `eval.Parsing` computes the standard UAS and LAS, while `eval.F1` computes Precision/Recall/F1 of various attributes based on the longest common subsequence.

Tree projectivization and deprojectivization (Nivre and Nilsson, 2005) can be performed using `transform.Proj` and `transform.Deproj`.

3 Design and Implementation

The primary focus of Udapi is simplicity of use and speed. The amount of effort spent on designing specialized data structures, micro-optimizing the speed and memory critical parts (e.g. loading

system	memory (MiB)	load (s)	save (s)	bench (s)
Treex	18,024	2,501	201	287
PyTreex	3,809	158	8	74
Udapi-Python	879	24	6	16
Udapi-Perl	**748**	**7**	3	11
Udapi-Java	1,323	9	**1**	**5**

Table 1: Memory and speed comparison. We measured performance of individual implementations on loading and saving from/to CoNLL-U, and on a benchmark composed of iterating over all nodes, reading and writing node attributes, changing the dependency structure, adding and removing nodes, and changing word order. We used `cs-ud-train-l.conllu` from UDv1.2 (68 MiB, 41k sentences, 800k words).

CoNLL-U, iterating over all nodes sorted by word order while allowing changes of the word order too) and other technical issues was much bigger than the effort spent on the use cases described in Section 2.

For example, to provide access to structured attributes FEATS and MISC (e.g. `node.feats['Case'] = 'Nom'`) while allowing access to the serialized data (e.g. `node.feats = 'Case=Nom|Person=1'`), Udapi maintains both representations (string and dict) and synchronizes them transparently, but lazily.

Table 1 shows a benchmark of 5 frameworks: Treex (Perl), PyTreex (Python 2) and three implementations of Udapi (Python 3, Perl, Java 8).[14]

The full description of the API is available online.[15] The following two sections summarize only the most important classes and methods.

3.1 Classes for data processing

Block. A block is the smallest processing unit that can be applied on UD data. Block classes implement usually some reasonably limited and well-defined tasks, often corresponding to the classical NLP components (tokenization, tagging, parsing…), but there can be blocks for purely technical tasks (such as for feature extraction).

---

[13] There are several treebanks which use ` `TeX-like quotes'' instead of the "quotes" used in the raw text or which normalize numbers by deleting the thousand separators. However, the UDv2 quidelines require word forms to match exactly the raw text.

[14] https://github.com/ufal/treex
https://github.com/ufal/pytreex
https://github.com/udapi/udapi-python
https://github.com/udapi/udapi-perl
https://github.com/udapi/udapi-java
[15] http://udapi.readthedocs.io

Run. The `Run` class instance corresponds to a sequence of blocks (also called scenario) that are to be applied on data one after another. Such scenarios can compose very complex NLP pipelines. This class offers also the support for the command-line interface `udapy`.

3.2 Classes for data representation

Document. A document consists of a sequence of bundles, mirroring a sequence of sentences in a typical natural language text. A document instance can be composed programatically or can be loaded from (or stored to) a CoNLL-U file.

Bundle. A bundle corresponds to a sentence, possibly in more forms or with different representations, such as sentence-tuples from parallel corpora, or paraphrases in the same language or alternative analyses (e.g. parses produced by different parsers). If there are more trees in a bundle, they must be distinguished by a so called *zone* (a label which contains the language code).

Root. A root is a special (artificial) node that is added to the top of a CoNLL-U tree in the Udapi model. The root serves as a representant of the whole tree (e.g. it bears the sentence's identifier). The root's functionality partially overlaps with functionality of nodes (e.g., it has methods `children` and `descendants`), but differs in other aspects (its lemma cannot be set, its linear position is always 0, it has methods for creating and accessing *multiword tokens*, computing the sentence text (detokenized), accessing the tree-level CoNLL-U comments, etc.).

Node. The `Node` class corresponds to a node of a dependency tree. It provides access to all the CoNLL-U-defined attributes. There are methods for tree traversal (`parent`, `root`, `children`, `descendants`); word-order traversal (`next_node`, `prev_node`); tree manipulation (`parent` setter) including word-order changes (`shift_after_node(x)`, `shift_before_subtree(x)`, etc.); and utility methods: `is_descendant_of(x)`, `is_nonprojective()`, `precedes(x)`, `is_leaf()`, `is_root()`, `get_attrs([])`, `compute_text()`, `print_subtree()`.

Some methods have optional arguments, e.g., `child = node.create_child(form="was", lemma="be")` for creating a new node with given attributes or `node.remove(`

children="rehang") for removing a node but keeping its children by re-attaching them to the parent of the removed node.[16]

4 Related work

Treex (Popel and Žabokrtský, 2010) is a Perl NLP framework focusing on MT and multi-layer annotation in the PDT (Bejček et al., 2013) style. It is the only framework we are aware of with at least partial support for UD and CoNLL-U. NLTK (Bird et al., 2009) is a popular framework focusing on teaching NLP and Python, with no UD support yet.[17] GATE (Cunningham et al., 2011)[18] is a family of Java tools for NLP and IR. There is a converter from CoNLL-U to GATE documents.[19]

Brat (Stenetorp et al., 2012) is an online editor (without full CoNLL-U support) and `conllu.js`[20] is a related JavaScript library used in the embedded CoNLL-U visualizations on the UD website.

5 Conclusion

Most of the current Udapi applications are focused on treebank developers. In future, we would like to focus also on other users, including NLP students, linguists and other researchers to make UD data more useful for them.

We hope Udapi will also serve as a common repository of interoperable NLP tools.

Acknowledgments

This work has been supported by projects GA15-10472S (Manyla), GAUK 1572314, and SVV 260 451. We thank the two anonymous reviewers for helpful feedback.

References

[Bejček et al.2013] Eduard Bejček, Eva Hajičová, Jan Hajič, Pavlína Jínová, Václava Kettnerová, Veronika Kolářová, Marie Mikulová, Jiří Mírovský, Anna Nedoluzhko, Jarmila Panevová, Lucie Poláková, Magda Ševčíková, Jan Štěpánek, and Šárka Zikánová. 2013. Prague Dependency Treebank 3.0. LINDAT/CLARIN digital library at the Institute of Formal and Applied Linguistics, Charles University in Prague.

---

[16] See footnote 3.
[17] `github.com/nltk/nltk/issues/875`
[18] `https://gate.ac.uk`
[19] `https://github.com/GateNLP/corpusconversion-universal-dependencies`
[20] `http://spyysalo.github.io/conllu.js/`

[Bird et al.2009] Steven Bird, Ewan Klein, and Edward Loper. 2009. *Natural Language Processing with Python*. O'Reilly Media, Inc., 1st edition.

[Bojar et al.2016] Ondřej Bojar, Ondřej Dušek, Tom Kocmi, Jindřich Libovický, Michal Novák, Martin Popel, Roman Sudarikov, and Dušan Variš. 2016. CzEng 1.6: Enlarged Czech-English Parallel Corpus with Processing Tools Dockered. In Petr Sojka, Aleš Horák, Ivan Kopeček, and Karel Pala, editors, *Text, Speech, and Dialogue: 19th International Conference, TSD 2016*, number 9924 in Lecture Notes in Computer Science, pages 231–238, Cham / Heidelberg / New York / Dordrecht / London. Masaryk University, Springer International Publishing.

[Cunningham et al.2011] Hamish Cunningham, Diana Maynard, Kalina Bontcheva, Valentin Tablan, Niraj Aswani, Ian Roberts, Genevieve Gorrell, Adam Funk, Angus Roberts, Danica Damljanovic, Thomas Heitz, Mark A. Greenwood, Horacio Saggion, Johann Petrak, Yaoyong Li, and Wim Peters. 2011. *Text Processing with GATE (Version 6)*.

[Nivre and Nilsson2005] Joakim Nivre and Jens Nilsson. 2005. Pseudo-projective dependency parsing. In *Proceedings of the 43rd Annual Meeting on Association for Computational Linguistics*, ACL '05, pages 99–106, Stroudsburg, PA, USA. Association for Computational Linguistics.

[Popel and Žabokrtský2010] Martin Popel and Zdeněk Žabokrtský. 2010. TectoMT: modular NLP framework. *Advances in Natural Language Processing*, pages 293–304.

[Stenetorp et al.2012] Pontus Stenetorp, Sampo Pyysalo, Goran Topić, Tomoko Ohta, Sophia Ananiadou, and Jun'ichi Tsujii. 2012. brat: a web-based tool for nlp-assisted text annotation. In *Proceedings of the Demonstrations at the 13th Conference of the European Chapter of the Association for Computational Linguistics*, pages 102–107. Association for Computational Linguistics.

[Straka et al.2016] Milan Straka, Jan Hajič, and Jana Straková. 2016. UDPipe: trainable pipeline for processing CoNLL-U files performing tokenization, morphological analysis, pos tagging and parsing. In *Proceedings of the Tenth International Conference on Language Resources and Evaluation (LREC'16)*, Paris, France, May. European Language Resources Association (ELRA).

Universal Dependencies for Greek

Prokopis Prokopidis
Institute for Language and
Speech Processing
Athena Research Center
Athens, Greece
prokopis@ilsp.gr

Haris Papageorgiou
Institute for Language and
Speech Processing
Athena Research Center
Athens, Greece
xaris@ilsp.gr

Abstract

This paper describes work towards the harmonization of the Greek Dependency Treebank with the Universal Dependencies v2 standard, and the extension of the treebank with enhanced dependencies. Experiments with the latest version of the UD_Greek resource have led to 88.94/87.66 LAS on gold/automatic POS, morphological features and lemmas.

1 Introduction

The Universal Dependencies (Nivre et al., 2016) community effort has led to the development and collection of a large number of treebanks adhering to common and extendible annotation guidelines. These guidelines aim to ease the annotation process and improve the accuracy of parsers and downstream NLP applications in generating useful and linguistically sound representations.

Greek is represented in the UD effort with UD_Greek[1]. In this paper, we provide more details on the annotated resource in section 2 and its conversion to the UD standard. In section 3 we discuss ongoing work for extending GDT with a subset of the enhanced dependencies proposed by Schuster and Manning (2016). Section 4 presents experiments with parsers trained on the different-sized versions of the resource and on manually/automatically annotated morphology and lemmas.

2 The Greek Dependency Treebank and its conversion to UD

UD_Greek is derived from the Greek Dependency Treebank (GDT, Prokopidis et al. (2005)), a resource developed and maintained by researchers at the Institute for Language and Speech Processing[2]. Although the conversion and harmonization to UD is work in progress since UD v1.1, the Greek dataset in the v2.0 release was the first one that involved extensive manual validation and correction of labeled dependencies generated from the orginial annotations.

The original annotation scheme used for the annotation of the resource was based on an adaptation of the guidelines for the Prague Dependency Treebank (Böhmová et al., 2003). Trees in the original data were headed by words bearing, in most cases, the `Pred` relation. Coordinating conjunctions and apposition markers headed participating tokens in relevant constructions. Prepositions and subordinating conjunctions acted as mediators between verbs/nouns and their phrasal and clausal dependents. The tagset used for the morphology layer in the original resource contained 584 combinations of basic POS tags and features that capture the rich morphology of the Greek language. As an example, the full tag `AjBaMaSgNm` for a word like *ταραχώδης/turbulent* denotes an adjective of basic degree, masculine gender, singular number and nominative case. The three last features are also used for nouns, articles, pronouns, and passive participles. Verb tags include features for tense and aspect, while articles are distinguished for definiteness. The top tree in Figure 1 presents an example of a dependency tree with basic POS tags.

Annotated documents in GDT are stored in XML files that integrate annotations for semantic roles and events. A procedure based on software described in Zeman et al. (2014) was used for rehanging nodes and changing labels in these files, so that annotations beyond the syntactic level were kept intact. The original heads and labels of the original annotation effort were stored as attributes of the XML elements corre-

---

Proceedings of the NoDaLiDa 2017 Workshop on Universal Dependencies (UDW 2017), pages 102–106,
Gothenburg, Sweden, 22 May 2017.

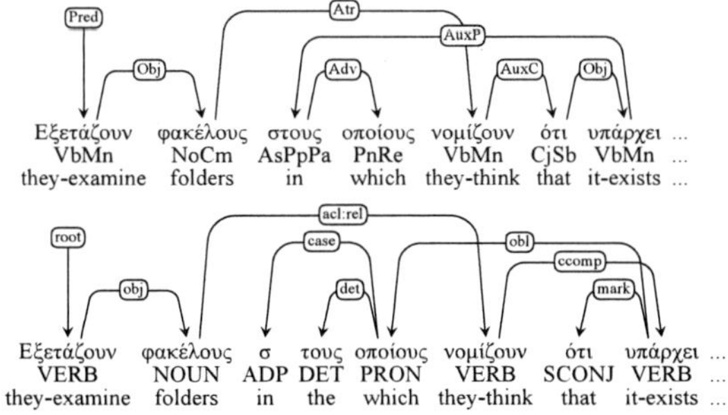

Figure 1: Annotation of a sentence fragment with a non-projective arc, according to the the original (top) and the current representation.

sponding to tree nodes. In view of the UD v2.0 release, the results of the automatic conversion were manually examined and corrected, in an effort focusing on errors related to core arguments of content words; heads of the copula; nodes participating in coordinating conjunctions; non-projective dependencies; and multi-word expressions acting as clause-introductory markers. Another difference to previous versions of the resource concerned preposition-article combinations (e.g. *στις/in-the/case/Prep3rdPersFemPlurAcc*). These multi-word tokens were split into words that were assigned morphological information and syntactic heads. The second tree in Figure 1 is an example involving several of the conversions mentioned above. The `acl:rel` relation in the example is a language specific extension used for the annotation of relative clauses. Another extension is `obl:arg`, which in the current version of the resource is used for prepositional arguments that cliticize and are described by many Greek grammars (e.g. Holton et al. (1997)) as indirect objects.

GDT is regularly updated with new material from different genres, and its current version comprises 178207/7417 tokens/sentences. The data in UD_Greek have also increased since v1.1 and currently[3] consist of 63441/2521 tokens/sentences. UD_Greek data are derived from annotated texts that are in the public domain, including Wikinews articles and European Parliament sessions. For the UD v2.* versions sentences are not shuffled and documents are not split across train/dev/test partitions. There are

10927/5894/6375 types/lemmas/hapax legomena in the resource, while the average sentence length is 25.17 tokens. Non-projective trees (12.38% of all sentences) allow for the intuitive representations of long-distance dependencies and non-configurational structures common in languages with flexible word order. The relatively free word order of Greek can also be inferred when examining typical head-dependent structures in the resource. Although determiners and adjectives almost always precede their nominal heads, the situation is different for arguments of verbs. Of the 2776 explicit subjects in UD_Greek, 32.89% occur to the right of their parent, while the percentage rises to 46.12% for subjects of verbs heading dependent clauses. The situation is more straightforward for non-pronominal objects, of which only 2.66% occur to the left of their head. Of those subjects and objects appearing in "non-canonical" positions, 21.58% and 29.63%, respectively, are of neuter gender. This fact can pose problems to parsing, since the case of nominative and accusative neuter homographs is particularly difficult to disambiguate, especially due to the fact that articles and adjectives often preceding them (e.g. *το/the κόκκινο/red βιβλίο/book*) are also invariant for these two case values.

3 Enhanced dependencies

A recent addition to the resource is semi-automatic annotation for the enhanced dependencies proposed by Schuster and Manning (2016). We have initially focused on a subset of these dependencies involving coordination and control structures.

For coordination structures, we have exploited the fact that conjunctions headed these constructions in the previous representation and that the ids of the heads of the conjuncts are still available in the current annotation files. We were thus able to convert trees like the one in Figure 2 to the enhanced dependency graph shown in the same example.

In the latest GDT version, no `ccomp/xcomp` distinction was included for Greek finite clauses that depend on verbs of obligatory subject or object control. We are currently using Lexis (Anagnostopoulou et al., 2000), a computational lexicon with syntactic and semantic information for Greek verbs, to annotate instances of these verbs with two extensions of the xcomp relation, `xcomp:sc` and `xcomp:oc`. These annotations allow us to gener-

---

[3]The dataset is available from `https://github.com/UniversalDependencies/UD_Greek/tree/dev`. The experiments described in Section 4 correspond to commit: `https://goo.gl/fhPmbN`.

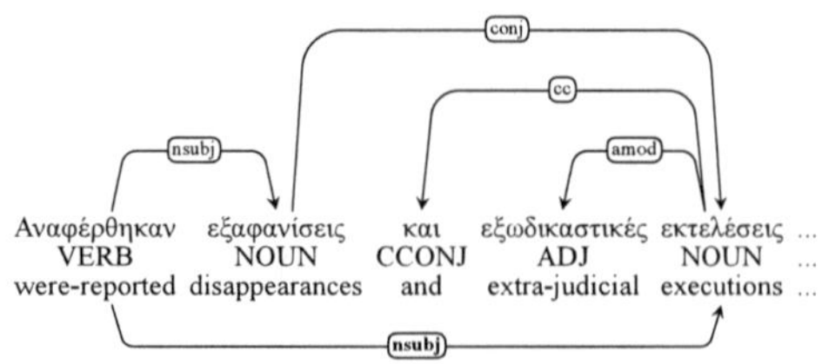

Figure 2: Enhanced dependency graph for a coordination structure.

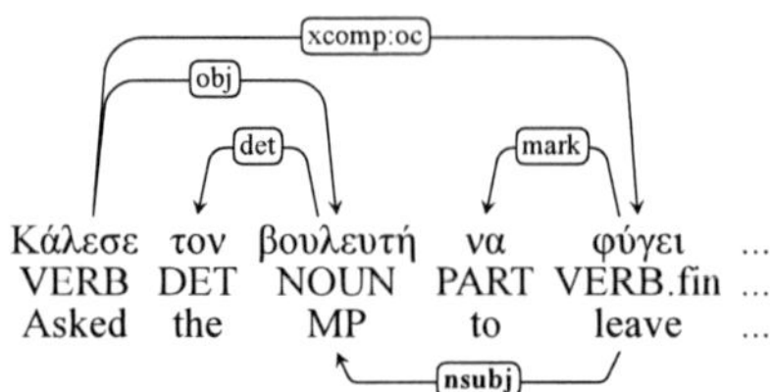

Figure 3: Enhanced dependency graph for an object control structure.

ate graphs like the object control one in Figure 3 and also the backward, subject control one in Figure 4.

4 Parsing experiments with the UD representation

In this section, we report on experiments with the current version of UD_Greek and its GDT superset. In all experiments reported below, we remove the annotations related to the enhanced dependencies described in Section 3, since they do not yet cover the whole resource. We examined parsing accuracy in scenarios involving manual and automatic annotations for morphology and lemmas. In the latter setting, POS tagging is conducted with a tagger (Papageorgiou et al., 2000) with an accuracy of 97.49 when only basic POS is considered. When all features (including, for example, gender and case for nouns, and aspect and tense for verbs) are taken into account, the tagger's accuracy drops to 92.54. As an indication of the relatively rich morphology of Greek, the tags/word ratio in the tagger's lexicon is 1.82. Tags for a word typically differ in only one or two features like case and gender for adjectives. However, distinct basic parts of speech (e.g. Vb/No) is also a possibility. Following POS tagging, a lemmatizer retrieves lemmas from a lexicon of 2M different entries. When a token under examination is associated in the lexicon with two or more lemmas, the lemmatizer uses information from the POS tags for

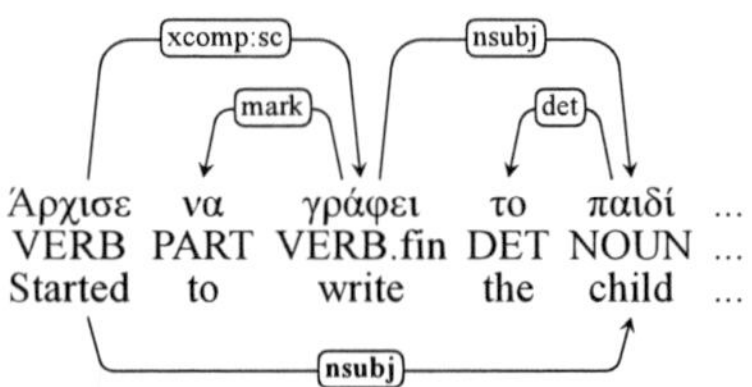

Figure 4: Enhanced dependency graph for a backward subject control structure.

disambiguation. For example, the token+POS input *εξετάσεις*/Vb guides the lemmatizer to retrieve the lemma *εξετάζω (examine)*, while the lemma *εξέταση (examination)* is returned for *εξετάσεις*/No.

We use the graph-based Mateparser (Bohnet, 2010) and the transition-based version of Bistparser (Kiperwasser and Goldberg, 2016). For the latter, we projectivise datasets by lifting non-projective arcs (Nivre and Nilsson, 2005), and we use 100-dimensional word-embeddings obtained with the `fastText` library (Bojanowski et al., 2016) from a 350M token corpus.

Table 1 summarizes the results. Using the whole resource with gold POS, morphological features and lemmas (GDT-MPL), the Mate and Bist LAS are 90.29/89.36, respectively. The difference between the two parsers on input with automatic annotations (GDT-APL) is smaller (88.82/88.36). When comparing the performance of both parsers on the different size datasets, the LAS improvement on the bigger dataset is more evident for Bistparser, with a 1.97% increase from the APL setting with the UD_Greek dataset (UD-APL). For both parsers, best LAS is observed for small sentences of 5-15 tokens long, with the accuracy remaining relatively stable for sentences of 15-25 tokens (cf. Fig. 5).

In related work, Prokopidis and Papageorgiou (2014) trained the Mateparser on a version of GDT of 130K tokens annotated according to the PDT-compatible representation, and reported a LAS of 80.16 on manually validated POS tags and lemmas. The automatically converted UD_Greek v1.* (59156/2411 tokens/sentences) has been used in evaluations for multilingual parsing, including the experiments by Straka et al. (2016), where 79.4/76.7 LAS were reported for manual/automatic POS tags, respectively.

	UD-MPL		UD-APL		GDT-MPL		GDT-APL	
	Bist	Mate	Bist	Mate	Bist	Mate	Bist	Mate
LAS	86.47	**88.94**	86.39	**87.66**	89.36	**90.29**	88.36	**88.82**
UAS	89.29	**90.78**	89.49	**90.49**	91.49	**92.01**	91.06	**91.38**
LACC	92.73	**93.68**	92.45	92.22	94.55	**94.70**	93.56	93.33

Table 1: Results from parsing UD_Greek and GDT with the Bist- and Mate parsers. UD_Greek contains 63K tokens, a subset of GDT's 178K tokens. (M/A)PL suffixes refer to training and testing on gold and automatic POS, morphological features and lemmas, respectively. All scores are calculated with punctuation excluded, on a test partition containing circa 10% of the tokens of each dataset.

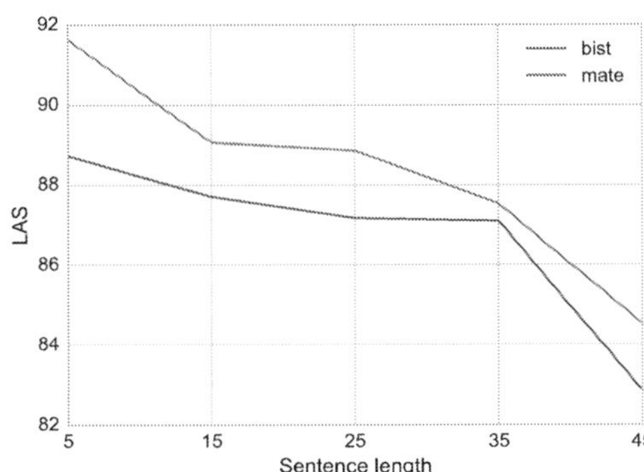

Figure 5: LAS relative to sentence length in the UD-APL setting.

5 Conclusions

We presented work for the harmonization of the syntactic trees in the Greek Dependency Treebank to the UD v.2 standard. We also discussed how we exploited previous annotations and a lexical resource to generate enhanced dependencies for the treebank. Finally, we reported a LAS of 88.94 for UD_Greek, by training the Mateparser on gold POS and lemmas. A 90.29 LAS on a larger version of the resource indicates that there is still room for accuracy improvements with additional data. While training on automatically preprocessed data, we obtain LAS scores (88.82) that are relatively high for morphologically rich languages like Greek. In future work, we plan to improve the enhanced dependencies annotation and augment the UD_Greek resource with sentences involving questions and commands.

References

Anagnostopoulou, D., E. Desipri, P. Labropoulou, E. Mantzari, and M. Gavrilidou (2000). Lexis - Lexicographical Infrastructure: Systematising the Data. In: *Computational Lexicography (COMLEX 2000)*.

Böhmová, A., J. Hajič, E. Hajičová, and B. Hladká (2003). The Prague Dependency Treebank: A Three-Level Annotation Scenario. In: *Treebanks: Building and Using Parsed Corpora*. Kluwer.

Bohnet, B. (2010). Very High Accuracy and Fast Dependency Parsing is Not a Contradiction. In: *Proceedings of the 23rd International Conference on Computational Linguistics*, pp. 89–97.

Bojanowski, P., E. Grave, A. Joulin, and T. Mikolov (2016). Enriching Word Vectors with Subword Information. In: *CoRR abs/1607.04606*.

Holton, D., P. Mackridge, and I. Philippaki-Warburton (1997). Greek: A comprehensive grammar of the modern language. London and New York: Routledge.

Kiperwasser, E. and Y. Goldberg (2016). Simple and Accurate Dependency Parsing Using Bidirectional LSTM Feature Representations. In: *Transactions of the Association for Computational Linguistics* 4, pp. 313–327.

Nivre, J., M.-C. de Marneffe, F. Ginter, Y. Goldberg, J. Hajic, C. D. Manning, R. McDonald, S. Petrov, S. Pyysalo, N. Silveira, R. Tsarfaty, and D. Zeman (2016). Universal Dependencies v1: A Multilingual Treebank Collection. In: *Proceedings of the Tenth International Conference on Language Resources and Evaluation (LREC 2016)*.

Nivre, J. and J. Nilsson (2005). Pseudo-Projective Dependency Parsing. In: *Proceedings of the 43rd Annual Meeting of the Association for Computational Linguistics (ACL)*, pp. 99–106.

Papageorgiou, H., P. Prokopidis, V. Giouli, and S. Piperidis (2000). A Unified POS Tagging Architecture and its Application to Greek. In: *Proceedings of the 2nd Language Resources and Evaluation Conference*. European Language Resources Association, pp. 1455–1462.

Prokopidis, P., E. Desypri, M. Koutsombogera, H. Papageorgiou, and S. Piperidis (2005). Theoretical and practical issues in the construction of a Greek Dependency Treebank. In: *Proceedings of the Fourth Workshop on Treebanks and Linguistic Theories*.

Prokopidis, P. and H. Papageorgiou (2014). Experiments for Dependency Parsing of Greek. In: *Proceedings of the First Joint Workshop on Statistical Parsing of Morphologically Rich Languages and Syntactic Analysis of Non-Canonical Languages*, pp. 90–96.

Schuster, S. and C. D. Manning (2016). Enhanced English Universal Dependencies: An Improved Representation for Natural Language Understanding Tasks. In: *Proceedings of the Tenth International Conference on Language Resources and Evaluation (LREC 2016)*.

Straka, M., J. Hajic, and J. Straková (2016). UDPipe: Trainable Pipeline for Processing CoNLL-U Files Performing Tokenization, Morphological Analysis, POS Tagging and Parsing. In: *Proceedings of the Tenth International Conference on Language Resources and Evaluation (LREC 2016)*.

Zeman, D., O. Dušek, D. Mareček, M. Popel, L. Ramasamy, J. Štěpánek, Z. Žabokrtský, and J. Hajič (2014). HamleDT: Harmonized multilanguage dependency treebank. In: *Language Resources and Evaluation* 48.4, pp. 601–637.

From Universal Dependencies to Abstract Syntax

Aarne Ranta
University of Gothenburg
aarne@chalmers.se

Prasanth Kolachina
University of Gothenburg
prasanth.kolachina@gu.se

Abstract

Abstract syntax is a tectogrammatical tree representation, which can be shared between languages. It is used for programming languages in compilers, and has been adapted to natural languages in GF (Grammatical Framework). Recent work has shown how GF trees can be converted to UD trees, making it possible to generate parallel synthetic treebanks for those 30 languages that are currently covered by GF. This paper attempts to invert the mapping: take UD trees from standard treebanks and reconstruct GF trees from them. Such a conversion is potentially useful in bootstrapping treebanks by translation. It can also help GF-based interlingual translation by providing a robust, efficient front end. However, since UD trees are based on natural (as opposed to generated) data and built manually or by machine learning (as opposed to rules), the conversion is not trivial. This paper will present a basic algorithm, which is essentially based on inverting the GF to UD conversion. This method enables covering around 70% of nodes, and the rest can be covered by approximative back up strategies. Analysing the reasons of the incompleteness reveals structures missing in GF grammars, but also some problems in UD treebanks.

1 Introduction

GF (Grammatical Framework (Ranta, 2011)) is a formalism for multilingual grammars. Similarly to UD (Universal Dependencies, (Nivre et al., 2016)), GF uses shared syntactic descriptions for multiple languages. In GF, this is achieved by using **abstract syntax trees**, similar to the internal representations used in compilers and to Curry's

tectogrammatical formulas (Curry, 1961). Given an abstract syntax tree, strings in different languages can be derived mechanically by **linearization functions** written for that language, similar to pretty-printing rules in compilers and to Curry's phenogrammatical rules. The linearization functions of GF are by design reversible to parsers, which convert strings to abstract syntax trees. Figure 1 gives a very brief summary of GF to readers unfamiliar with GF.

In UD, the shared descriptions are dependency labels and part of speech tags used in dependency trees. The words in the leaves of UD trees are language-specific, and languages can extend the core tagset and labels to annotate constructions in the language. The relation between trees and strings is not defined by grammar rules, but by constructing a set of example trees—a treebank. From a treebank, a parser is typically constructed by machine learning (Nivre, 2006). There is no mechanical way to translate a UD tree from one language to other languages. But such a translation can be approximated in different ways to bootstrap treebanks (Tiedemann and Agic, 2016).

GF's linearization can convert abstract syntax trees to UD trees (Kolachina and Ranta, 2016). This conversion can be used for generating multilingual (and parallel) treebanks from a given set of GF trees. However, to reach the full potential of the GF-UD correspondence, it would also be useful to go to the opposite direction, to convert UD trees to GF trees. Then one could translate standard UD treebanks to new languages. One could also use dependency parsing as a robust front-end to a translator, which uses GF linearization as a grammaticality-preserving backend (Angelov et al., 2014), or to a logical form generator in the style of (Reddy et al., 2016), but where GF trees give an accurate intermediate representation in the style of (Ranta, 2004). Figure 2 shows both of these scenarios, using the term **gf2ud** for the con-

107

Proceedings of the NoDaLiDa 2017 Workshop on Universal Dependencies (UDW 2017), pages 107–116,
Gothenburg, Sweden, 22 May 2017.

The abstract syntax defines a set of **categories**, such as CN (Common Noun) and AP (Adjectival Phrase), and a set of **functions**, such as ModCN (modification of CN with AP):

```
cat CN ; AP
fun ModCN : AP -> CN -> CN
```

A concrete syntax defines, for each category, a **linearization type**, and for each function, a **linearization function**; these can make use of **parameters**. For English, we need a parameter type Number (singular or plural). We define CN as a **table** (similar to an inflection table), which produces a string as a function Number (Number=>Str). As AP is not inflected, it is just a string. Adjectival modification places the AP before the CN, passing the number to the CN head of the construction:

```
param Number = Sg | Pl
lincat CN = Number => Str
lincat AP = Str
lin ModCN ap cn = \\n => ap ++ cn ! n
```

In French, we also need the parameter of gender. An AP depends on both gender and number. A CN has a table on Number like in English, but in addition, an inherent gender. The table and the gender are collected into a **record**. Adjectival modification places the AP after the CN, passing the inherent gender of the CN head to the AP, and the number to both constituents:

```
param Gender = Masc | Fem
```

```
lincat CN = {s : Number => Str ; g : Gender}
lincat AP = Gender => Number => Str
lin ModCN ap cn = {
  s = \\n => cn ! n ++ ap ! cn.g ! n ;
  g = cn.g
}
```

Context-free grammars correspond to a special case of GF where Str is the only linearization type. The use of tables (P=>T) and records ({a : A ; b : B}) makes GF more expressive than context-free grammars. The distinction between dependent and inherent features, as well as the restriction of tables to finite parameter types, makes GF less expressive than unification grammars. Formally, GF is equivalent to PMCFG (Parallel Multiple Context-Free Grammars) (Seki et al., 1991), as shown in (Ljunglöf, 2004), and has polynomial parsing complexity. The power of PMCFG has shown to be what is needed to share an abstract syntax across languages. In addition to morphological variation and agreement, it permits discontinuous constituents (used heavily e.g. in German) and reduplication (used e.g. in Chinese questions). The GF Resource Grammar Library uses a shared abstract syntax for currently 32 languages (Indo-European, Fenno-Ugric, Semitic and East Asian) written by over 50 contributors.

Software, grammars, and documentation are available in
`http://www.grammaticalframework.org`

Figure 1: GF in a nutshell. The text works out a simple GF grammar of adjectival modification in English and French, showing how the structure can be shared despite differences in word order and agreement.

version of Kolachina and Ranta (2016) and **ud2gf** for the inverse procedure, which is the topic of this paper.

GF was originally designed for multilingual generation in controlled language scenarios, not for wide-coverage parsing. The GF Resource Grammar Library (Ranta, 2009) thus does not cover everything in all languages, but just a "semantically complete subset", in the sense that it provides ways to express all kinds of content, but not necessarily all possible ways to express it. It is has therefore been interesting to see how much of the syntax in UD treebanks is actually covered, to assess the completeness of the library. In the other direction, some of the difficulties in ud2gf mapping suggest that UD does not always annotate syntax in the most logical way, or in a way that is maximally general across languages.

The work reported in this paper is the current status of work in progress. Therefore the results are not conclusive: in particular, we expect to improve the missing coverage in a straightforward way. The most stable part of the work is the annotation algorithm described in Sections 3 an 4. It is based on a general notation for dependency configurations, which can be applied to any GF grammar and to any dependency annotation scheme—not only to the UD scheme. The code for the algorithm and the annotations used in experiments is available open source.[1]

The structure of the paper is as follows: Section 2 summarizes the existing gf2ud conversion and formulates the problem of inverting it. Section 3 describes a baseline bottom-up algorithm for translation from UD trees to GF trees. Section 4 presents some refinements to the basic algorithm. Section 5 shows a preliminary evaluation with UD treebanks for English, Finnish, and Swedish. Section 6 concludes.

2 From gf2ud to ud2gf

The relation between UD and GF is defined declaratively by a set of **dependency configurations**. These configurations specify the dependency labels that attach to each subtree in a GF tree. Figure 3 shows an abstract syntax specification to-

---

[1] `https://github.com/GrammaticalFramework/gf-contrib/tree/master/ud2gf`

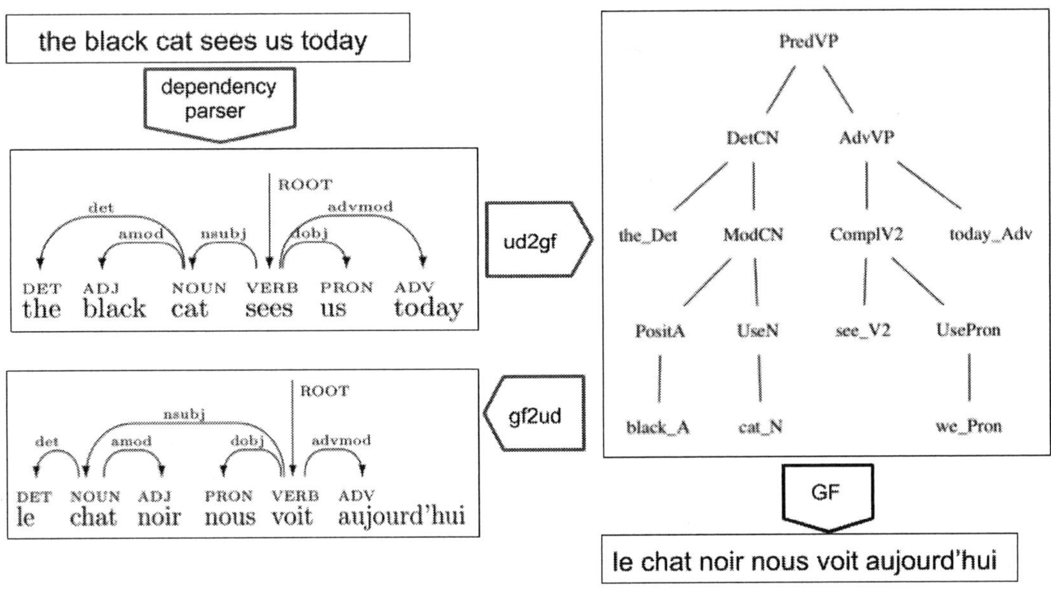

Figure 2: Conversions between UD trees, GF trees, and surface strings in English and French.

gether with a dependency configuration, as well as a GF tree with corresponding labels attached.

Consider, for example, the second line of the "abstract syntax" part of Figure 3, with the symbol ComplV2. This symbol is one of the **functions** that are used for building the abstract syntax tree. Such a function takes a number of trees (zero or more) as arguments and combines them to a larger tree. Thus ComplV2 takes a V2 tree (two-place verb) and an NP tree (noun phrase) to construct a VP tree (verb phrase). Its name hints that it performs complementation, i.e. combines verbs with their complements. Its dependency configuration head dobj specifies that the first argument (the verb) will contain the label head in UD, whereas the second argument (the noun phrase) will contain the label dobj (direct object). When the configuration is applied to a tree, the head labels are omitted, since they are the default. Notice that the order of arguments in an abstract syntax tree is independent of the order of words in its linearizations. Thus, in Figure 2, the object is placed after the verb in English but before the verb in French.

The algorithm for deriving the UD tree from the annotated GF tree is simple:

- for each leaf X (which corresponds to a lexical item)
    - follow the path up towards the root until you encounter a label L
    - from the node immediately above L, follow the **spine** (the unlabelled branches) down to another leaf Y
    - Y is the head of X with label L

It is easy to verify that the UD trees in Figure 2 can be obtained in this way, together with the English and French linearization rules that produce the surface words and the word order. In addition to the configurations of functions, we need **category configurations**, which map GF types to UD part of speech (POS) tags.

This algorithm covers what Kolachina and Ranta (2016) call **local abstract configurations**. They are sufficient for most cases of the gf2ud conversion, and have the virtue of being compositional and exactly the same for all languages. However, since the syntactic analysis of GF and UD are not exactly the same, and within UD can moreover differ between languages, some **non-local** and **concrete** configurations are needed in addition. We will return to these after showing how the local abstract configurations are used in ud2gf.

The path from GF trees to UD trees (**gf2ud**) is deterministic: it is just linearization to an annotated string representing a dependency tree. It defines a relation between GF trees and UD trees: *GF tree t produces UD tree u*. Since the mapping involves loss of information, it is many-to-

```
abstract syntax                          dependency configuration

PredVP   : NP   -> VP   -> Cl       nsubj  head
ComplV2  : V2   -> NP   -> VP       head   dobj
AdvVP    : VP   -> Adv  -> VP       head   advmod
DetCN    : Det  -> CN   -> NP       det    head
ModCN    : AP   -> CN   -> CN       amod   head
UseN     : N          -> CN        head
UsePron  : Pron -> NP              head
PositA   : A          -> AP         Head

cat A                               ADJ
cat Adv                             ADV
cat Det                             DET
cat N                               NOUN
cat Pron                            PRON
cat V2                              VERB
```

Figure 3: Annotating a GF tree with dependency labels. The label `dobj` results from the annotation of the `ComplV2` function. The category annotation (`cat`) are used in Figures 1 and 3 to map between GF categories and UD POS tags.

one. The opposite direction, ud2gf, is a nondeterministic search problem: *given a UD tree u, find all GF trees t that can produce u.* The first problem we have to solve is thus

> **Ambiguity**: a UD tree can correspond to many GF trees.

More problems are caused by the fact that GF trees are formally generated by a grammar whereas UD trees have no grammar. Thus a UD tree may lack a corresponding GF tree for many different reasons:

> **Incompleteness**: the GF grammar is incomplete.
> **Noise**: the UD tree has annotation errors.
> **Ungrammaticality**: the original sentence has grammar errors.

Coping with these problems requires **robustness** of the ud2gf conversion. The situation is similar to the problems encountered when GF is used for wide-coverage parsing and translation (Angelov et al., 2014). The solution is also similar, as it combines a declarative rule-based approach with disambiguation and a back-up strategy.

3   The ud2gf basic algorithm

The basic algorithm is illustrated in Figure 4

Its main data-structure is an **annotated dependency tree**, where each node has the form

$$< L, t, ts, C, p > \text{ where}$$

- L is a dependency label (always the same as in the original UD tree)
- t is the current GF abstract syntax tree (iteratively changed by the algorithm)
- ts is a list of alternative GF abstract syntax trees (iteratively changed by the algorithm)
- C is the GF category of t (iteratively changed by the algorithm)
- p is the position of the original word in the UD tree (always the same as in the original UD tree)

Examples of such nodes are shown in Figure 4, in the tree marked (5) and in all trees below it.

The algorithm works in the following steps, with references to Figure 4:

1. **Restructuring**. Convert the CoNLL graph (marked (2) in Figure 4) to a tree data-structure (3), where each node is labelled by a dependency label, lemma, POS tag, and word position. This step is simple and completely deterministic, provided that the graph is a well-formed tree; if it

Restructuring and lexical annotation

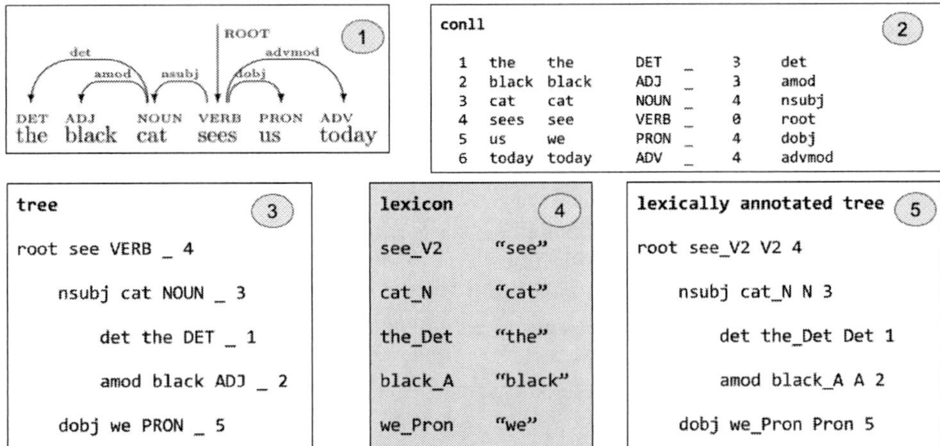

A node annotation by endo- and exocentric functions

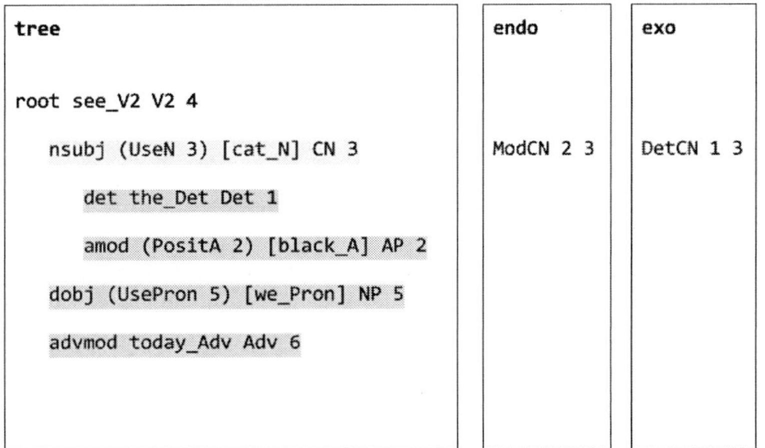

The final annotated tree

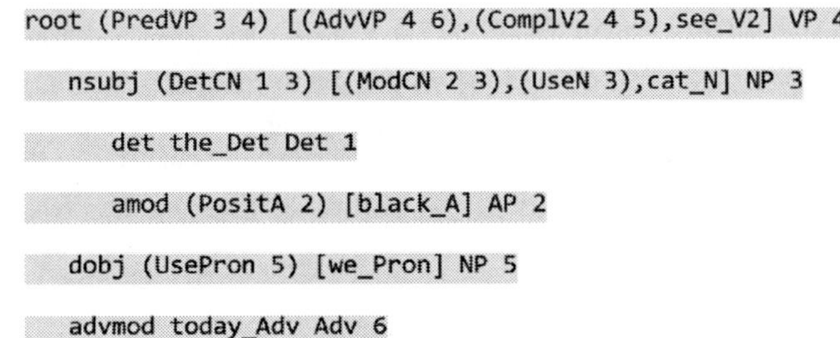

Figure 4: Steps in ud2gf

isn't, the conversion fails[2].

2. **Lexical annotation**. Preserve the tree structure in (3) but change the structure of nodes to the one described above and shown in (5). This is done by using a GF lexicon (4), and a category configuration, replacing each lemma with a GF abstract syntax function and its POS with a GF category.[3]

3. **Syntactic annotation**. The GF trees t in the initial tree (5) are lexical (0-argument) functions. The syntactic annotation step annotates the tree recursively with applications of syntactic combination functions. Some of them may be **endofunctions** (i.e. **endocentric** functions), in the sense that some of the argument types is the same as the value type. In Figure 3, the functions AdvVP and ModCN are endocentric. All other functions are **exofunctions** (i.e. **exocentric** functions), where none of the argument types is the same as the value type. In the syntactic annotation, it is important to apply endofunctions before exofunctions, because exofunctions could otherwise block later applications of endofunctions.[4] The algorithm is a depth-first postorder traversal: for an annotated tree $T = (N\,T_1 \ldots T_n)$, where $N = <L, t, ts, C, p>$,

- syntax-annotate the subtrees $T_1, \ldots, T_n$
- apply available combination functions to N:
    - if an endofunction $f : C \to C$ applies, replace $< t, ts >$ with $< ((ft), \{t\} \cup ts >$
    - else, if an exofunction $f : C \to C'$ applies, replace $< t, ts, C >$ with $< (ft), \{t\} \cup ts, C' >$

where a function $f : A \to B$ **applies** if $f = (\lambda x)(g \ldots x \ldots)$ where g is an endo- or exocentric function on C and all other argument places than x are filled with GF trees from the subtrees of T. Every subtree can be used at most once.

An example of syntactic annotation is shown in the middle part of Figure 4. The node for the word *cat* at position 3 (the second line in the tree) has one applicable endofunction, ModCN (adjectival modification), and one exofunction, DetCN (determination). Hence the application of the endofunction ModCN combines the AP in position 2 with the CN in position 3. For brevity, the subtrees

that the functions can apply to are marked by the position numbers. [5] Hence the tree

```
DetCN 1 3
```

in the final annotated tree actually expands to

```
DetCN the_Det
   (ModCN (PositA black_A) (UseN cat_N))
```

by following these links. The whole GF tree at the root node expands to the tree shown in Figures 2 and 3.

4 Refinements of the basic algorithm

We noted in Section 2 that ud2gf has to deal with ambiguity, incompleteness, noise, and ungrammaticality. The basic algorithm of Section 3 takes none of these aspects into account. But it does contain what is needed for ambiguity: the list ts of previous trees at each node can also be used more generally for storing alternative trees. The "main" tree t is then compared and ranked together with these candidates. Ranking based on tree probabilities in previous GF treebanks, as in (Angelov, 2011), is readily available. But an even more important criterion is the **node coverage** of the tree. This means penalizing heavily those trees that don't cover all nodes in the subtrees.

This leads us to the problem of incompleteness: what happens if the application of all possible candidate functions and trees still does not lead to a tree covering all nodes? An important part of this problem is due to **syncategorematic words**. For instance, the copula in GF is usually introduced as a part of the linearization, and does not have a category or function of its own.[6] To take the simplest possible example, consider the adjectival predication function and its linearization:

```
fun UseAP : AP -> VP
lin UseAP ap = \\agr => be agr ++ ap
```

where the agreement feature of the verb phrase is passed to an auxiliary function be, which produces the correct form of the copula when the subject is added. The sentence *the cat is black* has the following tree obtained from UD:

---

[2]This has never happened with the standard UD treebanks that we have worked with.

[3]The GF lexicon is obtained from the GF grammar by linearizing each lexical item (i.e. zero-place function) to the form that is used as the lemma in the UD treebank for the language in question.

[4]This is a simplifying assumption: a chain of two or more exofunctions could in theory bring us back to the same category as we started with.

[5]If the argument has the same node as the head (like 3 here), the position refers to the next-newest item on the list of trees.

[6]This is in (Kolachina and Ranta, 2016) motivated by cross-lingual considerations: there are languages that don't need copulas. In (Croft et al., 2017), the copula is defined as a **strategy**, which can be language-dependent, in contrast to **constructions**, which are language-independent. This distinction seems to correspond closely to concrete vs. abstract syntax in GF.

```
root (PredVP 2 4) [UseAP...black_A] S 4
  nsubj (DetCN 1 2) [UseN 2,cat_N] 2
    det the_Det Det 1
  cop "be" String 3 ***
```

The resulting GF tree is correct, but it does not cover node 3 containing the copula.[7] The problem is the same in gf2ud (Kolachina and Ranta, 2016), which introduces language-specific concrete annotations to endow syncategorematic words with UD labels. Thus the concrete annotation

```
UseAP head {"is","are","am"} cop head
```

specifies that the words *is,are,am* occurring in a tree linearized from a `UseAP` application have the label cop attached to the head.

In ud2gf, the treatment of the copula turned out to be simpler than in gf2ud. What we need is to postulate an abstract syntax category of copulas and a function that uses the copula. This function has the following type and configuration:

```
UseAP_ : Cop_ -> AP -> VP ; cop head
```

It is used in the basic algorithm in the same way as ordinary functions, but eliminated from the final tree by an explicit definition:

```
UseAP_ cop ap = UseAP ap
```

The copula is captured from the UD tree by applying a category configuration that has a condition about the lemma:[8]

```
Cop_ VERB lemma=be
```

This configuration is used at the lexical annotation phase, so that the last line of the tree for *the cat is black* becomes

```
cop be Cop_ 3
```

Hence the final tree built for the sentence is

```
PredVP (DetCN the_Det (UseN cat_N))
  (UseAP_ be (PositA black_A))
```

which covers the entire UD tree. By applying the explicit definition of `UseAP_`, we obtain the standard GF tree

```
PredVP (DetCN the_Det (UseN cat_N))
  (UseAP (PositA black_A))
```

Many other syncategorematic words—such as negations, tense auxiliaries, infinitive marks—can

be treated in a similar way. The eliminated constants are called **helper functions** and **helper categories**, and for clarity suffixed with underscores.

Another type of incomplete coverage is due to missing functions in the grammar, annotation errors, and actual grammar errors in the source text. To deal with these, we have introduced another type of extra functions: **backup functions**. These functions collect the uncovered nodes (marked with ***) and attach them to their heads as adverbial modifiers. The nodes collected as backups are marked with single asterisks (*). In the evaluation statistics, they are counted as **uninterpreted nodes**, meaning that they are not covered with the standard GF grammar. But we have added linearization rules to them, so that they are for instance reproduced in translations. Figure 5 gives an example of a UD tree thus annotated, and the corresponding translations to Finnish and Swedish, as well as back to English. What has happened is that the temporal modifier formed from the bare noun phrase *next week* and labelled `nmod:tmod` has not found a matching rule in the configurations. The translations of the resulting backup string are shown in brackets.

5 First results

The ud2gf algorithm and annotations are tested using the UD treebanks (v1.4)[9]. The training section of the treebank was used to develop the annotations and the results are reported on the test section. We evaluated the performance in terms of coverage and interpretability of the GF trees derived from the translation. The coverage figures show the percentage of dependency nodes (or tokens) covered, and interpreted nodes show the percentage nodes covered in "normal" categories, that is, other than the Backup category. The percentage of interpreted nodes is calculated as the number of nodes in the tree that use a Backup function to cover all its children. Additionally, the GF trees can be translated back into strings using the concrete grammar, allowing for qualitative evaluation of the translations to the original and other languages.[10]

We performed experiments for three languages: English, Swedish and Finnish. Table 1 show the scores for the experiments using the gold UD

---

[7]We use *** to mark uncovered nodes; since *be* has no corresponding item in the GF lexicon, its only possible categorization is as a `String` literal.

[8]The simplicity is due to the fact that the trees in the treebank are lemmatized, which means that we need not match with all forms of the copula.

[9]`https://github.com/UniversalDependencies/`, retrieved in October 2016

[10]A quantitative evaluation would also be possible by standard machine translation metrics, but has not been done yet.

```
I have a change in plans next week .

root have_V2 : V2 2                      I have a change in plans "."
  nsubj i_Pron : Pron 1                  [ next week ]
  dobj change_N : N 4
    det IndefArt : Quant 3               minulla on muutos suunnitelmissa "."
    nmod plan_N : N 6                    [ seuraava viikko ]
      case in_Prep : Prep 5
  nmod:tmod Backup week_N : N 8 *        jag har en ändring i planer "."
    amod next_A : A 7 *                  [ nästa vecka ]
  punct "." : String 9
```

Figure 5: A tree from the UD English training treebank with lexical annotations and backups marked, and the resulting linearizations to English, Finnish, and Swedish.

language	#trees	#confs	%cov'd	%int'd
English	2077	31	94	72
Finnish	648	12	92	61
Finnish*	648	0	74	55
Swedish	1219	26	91	65
Swedish*	1219	0	75	57

Table 1: Coverage of nodes in each test set (L-ud-test.conllu). L* (Swedish*, Finnish*) is with language-independent configurations only. #conf's is the number of language-specific configurations. %cov'd and %int'd are the percentages of covered and interpreted nodes, respectively.

rule type	number
GF function (given)	346
GF category (given)	109
backup function	16
function config	128
category config	33
helper function	250
helper category*	26

Table 2: Estimating the size of the project: GF abstract syntax (as given in the resource grammar library) and its abstract and concrete configurations. Helper category definitions are the only genuinely language-dependent configurations, as they refer to lemmas.

trees. Also shown are the number of trees (i.e. sentences) in the test set for each language. The results show an incomplete coverage, as nodes are not yet completely covered by the available Backup functions. As a second thing, we see the impact of language-specific configurations (mostly defining helper categories for syncategorematic words) on the interpretability of GF trees. For example, in Swedish, just a small number of such categories (26) increases the coverage significantly. Further experiments also showed an average increase of 4-6% points in interpretability scores when out-of-vocabulary words were handled using additional functions based on the part-of-speech tags; in other words, more than 10% of uninterpreted nodes contained words not included in the available GF lexica.

Table 2 shows how much work was needed in the configurations. It shows the number of GF functions (excluding the lexical ones) and language-independent configurations. It reveals that there are many GF functions that are not yet reached by configurations, and which would be likely to increase the interpreted nodes. The helper categories in Table 2, such as Copula, typically refer to lemmas. These categories, even though they can be used in language-independent helper rules, become actually usable only if the language-specific configuration gives ways to construct them.

A high number of helper functions were needed to construct tensed verb phrases (VPS) covering all combinations of auxiliary verbs and negations in the three languages. This is not surprising given the different ways in which tenses are realized across languages. The extent to which these helper functions can be shared across languages depends on where the information is annotated in the UD tree and how uniform the annotations are; in English, Swedish, and Finnish, the compound tense systems are similar to each other, whereas negation mechanisms are quite different.

Modal verbs outside the tense system were another major issue in gf2ud (Kolachina and Ranta, 2016), but this issue has an easier solution in ud2gf. In GF resource grammars, modal verbs are a special case of VP-complement verbs (VV), which also contains non-modal verbs. The complementation function `ComplVV` hence needs two configurations:

```
ComplVV : VV->VP->VP ; head xcomp
ComplVV : VV->VP->VP ; aux  head
```

The first configuration is valid for the cases where the VP complement is marked using the `xcomp` label (e.g. *want to sleep*). The second one covers the cases where the VP complement is treated as the head and the VV is labelled aux (e.g. *must sleep*). The choice of which verbs are modal is language-specific. For example, the verb *want* marked as VV in GF is non-nodal in English but translated in Swedish as an auxiliary verb *vilja*. In gf2ud, modal verbs need non-local configurations, but in ud2gf, we handle them simply by using alternative configurations as shown above.

Another discrepancy across languages was found in the treatment of progressive verb phrases (e.g. *be reading*, Finnish *olla lukemassa*). in English the verb *be* is annotated as a child of the content verb with the aux label. In Finnish, however the equivalent verb *olla* is marked as the head and the content verb as the child with the `xcomp` label. This is a case of where the content word is not chosen to be the head, but the choice is more syntax-driven.

6 Conclusion

The main rationale of relating UD with GF is their complementary strengths. Generally speaking, UD strengths lie in parsing and GF strengths in generation. UD pipelines are robust and fast at analyzing large texts. GF on the other hand, allows for accurate generation in multiple languages apart from compositional semantics. This suggests pipelines where UD feeds GF.

In this paper, we have done preparatory work for such a pipeline. Most of the work can be done on a language-independent level of abstract syntax configurations. This brings us currently to around 70–75 % coverage of nodes, which applies automatically to new languages. A handful of language-specific configurations (mostly for syncategorematic words) increases the coverage to 90–95%. The configuration notation is generic

property	UD	GF
parser coverage	robust	brittle
parser speed	fast	slow
disambiguation	cont.-sensitive	context-free
semantics	loose	compositional
generation	?	accurate
new language	low-level work	high-level work

Table 3: Complementary strengths and weaknesses of GF and UD. UD strengths above the dividing line, GF strengths below.

and can be applied to any GF grammar and dependency scheme.

Future work includes testing the pipeline in applications such as machine translation, abstractive summarization, logical form extraction, and treebank bootstrapping. A more theoretical line of work includes assessing the universality of current UD praxis following the ideas of Croft et al. (2017). In particular, their distinction between **constructions** and **strategies** seems to correspond to what we have implemented with shared vs. language-specific configurations, respectively.

Situations where a shared rule would be possible but the treebanks diverge, such as the treatment of VP-complement verbs and progressives (Section 5), would deserve closer inspection. Also an analysis of UD Version 2, which became available in the course of the project, would be in place, with the expectation that the differences between languages decrease.

Acknowledgements

We want to thank Joakim Nivre and the anonymous referees for helpful comments on the work. The project has been funded by the REMU project (Reliable Multilingual Digital Communication, Swedish Research Council 2012-5746).

References

Krasimir Angelov, Björn Bringert, and Aarne Ranta. 2014. Speech-enabled hybrid multilingual translation for mobile devices. In *Proceedings of the Demonstrations at the 14th Conference of the European Chapter of the Association for Computational Linguistics*, pages 41–44, Gothenburg, Sweden, April. Association for Computational Linguistics.

Krasimir Angelov. 2011. *The Mechanics of the Grammatical Framework*. Ph.D. thesis, Chalmers University of Technology.

William Croft, Dawn Nordquist, Katherine Looney, and Michael Regan. 2017. Linguistic Typology meets Universal Dependencies. In *Treebanks and Linguistic Theories (TLT-2017)*, pages 63–75, Bloomington IN, January 20–21.

Haskell B. Curry. 1961. Some Logical Aspects of Grammatical Structure. In *Structure of Language and its Mathematical Aspects: Proceedings of the Twelfth Symposium in Applied Mathematics*, pages 56–68. American Mathematical Society.

Prasanth Kolachina and Aarne Ranta. 2016. From Abstract Syntax to Universal Dependencies. *Linguistic Issues in Language Technology*, 13(2).

Peter Ljunglöf. 2004. *The Expressivity and Complexity of Grammatical Framework*. Ph.D. thesis, Department of Computing Science, Chalmers University of Technology and University of Gothenburg.

Joakim Nivre, Marie-Catherine de Marneffe, Filip Ginter, Yoav Goldberg, Jan Hajic, Christopher D. Manning, Ryan McDonald, Slav Petrov, Sampo Pyysalo, Natalia Silveira, Reut Tsarfaty, and Daniel Zeman. 2016. Universal Dependencies v1: A Multilingual Treebank Collection. In *Proceedings of the Tenth International Conference on Language Resources and Evaluation (LREC 2016)*, Paris, France, May. European Language Resources Association (ELRA).

Joakim Nivre. 2006. *Inductive Dependency Parsing*. Springer.

Aarne Ranta. 2004. Computational Semantics in Type Theory. *Mathematics and Social Sciences*, 165:31–57.

Aarne Ranta. 2009. The GF Resource Grammar Library. *Linguistic Issues in Language Technology*, 2(2).

Aarne Ranta. 2011. *Grammatical Framework: Programming with Multilingual Grammars*. CSLI Publications, Stanford.

Siva Reddy, Oscar Täckström, Michael Collins, Tom Kwiatkowski, Dipanjan Das, Mark Steedman, and Mirella Lapata. 2016. Transforming Dependency Structures to Logical Forms for Semantic Parsing. *Transactions of the Association for Computational Linguistics*, 4.

Hiroyuki Seki, Takashi Matsumura, Mamoru Fujii, and Tadao Kasami. 1991. On multiple context-free grammars. *Theoretical Computer Science*, 88(2):191–229.

Jörg Tiedemann and Zeljko Agic. 2016. Synthetic treebanking for cross-lingual dependency parsing. *The Journal of Artificial Intelligence Research (JAIR)*, 55:209–248.

Empirically sampling Universal Dependencies

Natalie Schluter
IT University of Copenhagen
natschluter@itu.dk

Željko Agić
IT University of Copenhagen
zeag@itu.dk

Abstract

Universal Dependencies incur a high cost in computation for unbiased system development. We propose a 100% empirically chosen small subset of UD languages for efficient parsing system development. The technique used is based on measurements of model capacity globally. We show that the diversity of the resulting representative language set is superior to the requirements-based procedure.

1 Introduction

The development of natural language parsing systems has historically relied mainly on the central benchmarking dataset the Penn Treebank, as well as, to a lesser extent, a restrictive selection of very well-resourced languages like German and Chinese. This is problematic in that (1) the development of the technology risks being highly biased towards English and other resource-rich languages and their particular annotations for syntax, (2) the technology is inadequately benchmarked against a central group of languages that do not reflect the linguistic diversity required to adequately evaluate parsing systems with respect to language in general, and (3) the development of linguistic resources for unrepresented or poorly represented languages continues to be erroneously regarded as independent of the development of parsing systems, rather than integral to it.

The Universal Dependencies (UD) project (Nivre et al., 2016), has made great strides towards remedying this situation, by providing a single unified syntactic framework and related support for treebank development. The Universal Dependencies 1.4 resource now comprises 64 different treebanks covering 47 different languages (Nivre et al., 2017), and these numbers continue rising (v2.0 is set to add three languages and six treebanks). Parsing scores are now expected to be re-ported over all (modern) languages if not all treebanks as macroaverages of scores.

With this added diversity in treebanks and languages, and with a growing trend towards more computationally intensive learning algorithms that promise greater accuracy (such as neural networks), feasible parser development should be a rising concern. The availability of computational resources to develop–that is, to train across all interesting parameter/hyper-parameter settings–neural network models for 64 treebanks within a reasonable amount of time will counteract progress and shut out researchers without adequate computational resources. Moreover, there are environmental concerns for the inefficient use of power in the language-exhaustive development of these resources.

In this paper, we provide an entirely empirically motivated sub-sample of nine languages that can can be used to develop monolingual parsing resources. The method uses delexicalised parser performance as a measure of similarity to construct a language similarity network. The network is naturally partitioned into language groups using a standard network clustering algorithm, which does not take the number of clusters as a parameter. The clusters are assumed to be diverse between them but coherent within them, with respect to their individual parser models. Using this technique, the mean and standard deviation of monolingual unlabeled accuracy scores for cluster representatives are found to be close to the true average and standard deviation. Future monolingual parsing systems can extrapolate parser performance over the entire set of languages, using only the set of nine representative languages listed in Table 1, which interestingly excludes English, Chinese, German, and Czech.

Efficient parser development for UD languages.
As an efficient alternative to exhaustive parameter search across 47 languages (or 64 treebanks), the

Proceedings of the NoDaLiDa 2017 Workshop on Universal Dependencies (UDW 2017), pages 117–122,
Gothenburg, Sweden, 22 May 2017.

1. Polish	6. Coptic
2. Italian	7. Hebrew
3. Norwegian	8. Indonesian, and
4. Old Church Slavonic	9. Dutch
5. Sanskrit	

Table 1: Representative languages for UD parsing resource development.

method we propose for the development of parsing resources is the following:

1. **Development**: develop parsing resources over only the nine languages in Table 1, optimising for average and standard deviation of unlabeled attachment across all languages.

2. **Full testing**: using the parameters discovered in step (1), report final average parsing scores and standard deviation over *all* UD languages.

In Section 3 we will outline the network analytic method for determining these nine representative languages empirically. First we discuss the only preceding approach to sampling UD languages for parser development; the approach is essentially non-empirical.

2   Related work

De Lhoneux and Nivre (2016) presented the first approach to language sampling from UD. They hand-picked a set of representative languages based on the following requirements:

1. **Language family**: include exactly one language from each of 8 coarse-grained language families, and no more than one from each of 15 fine-grained language families,

2. **Morphological diversity**: include at least one isolating, one morphologically rich and one inflecting language,

3. **Treebank size and domain**: ensure varied treebank size and domain,

4. **Non-projectivity**: include one language with a large amount of non-projective trees.

De Lhoneux and Nivre (2016) also considered the quality of treebanks and selected those languages that had as few annotation inconsistencies as possible. To ensure comparability, they also only consider treebanks with morphological features. They selected eight languages: Czech, Chinese, Finnish, English, Ancient Greek-PROIEL, Kazakh, Tamil, and Hebrew (cf. Table 2).

Our method differs in that it is entirely empirical, based on delexicalised parsing model similarity. Note that we also control for treebank size and exclude all morphological information.

3   Methodology

Delexicalised and projection-based parser approaches form the state-of-the-art for cross-lingual dependency parsing systems (Rasooli and Collins, 2015). Moreover, as shown by Agić et al. (2016) in upper-bound experiments, languages that are well-known to hold similar syntactic behaviours to one another, given that they come from the same language family, often generate better cross-lingual parsers for one another.

In our approach, we use delexicalised cross-lingual parsing scores to the indicate parser generalisation capacity from one language to another. As such, these parsing scores can be seen as a sort of similarity score between languages. The more similar the POS sequences and associated syntactic structures are between languages, the more similar the optimal parsing model to parse them and the better the resultant delexicalised parsing scores between them. We call this similarity score, (optimal) **model similarity**.

We need a global account of model similarity between UD languages in order to select a naturally small representative subset of UD languages based on maximal coverage of model capacities.

Building the network.   We first create a complete weighted directed network $G = (V, E, w)$ to reflect model similarity. Each node in V represents a language from the UD dataset. We make arcs between all ordered pairs of nodes and decorate each arc with a weight as follows.

For a pair of languages L_1 and L_2 in our dataset, the arc (L_1, L_2) is the unlabeled attachment score of the delexicalised parser trained on L_1 and evaluated on L_2. In Section 4, we give the precise parameters of these experiments. The network thus created can be seen to roughly model the flow of model similarity. In order to transform these edge weights into probabilities, which our clustering algorithm requires, we put the set of outgoing weights of a node through soft-max at temperature

	language	flow	rank			language	flow	rank
	Cluster 1					**Cluster 4**		
pl	Polish	0.134645	2	cu	Old Church Slavonic	0.0242178	10
sl	Slovenian	0.120378	3	got	Gothic	0.0212005	12
bg	Bulgarian	0.0772124	5	la	Latin	0.00163673	28
uk	Ukrainian	0.0324838	8	grc	Ancient Greek	0.000146437	40
cs	Czech	0.0226545	11		**Cluster 5**		
sk	Slovak	0.0105861	17	sa	Sanskrit	0.0171218	15
hr	Croatian	0.00662242	19	tr	Turkish	0.00405451	22
de	German	0.00651388	20	ta	Tamil	0.00218517	25
ru	Russian	0.00620382	21	hi	Hindi	0.00175879	27
el	Greek	0.0039794	23	ug	Uyghur	0.00105993	30
et	Estonian	0.00267263	24	eu	Basque	0.000897161	31
fi	Finnish	0.000232028	38	kk	Kazakh	0.00084926	32
lv	Latvian	3.36723e-05	43	hu	Hungarian	0.000793513	33
				ja	Japanese	0.000640374	35
				gl	Galician	6.85458e-05	42
	Cluster 2			zh	Chinese	4.28534e-06	46
it	Italian	0.180703	1	swl	Swedish Sing	5.57449e-07	47
ca	Catalan	0.0894462	4		**Cluster 6**		
es	Spanish	0.0753139	6	cop	Coptic	0.0260177	9
fr	French	0.0598804	7		**Cluster 7**		
pt	Portuguese	0.0133104	16	he	Hebrew	0.000642038	34
ro	Romanian	0.00190421	26	ga	Irish	0.000452355	37
vi	Vietnamese	0.000169612	39	fa	Persian	3.26755e-05	44
				ar	Arabic	1.8784e-05	45
	Cluster 3				**Cluster 8**		
no	Norwegian	0.020558	13	id	Indonesian	0.000609376	36
sv	Swedish	0.019848	14		**Cluster 9**		
da	Danish	0.00897288	18	nl	Dutch	0.000105621	41
en	English	0.00116163	29				

Table 2: Language clusters, flow (centrality) and rankings, given temperature $\tau = 0.025$. The most central languages for clusters are highlighted in blue. Red rows are the languages chosen by de Lhoneux and Nivre (2016). And the one purple language, Hebrew, was chosen by both methods.

τ, to be determined with respect to true parsing score aggregates later.

Our goal is to use the network to determine the language representatives of the UD dataset. To do this, we run the Infomap network clustering algorithm and then extract the most important languages from each cluster.

Clustering the network naturally. We need to now cluster the nodes of the network, given its structure, but without supplying the number of languages as a parameter, in order for the output modular structure the be completely data-driven.

Infomap[1] poses the problem of the clustering of nodes in a weighted directed network as the dual of the problem of minimising the description length of a random walker's movements on a network. Intuitively, the description parts corresponding to various regions of the network may be compressed if the random walker spends longer of periods of time there.

The description of the network (the map equation) to be minimised is

$$L(M) := q_\curvearrowright H(Q) + \sum_{i=1}^{m} p_{i\circlearrowright} H(P_i)$$

where $q_\curvearrowright$ is the total given probability that the random walker enters some new cluster; $H(Q)$ is entropy of the modular structure of the network; $p_{i\circlearrowright}$ is the probability that some node in cluster i is visited together with the probability of exiting cluster i; and $H(P_i)$ the entropy of the internal network structure in cluster i.

The interested reader is referred to Rosvall et al. (2009) for more details. Infomap outputs three pieces of information that we need here: (1) The number of clusters, (2) the cluster that each node belongs to, and (3) the flow of each node in the network as determined by the random walk traversals. The larger the flow, the more central a node is within the network.

---

[1] http://www.mapequation.org/code.html

Extracting representative languages. For each cluster, the most representative (central) language of the cluster is considered to be the node with the highest flow. In terms of the random walker in the network structure, these are the nodes that are traversed the most within their own clusters, meaning that correspond to languages with highest cluster-wide model similarity. In this sense, they can act as **cluster representatives**.

Calculating parsing score aggregates. In order to fit the modular structure of the network to the true parsing score aggregates we carry out an exhaustive search for optimal temperature within the interval $\tau \in (0,1]$ at increments of 0.005. The value τ is optimal when

$$|\mu - \mu_\tau| + |\sigma - \sigma_\tau| \qquad (1)$$

is minimised, where μ and σ are the true macro-average of unlabeled parsing accuracy score mean and standard deviation, and μ_τ and σ_τ are found in the same way except that parsing scores for non-cluster representatives are replaced by that of their unique cluster representatives. This corresponds to a weighted average and standard deviation of scores of cluster representatives based on cluster size.

4 Data preparation

We used UD v1.4 in our experiment. Out of the 64 treebanks it offers, we select the 47 canonical ones for the 47 languages represented in the release.

We filter out all but the following CoNLL-U features from the dataset:[2] ID, UPOSTAG, HEAD, and DEPREL. Note that all our parsers are delexicalised following McDonald et al. (2013), that is, we exclude all lexical information and learn parses over POS sequences. We also filter out all multi-word tokens.

All training data is sub-sampled up to 10k sentences so as to avoid the bias towards the largest training sets.[3] Then, we train our delexicalized models using the graph-based parser MATE with default settings (Bohnet, 2010).

All our parsers assign labels, but here we evaluate for UAS only. While LAS and UAS are the two

most highly correlated dependency parsing metrics as per Plank et al. (2015), we find that the latter offers a bit more stability in constructing our similarity network. The aggregates over the 47 UD languages are: average UAS 74.45, and standard deviation UAS 9.4. An optimal language sampling method extrapolates to these aggregates as closely as possible.

5 Method visualisation and discussion

In Figure 1, on the left y-axis, we see the number of clusters generated in the network for varying temperature levels. On the right y-axis, we see the parsing score estimate over cluster representatives for varying temperatures. Equation (1) is minimised when $\tau = 0.025$ and this yields nine separate clusters for our model similarity network. The error for this temperature is 5.05 (with $|\mu - \mu_\tau| = 3.5$ and $|\sigma - \sigma_\tau| = 1.55$) as reported in Table 3.

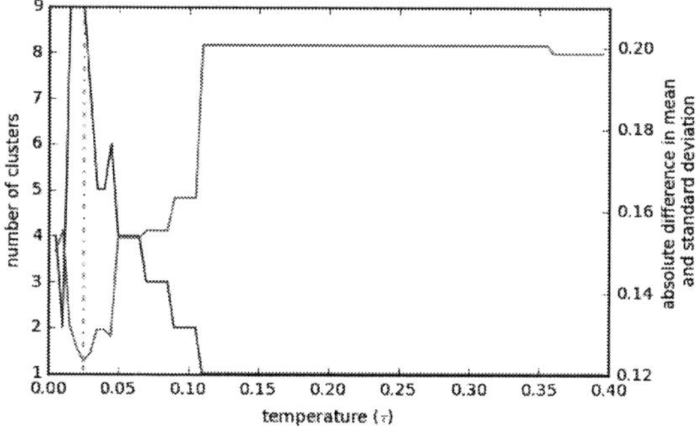

Figure 1: Number of clusters over varying temperatures, with respect to soft-max temperature. Optimal temperature at $\tau = 0.025$ (dotted green line). The number of clusters and error remain unchanged for $\tau > 0.4$.

Visualising the model similarity network. A visualisation of the network for $\tau = 0.025$ is given in Figure 2. We notice that, as expected, many of the clusters follow language family closely, but there are a number of outliers. For instance, Dutch is entirely alone in its cluster and Vietnamese is grouped together with the Romance languages.

Language centrality. In Table 2, we also see the rank of languages in terms of their centrality (flow score) in the network. The centrality score in our case provides an indication of model similarity between parsers trained on the language in ques-

---

[2]http://universaldependencies.org/format.html

[3]Czech, the largest training set in our UD subset, is 4.5x larger than each of the 12 languages that follow it.

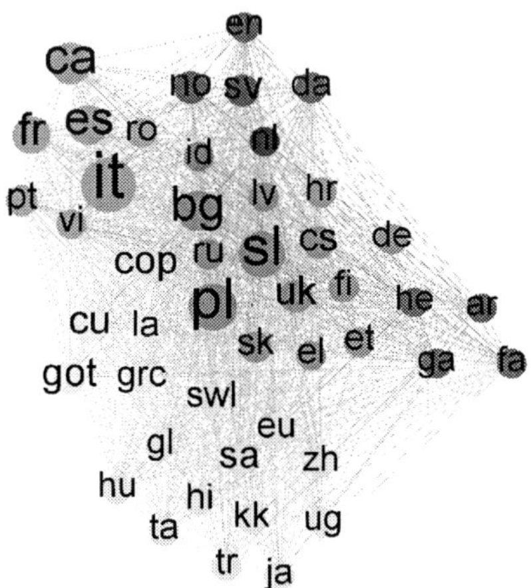

Figure 2: Visualisation of the model similarity network. Node centrality corresponds to node size.

tion and those of all other languages in the network. Surprisingly, English is ranked in 29th position, which provides simple empirical evidence that parsing resources developed mainly on and optimised for English risk suboptimal overall performance. Interestingly, other well-studied languages like Chinese and Arabic have considerably low rank both in the entire networks well as in their respective clusters.

In Table 2 we have also highlighted the representative languages chosen by de Lhoneux and Nivre (2016). We see that according to our empirical model, the languages they chose reflect neither the centrality nor the diversity intended.

Comparing extrapolations. The error for de Lhoneux and Nivre's (2016) representative set is given in Table 4. We see that total error is lower in the parsing model similarity method we describe here. However, because of the combined optimisation of mean and standard deviation, our sample over-estimates general performance, while de Lhoneux and Nivre (2016)'s sample underestimates the reliability of the parser to achieve the mean performance.

6 Concluding remarks

We have shown the first 100% empirical method for determining a small representative sample of UD languages for parser development, and have proposed an associated methodology. In particular, for the Universal Dependencies v1.4, we given a specific subset of nine languages on which pars-

language	cluster size	score
Polish	13	84.91
Italian	7	85.11
Norwegian	4	79.99
Old Church Slav.	4	73.72
Sanskrit	12	66.10
Coptic	1	85.01
Hebrew	4	79.60
Indonesian	1	77.73
Dutch	1	75.05
average	77.96 (error = 3.5)	
std	7.85 (error = 1.55)	
total error	**5.05**	

Table 3: UAS contributions and aggregates of our representative UD languages. The contributions (cluster size) * score are collected over the 9 sampled languages and normalised over the 47 languages.

language	score
Czech	78.49
Chinese	68.08
Finnish	68.00
English	79.71
Anc. Greek-P.	62.37
Kazakh	69.29
Tamil	71.39
Hebrew	79.60
average	72.12 (error = 2.33)
std	6.45 (error = 2.95)
total error	5.28

Table 4: UAS and aggregates of de Lhoneux and Nivre's (2016) representative UD languages. The score aggregates are calculated over the 8 sampled languages.

ing systems can be developed efficiently.

The language clusters presented here have many similarities with well-studied language family distinctions, but also many differences. These clusters could provide an interesting technology-motivated study of syntactic similarity between languages.

References

Željko Agić, Anders Johannsen, Barbara Plank, Héctor Martínez Alonso, Natalie Schluter, and Anders Søgaard. 2016. Multilingual projection for parsing truly low-resource languages. *Transactions of the Association for Computational Linguistics*, 4:303–312.

Bernd Bohnet. 2010. Top accuracy and fast dependency parsing is not a contradiction. In *Proceedings of the 23rd International Conference on Computa-*

tional Linguistics (Coling 2010), pages 89–97, Beijing, China, August. Coling 2010 Organizing Committee.

Miryam de Lhoneux and Joakim Nivre. 2016. Ud treebank sampling for comparative parser evaluation. In *Proceedings of SLT 2016*.

Ryan McDonald, Joakim Nivre, Yvonne Quirmbach-Brundage, Yoav Goldberg, Dipanjan Das, Kuzman Ganchev, Keith Hall, Slav Petrov, Hao Zhang, Oscar Täckström, Claudia Bedini, Núria Bertomeu Castelló, and Jungmee Lee. 2013. Universal dependency annotation for multilingual parsing. In *Proceedings of the 51st Annual Meeting of the Association for Computational Linguistics (Volume 2: Short Papers)*, pages 92–97, Sofia, Bulgaria, August. Association for Computational Linguistics.

Joakim Nivre, Marie-Catherine de Marneffe, Filip Ginter, Yoav Goldberg, Jan Hajic, Christopher D. Manning, Ryan McDonald, Slav Petrov, Sampo Pyysalo, Natalia Silveira, and et al. 2016. Universal dependencies v1: A multilingual treebank collection. In *Proceedings of the 10th International Conference on Language Resources and Evaluation (LREC 2016)*.

Joakim Nivre, Željko Agić, Lars Ahrenberg, Maria Jesus Aranzabe, Masayuki Asahara, Aitziber Atutxa, Miguel Ballesteros, John Bauer, Kepa Bengoetxea, Riyaz Ahmad Bhat, Eckhard Bick, Cristina Bosco, Gosse Bouma, Sam Bowman, Marie Candito, Gülşen Cebirolu Eryiit, Giuseppe G. A. Celano, Fabricio Chalub, Jinho Choi, Çar Çöltekin, Miriam Connor, Elizabeth Davidson, Marie-Catherine de Marneffe, Valeria de Paiva, Arantza Diaz de Ilarraza, Kaja Dobrovoljc, Timothy Dozat, Kira Droganova, Puneet Dwivedi, Marhaba Eli, Tomaž Erjavec, Richárd Farkas, Jennifer Foster, Cláudia Freitas, Katarína Gajdošová, Daniel Galbraith, Marcos Garcia, Filip Ginter, Iakes Goenaga, Koldo Gojenola, Memduh Gökrmak, Yoav Goldberg, Xavier Gómez Guinovart, Berta Gonzáles Saavedra, Matias Grioni, Normunds Grūzītis, Bruno Guillaume, Nizar Habash, Jan Hajič, Linh Hà M, Dag Haug, Barbora Hladká, Petter Hohle, Radu Ion, Elena Irimia, Anders Johannsen, Fredrik Jørgensen, Hüner Kaşkara, Hiroshi Kanayama, Jenna Kanerva, Natalia Kotsyba, Simon Krek, Veronika Laippala, Phng Lê Hng, Alessandro Lenci, Nikola Ljubešić, Olga Lyashevskaya, Teresa Lynn, Aibek Makazhanov, Christopher Manning, Cătălina Mărănduc, David Mareček, Héctor Martínez Alonso, André Martins, Jan Mašek, Yuji Matsumoto, Ryan McDonald, Anna Missilä, Verginica Mititelu, Yusuke Miyao, Simonetta Montemagni, Amir More, Shunsuke Mori, Bohdan Moskalevskyi, Kadri Muischnek, Nina Mustafina, Kaili Müürisep, Lng Nguyn Th, Huyn Nguyn Th Minh, Vitaly Nikolaev, Hanna Nurmi, Stina Ojala, Petya Osenova, Lilja Øvrelid, Elena Pascual, Marco Passarotti, Cenel-Augusto Perez, Guy Perrier, Slav Petrov, Jussi Piitulainen, Barbara Plank, Martin Popel, Lauma Pretkalnia, Prokopis Proko-pidis, Tiina Puolakainen, Sampo Pyysalo, Alexandre Rademaker, Loganathan Ramasamy, Livy Real, Laura Rituma, Rudolf Rosa, Shadi Saleh, Manuela Sanguinetti, Baiba Saulīte, Sebastian Schuster, Djamé Seddah, Wolfgang Seeker, Mojgan Seraji, Lena Shakurova, Mo Shen, Dmitry Sichinava, Natalia Silveira, Maria Simi, Radu Simionescu, Katalin Simkó, Mária Šimková, Kiril Simov, Aaron Smith, Alane Suhr, Umut Sulubacak, Zsolt Szántó, Dima Taji, Takaaki Tanaka, Reut Tsarfaty, Francis Tyers, Sumire Uematsu, Larraitz Uria, Gertjan van Noord, Viktor Varga, Veronika Vincze, Jonathan North Washington, Zdeněk Žabokrtský, Amir Zeldes, Daniel Zeman, and Hanzhi Zhu. 2017. Universal dependencies 2.0. LINDAT/CLARIN digital library at the Institute of Formal and Applied Linguistics, Charles University in Prague.

Barbara Plank, Héctor Martínez Alonso, Željko Agić, Danijela Merkler, and Anders Søgaard. 2015. Do dependency parsing metrics correlate with human judgments? In *Proceedings of the Nineteenth Conference on Computational Natural Language Learning*, pages 315–320, Beijing, China, July. Association for Computational Linguistics.

Mohammad Sadegh Rasooli and Michael Collins. 2015. Density-driven cross-lingual transfer of dependency parsers. In *Proceedings of the 2015 Conference on Empirical Methods in Natural Language Processing*, pages 328–338, Lisbon, Portugal, September. Association for Computational Linguistics.

Martin Rosvall, Daniel Axelsson, and Carl T. Bergstrom. 2009. The map equation. *Eur. Phys. J. Special Topics*, 178.

Gapping Constructions in Universal Dependencies v2

Sebastian Schuster   **Matthew Lamm**   **Christopher D. Manning**
Department of Linguistics and Department of Computer Science
Stanford University, Stanford, CA 94305
{sebschu,mlamm,manning}@stanford.edu

Abstract

In this paper, we provide a detailed account of sentences with gapping such as *"John likes tea, and Mary coffee"* within the Universal Dependencies (UD) framework. We explain how common gapping constructions as well as rare complex constructions can be analyzed on the basis of examples in Dutch, English, Farsi, German, Hindi, Japanese, and Turkish. We further argue why the adopted analysis of these constructions in UD version 2 is better suited for annotating treebanks and parsing than previous proposals, and we discuss how gapping constructions can be analyzed in the *enhanced* UD representation, a graph-based semantic representation for shallow computational semantics tasks.

1 Introduction

An important property of natural languages is that speakers can sometimes omit redundant material. One example of this phenomenon is so-called gapping constructions (Ross, 1970). In such constructions, speakers elide a previously mentioned verb that takes multiple arguments, which leaves behind a clause without its main predicate. For example, in the sentence *"John likes tea, and Mary coffee"*, the verb *likes* was elided from the second conjunct.

Sentences with gapping pose practical as well as theoretical challenges to natural language processing tasks. From a practical point of view, it is challenging for natural language processing systems to resolve the gaps, which is necessary to interpret these sentences and extract information from them. Further, these sentences are hard for statistical parsers to parse as part of their structure deviates significantly from canonical clause structures.

From a more theoretical point of view, these constructions pose challenges to designers of dependency representations. Most dependency representations that are used in natural language processing systems (e.g., the adaptation of Mel'čuk (1988) for the CoNLL-08 shared task (Surdeanu et al., 2008); de Marneffe et al. (2006); Nivre et al. (2016)) are concerned with providing surface syntax descriptions without stipulating any additional transformations or empty nodes. Further, virtually all dependency representations consider a verb (either the inflected or the main verb) to be the head of a clause. Consequently, the verb governs all its arguments and modifiers. For these reasons, it is challenging to find a good representation of clauses in which a verb that has multiple dependents was elided, because it is not obvious where and how the remaining dependents should be attached in these cases.

In recent years, the Universal Dependencies (UD) representation (Nivre et al., 2016) has become the dominant dependency representation for annotating treebanks in a large variety of languages. The goal of the UD project is to provide guidelines for cross-linguistically consistent treebank annotations for as many languages as possible. Considering that gapping constructions appear in many languages, these guidelines necessarily also have to include guidelines on how to analyze gapping constructions. While the official guidelines[1] provide basic instructions for the analysis of gapping constructions, they lack a detailed discussion of cross-linguistically attested gapping constructions and a thorough explanation why the adopted guidelines should be preferred over other proposals. The purpose of the present paper is therefore to discuss in detail how different gapping constructions can be analyzed in a variety of lan-

---

[1] See http://universaldependencies.org/u/overview/specific-syntax.html#ellipsis. The first and the last author were both involved in developing these guidelines.

123

Proceedings of the NoDaLiDa 2017 Workshop on Universal Dependencies (UDW 2017), pages 123–132,
Gothenburg, Sweden, 22 May 2017.

guages and to provide a theoretical comparison of different proposals based on these examples. We further discuss how gapping constructions should be represented in the *enhanced* Universal Dependencies representation, which aims to be a better representation for shallow natural language understanding tasks and how these design choices can potentially help in downstream tasks.

For the purpose of this paper, we consider constructions in which a verb that has multiple dependents was elided, including classic cases of gapping (Ross, 1970). Throughout this paper, we call the elided material (a verb and occasionally also some of its arguments) the GAP. Further, we refer to the dependents of the gap as ORPHANS or REMNANTS, and we refer to the dependents of the verb in the clause with the overt verb as the COR-RESPONDENTS, as illustrated with the following annotated sentence.

John	likes	tea	and	Mary	coffee
CORRE- SPONDENT	OVERT VERB	CORRE- SPONDENT		ORPHAN/ REMNANT	ORPHAN/ REMNANT

2 Coordination, ellipsis, and gapping in UD v2

Before we discuss how gapping constructions are analyzed in UD v2, we give a brief overview how UD analyzes coordinated clauses and other forms of elliptical constructions.

Coordinated clauses are analyzed like all other types of coordination: By convention, the head of the first conjunct is always the head of the coordinated construction and all other conjuncts are attached to the head of the first conjunct with a `conj` relation. If there is an overt coordinating conjunction, it is attached to the head of the succeeding conjunct. This captures the fact that the coordinating conjunction forms a syntactic unit with the succeeding conjunct (Gerdes and Kahane, 2015). A sentence with two coordinated clauses is then analyzed as follows.

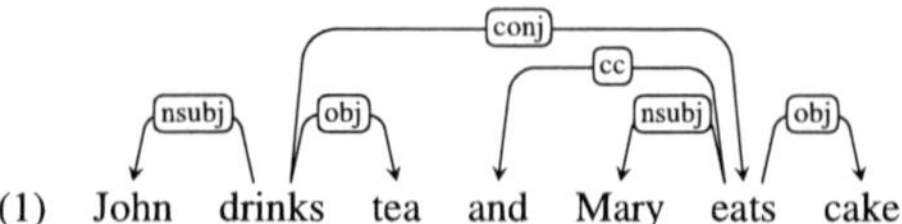

For constructions in which a head nominal was elided, UD promotes the highest dependent according to the hierarchy `amod` > `nummod` > `det` > `nmod` > `case`. The promoted dependent is attached to the governor of the elided nominal with

the same relation that would have been used if the nominal had not been elided. All the other dependents of the elided noun are attached to the promoted dependent with their regular relations. For example, in the second conjunct of the following sentence, the head noun *bird* was elided. We therefore promote the determiner *some* to serve as the object of *saw*.

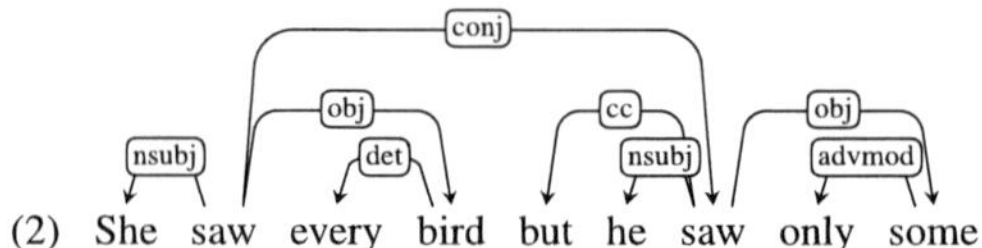

In some cases of ellipsis, a verb phrase is elided but there is still an overt copula or auxiliary verb. In these cases, we promote the copula or auxiliary verb to be the head of the clause and attach all orphans to the auxiliary.

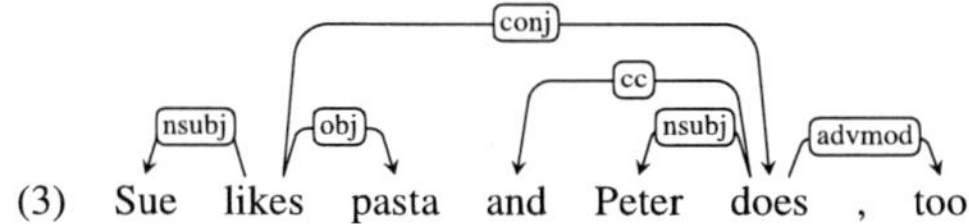

For the constructions we are mainly concerned with in this paper, i.e., gapping constructions in which the governor of multiple phrases was elided, UD v2 adopts a modified version of a proposal by Gerdes and Kahane (2015). We promote the orphan whose grammatical role dominates all other orphans according to an adaptation of the obliqueness hierarchy,[2] to be the head of the conjunct. The motivation behind using such a hierarchy instead of a simpler strategy such as promoting the leftmost phrase is that it leads to a more parallel analysis across languages that differ in word order. We attach all other orphans except for coordinating conjunctions using the special `orphan` relation. Coordinating conjunctions are attached to the head of the following conjunct with the `cc` relation. This leads to the analysis in (4) of a sentence with three conjuncts of which two contain a gap.

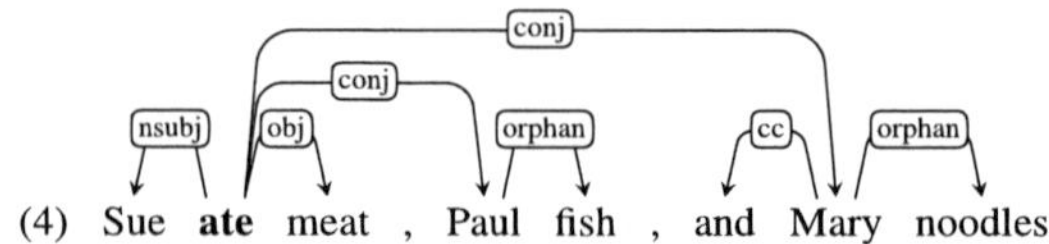

---

[2]Our adaptation prioritizes phrasal over clausal dependents. Translated to UD relations, our adaptation of the obliqueness hierarchy is as follows: `nsubj` > `obj` > `iobj` > `obl` > `advmod` > `csubj` > `xcomp` > `ccomp` > `advcl`. See, for example, Pollard and Sag (1994) for a motivation behind this ordering.

The motivation behind using a special `orphan` relation is that it indicates that the clause contains a gap. If we used a regular relation, it might not be clear that a predicate was elided. For example, if instead, we attached the orphaned subject to the orphaned object using an `nsubj` relation, one could confuse gapping constructions with copular constructions, especially in languages with zero-copula.

In the rest of this paper, we argue in favor of this proposal for several reasons. First, as we show in the following section, it can be used to analyze a wide range of gapping constructions in many different languages. Second, as we argue in Section 4, there is evidence that the conjunct with the gap forms a syntactic unit, and this fact is captured by the adopted analysis. Finally, as discussed in Section 6, this representation is potentially better suited for automatic parsing than previous proposals.

3 Gapping constructions

We now discuss how a range of attested gapping constructions in a variety of languages can be analyzed according to the above proposal.

3.1 Single verbs

The most common form of gapping constructions are two or more conjoined clauses in which a single inflected verb is missing in all but one of the conjuncts. As illustrated in (4), in SVO languages such as English, the overt verb typically appears in the first conjunct and is elided from all subsequent conjuncts. In languages with other word orders, the overt verb can also appear exclusively in the last conjunct. For example, in the following sentence in Japanese (an SOV language), the verb appears in the last conjunct and the gap in the first conjunct.

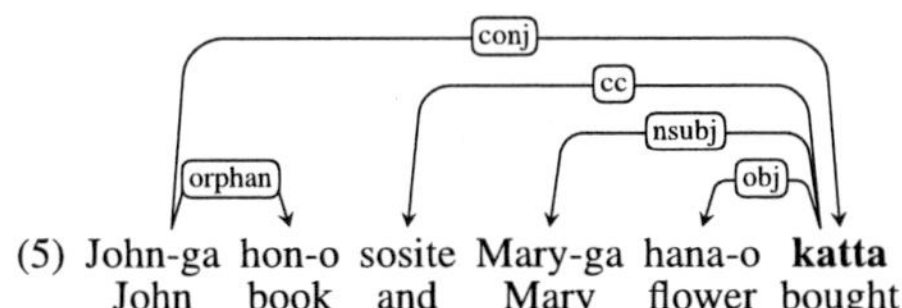

(5) John-ga hon-o sosite Mary-ga hana-o **katta**
John book and Mary flower bought

'John bought books, and Mary flowers.' (Kato, 2006)

In some languages with flexible word orders such as Turkish, the overt verb can appear in the first or the last conjunct. The orphans typically appear in the same order as the correspondents in the other conjunct as in (6a-d) (Bozsahin, 2000).

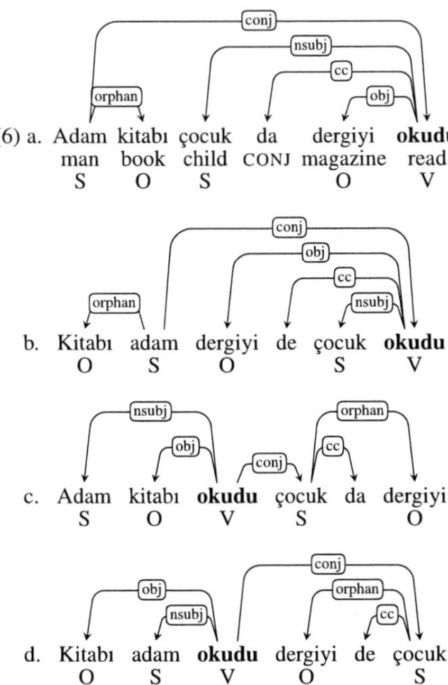

(6) a. Adam kitabı çocuk da dergiyi **okudu**
man book child CONJ magazine read
S O S O V

b. Kitabı adam dergiyi de çocuk **okudu**
O S O S V

c. Adam kitabı **okudu** çocuk da dergiyi
S O V S O

d. Kitabı adam **okudu** dergiyi de çocuk
O S V O S

'The man read the book, and the child the magazine.'
(Bozsahin, 2000)

As mentioned above, in order to achieve higher cross-linguistic consistency, the first conjunct is always the head of a coordinated structure in UD. Therefore, the head of the first conjunct is always the head of the coordination, but the internal structure of each conjunct is the same for all four variants in (6).

In some cases, e.g., in certain discourse settings, the clause with the gap is not part of the same sentence as the clause with the overt verb (Gerdes and Kahane, 2015). In these cases, we promote one of the orphans to be the root of the second sentence; the internal structure of the two clauses is the same as when they are part of an intra-sentential coordination.

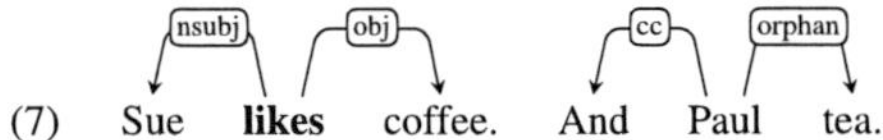

(7) Sue **likes** coffee. And Paul tea.

Further, conjuncts with a gap can also contain additional types of arguments or modifiers. For example, in the sentence in (8), the oblique modifier *for good* does not correspond to any phrase in the first conjunct.

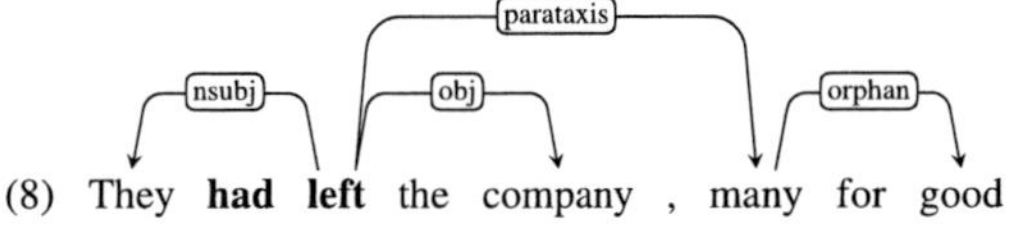

(8) They **had left** the company , many for good

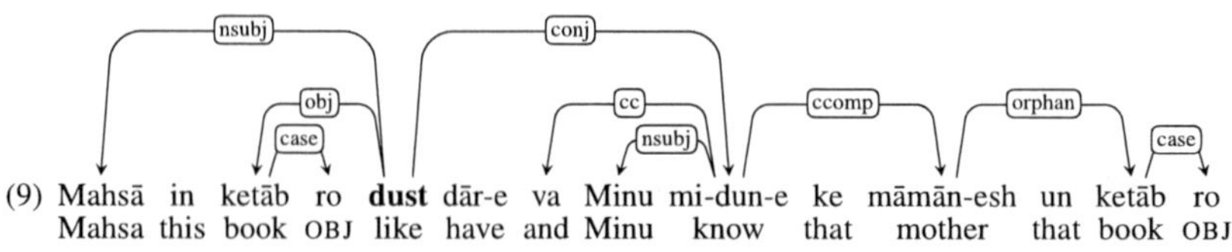

(9) Mahsā in ketāb ro **dust** dār-e va Minu mi-dun-e ke māmān-esh un ketāb ro
    Mahsa this book OBJ like have and Minu know that mother that book OBJ

'Mahsa likes this book and Minu knows that her mother (likes) that book' (Farudi, 2013)

Figure 1: Basic UD tree of a Farsi sentence with a gap within an embedded clause.

3.2 Verbs and their arguments or modifiers

Many languages also allow gapping of verbs along with their arguments or modifiers as illustrated in the following two examples in Hindi (10) and English (11).

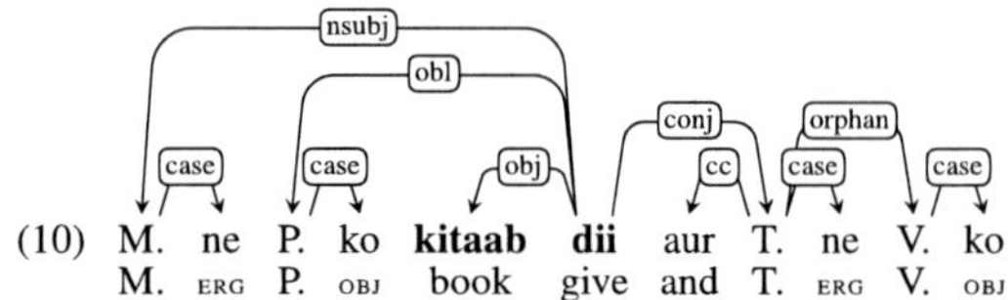

(10) M. ne P. ko **kitaab** **dii** aur T. ne V. ko
     M. ERG P. OBJ book give and T. ERG V. OBJ

'Manu gave a book to Pari and Tanu to Vimla' (Kush, 2016)

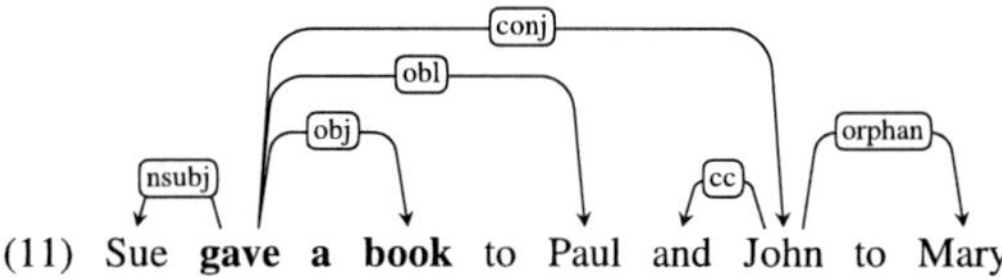

(11) Sue **gave a book** to Paul and John to Mary

We analyze these cases as analogous to sentences in which only a verb was elided. The subject is promoted to be the head of the second conjunct and the oblique argument is attached with an orphan dependency.

3.3 Verbs and clausal complements

Ross (1970) points out that gaps can also correspond to a finite verb and one or more embedded verbs. For example, in the following sentence, it is possible to elide the matrix verb and all or some of the embedded verbs.

(12) I want to try to begin to write a novel, ...
    a. ... and Mary to try to begin to write a play.
    b. ... and Mary to begin to write a play.
    c. ... and Mary to write a play.
    d. ... and Mary a play.   Ross (1970)

In all of these variants, the matrix verb was elided from the second conjunct. While this is an example of subject control and therefore *Mary* is also the subject of all the embedded verbs, it would be misleading to attach *Mary* to one of the embedded verbs because this would hide the fact that the matrix verb was elided. For this reason, we treat *Mary* as the head of the second conjunct and attach the remainder of the embedded clause with an orphan relation.

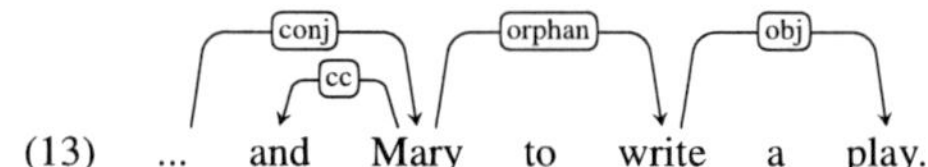

(13) ... and Mary to write a play.

3.4 Non-contiguous gaps

In the previous examples, the gap corresponds to a contiguous sequence in the first conjunct. However, as highlighted by the following examples, this is not always the case.

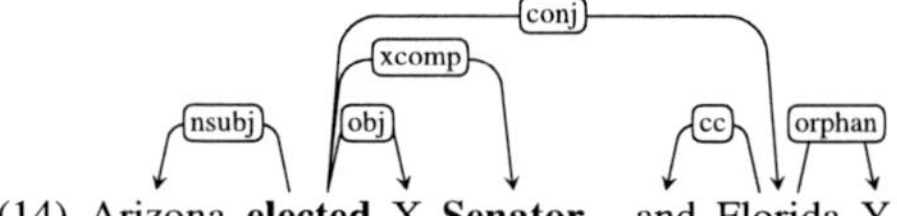

(14) Arizona **elected** X **Senator** , and Florida Y

(adapted from an example in Jackendoff (1971))

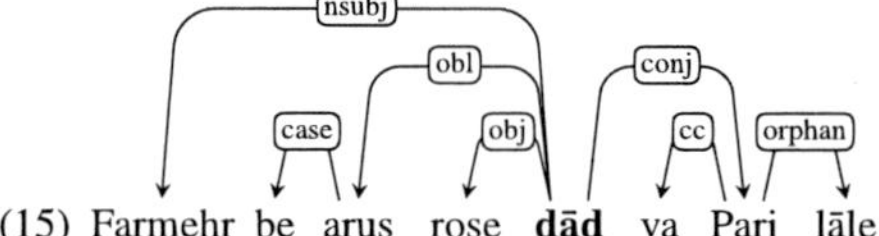

(15) Farmehr be arus rose **dād** va Pari lāle
     Farmehr to bride roses gave and Pari tulips

'Farmehr gave roses to the bride and Pari (gave) tulips (to the bride).'   (Farudi, 2013)

While the interpretation of the second conjunct is only possible if one fills both gaps, we are also in these cases primarily concerned with the elided verb because neither of the phrases in the second conjunct depend on the second gap. We can therefore analyze constructions with non-contiguous gaps in a similar manner as constructions with contiguous gaps, namely by promoting one orphan to be the head of the conjunct and attaching all other orphans to this head.

3.5 Gaps in embedded clauses

Farudi (2013) notes that in Farsi, gaps can appear in embedded clauses even if the corresponding verb in the first conjunct is not part of an embedded clause. For example, in (9) in Figure 1,

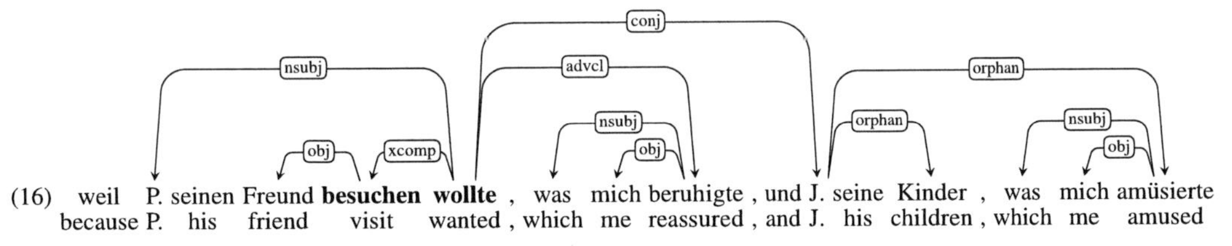

"because Peter wanted to visit his friend which reassured me, and Johann (wanted to visit) his children, which amused me"

(Wyngaerd, 2007)

Figure 2: Basic UD tree of a German subordinate clause with an adverbial clause modifying a gap.

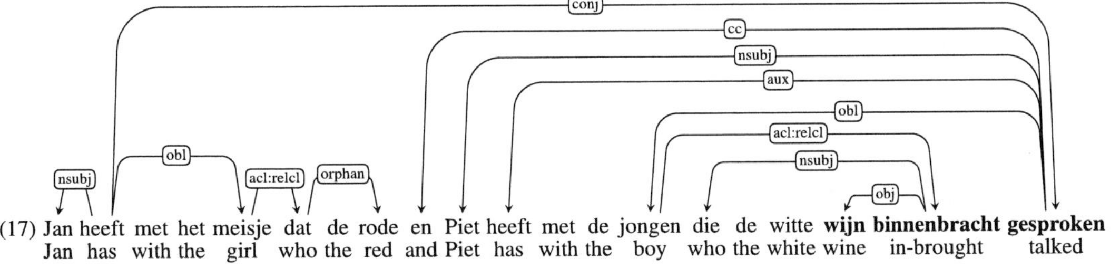

'Jan (talked) to the girl who (brought in) the red (wine), and Piet talked to the boy who brought in the white wine.'

(Wyngaerd, 2007)

Figure 3: Basic UD tree of a Dutch sentence with a gap in a relative clause.

dust ('like') is the main verb of the highest clause of the first conjunct but in the second conjunct, the verb was elided from a clause embedded under *mi-dun-e* ('think'). In these cases, we consider the matrix verb to be the head of the second conjunct as we would if there was no gap, and we promote the subject of the embedded clause (*māmān-esh*) to be the head of the embedded clause. We attach the remaining orphans to the subject with the `orphan` relation.

Note that this construction is different from constructions in which parenthetical material (Pollard and Sag, 1994) appears in the second conjunct, as in the following English example.

(18)   [...] I always had a pretty deep emotional connection to him, and I think he to me.[3]

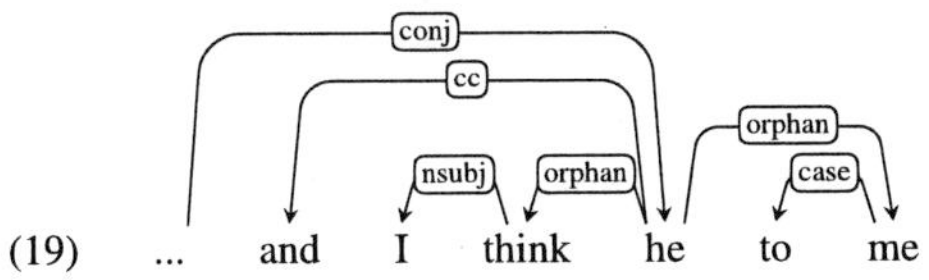

In these cases, we promote the subject of the second conjunct (*he*) and attach the parenthetical *I think* as well as *to him* to the subject.

---

[3] Source: hhttp://www.ttbook.org/book/transcript/transcript-humour-healing-marc-maron

3.6 Relative clauses

Several Germanic languages such as German and Dutch show more complex gapping behaviors in sentences with adverbial and relative clauses. For example, Wyngaerd (2007) points out that German also allows a verbal gap in clauses modified by an adverbial clause such as the one in Figure 2. In this example, the two verbs *besuchen wollte* ('wanted to visit') are missing from the second clause, which leaves three orphans, namely a subject, a direct object, and an adverbial clause without a governor. As in the case of two orphaned constituents, we promote the subject to be the head of the clause as it is the highest type of argument in the obliqueness hierarchy, and we attach the two other constituents to the subject with an `orphan` relation.

Dutch even allows gaps to appear within relative clauses that modify a constituent in each of the conjuncts. In the example sentence in Figure 3, there are in total two elided verbs, and one elided noun. First, the left conjunct is missing the main verb *gesproken* ('talked') in its matrix clause; second, the relative clause of the object in the first conjunct is missing its verb *binnenbracht* ('brought in'); and third, the noun *wijn* ('wine') was elided from the object in the relative clause. The matrix clause of the first conjunct still contains an auxiliary which we promote to be the head of the first conjunct. We further promote the subject of the relative clause, i.e., the relative pronoun, to be the head of the relative clause, and we attach the adjective, which modifies the elided noun, to the promoted subject with an `orphan` relation.

4 Dependency structure

In the previous section, we showed that the adopted *orphan* analysis can be used to consistently annotate a large number of attested gapping constructions in different languages, which is an important consideration in deciding on an analysis. A second important question is whether our adopted analysis leads to sensible tree structures. Our analysis indicates that a conjunct with a gap forms a syntactic unit, which raises the question whether there is evidence for such a structure.

Many constituency tests such as topicalization, clefting, and stripping suggest that conjuncts with a gap often do not qualify as a constituent. For example, Osborne (2006a) argues against treating the gapping in (20) as the coordination of *[the dog a bone]* and *[the man a flower]*, which would suggest that both conjuncts are constituents. He bases his argument on the observation that the former conjunct fails most constituency tests when it is used in a sentence without coordination (21).

(20)   She gave the dog a bone, and the man a flower.

(21)   a. *The dog a bone, she gave. (Topicalization)

     b. *It was the dog a bone that she gave. (Clefting)

     c. ?She gave a dog a bone, not a cat some fish. (Stripping)

However, this argument is based on the assumption that *[the dog a bone]* and *[the man a flower]* form a coordinate structure. If we assume instead that the second conjunct is a clause with elided nodes, then none of the above tests seem applicable. At the same time, as already mentioned above, Gerdes and Kahane (2015) point out that phrases such as *"and the man a flower "* can be uttered by a speaker in response to someone else uttering a phrase such as *"she gave the dog a bone"*. They take this behavior as evidence for treating the entire conjunct with a gap (including the conjunction) as a syntactic unit.

Such an analysis is also in line with most accounts of gapping in the generative literature. While there is disagreement on what the deep structure of sentences with gapping should look like and what transformations are employed to derive the surface structure, there is broad consensus that all remnants are part of the same phrase (e.g., Coppock (2001); Johnson (2009)). We take all of these facts as weak evidence for treating conjuncts with gaps as syntactic units.

This argument based on constituency criteria might seem surprising considering that such evidence was dismissed when deciding on analyses for other constructions in UD, such as prepositional phrases. One of the major criticisms of UD has been that we attach prepositions to their complement instead of treating them as heads of prepositional phrases because this decision appears to be misguided when one considers constituency tests (see, e.g., Osborne (2015)). However, this decision should not be interpreted as UD completely ignoring constituency. It is true that following Tesnière (1959), UD treats content words with their function words as dissociated nuclei and thus ignores the results of constituency tests for determining the attachment of function words – an approach that is also taken by some generative grammarians, for example, in the form of the notion of extended projection by Grimshaw (1997). But importantly, UD still respects the constituency of nominals, clauses and other larger units. For this reason, it is important to have an analysis of gapping that respects larger constituent boundaries as it is the case with the adopted "orphan" analysis.

5 Enhanced representation

One of the drawbacks of the adopted analysis is that the `orphan` dependencies do not encode information on the type of argument of each remnant, which complicates extracting relations between content words in downstream tasks. However, UD also defines an *enhanced* representation, which may be a graph instead of a tree and which may contain additional nodes and relations (Nivre et al., 2016; Schuster and Manning, 2016). The purpose of this representation is to make implicit relations between words more explicit in order to facilitate shallow natural language understanding tasks such as relation extraction. One property of the *enhanced* representation is that it resolves gaps by adding nodes to *basic* UD trees. Remnants attach to these additional nodes with meaningful re-

lations just as if nothing had been elided,[4] thus
solving the issue of the uninformative `orphan` dependencies. The general idea is to insert as many
nodes as required to obtain a structure without
orphans while keeping the number of additional
nodes to a minimum. On top of additional nodes,
we add relations between new nodes and existing content words so that there exist explicit relations between each verb and its arguments and
modifiers. We now illustrate how different cases
of gapping can be analyzed in the *enhanced* representation based on the following representative
examples

The simplest cases are constructions in which a
single verb was elided. In these cases, we insert a
copy node[5] of the elided verb at the position of the
gap, make this node the head of the conjunct, and
attach all orphans to this copy node. For example,
for the following sentence, we insert the copy node
likes' and attach *Mary* as a subject and *coffee* as an
object.

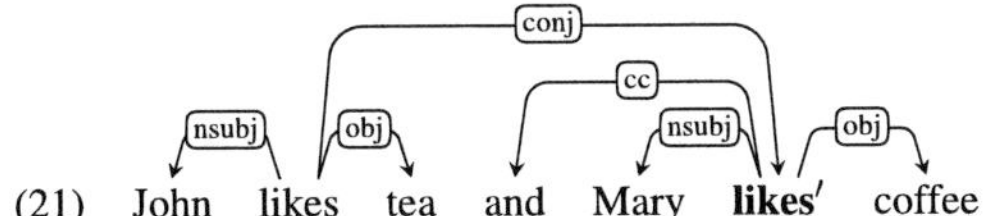

(21)   John   likes   tea   and   Mary   **likes'**   coffee

Similarly, we insert a copy node as the new root of
a sentence in cases in which the leftmost conjunct
contains a gap as, for example, in (5).

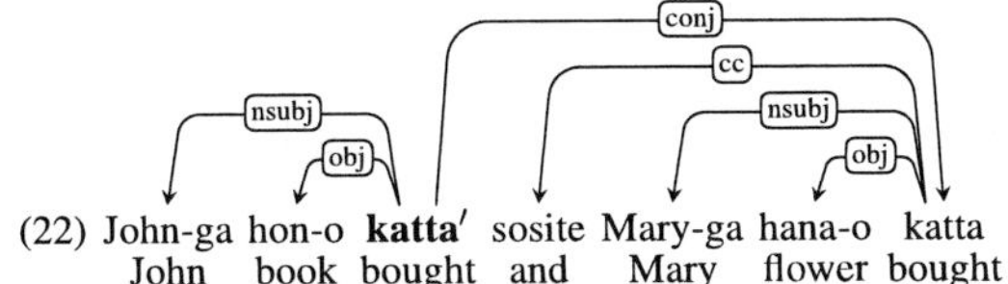

(22) John-ga hon-o **katta'** sosite Mary-ga hana-o katta
     John   book bought and   Mary   flower bought

'John bought books, and Mary bought flowers.'
(adapted from Kato (2006))

In cases in which arguments or modifiers were
elided along with the verb, we still only insert one
copy node for the main verb. However, in order
to make the relation between the verb and all of
its arguments explicit, we also add relations between the new copy node and existing arguments
and meaningful modifiers. In (23), we add a copy

---

[4]A similar analysis was used in the tectogrammatical
layer of the Prague Dependency Treebank (Bejček et al.,
2013).

[5]Similar copy nodes are already used for some cases of reduced conjunctions in the *collapsed* and *CCprocessed* Stanford Dependencies representations (de Marneffe and Manning, 2008) and in the *enhanced* UD representation (Schuster
and Manning, 2016).

node for the elided verb *elected* and a relation between the copy node and *Senator*.

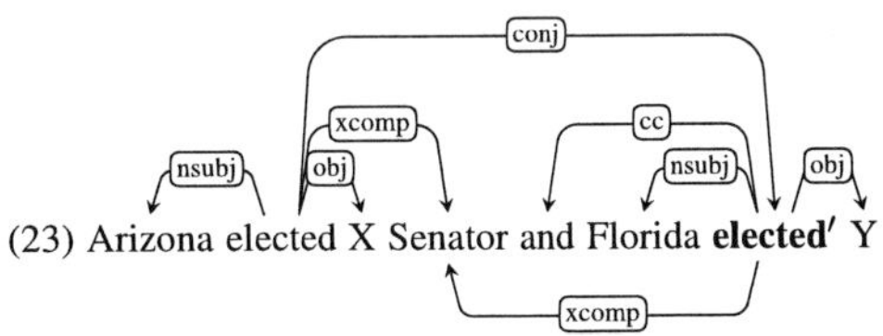

(23) Arizona elected X Senator and Florida **elected'** Y

In cases in which a finite verb was elided along
with one or more embedded verbs, as in the sentence *"I want to try to begin to write a novel, and
Mary a play."*, we insert one copy node for each
elided verb. However, unlike in the previous example, we do not add relations between the copy
nodes and the semantically vacuous function word
to because it is not required for the interpretation
of the sentence.

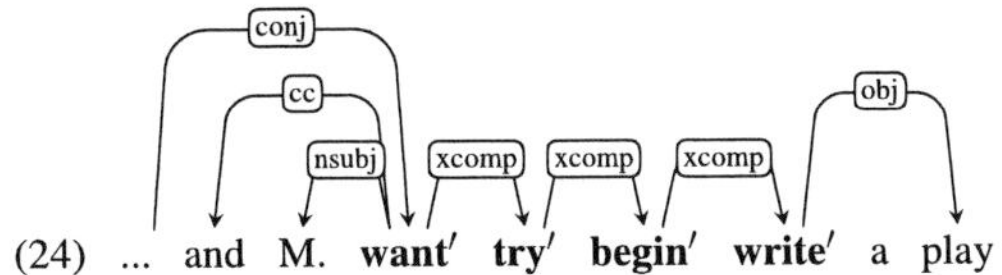

(24)   ...   and   M.   **want'**   **try'**   **begin'**   **write'**   a   play

The motivation behind these design choices is to
have direct and meaningful relations between content words. Many shallow natural language understanding systems, which make use of UD such as
open relation extraction systems (Mausam et al.,
2012; Angeli et al., 2015) or semantic parsers (Andreas et al., 2016; Reddy et al., 2017), use dependency graph patterns to extract information from
sentences. These patterns are typically designed
for prototypical clause structures, and by aug-
menting the dependency graph as described above,
many patterns that were designed for canonical
clause structures also produce the correct results
when applied to sentences with gapping constructions.

6   Comparison to other proposals

6.1   Remnant analysis

The first version of the UD guidelines (Nivre et al.,
2016) proposed that orphans should be attached to
their correspondents with the special `remnant` relation. This proposal is very similar to the analysis
of string coordination by Osborne (2006b), which
adds special orthogonal connections between orphans and correspondents. According to the "remnant" proposal, a sentence with a single verb gap
is analyzed as follows.

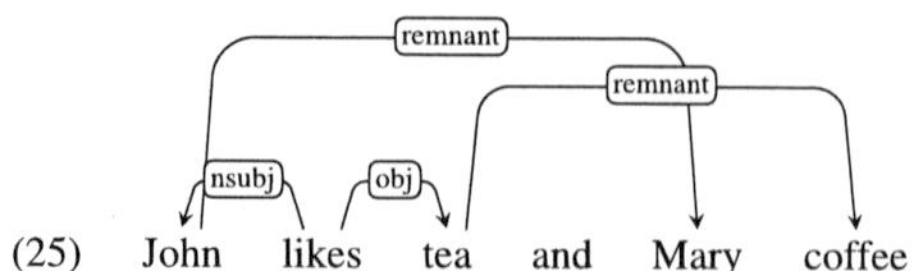

(25) John likes tea and Mary coffee

This is arguably a more expressive analysis than the "orphan" analysis because there is a direct link between each orphan and its correspondent, and one is able to determine the type of argument of each orphan by considering the type of argument of its correspondent. However, this analysis comes with several problems. First, it makes it impossible to analyze sentences with orphans that do not have a correspondent such as the sentence with an additional modifier in (8), or sentences whose correspondents appear in a previous sentence as in (7). Second, the `remnant` relations appear to be an abuse of dependency links as they are clearly not true syntactic dependency relations but rather a kind of co-indexing relation between orphans and correspondents. Further, such an analysis introduces many long-distance dependencies and many non-projective dependencies, both of which are known to lower parsing performance (McDonald and Nivre, 2007). Lastly, as mentioned above, *and Mary coffee* forms a syntactic unit, which is not captured by this proposal.

6.2   Gerdes and Kahane (2015)

Gerdes and Kahane (2015) propose a graph-based analysis of gapping constructions, which inspired the analysis of gapping constructions in UD v2. Their proposal is, by and large, a combination of the "remnant" analysis and the "orphan" analysis that we described in this paper. They further add a `lat-NCC` (lateral non-constituent coordination) relation between the correspondents in the clause with the overt verb. According to their proposal, we would analyze a sentence with a single verb gap as follows.[6]

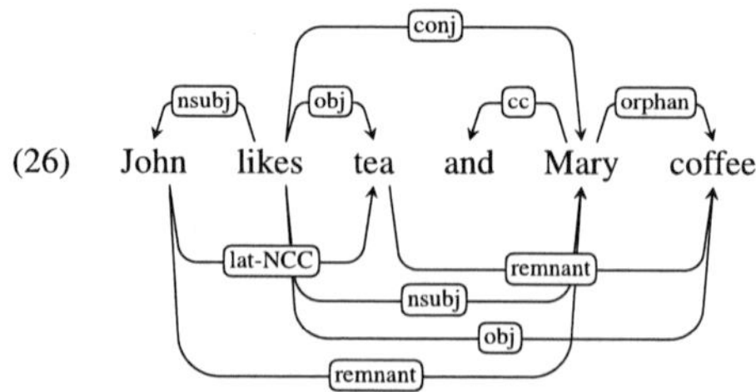

(26) John likes tea and Mary coffee

The advantage of this proposal is that it captures two different things: The `orphan` relation captures

the fact that *and Mary coffee* forms a syntactic unit and the `remnant` relations allow one to determine the type of argument of each orphan. Nevertheless, this proposal also comes with several drawbacks. First, this analysis leads to graphs that are no longer trees and it is therefore not suited for the *basic* UD representation, which is supposed to be a strict surface syntax tree (Nivre et al., 2016). This would not be an issue for the *enhanced* representation, which may be a graph instead of a tree, but the `remnant` relations in this analysis can lead to the same problem as mentioned above. That is, if an orphan does not have a correspondent within the same sentence, we cannot use this type of dependency. Further, the copy nodes in our *enhanced* representation capture the fact that this sentence is describing two distinct "liking" events, which is not captured in this analysis. Finally, while their `lat-NCC` relation seems unproblematic from a theoretical point of view, we do not see its advantage in practice. For these reasons, we adopt only part of their proposal for the *basic* representation and introduce copy nodes in the *enhanced* representation.

6.3   Composite relations

Joakim Nivre and Daniel Zeman developed a third proposal[7] as part of the discussion of the second version of the UD guidelines. Their proposal is based on composite relations such as `conj>nsubj`, which indicates which relations would be present along the dependency path from the first conjunct to the orphan if there was no gap. For example, `X conj>nsubj Y` indicates that there would have been a `conj` relation between X and an elided node, and an `nsubj` relation between the elided node and Y. According to this proposal, we would analyze a sentence with a single verb gap as follows.

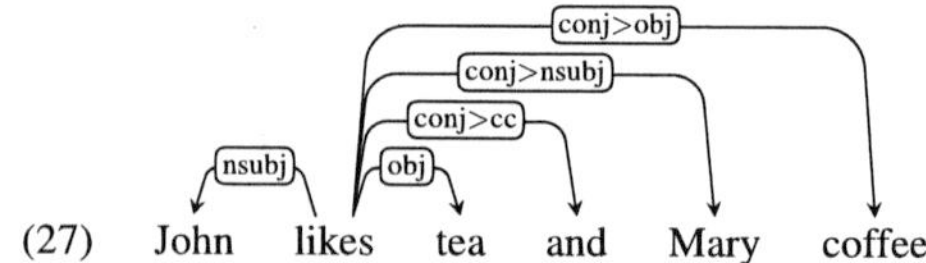

(27) John likes tea and Mary coffee

The advantages of this proposal are that the relation names provide much more information on the type of dependent than the generic `orphan` relation, and that in most cases, the *enhanced* representation can be deterministically obtained by

---

[6]We translated their relation names to the appropriate UD relations to make it easier to compare the various proposals.

[7]See http://universaldependencies.org/v2_prelim/ellipsis.html for a more detailed description of their proposal.

splitting up the relation name and inserting a copy of the governor of the composite relation. For example, for the above sentence, one could obtain the *enhanced* representation by copying *likes* and attaching *and*, *Mary*, and *coffee* with a *cc*, *nsubj*, *obj* relation, respectively.

However, this representation also comes with several drawbacks. First, it drastically increases the size of the relation domain as in theory, an unbounded number of relations can be concatenated. For example, in the sentence in (12d), we would end up with a `conj>xcomp>xcomp>xcomp>obj` relation[8] between *want* and *play*. This is highly problematic from a practical point of view as virtually all existing parsers assume that there is a finite set of relations than can appear between two words. Further, such an analysis also introduces many more long-distance dependencies. For these reasons, it seems unlikely that a parser would be able to produce this representation (and consequently also not the *enhanced* representation) with high accuracy. Finally, also in this case, the second conjunct does not form a syntactic unit.

To summarize this comparison, the main drawback of the *orphan* analysis is that it does not capture any information about the type of arguments in the basic representation. Despite this drawback, we believe that the analysis of gapping constructions in UD version 2 is better with regard to theoretical and practical considerations than any of the previous proposals, because (a) it can be used to analyze sentences in which orphans do not have correspondents; (b) it does not increase the number of relations; (c) it does not introduce additional long-distance dependencies or non-projective dependencies; and (d) it captures the fact that the second conjunct forms a syntactic unit.

---

[8]As pointed out by a reviewer, one could limit the relation name to the first and last relation in the hypothetical dependency path, e.g., `conj>obj` in this example. While this would put an upper bound on the number of relations, it would no longer be possible to deterministically obtain the *enhanced* representation in these cases. Further, we would assign the same relation label to different arguments in some cases. For example, we would add a `conj>obj` relation between *want* and *John* and between *want* and *play* in the analysis of the following sentence despite the fact that these two phrases are arguments to different verbs.

(28) Mary wants Tim to write a novel, and (wants) John (to write) a play.

7 Conclusion and future directions

We discussed which kind of gapping constructions are attested in a variety of languages, and we provided a detailed description how these constructions can be analyzed within the UD version 2 framework. We further explained how sentences with gaps can be analyzed in the *enhanced* UD representation, and we argued why we believe that the current proposal gives the best tradeoff between theoretical and practical considerations.

While we discussed what *enhanced* UD graphs of sentences with gapping should look like, we did not provide any methods of obtaining these graphs from sentences or basic UD trees. One future direction is therefore to develop methods to automatically obtain this representation.

Acknowledgments

We thank the entire UD community for developing the guidelines and for providing feedback to various proposals as part of the the discussion of the second version of the UD guidelines. We also thank Joakim Nivre for providing comments on an early draft of this paper. Further, we thank the anonymous reviewers for their thoughtful feedback. We especially appreciated the thorough and insightful feedback by the second reviewer, and while we were not able to incorporate all of it due to space and time constraints, we hope to address most of the remaining points in future versions of this work. This work was supported in part by gifts from Google, Inc. and IPSoft, Inc. The first author is also supported by a Goodan Family Graduate Fellowship.

References

Jacob Andreas, Marcus Rohrbach, Trevor Darrell, and Dan Klein. 2016. Learning to compose neural networks for question answering. In *Proceedings of the 2016 Conference of the North American Chapter of the Association for Computational Linguistics: Human Language Technologies (NAACL 2016)*.

Gabor Angeli, Melvin Johnson Premkumar, and Christopher D Manning. 2015. Leveraging linguistic structure for open domain information extraction. *Proceedings of the 53rd Annual Meeting of the Association for Computational Linguistics and the 7th International Joint Conference on Natural Language Processing of the Asian Federation of Natural Language Processing (ACL-IJCNLP)*.

Eduard Bejček, Eva Hajičová, Jan Hajič, Pavlína Jínová, Václava Kettnerová, Veronika Kolářová,

Marie Mikulová, Jiří Mírovský, Anna Nedoluzhko, Jarmila Panevová, Lucie Poláková, Magda Ševčíková, Jan Štěpánek, and Šárka Zikánová. 2013. Prague Dependency Treebank 3.0. LINDAT/CLARIN digital library at the Institute of Formal and Applied Linguistics, Charles University.

Cem Bozsahin. 2000. Gapping and word order in Turkish. In *Proceedings of the 10th International Conference on Turkish Linguistics.*

Elizabeth Coppock. 2001. Gapping: In defense of deletion. In Mary Andronis, Christopher Ball, Heidi Elston, and Sylvain Neuvel, editors, *Papers from the 37th Meeting of the Chicago Linguistic Society*, Chicago. Chicago Linguistic Society.

Marie-Catherine de Marneffe and Christopher D. Manning. 2008. Stanford typed dependencies manual. Technical report, Stanford University.

Marie-Catherine de Marneffe, Bill MacCartney, and Christopher D. Manning. 2006. Generating typed dependency parses from phrase structure parses. In *Proceedings of the 5th International Conference on Language Resources and Evaluation (LREC 2006).*

Annahita Farudi. 2013. *Gapping in Farsi: A Crosslinguistic Investigation*. Ph.D. thesis, MIT.

Kim Gerdes and Sylvain Kahane. 2015. Non-constituent coordination and other coordinative constructions as dependency graphs. In *Proceedings of the Third International conference on Dependency Linguistics (Depling 2015).*

Jane Grimshaw. 1997. Projection, heads, and optimality. *Linguistic Inquiry*, 28(3):373–422.

Ray S. Jackendoff. 1971. Gapping and related rules. *Linguistic Inquiry*, 2(1):21–35.

Kyle Johnson. 2009. Gapping is not (VP-) ellipsis. *Linguistic Inquiry*, 40(2):289–328.

Kumiko Kato. 2006. *Japanese Gapping in Minimalist Syntax*. Ph.D. thesis, University of Washington.

Dave Kush. 2016. Notes on gapping in Hindi-Urdu: Conjunct size and focus parallelism. *Linguistic Analysis*, 40(3-4):255–296.

Mausam, Michael Schmitz, Robert Bart, Stephen Soderland, and Oren Etzioni. 2012. Open language learning for information extraction. In *Proceedings of Conference on Empirical Methods in Natural Language Processing and Computational Natural Language Learning (EMNLP-CoNLL).*

Ryan McDonald and Joakim Nivre. 2007. Characterizing the errors of data-driven dependency parsing models. In *Proceedings of the 2007 Joint Conference on Empirical Methods in Natural Language Processing and Computational Natural Language Learning (EMNLP-CoNLL).*

Igor A. Mel'čuk. 1988. *Dependency Syntax: Theory and Practice*. State University of New York Press, Albany.

Joakim Nivre, Marie-Catherine de Marneffe, Filip Ginter, Yoav Goldberg, Jan Hajič, Christopher D. Manning, Ryan McDonald, Slav Petrov, Sampo Pyysalo, Natalia Silveira, Reut Tsarfaty, and Daniel Zeman. 2016. Universal Dependencies v1: A multilingual treebank collection. In *Proceedings of the Tenth International Conference on Language Resources and Evaluation (LREC 2016).*

Timothy Osborne. 2006a. Gapping vs. non-gapping coordination. *Linguistische Berichte*, 207:307–337.

Timothy Osborne. 2006b. Shared material and grammar: Toward a dependency grammar theory of non-gapping coordination for english and german. *Zeitschrift für Sprachwissenschaft*, 25(1).

Timothy Osborne. 2015. Diagnostics for constituents: Dependency, constituency, and the status of function words. In *Proceedings of the Third International Conference on Dependency Linguistics (Depling 2015).*

Carl Pollard and Ivan A. Sag. 1994. *Head-driven phrase structure grammar*. University of Chicago Press.

Siva Reddy, Oscar Täckström, Slav Petrov, Mark Steedman, and Mirella Lapata. 2017. Universal semantic parsing. *arXiv preprint arXiv:1702.03196.*

John Robert Ross. 1970. Gapping and the order of constituents. In Manfred Bierwisch and Karl Erich Heidolph, editors, *Progress in Linguistics*. De Gruyter, The Hague.

Sebastian Schuster and Christopher D. Manning. 2016. Enhanced English Universal Dependencies: An improved representation for natural language understanding tasks. In *Proceedings of the Tenth International Conference on Language Resources and Evaluation (LREC 2016).*

Mihai Surdeanu, Richard Johansson, Adam Meyers, Lluís Màrquez, and Joakim Nivre. 2008. The CoNLL-2008 Shared Task on Joint Parsing of Syntactic and Semantic Dependencies. In *Proceedings of the Twelfth Conference on Computational Natural Language Learning (CoNLL 2008).*

Lucien Tesnière. 1959. *Eléments de Syntaxe Structurale*. Klincksieck, Paris.

G. Vanden Wyngaerd. 2007. Gapping constituents. Ms., FWO/K.U. Brussel.

Toward Universal Dependencies for Ainu

Hajime Senuma
University of Tokyo
National Institute of Informatics
senuma@nii.ac.jp

Akiko Aizawa
National Institute of Informatics
University of Tokyo
aizawa@nii.ac.jp

Abstract

Ainu is a language spoken by the Ainu people, a minority ethnic group in Japan. The development of syntactic corpora for Ainu is crucial both for the advancement of linguistic theories and for language revitalization. To solve the situation, we experimentally annotated a short poem of Ainu with Universal Dependencies version 2 scheme. In this paper, we report several language-specific suggestions for the UD annotation of Ainu, obtained through the experience of the initial experiments.

1 Introduction

"In the beginning was the Word"—assuming we have the definition of *word* in the first place. For many languages, the boundary between words and sentences is clear in many cases, not to say in most cases. For some languages, however, it is inherently ambiguous. More than one hundred years ago, linguists heatedly discussed a construction called *noun incorporation*, in which nouns and verbs are combined to form *one* word which has information comparable to a sentence, as a challenging phenomenon to identify such a boundary (Kroeber, 1910; Sapir, 1911; Kroeber, 1911). Even in this age the discussion is not resolved at all but further complicated (Mithun, 1984; Baker, 1988; Baker, 1996; Massam, 2001). Massam (2009, p. 1091) claimed that "[noun incorporation] studies all by themselves provide us with a microcosm of linguistic theory, demonstrating the struggle by linguists to answer major questions such as what constitutes a construction, what are the differences between words and sentences, and what is the relation between meaning and form."

Ainu is one of the representative languages equipped with noun incorporation and *polysynthesis* (words are synthesized by many morphemes), and it has been used as an important tool to uncover the universal nature of human languages (Baker, 1996). It has been spoken by the Ainu, an indigenous people in Japan who originally inhabited islands around the border of what is now Japan and Russia. It is a *language isolate* in the sense that no languages are confirmed to be genetically related to Ainu. The language is in need of linguistic resources, not only for its typological importance, but also for language preservation and revival; Ethnologue classified Ainu as *nearly extinct* (Lewis et al., 2016) and constant effort has been taken to revitalize it (Sato, 2012).

Unfortunately, to the best of our knowledge, there is no syntactically annotated corpus on Ainu thus far. Momouchi et al. (2008) annotated some Ainu poems of Ainu Shinyoshu only with part of speeches and parallel Japanese translation. Bugaeva (2011b) released a freely-accessible dictionary with in-depth glossing for sentence examples but the glossing system is mainly for traditional typological purposes. If we have syntactic annotations, they will enable us to develop advanced natural language processing (NLP) tools and may also serve as an educational tool to explain unique phenomena in Ainu clearly.

Considering the recent revival of dependency grammar (Tesnière, 1959; Tesnière, 2015; Hays, 1960) by theoretical refinement (Järvinen and Tapanainen, 1998; Kuhlmann, 2013; Nivre, 2015) and success in statistical/neural dependency parsing (McDonald et al., 2005; Nivre et al., 2007; Chen and Manning, 2014; Kiperwasser and Goldberg, 2016), Universal Dependencies (UD) is a natural choice to syntactically annotate Ainu texts. One notable feature of modern dependency theory such as UD is its simplicity in the annotation scheme (Nivre, 2015). Because Ainu is a complex language the theoretical aspect of which is not yet fully understood, it is crucial to make its annotation as easy as possible.

In addition, Tesnière (1959, Chapter 276) claimed that dependency diagrams are a useful tool for pedagogical purposes, e.g., deeper analysis of

Proceedings of the NoDaLiDa 2017 Workshop on Universal Dependencies (UDW 2017), pages 133–139,
Gothenburg, Sweden, 22 May 2017.

sentences and learning new languages. On top of that, it should be accessible to Japanese students, because Japanese junior high school curriculum includes the *kakari-uke* theory, a variant of the dependency theory independently developed by Hashimoto (1932).

Note that within the UD framework we do not annotate noun incorporation and treat complex verbs formed by noun incorporation as ordinary one-word verbs, as the framework adopted the *lexical integrity principle* and separated morphology as being fundamentally different from syntax (de Marneffe et al., 2014). We will try to discover the nature of noun incorporation only when we resolve the problems of syntactic side. Practically speaking, this treatment will not be so problematic for Ainu, because it is in poetry where noun incorporation is highly productive and for day-to-day speech, noun incorporation is usually used only for idiomatic expressions. Still, annotating Ainu is by no means trivial. As we will see below, there are several unique constructions other than noun incorporation and we will discuss how to annotate them in UD.

To endeavor to develop the UD corpus of Ainu, as an initial effort, we examined a short poem in a collection of Ainu poetry and experimentally annotated texts with UD. This tiny experimental "corpus" contains only 36 sentences and 516 words in total but through this experiment we devised a prototype of the annotation scheme for Ainu. In this paper, we report several findings which may lead toward the complete corpus in the future.

2 Notation

For glossing, we adopted the Leipzig Glossing Rules (Comrie et al., 2008) with the following additions: n-VAL for valency (e.g., 1VAL indicates monovalent verbs) and INT for intensifiers.

We omitted the `root` dependency from each dependency diagram if visually redundant.

3 Resources

3.1 Source text

We used the poetry *Ainu Shin'yōshū* "Ainu Godly Tales" written by a female poet Yukie Chiri (Chiri, 1923) as our raw corpus. It contains 13 short traditional Ainu poems (*kamuyyukar* "godly tales") in romanized form as well as Japanese translations by herself. In Japan, it has been recognized as a great masterpiece and now published from Iwanami Bunko, a series of paperbacks for literary classics, similar to Penguin Classics and Reclam. The English translation of the poetry by Peterson (2013) is openly accessible.[1]

We chose the work as our text because of the following reasons:

1. It is now under public domain and freely available from Aozora Bunko.[2]

2. It uses Classical Ainu, a register of Ainu which exhibits noun incorporation more extensively than colloquial one.

3. It was compiled by a native speaker.

In this experimental annotation, we used the sixth poem *Pon Horkewkamuy Yayeyukar: "Hotenao"* "A little wolf-god recites a song about himself: 'Hotenao' " ("6: The Song the Wolf Cub Sang" in Peterson (2013)'s translation) as reference.

The result was uploaded as the first author's GitHub project under CC BY 4.0.[3]

3.2 Orthography

Traditionally the Ainu language has no writing systems. From the 19th century, however, two writing systems have been co-developed: one with Latin characters and the other with Japanese katakana. While katakana system has an advantage that it is easy for Japanese people to learn, it has a disadvantage that it generates ambiguity for some cases. For instance, modern katakana orthography adopted by the Foundation of Research and Promotion of Ainu Culture (FRPAC) uses the same character ッ for germination and a consonantal syllable *t*, resulting that both *makkosanpa* "to brighten suddenly" (Tamura, 1996, p. 376) and *matkosanpa* "to wake up suddenly" (Tamura, 1996, p. 380) are written as マッコサンパ. On the other hand, the Latin-based writing system has less ambiguity and thus is suitable for research purposes, while elderly people and children in Japan may feel difficulty to learn it.

The original text of our corpus was written in Latin characters following Kyōsuke Kindaichi's romanization style. We, however, manually converted it into modern (Latin-based) romanization style because doing so will be useful for further research analysis as it is adopted by modern scholars (Tamura, 2000; Sato, 2008) and also for being read

---

[1]http://www.okikirmui.com
[2]http://www.aozora.gr.jp/cards/001529/
files/44909_29558.html
[3]https://github.com/hajimes/ud-ainu

by beginners of Ainu as it is adopted in textbooks for non-experts by FRPAC (2011). Although there are several minor differences between these work, we basically followed FRPAC (2011) where there are conflicts. To name a few, 1. we use "=" as a delimiter between pronominal morphemes and other words (like *ku=kor* "I=have"), 2. the first letter of each sentence is *not* capitalized, and 3. we prefer to retain morphological values (e.g., *sanpa* because it consists of *san* and *pa*, in spite that its sound is *sampa*). We also corrected errors in the original text by using critical studies on the work (Kirikae, 2003; Sato, 2004).

Tokenization is relatively simple with the exception of treatment for pronominal clitics. See Section 4 for the topic.

3.3 Dictionary and referential textbook

For dictionary and reference, we mainly referred to Tamura (1996) and Tamura (2000) (English translation of Tamura (1988)), respectively. Strictly speaking, Tamura (1996) deals with the Saru dialect while our text is in the Horobetsu dialect, but two dialects are so close that they have few differences in vocabulary and no grammatical differences.

We also used other dictionaries, e.g., Nakagawa (1995), Kayano (2002), and Bugaeva (2011b). For reference, we also consulted Refsing (1986), Shibatani (1990), and Sato (2008).

4 Pronominal Clitics and Polypersonal Agreement

Polysynthesis often comes with *polypersonal agreement* and Ainu is no exception. Ainu verbs are obligatorily inflected with subject and object. For example, a prefix *e=un=* denotes 2SG>1PL.EXCL "you (but not you all) [hit, took care of, etc.] us (but not including you)".

It is highly controversial whether these pronominal morphemes are words, clitics (that is, relatively dependent elements which are still separable from other words), or affixes (that is, partial elements of other words). Bugaeva (2011a, Section 2.3) argued that *=an* and *=as* are words, *a=* and *eci=* are clitics, and *ku=*, *ci=*, *e=*, *en=*, *un=*, *i=* are "fully-fledged prefixes". We applied the classical test of cliticness (Zwicky, 1985) and decided to treat all of these morphemes as clitics. We annotated them with PART (particles) for their part-of-speech category and used the aux relation when they depend on verbs and nmod:poss when nouns.

For convenience, we treated delimiters "=" as if they are a part of pronominal clitics. For example, *sap=as* "go=I" is tokenized as *sap* and *=as* rather than *sap*, =, and *as*. This style is consistent with Tamura (1996) and the glossary of FRPAC (2011) in which pronominal clitics are affixed with the delimiters in their entries.

5 Relative Clauses as Adjectival Expressions

In light of syntactic categories (or parts-of-speech), the most noticeable feature of Ainu is a lack of adjectives. Instead, the language employs relative clause constructions to obtain the same effect. This phenomenon is similar to Arapaho (Wagner et al., 2016).

For example, since Ainu is SOV in most cases,

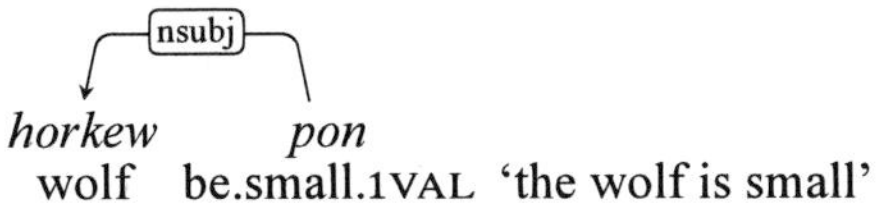

horkew   pon
wolf   be.small.1VAL   'the wolf is small'

On the other hand, if we place the verb at the preceding position of the noun, it acts as relative clause modification.

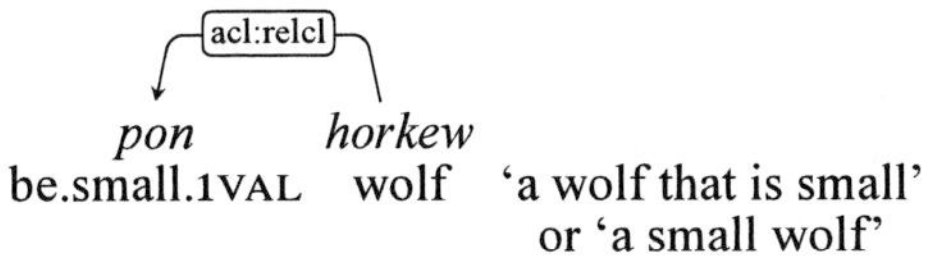

pon   horkew
be.small.1VAL   wolf   'a wolf that is small'
or 'a small wolf'

For *alienable* nouns, pronominal possession is also expressed by relative clause-like construction. For example (Tamura, 2000, p. 87),

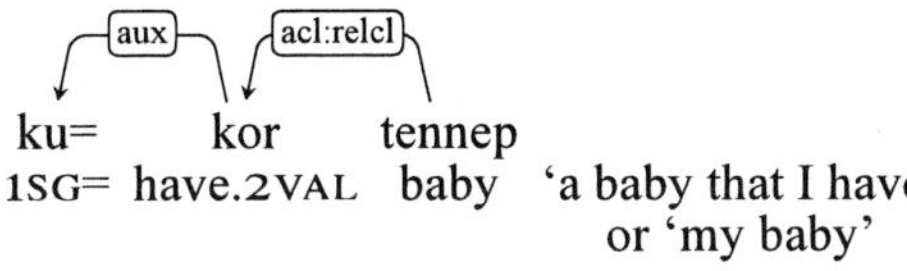

ku=   kor   tennep
1SG=   have.2VAL   baby   'a baby that I have'
or 'my baby'

A condition to form relative clauses is that the remaining number of slots of a verb expression must be one, so it actively interacts with the valency property of verbs.

6 Pronominal Arguments

In traditional understanding, Ainu has polypersonal agreement and we have the following analysis (the phrase is a shortened form of a sentence ky-6-33 *eani anak pon horkew sani e=ne ruwe tasi an ne* in our corpus):

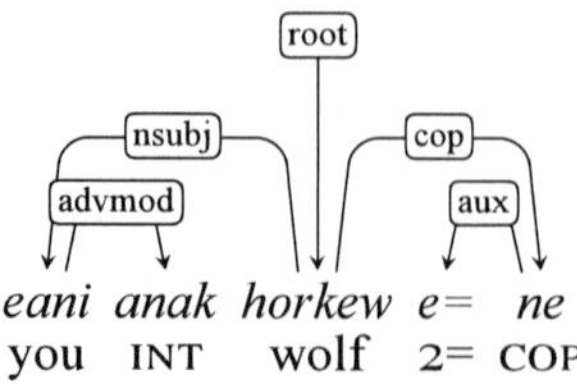

'You are a wolf'

Here, *eani* is used as a common pronoun (PRON) and a clitic *e=* is used as an auxiliary item (PART) to the verb. The problem is that in almost all cases explicit pronominal arguments like *eani* is omitted. In 516 words of our corpus, these "pronouns" occurred only once. To make the matter worse, these "pronouns" often behave like adverbials rather than nominals.

Because of this, several linguists (cf. Baker (1996)) claimed that the clitics are "true" arguments to verbs in these polysynthetic languages and the pronoun-like words such as *eani* in Ainu are mere adjuncts. According to Baker, this analysis was already pointed out by Wilhelm von Humboldt for Aztec in the 1830s but it was not until Eloise Jelinek discussed the matter in the 1980s that the analysis is widely recognized. Although Baker's analysis is based on Chomskyian constituency framework, if we somehow apply their discussion to our text, we may have the following analysis:

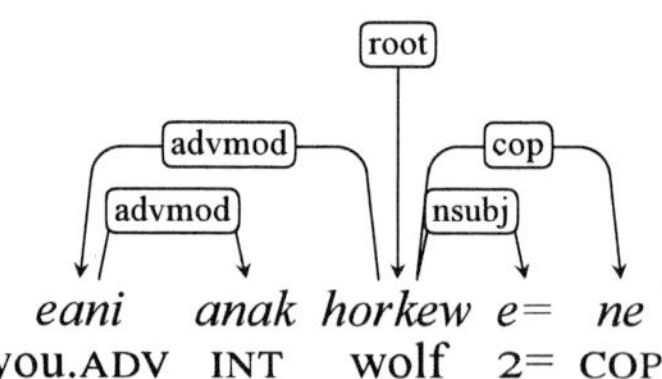

'Speaking of you, you are a wolf.'

In our annotation scheme, however, we maintain the first conservative approach. This approach has an advantage that it can consistently annotate a subtype of Ainu which adopted several constructions from Japanese and was used in some dialects. Izutsu (2006) reported that in some dialects the construction of Ainu sentence became close to the Japanese language and they lack pronominal clitics even though in original Ainu they are mandatory. Instead, they used pronoun-like words such as *eani* as true core arguments to verbs. If we adopted the first annotation scheme, there is no difficulty to handle this exceptional situation as:

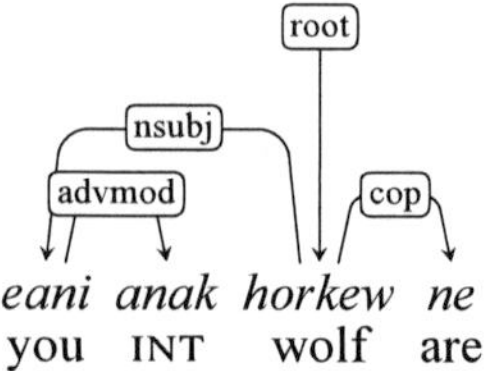

7 Language-Specific Features

7.1 Person: Fourth person

The Ainu language has a peculiar set of pronominal clitics: subject postfix *=an* for monovalent (intransitive) verbs, subject prefix *a=* for polyvalent (transitive) verbs, and object prefix *i=*. It fulfills various rolls depending on the context (Tamura, 2000, pp. 63–80): 1. most commonly first person plural (1PL) inclusive (whereas an ordinary prefix *ci=* for 1PL exclusive); 2. first person singular (1SG) in quotational sentences (such as "I" in "He said 'I saw the man.' "); 3. 1SG in oral literature, because the Ainu literature often employs the style with which someone talks about himself/herself in quotational sentences, 4. general laws ("In general, people do ..."); 5. indefinite person; 6. used for passive construction; and 7. at least in the Saru dialect, traditionally used as second person polite form from females to males of higher position such as their own husbands and village-leaders.

There is no unanimous agreement what we should call these pronouns. Nakagawa (1995) used the term "fourth person", while Tamura (2000) used "indefinite person" and Shibatani (1990), Sato (2008), and Bugaeva (2011a) used "first person plural inclusive".

In our scheme, we used Person=4 for expedience, as available in UD version 2. Whereas UD defines Person=4 as "a third person argument morphologically distinguished from another third person argument" that is suitable for Ainu to some extent, its usage in Navajo, cited as a typical example, is much different from that in Ainu. One possible solution (owing to Francis Tyers) is to annotate it as first person inclusive with Clusive=Inc. We hope to gain insights from research into other languages in the future.

7.2 Number: pluractional

In Ainu, some verbs are inflected by pluractionality, that is, the plurality of actions.

For example, *tuypa*, the pluractional form of *tuye* "to cut" indicates (Tamura, 2000, Section 4.3.2.4): 1. two or more people do cutting, 2. one person cuts two or more objects, or 3. one person cuts one object more than once.

Pronominal clitics may enforce pluractionality. Our corpus contains a phrase *pis ta sap=as* "I go to the beach" where *sap* "to go" is in a pluractional form though the action is semantically singular. This is possibly because, as we stated in previous section, in the oral literature 1PL inclusive (*=as*) is used as 1SG.

To annotate this phenomenon, following the tradition of Ainu studies in which it is treated as number, we tentatively used a language-specific feature `Number=Pluract`. However, this phenomonenon clearly deviates from number, which basically serves as an agreement system between nouns, often purely syntactically, rather than semantically. In the literature of typology there seems to be a difference of opinion as to whether pluractionality is related to aspect or it is an independent feature. We will make further research on this point, and we may adopt either `Aspect=Pluract` or `Pluract=Yes` in the future.

7.3 Valency

Valency (number of core arguments attachable to verbs) enjoys the central role in the Ainu morphology and syntax. Morphologically it governs the system of noun incorporation. It also affects syntactic phenomena such as selection of pronominal clitics and construction of relative clauses.

Commonly used valency are monovalent (intransitive), divalent (monotransitive), and trivalent (ditransitive). In addition, avalent verbs are not so rare, e.g., *sirkunne* (it expresses a sentential phrase "it is dark" by one word). The maximum of valency in Ainu is not known but Bugaeva (2015, p. 828) reported the existence of a tetravalent verb (`Valency=4`) *korere* "to make somebody give something to somebody".

In the above example, *kor-e-re* is formed by doubly suffixing causatives: "have-CAUS-CAUS". Here *e* / *re* (allophones of *te*) add valency and causativity. The degree of modification depends on morpheme; for example, while *te* obligatorily increases valency, an indefinite causative morpheme *yar* does not change it. Turkish has a similar system, which allows multiple causative voices. In Ainu, however, causative is just a part of verb formation and has no special status.

The morphological system of Ainu (notably Classical Ainu) productively affects the valency of verbs: e.g., valency-increasing operators such as causative suffixes and applicative prefixes (such as instrumental *e-*, adding an argument slot meaning 'by using') and valency-decreasing ones such as incorporated nouns and reflexive prefixes.

To annotate this phenomenon, we used a language-specific feature `Valency=0`, `Valency=1`, etc. Possibly we may borrow the terminology of UniMorph (Sylak-Glassman et al., 2015) features, that is, `Valency: DITR, IMPRS, INTR, TR` in the future.

7.4 Inalienable possession

The only inflectional system of Ainu nouns is by inalienable possession, with the form similar to ezāfe in Persian (Bugaeva, 2011a, p. 520).

Only a handful of nouns are classified as being inalienable, e.g., body parts (including names) and family members. They are inflected if being possessed by someone. For instance, *re* "name" is inflected to *réhe*; and with 1SG pronominal clitic *ku=*, we obtain *ku=réhe* "my name".

Likewise, a class of nouns called *locative nouns* has possessed forms. For example, a locative noun *or* is used as a concept of "place" as in *atuy or un* "sea place to", that is, "into the sea", while its possessed form *oro* is used to indicate "its place" as in *oro wano* "its.place from", that is, "from there".

Several nouns act as *nominalizer* in their possessed forms. For instance, *hawe*, the inflected form of *haw* "voice", is used as a nominalizer related to auditory sense, as in *itak=as hawe* "speak=I fact" or "the fact that I speak'. Unlike relative clauses (see Section 5), these nominals are prefixed only by complete sentences, and thus we used `acl` relationship to mark the dependency rather than `acl:relcl`.

To annotate this phenomenon, we used a language-specific feature `Possessed=Yes`.

8 Conclusion

This paper proposed several UD annotation schemes for Ainu as a prototype, obtained through experimental annotation for a short poem. We plan to annotate the whole collection of poetry by using this scheme and publish it as an open-source corpus. We hope this endeavor serves as a basis for building huge corpora of Ainu in the future.

Acknowledgements

This work was supported by CREST, Japan Science and Technology Agency. We thank two anonymous reviewers for their helpful comments, especially for indicating relation to Arapaho. We are also deeply indebted to Francis Tyers for the substantial improvement of this paper including suggestions for the future treatment of fourth person, pluractionality, and valency.

References

Mark C. Baker. 1988. *Incorporation*. Chicago University Press.

Mark C. Baker. 1996. *The Polysynthesis Parameter*. Oxford University Press.

Anna Bugaeva. 2011a. A diachronic study of the impersonal passive in Ainu. In *Impersonal Constructions: A Cross-Linguistic Perspective*, Studies in Language Companion, pages 517–546. John Benjamins.

Anna Bugaeva. 2011b. Internet Applications for Endangered Languages: A Talking Dictionary of Ainu. *Waseda Institute for Advanced Study Research Bulletin*, 3:73–81.

Anna Bugaeva. 2015. Valency classes in Ainu. In Bernard Comrie and Andrey Malchukov, editors, *Valency Classes in the World's Languages*. Mouton de Gruyter.

Danqi Chen and Christopher D. Manning. 2014. A Fast and Accurate Dependency Parser using Neural Networks. In *Proceedings of the 2014 Conference on Empirical Methods in Natural Language Processing (EMNLP)*, pages 740–750, Stroudsburg, PA, USA. Association for Computational Linguistics.

Yukie Chiri. 1923. *Ainu Shin'yōshū [Collection of Ainu Kamuyyukar]*. Kyodo Kenkyusha.

Bernard Comrie, Martin Haspelmath, and Balthasar Bickel. 2008. The Leipzig Glossing Rules. Technical report, Max Planck Institute for Evolutionary Anthropology and University of Leipzig.

Marie-Catherine de Marneffe, Timothy Dozat, Natalia Silveira, Katri Haverinen, Filip Ginter, Joakim Nivre, and Christopher D. Manning. 2014. Universal Stanford Dependencies: A cross-linguistic typology. In *In Proceedings of the Ninth International Conference on Language Resources and Evaluation (LREC'14)*, pages 4585–4592.

FRPAC. 2011. *Chūkyū Ainugo: Horobetsu [Intermediate Ainu: Horobetsu Dialect]*. FRPAC (The Foundation of Research and Promotion of Ainu Culture).

Shinkichi Hashimoto. 1932. *Kokugogaku Gairon [Elements of Japanese Linguistics]*. Iwanami Shoten.

David G. Hays. 1960. Grouping and Dependency Theories. In *Proceedings of the National Symposium on Machine Translation*, pages 258–266.

Katsunobu Izutsu. 2006. Ainugo no Hinshi Bunrui Saikō: Iwayuru Ninshō Daimeishi o Megutte [Ainu Parts of Speech Revisited: with Special Reference to So-called Personal Pronouns]. *Journal of Hokkaido University of Education: Humanities and Social Sciences*, 56(2):13–27.

Timo Järvinen and Pasi Tapanainen. 1998. Towards an implementable dependency grammar. In *Processing of Dependency-Based Grammars: Proceedings of the Workshop, COLING-ACL'98*, pages 1–10.

Shigeru Kayano. 2002. *Kayano Shigeru no Ainugo Jiten [The Ainu Dictionary by Shigeru Kayano]*. Sanseido, 2nd edition.

Eliyahu Kiperwasser and Yoav Goldberg. 2016. Easy-First Dependency Parsing with Hierarchical Tree LSTMs. *Transactions of the Association for Computational Linguistics*, 4:445–461.

Hideo Kirikae. 2003. *Ainu Shin'yōshu Jiten [Lexicon to Ainu Shin'yōshū]*. Daigaku Shorin.

A. L. Kroeber. 1910. Noun incorporation in American languages. In *Verhandlungen der XVI Internationaler Amerikanisten-Kongress [Reprinted in The Collected Works of Edward Sapir, Vol. 5, 1990]*, pages 569–576. Hartleben.

A. L. Kroeber. 1911. Incorporation as a Linguistic Process. *American Anthropologist*, 13(4):577–584.

Marco Kuhlmann. 2013. Mildly Non-Projective Dependency Grammar. *Computational Linguistics*, 39(2):355–387, June.

M. Paul Lewis, Gary F. Simons, and Charles D. Fennig. 2016. *Ethnologue: Languages of the World, Nineteenth edition*. SIL International.

Diane Massam. 2001. Pseudo Noun Incorporation in Niuean. *Natural Language and Linguistic Theory*, 19(1):153–197.

Diane Massam. 2009. Noun Incorporation: Essentials and Extensions. *Linguistics and Language Compass*, 3(4):1076–1096.

Ryan McDonald, Fernando Pereira, Kiril Ribarov, and Jan Hajič. 2005. Non-projective Dependency Parsing using Spanning Tree Algorithms. In *Proceedings of the Conference on Human Language Technology and Empirical Methods in Natural Language Processing - HLT '05*, pages 523–530. Association for Computational Linguistics.

Marianne Mithun. 1984. The Evolution of Noun Incorporation. *Language*, 60(4):847–894.

Yoshio Momouchi, Yasunori Azumi, and Yukio Kadoya. 2008. Research Note: Construction and Utilization of Electronic Data for Ainu Shin-yosyu. *Bulletin of the Faculty of Engineering at Hokkai-Gakuen University*, 35:159–171.

Hiroshi Nakagawa. 1995. *Ainugo Chitose Hōgen Jiten [The Ainu–Japanese Dictionary: Chitose Dialect]*. Sōfūkan.

Joakim Nivre, Johan Hall, Jens Nilsson, Atanas Chanev, Gülşen Eryiğit, Sandra Kübler, Svetoslav Marinov, and Erwin Marsi. 2007. MaltParser:

A language-independent system for data-driven dependency parsing. *Natural Language Engineering*, 13(2):95–135, June.

Joakim Nivre. 2015. Towards a Universal Grammar for Natural Language Processing. In *Computational Linguistics and Intelligent Text Processing: 16th International Conference, CICLing 2015, Cairo, Egypt, April 14-20, 2015, Proceedings, Part I*, pages 3–16. Springer International Publishing.

Benjamin Peterson. 2013. *The Song The Owl God Sang: The collected Ainu legends of Chiri Yukie*. BJS Books.

Kirsten Refsing. 1986. *The Ainu Language: The Morphology and Syntax of the Shizunai Dialect*. Aarhus University Press.

Edward Sapir. 1911. The Problem of Noun Incorporation in American Languages. *American Anthropologist*, 13:250–282.

Tomomi Sato. 2004. Chiri Yukie Ainu Shinyōshu no Nandoku Kasho to Tokui na Gengo Jirei o Megutte [Notes on Some Linguistic Problems and the Interpretation of Lines Doubtful in Yukie Chiri's Ainu sin'yôshû]. *The Annual Reports on Cultural Science, Hokkaido University*, 10.

Tomomi Sato. 2008. *Ainugo Bunpō no Kiso [The Basics of the Ainu Grammar]*. Daigaku Shorin.

Tomomi Sato. 2012. Ainugo no Genjō to Fukkō [The Present Situation of the Ainu Language and Its Revitalization]. *Gengo Kenkyu*, 142:29–44.

Masayoshi Shibatani. 1990. *The Languages of Japan*. Cambridge University Press.

John Sylak-Glassman, Christo Kirov, David Yarowsky, and Roger Que. 2015. A Language-Independent Feature Schema for Inflectional Morphology. In *Proceedings of the 53rd Annual Meeting of the Association for Computational Linguistics and the 7th International Joint Conference on Natural Language Processing (Volume 1: Long Papers)*, pages 674–680.

Suzuko Tamura. 1988. Ainugo [The Ainu Language]. In *Gengogaku Daijiten*, volume 1, pages 6–94. Sanseidō.

Suzuko Tamura. 1996. *Ainugo Saru Hōgen Jiten [The Ainu–Japanese Dictionary: Saru Dialect]*. Sōfūkan.

Suzuko Tamura. 2000. *The Ainu Language*. ICHEL Linguistic Studies. Sanseidō.

Lucien Tesnière. 1959. *Éléments de syntaxe structurale [Elements of structural syntax]*. C. Klincksieck, Paris.

Lucien Tesnière. 2015. *Elements of Structural Syntax*. John Benjamins Publishing Company, Amsterdam. Translated by Timothy Osborne and Sylvain Kahane.

Irina Wagner, Andrew Cowell, and Jena D. Hwang. 2016. Applying Universal Dependency to the Arapaho Language. In *Proceedings of the 10th Linguistic Annotation Workshop held in conjunction with ACL 2016 (LAW-X 2016)*, pages 171–179, Stroudsburg, PA, USA. Association for Computational Linguistics.

Arnold M. Zwicky. 1985. Clitics and Particles. *Language*, 61(2):283–305.

Automatic Morpheme Segmentation and Labeling in Universal Dependencies resources

Miikka Silfverberg and **Mans Hulden**
Department of Linguistics
University of Colorado
{miikka.silfverberg,mans.hulden}@colorado.edu

Abstract

Newer incarnations of the Universal Dependencies (UD) resources feature rich morphological annotation on the word-token level as regards tense, mood, aspect, case, gender, and other grammatical information. This information, however, is not aligned to any part of the word forms in the data. In this work, we present an algorithm for inferring this latent alignment between morphosyntactic labels and substrings of word forms. We evaluate the method on three languages where we have manually labeled part of the Universal Dependencies data—Finnish, Swedish, and Spanish—and show that the method is robust enough to use for automatic discovery, segmentation, and labeling of allomorphs in the data sets. The model allows us to provide a more detailed morphosyntactic labeling and segmentation of the UD data.

1 Introduction

Recent versions of Universal Dependencies (UD) (Nivre et al., 2017) provide not only part-of-speech labeling, but also universal lexical and inflectional features on most word forms. Table 1 illustrates a few example words from the three experiment languages used in this paper.[1]

A noteworthy aspect of this layout of the data is that it provides for an interesting inference problem in the realm of weakly supervised learning of inflectional morphology.[2] First, we note that

---

[1]We have deviated slightly from the original annotation, incorporating the lemma as a feature for each word, the need for which will be explained in the technical portion of the paper.

[2]A similar annotation is provided in the SIGMORPHON shared task (Cotterell et al., 2016a) data set, although without implicit token frequency information since the data comes in the form of inflection examples mostly from Wiktionary.

the feature-value pairs in the annotation correspond mostly to individual allomorphs in the surface form of the word. For example, in the Spanish word **asignados** (Table 1), a standard analysis would be that the **asign-** part corresponds to the stem, the **-ad-** corresponds to `VerbForm=Part` and `Tense=Past`, the **-o-** to `Gender=Masc` and the **-s** to `Number=Plur`. The inference problem is then: given many annotated word forms with morphosyntactic features which are not matched to any substrings in the word, find a globally satisfactory segmentation of all word forms and associate the morphosyntactic labels in each word with these segmented substrings.

2 Related Work

Morphological segmentation, particularly in unsupervised scenarios, is a standard problem in NLP, and has been explored in numerous works (Goldsmith (2001), Creutz and Lagus (2005), Poon et al. (2009), Dreyer and Eisner (2011) inter alia). We recommend Ruokolainen et al. (2016) for an overview. Likewise, semi-supervised, or minimally supervised models—where the supervision usually implies access to some small number of segmented words—have also been widely investigated (Dasgupta and Ng, 2007; Kohonen et al., 2010; Grönroos et al., 2014; Sirts and Goldwater, 2013). Many approaches also take advantage of a semantic signal, or a proxy for semantic similarity between words such as Latent Semantic Analysis (Schone and Jurafsky, 2000) or its more modern counterpart, word embeddings (Soricut and Och, 2015). The specific formulation of an inference problem like the one presented in this paper has to our knowledge not been directly addressed previously, probably due to the necessity of annotated resource schemas such as those present in UD 2.0. A related problem, dealt with in Cotterell et al. (2016b) and Kann et al. (2016), concerns simultaneous segmentation and canonicalization—

Proceedings of the NoDaLiDa 2017 Workshop on Universal Dependencies (UDW 2017), pages 140–145,
Gothenburg, Sweden, 22 May 2017.

Finnish	jäällä	Noun|Lemma=jää|Case=Ade|Number=Sing
Spanish	asignados	Verb|Lemma=asignar|Gender=Masc|Number=Plur|Tense=Past|VerbForm=Part
Swedish	innebär	Verb|Lemma=innebära|Mood=Ind|Tense=Pres|VerbForm=Fin|Voice=Act

Table 1: Examples of the modified UD annotations used for inference of segmentation and labeling.

a task where allomorphs are both segmented and rendered as a single canonical form, e.g. **communism** $\mapsto$ **commune ism**. This task was addressed in an entirely supervised scenario, however, and so the results are not directly comparable.

3 The Segmentation and Labeling Problem

As implied above, the current labeling of the UD data provides significant constraints and a supervision signal that can guide us in the inference process. One strong linguistically informed bias is that labels, i.e. abstractions of morphemes such as Number=Sing, Gender=Masc, should be assigned to substrings in such a way as to co-occur only with a small number of distinct strings throughout the data. This corresponds to the idea that each morpheme be realized as a limited number of distinct allomorphs. For example, the English pluralizer morpheme by and large occurs as only three allomorphs, **-s,-es,** $\varnothing$. Another intuition is the inverse of the previous one: that each allomorph only co-occur with a limited number of labels. For example, the **-s** allomorph in English serves mainly two distinct functions: a pluralizer and the third person present tense marker. We expect rampant ambiguity not to be present in the morphology of a language. On the whole, since most labels are seen a large number of times, we can develop a model that leverages this information to favor correspondences that are systematic in the data. Figure 1 illustrates a linguistically sound correspondence over several word forms that involve two stems in Spanish.

The intuition behind our model is that we'd like to find a segmentation of all words in the data into constituent allomorphs, and provide a label for each allomorph that fulfills the properties above. To perform this, we take advantage of the fact that we already know which morphemes (feature-value pairs) are present in each word (although some of these labels will correspond to null allomorphs).

In general, we want to explore the space of all possible segmentations and labelings in the data and find one that optimizes some objective func-

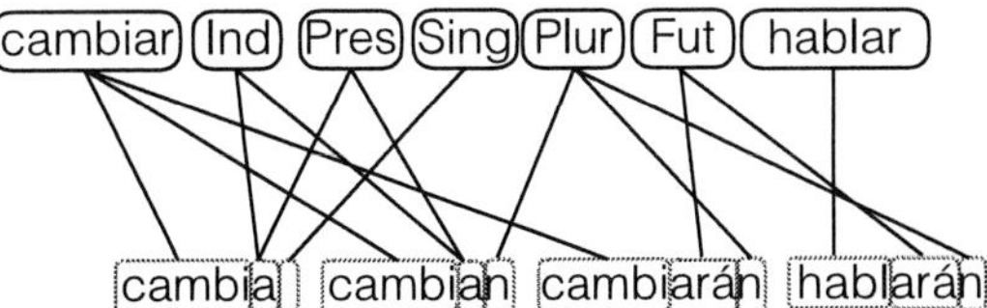

Figure 1: Morphosyntactic features are assigned corresponding substrings where re-use of the same label-substring correspondences is encouraged by the model. Note that some labels (such as Sing here) can be assigned to empty substrings.

tion $\mathcal{C}$, based on the above observations. A given proposal segmentation S and labeling F of the data gives us a joint distribution $P_{S,F}$ over pairs of substrings $s \in \Sigma^*$ and labels $l \in \mathcal{Y}$, where $\mathcal{Y}$ is the set of labels (feature-value pairs) used in the data. We can formalize a cost function $\mathcal{C}(S, F)$ based on the distribution $P(S, F)$. This cost function could take many linguistically motivated specific forms: simply minimizing the total number of resulting distinct allomorphs in the data, minimizing the joint entropy of the labels and the allomorphs, maximizing the mutual information of the allomorphs and the labels, etc. Below, we use a specific cost function that maximizes a measure of symmetric conditional probability between segments and labels.

4 Model

4.1 Definitions

Let $\mathcal{D} = \{(x_1, y_1), ..., (x_k, y_k)\}$ be a collection of word forms x_i and sets of associated morphological features y_i, for example

dogs {lemma=dog,num=plural}

As explained in Section 3, we learn a segmentation $S = \{s^1, ..., s^k\}$ of words in $\mathcal{D}$, where each $s^i = (s^i_i ... s^i_n)$ is a segmentation of word x_i into substrings, and a set of feature assignments $F = \{f_i : y_i \to s^i | 1 \leq i \leq k\}$ of morphological features in y_i onto substrings in s^i.

Because of the existence of unmarked morphological features, such as singular number of nouns in English, we have to allow assignment of morphological features to a zero morpheme. We accomplish this by adding an empty substring to each segmentation.

Each segmentation and label assignment of the data set $\mathcal{D}$ defines joint counts $c(s, f)$ of substrings s and morphological features f as in Equation 1.

$$c(s, f) = \|\{s_j^i | s_j^i = s \text{ and } f_i(f) = s_j^i\}\| \quad (1)$$

Using $c(s, f)$ we express the probability of the co-occurrence of a feature and substring in Equation 2.

$$\mathrm{P}(s, f) \propto c(s, f) + \alpha B(s, f) \quad (2)$$

The function B in Equation 2 expresses a prior belief about the joint counts of segments and labels, and hyper-parameter α controls the weight of the prior information (Goldwater and Griffiths, 2007). A large α will result in $\mathrm{P}(s, f)$ which very closely reflects the prior belief while a smaller α lets P adapt more closely to the current segmentation and label assignment. We set α to 0.1 in all experiments.

We use the joint distribution of substrings and labels in the unsegmented data set $\mathcal{D}$ as prior information. Thus $B(s, f) = \#(s, f)/\#(f)$, where $\#(s, f)$ is the count of substrings s in words with morphological feature f and $\#(f)$ is the count of feature f in $\mathcal{D}$.

For lemma features, for example `lemma=dog`, we add an additional factor to the co-occurrence probability $\mathrm{P}(s, f)$ as shown in Equation 3. The quantity $\mathrm{d}(s, f)$ represents the edit distance of the substring s and the lemma corresponding to f. For example, d(**do**,`lemma=dog`) = 1. This allows us to model the fact that the stem and lemma of a word form often share a long common substring.

$$\mathrm{P}(s, f) \propto (c(s, f) + \alpha B(s, f)) \cdot 2^{-\mathrm{d}(s, f)} \quad (3)$$

4.2 Objective Function

Our objective function is the *symmetric conditional probability* over segments s and morphological features f defined by Equation 4

$$\mathcal{C}(S, F) = \prod_{s \in \Sigma^*, f \in \mathcal{Y}} \mathrm{P}(s|f)\mathrm{P}(f|s) \quad (4)$$

Symmetric conditional probability was introduced by da Silva et al. (1999) for multi-word expression extraction. The measure is intuitively appealing for our purposes since it is maximized when each morphological feature is associated with exactly one allomorph, and this allomorph, in

turn, only occurs with the specific morphological feature.[3]

4.3 Inference

The space of possible segmentations and label assignments to each allomorph segment is very large except for toy data sets. Therefore, an exact solution to the optimization problem presented in Section 4.2 is infeasible. Instead, we use Gibbs sampling to explore the space of possible segmentations S and feature assignments A of our data set $\mathcal{D}$ with the intent of finding the segmentation S_{max} and assignment A_{max} which maximize the symmetric conditional probability of segments and features.

Gibbs sampling in this context proceeds by sampling a new segmentation S' and assignment A' from the current segmentation S and assignment A, and then either rejecting the old segmentation and assignment in favor of the new one with probability $(\mathcal{C}(A', S')/\mathcal{C}(A, S))^{\beta}$, or keeping the old segmentation and assignment. We set the hyper-parameter β to 2 in all experiments and run the Gibbs sampler on the data set $\mathcal{D}$ until the value of the objective function $\mathcal{C}$ has converged.

A new segmentation S' and label assignment A' can be sampled from an existing segmentation S and assignment A in two steps. First, randomly choose a word x_i from the data set. Using its current segmentation s^i in S, form the set of new segmentation candidates C by (1) joining two segments in s^i, (2) splitting one of the segments in s^i, or (3) moving a segment boundary in s^i one step to the left or right. The set C is illustrated in Figure 2.[4] Then randomly sample a new segmentation c from C.

Next, assign the labels in y_i to the segments of c in the following way. Iteratively, choose the substring $s \in c$ and feature $f \in y_i$ of maximal symmetric conditional probability $P(s|f)P(f|s)$, provided that no features have yet been assigned to s, and f has not been assigned to a substring. When each substring in c has been assigned exactly one label, assign remaining labels to substrings in c which maximize the symmetric conditional probability.

---

[3]This is, of course, not true in general because morphemes often have more than one allomorph. Nevertheless, the number of allomorphs is small for most stems and affixes.

[4]We assume that every non-empty segment has a corresponding morphological feature. Therefore, we filter out segmentations where the number of segments exceeds the number of morphological features y_i for the given word x_i.

(a)	Finnish	Spanish	Swedish
Recall	87.43	84.38	88.71
Precision	94.63	88.63	94.01
F_1-score	**90.89**	**86.45**	**91.28**
Morfessor baseline			
Recall	80.65	81.32	90.82
Precision	76.92	73.64	75.58
F_1-score	78.74	77.29	82.50

(b)	Finnish	Spanish	Swedish
Recall	62.79	50.10	55.87
Precision	71.06	54.22	61.82
F_1-score	**66.67**	**52.08**	**58.69**
Morfessor baseline			
Recall	30.51	25.93	44.13
Precision	28.45	22.24	32.92
F_1-score	29.45	23.94	37.71

(c)	Finnish	Spanish	Swedish
Recall	80.07	73.49	88.26
Precision	90.62	79.54	97.66
F_1-score	**85.02**	**76.39**	**92.73**
Morfessor baseline			
Recall	74.96	48.34	83.10
Precision	69.90	41.47	62.00
F_1-score	72.34	44.64	71.01

Table 2: Results for (a) morpheme boundaries; (b) unlabeled morphemes; (c) labeled morphemes.

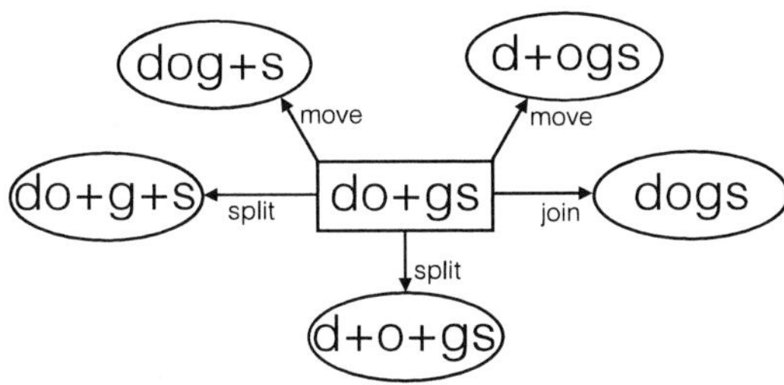

Figure 2: The set of new segmentation candidates for word *dogs* given the old segmentation *do+gs*. Each of the new segmentations is equally probable.

5   Experiments

We conduct experiments by running Gibbs sampling on words and morphological labels in the combined training and test data (without manual segmentations and label assignments). We then compare the segmentations and label assignments, discovered by the system, with the manually prepared annotations in the test data.

5.1   Baseline

As a baseline, we use the Morfessor system (Creutz and Lagus, 2005) for unsupervised segmentation.[5] We then assign labels to substrings as explained in Section 4.3. However, as we cannot control the number of segments given by Morfessor, we may end up with substrings to which we cannot assign morphological features. This happens in the case where the number of substrings given by Morfessor exceeds the number of morphological features for the word.

5.2   Data and Evaluation

We use three treebanks from the Universal Dependency v1.4 resource for experiments: UD-Finnish, UD-Spanish and UD-Swedish. We use the first 10,000 word forms from the training sets of each treebank for training (these contain 5,892 unique word forms for Finnish, 3,624 unique word form for Swedish and 4,092 unique word forms for Spanish) and the first 300 words from the test sets of each treebank for testing (these contain 253 unique word forms for Finnish, 172 unique word forms for Swedish and 278 unique word forms for Spanish). Punctuation and numbers were excluded from the training and test sets.

We remove a number of UD labels which do not express morphological categories, for example style=arch and abbr=yes.[6]

The test sets were manually segmented and morphological features were manually assigned to the segments by competent language speakers. The average number of morphemes per word in the test sets are 1.9 for Finnish, 1.7 for Spanish and 1.4 for Swedish, respectively.

We evaluate our system with regard to recall, precision and F_1-score for (1) morpheme boundaries including word boundaries, (2) unlabeled morphemes, and (3) labeled morphemes. In the case of labeled morphemes, a single substring can be counted multiple times if it has been assigned multiple morphological features. That is, even when the system fails to predict some of the morphological features correctly for a given substring, it will still receive a score for the features it did manage to predict correctly.

5.3   Results

Results are shown in Figures 2 (a), (b), and (c). The advantage given by leveraging the weak labeling in UD is visible in that the proposed system clearly outperforms the unsupervised Morfessor baseline for all languages.

Results for labeled morphemes are substantially

---

[5]We use revision 4219fbcc27ee0f5e3a4dca8de9f7ffc7a5bfe5e0 of https://github.com/aalto-speech/morfessor and default settings for all hyperparameters.

[6]Our data sets and code are publicly available at https://github.com/mpsilfve/ud-segmenter.

better than for unlabeled morphemes because the same substring can be scored as correct multiple times if it is associated to several morphological features. Moreover, the F_1-score for labeled morphemes is computed over both non-empty and empty substrings because morphological features can be realized as a zero morpheme. In contrast, the unlabeled morpheme F_1-score only considers non-empty substrings—i.e. the unlabeled segmentation is not rewarded for declaring empty allomorphs.

Overall, our system performs well on Finnish and Swedish but performance is markedly worse on Spanish—although an error analysis reveals that many of the incorrect segmentations in Spanish are linguistically defensible.

6 Discussion & Future Work

The system is immediately deployable for all UD languages and provides a segmentation and labeling of allomorphs, which may be useful for other downstream tasks. While the segmentation is not linguistically perfect, it is consistent. We also note that in many cases it is not linguistically clear-cut where morpheme boundaries should be drawn. An illustrative example is provided by Spanish verb forms where the infinitive, future, and conditional forms always contain an **-ar**, **-er**, or **-ir** substring, e.g. **habla̲r̲**, **come̲r̲**, **vivi̲r̲**. Traditionally, the verb stem itself is not assumed to include these since, for example, subjunctive and some preterite forms surface without the vowel or the **r**: **hablé**, **comía**, **viva**. From an information-theoretic point of view, it is unclear which stem shape is an appropriate linguistic choice to declare. This is due to the fact that most witnessed forms in the data retain at least the vowel because present indicative forms are quite frequent, e.g. **hablan** (3P-PL) or **hablamos** (1P-PL), etc. Indeed, our algorithm chooses to include the vowel, probably because of the overwhelming frequency of present tense forms.

Our algorithm generally performs quite well on Finnish, however, there are a number of problematic morphological features which cause segmentation errors. For example, plural number for nouns, adjectives and pronouns is a source of errors. In Finnish, plural number in nouns and adjectives is realized by three different affixes **-i-**, **-j-** and **-t**. Pronouns are also marked for number in the UD data set but these affixes are not present in pronouns. Instead, plural number is realized as

the zero morpheme in our gold standard segmentation. This means that there is a large number of different realizations for plural number, which may explain the fact that our system quite often incorrectly assigns plural number to the zero morpheme. Another problem is caused by illative case which is realized as **-Vn** or **-hVn** where **V** refers to the last vowel of the preceding word stem. As in the case of plural number, this leads to a large amount of different realizations for illative case. All of these, nevertheless, share the final suffix **-n**. Therefore, our system often prefers to drop all non-final characters and incorrectly marks illative case as **-n**.

The most frequent error in the Swedish data set is that the definite noun markers (**-en**, **-et**, **-n**) and adjective markers (**-a**) are assigned to the zero morpheme. This may be related to the fact that pronouns, which are quite common in the data set, are marked for definiteness but do not always carry the same affixes as nouns. For example, the Swedish pronoun **dessa** is definite but carries none of the definiteness markers for nouns. This can most likely be addressed by invoking separate models per part of speech so that the model is not confused by similar suffixes occurring with entirely different tags.

The majority of segmentation errors seem stem from the tendency of the SCP scoring to strongly prefer one-to-one correspondences between allomorphs and morphological features. Situations where a morphological feature can be realized by a large number of different allomorphs present problems. At the present time, solving these problems remains future work. To this end, we plan to experiment with different cost functions as the SCP appears to perform best on agglutinative languages where the one-to-one assumption holds stronger than for fusional languages. Likewise, root-and-pattern morphologies, such as found in the Semitic languages, have not been considered here since this would require permitting that allomorphs be discontinuous in a word form. Extending the model to handle such phenomena is straightforward, but requires associating labels with subsequences instead of substrings, which in turn greatly enlarges the search space, and requires efficiency improvements in the sampler to be able to handle large data sets where discontinuous morphemes are present.

References

Ryan Cotterell, Christo Kirov, John Sylak-Glassman, David Yarowsky, Jason Eisner, and Mans Hulden. 2016a. The SIGMORPHON 2016 shared task—morphological reinflection. In *Proceedings of the 14th SIGMORPHON Workshop on Computational Research in Phonetics, Phonology, and Morphology*, pages 10–22, Berlin, Germany, August. Association for Computational Linguistics.

Ryan Cotterell, Tim Vieira, and Hinrich Schütze. 2016b. A joint model of orthography and morphological segmentation. In *Proceedings of the 2016 Conference of the North American Chapter of the Association for Computational Linguistics: Human Language Technologies*, pages 664–669, San Diego, California, June. Association for Computational Linguistics.

Mathias Creutz and Krista Lagus. 2005. Unsupervised morpheme segmentation and morphology induction from text corpora using Morfessor 1.0. Technical Report A81, Helsinki University of Technology.

Joaquim Ferreira da Silva, Gaël Dias, Sylvie Guilloré, and José Gabriel Pereira Lopes. 1999. Using Local-Maxs algorithm for the extraction of contiguous and non-contiguous multiword lexical units. In *Progress in Artificial Intelligence: 9th Portuguese Conference on Artificial Intelligence, EPIA '99 Évora, Portugal, September 21–24, 1999 Proceedings*, pages 113–132. Springer Berlin Heidelberg, Berlin, Heidelberg.

Sajib Dasgupta and Vincent Ng. 2007. High-performance, language-independent morphological segmentation. In *Human Language Technologies 2007: The Conference of the North American Chapter of the Association for Computational Linguistics; Proceedings of the Main Conference*, pages 155–163, Rochester, New York, April. Association for Computational Linguistics.

Markus Dreyer and Jason Eisner. 2011. Discovering morphological paradigms from plain text using a Dirichlet process mixture model. In *Proceedings of EMNLP 2011*, pages 616–627, Edinburgh. Association for Computational Linguistics.

John Goldsmith. 2001. Unsupervised learning of the morphology of a natural language. *Computational linguistics*, 27(2):153–198.

Sharon Goldwater and Tom Griffiths. 2007. A fully Bayesian approach to unsupervised part-of-speech tagging. In *Proceedings of the 45th Annual Meeting of the Association of Computational Linguistics*, pages 744–751, Prague, Czech Republic, June. Association for Computational Linguistics.

Stig-Arne Grönroos, Sami Virpioja, Peter Smit, and Mikko Kurimo. 2014. Morfessor FlatCat: An HMM-based method for unsupervised and semi-supervised learning of morphology. In *Proceedings of COLING 2014, the 25th International Conference on Computational Linguistics*, pages 1177–1185, Dublin, Ireland, August. Dublin City University and Association for Computational Linguistics.

Katharina Kann, Ryan Cotterell, and Hinrich Schütze. 2016. Neural morphological analysis: Encoding-decoding canonical segments. In *Proceedings of the 2016 Conference on Empirical Methods in Natural Language Processing*, pages 961–967, Austin, Texas, November. Association for Computational Linguistics.

Oskar Kohonen, Sami Virpioja, and Krista Lagus. 2010. Semi-supervised learning of concatenative morphology. In *Proceedings of the 11th Meeting of the ACL Special Interest Group on Computational Morphology and Phonology (SIGMORPHON)*, pages 78–86. Association for Computational Linguistics.

Joakim Nivre, Željko Agić, Lars Ahrenberg, Maria Jesus Aranzabe, Masayuki Asahara, Aitziber Atutxa, et al. 2017. Universal dependencies 2.0. LINDAT/CLARIN digital library at the Institute of Formal and Applied Linguistics, Charles University in Prague.

Hoifung Poon, Colin Cherry, and Kristina Toutanova. 2009. Unsupervised morphological segmentation with log-linear models. In *Proceedings of Human Language Technologies: The 2009 Annual Conference of the North American Chapter of the Association for Computational Linguistics*, pages 209–217. Association for Computational Linguistics.

Teemu Ruokolainen, Oskar Kohonen, Kairit Sirts, Stig-Arne Grönroos, Mikko Kurimo, and Sami Virpioja. 2016. A comparative study of minimally supervised morphological segmentation. *Computational Linguistics*, 42(1):91–120.

Patrick Schone and Daniel Jurafsky. 2000. Knowledge-free induction of morphology using latent semantic analysis. In *Proceedings of the 2nd workshop on Learning language in logic and the 4th conference on Computational natural language learning*, pages 67–72. Association for Computational Linguistics.

Kairit Sirts and Sharon Goldwater. 2013. Minimally-supervised morphological segmentation using adaptor grammars. *Transactions of the Association for Computational Linguistics*, 1:255–266.

Radu Soricut and Franz Och. 2015. Unsupervised morphology induction using word embeddings. In *Proceedings of the 2015 Conference of the North American Chapter of the Association for Computational Linguistics: Human Language Technologies*, pages 1627–1637, Denver, Colorado, May–June. Association for Computational Linguistics.

A Systematic Comparison of Syntactic Representations of Dependency Parsing

Guillaume Wisniewski
LIMSI, CNRS, Univ. Paris-Sud
Université Paris-Saclay
91 405 Orsay, France
guillaume.wisniewski@limsi.fr

Ophélie Lacroix
DIKU, University of Copenhagen
University Park 5
2100 Copenhagen
lacroix@di.ku.dk

Abstract

We compare the performance of a transition-based parser in regards to different annotation schemes. We propose to convert some specific syntactic constructions observed in the universal dependency treebanks into a so-called more standard representation and to evaluate parsing performances over all the languages of the project. We show that the "standard" constructions do not lead systematically to better parsing performance and that the scores vary considerably according to the languages.

1 Introduction

Many treebanks have been developed for dependency parsing, following different annotations conventions. The divergence between the guidelines can results from both the theoretical linguistic principles governing the choices of head status and dependency inventories or to improve the performance of down-stream applications (Elming et al., 2013). Therefore it is difficult to compare parsing performance across languages or even across the different corpora of a single language.

Two projects of unified treebanks have recently emerged: the HamleDT (Zeman et al., 2014) and the Universal Dependency Treebank (UDT) (McDonald et al., 2013). They aim at harmonizing annotation schemes (at the level of PoS-tags and dependencies) between languages by converting existing treebanks to the new scheme. These works have led to the creation of the Universal Dependencies (UD) project (Nivre et al., 2016) that gathers treebanks for more than 45 languages (v1.3).

The UD annotation scheme has been designed to facilitate the transfer of annotations across languages: similar syntactic relations are represented by similar syntactic structures in different languages, and relations tend to hold between content

words rather than through function words. However, (Schwartz et al., 2012) showed that, for English, some of the choices made to increase the sharing of structures between languages actually hurts parsing performance. Since then the UD scheme has been hypothesized to be sub-optimal for (monolingual) parsing.

In this work, we propose to systematically compare the parsing performance of alternative syntactic representations over all the languages of the UD project. We design a set of rules[1] to automatically modify the representation of several syntactic constructions of the UD to alternative representations proposed in the literature (§ 3) and evaluate whether these transformations improve parsing performance or not (§ 4). Further we try to relate the choice of the syntactic representation to different measure of *learnability* to see if it is possible to predict which representation will achieve the best parsing performance.

2 Related Work

Since (Nilsson et al., 2006) many works have shown that well-chosen transformations of syntactic representations can greatly improve the parsing accuracy achieved by dependency parsers. (Schwartz et al., 2012) shows that "selecting one representation over another may affect parsing performance". Focusing on English, they compare parsing performance through several alternatives and conclude that parsers prefer attachment via function word over content-word attachments. They argue that the *learnability* of a representation, estimated by the accuracy within this representation is a good criterion for selecting a syntactic representation among alternatives.

More recently, (de Lhoneux and Nivre, 2016)

---

[1]Source code to transform between the various dependency structures we consider can be downloaded from https://perso.limsi.fr/wisniews/recherche/
#dependency-transformations

Proceedings of the NoDaLiDa 2017 Workshop on Universal Dependencies (UDW 2017), pages 146–152,
Gothenburg, Sweden, 22 May 2017.

studies the representation of verbal constructions to see if parsing works better when auxiliaries are the head of auxiliary dependency relations, which is not the case in UD. They highlight that the parsing benefits from the disambiguation of PoS tags for main verbs and auxiliaries in UD PoS tagset even if the overall parsing accuracy decreases.

To the best of our knowledge, (Rosa, 2015) is the only work to study the impact of the annotation scheme on the performance of transferred parsers. It compares the Prague annotation style used in the HamleDT (Zeman et al., 2014) with the Stanford style (De Marneffe and Manning, 2008) that has inspired the UD guidelines and shows that Prague style results in better parsing performance. Nevertheless — with a particular focus on the adposition attachment case — the Stanford style is advantageous for delexicalized parsing transfer.

Finally, (Silveira and Manning, 2015) performs an analysis very similar to ours and find that, for English, UD is a good parsing representation. More recently, (Kohita et al., 2017) shows that it is possible to improve parsing performance for a wide array of language by converting the dependency structure back-and-forth.

3 Conversion

We consider several alternatives to the UD annotation scheme. Most have been proposed by (Schwartz et al., 2012) or have been discussed when defining annotations of the UD (e.g. when abandoning the so-called "standard" scheme of the UDT for the content-head scheme now used in the UD). The transformations are summarized in the upper part of Table 1. We omit the transformation of verb groups that is already analyzed in detail in (de Lhoneux and Nivre, 2016). In contrast to most works analyzing the impact of annotation conventions, the alternative representations we consider are defined by selecting dependencies according to their label and transforming them rather than by modifying the tree-to-dependency conversion scheme. It is therefore possible to apply them to any language of the UD initiative.

3.1 From Simple Conversions...

The syntactic relations that we transform are mostly represented with only one dependency which can be identified by its label. In this case the conversion simply consists in inverting the role of the tokens involved in the main dependency rep-

resenting the syntactic relation: the dependent becomes the head and the head becomes the dependent. Given an original dependency $w_i \curvearrowright w_j$ in which w_i is the head (i.e. w_i receive a dependency from another word w_h): *i)* the dependency is replaced by $w_i \curvearrowleft w_j$, *ii)* the former head of w_i, named w_h, become the new head of w_j. These transformations applies to relations such as the clause subordinates (`mark`), the determiners (`det`) or the case markings (`case`).

3.2 ...to Non-Projectivity...

However, more than two tokens are frequently involved in the sub-structure carried by the dependency in question. In that case, the conversion may create non-projective dependencies (i.e. crossing between dependencies). Figure 1 illustrates this problem. Let $w_i \curvearrowright w_j$ be the original dependency we want to invert, w_i being the head and w_j the dependent. If the head w_i has a child w_k, i.e. there is a w_k such as $w_i \curvearrowright w_k$, and the tokens are ordered such as k<j<i or i<j<k then a crossing between the dependencies[2] will appear when inverting the role of w_i and w_j. To avoid introducing a non-projectivity, it is necessary to attach the former child w_k of w_i to w_j.

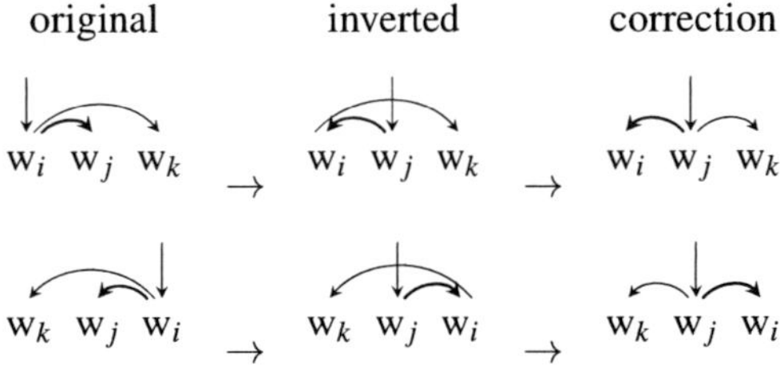

Figure 1: Cases of non-projectivity caused by conversion, and correction. The main (bold) dependency $w_i \curvearrowright w_j$ is the one to invert. When inverting, w_j becomes the root of the sub-structure.

3.3 ... and Particular Cases

Noun Sequences For noun sequences (`mwe`, `name` and `goeswith`), we systematically consider the first word of the sequence as the head, and, when the sequence contains several words, attach each word to its preceding word, while, in UD guidelines, noun sequences are annotated in a flat, head-initial structure, in which all words in the name modify the first one (see Figure 3.3).

---

[2]A crossing generally appears between the dependency going from w_i to his child w_k and the root dependency, now

Syntactic Functions		Annotation Scheme	
	UD relations	UD	Alternative
Clause subordinates	mark	to read	to read
Determiners	det	the book	the book
Noun sequences	mwe+goeswith, name	John Jr. Doe	John Jr. Doe
Case marking	case	of Earth	of Earth
Coordinations	cc+conj	me and you	me and you
Copulas	cop+auxpass	is nice	is nice
Verb groups	root+aux	have been done	have been done

Table 1: Annotation scheme in the UD treebanks and standard alternatives.

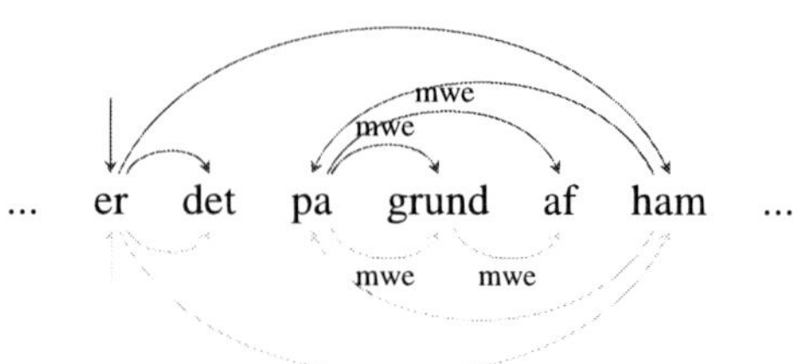

Figure 2: Multi-word expression conversion for the danish phrase 'it is because of him'. The dependencies following the UD conventions are represented in blue above the words; the alternative structure is represented in green below the words.

Copulas In copula constructions (cop and auxpass dependencies), the head of the dependency is generally the root of the sentence (or of a subordinate clause). The transformation of a copula dependency $w_i \curvearrowright w_j$ between the the i-th and j-th word of the sentence consists in inverting the dependency (as for mark and case), making w_j the root of the sentence and attaching all words that were modifying w_i to w_j with a dependency not related to nouns such as det, amod, or nmod. The last step allows us to ensure the coherence of the annotations (with respect, for instance, to the final punctuation).

Coordinations For coordinating structures (cc and conj dependencies), in the UD scheme, the first conjunct[3] is taken as the head of the coordina-

tion and all the other conjuncts depend on it via the conj relation, and each coordinating conjunction[4] is attached to the first conjunct with a cc relation.[5] As an alternative, we define the first coordinating conjunction as the head and attach all conjuncts to it (see Figure 3).

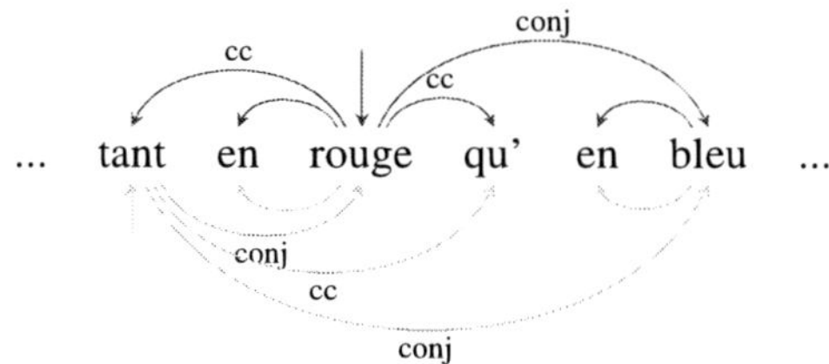

Figure 3: Coordination conversion for the French phrase 'as well in red as in blue'. The dependencies following the UD conventions are represented in blue above the words; the alternative structure is represented in green below the words.

4 Experimental Settings

To evaluate the proposed transformations, we follow the approach introduced in (Schwartz et al., 2012) consisting in comparing the original and the transformed data on their respective references.

4.1 Data

We experiment on data from the v1.3 of the Universal Dependency project (Nivre et al., 2016), using the official split into train, validation and test sets. We apply separately the 7 transformations described in Section 3 on the 38 languages of the

---

arriving on w_j, i.e. coming from the former head of w_i.

[3] Typically a noun for instance (but could also be a verb or an adjective) for which the incoming dependency could be labeled with dobj, root, amod, etc.

[4] Often PoS-tagged with a CONJ such as *and*, *or*, etc.

[5] Recall that we are considering the version 1 guidelines; the definition of the cc relation has changed in version 2.

UD, resulting in the creation of 266 transformed corpora, 44 of which were identical to the original corpora as the transformation can not be applied (e.g. there are no multi-word expressions in Chinese). These corpora are not included in the different statistics presented in this Section.

For each configuration (i.e. a language and a transformation), a dependency parser is trained on the original data annotated with UD convention (denoted UD) and the transformed data (denoted `transformed`). Parsing performance is estimated using the usual Unlabeled Attachment Score (UAS, excluding punctuation). Reported scores are averaged over three trainings.

4.2 Parser

We use our own implementation of the arc-eager dependency parser with a dynamic oracle and an averaged perceptron (Aufrant and Wisniewski, 2016), using the features described in (Zhang and Nivre, 2011) which have been designed for English. Preliminary experiments show that similar results are achieved with other implementation of transition-based parsers (namely with the Malt-Parser (Nivre, 2003)).

5 Results

Figure 4 shows the distribution of differences in UAS between a parser trained on the original data and a parser trained on the transformed data (positive differences indicates corpora for which the UD annotation scheme results in better predictions). As expected, the annotation scheme has a large impact on the quality of the prediction, with an average difference in scores of 0.66 UAS points and variations as large as 8.1 UAS points.

However, contrary to what is usually believed, the UD scheme appears to achieve, in most cases, better prediction performance than the proposed transformations: in 58.1% of the configurations, the parser trained and evaluated on transformed data is outperformed by the parser trained on the original UD data. More precisely, the difference in UAS is negative in 93 configurations and positive in 129 configurations. Table 2 details for each transformation the percentage of languages for which the UD scheme results in better predictions. The `cc` dependency (conjunction), and to a lesser extent the `det` dependency, are easier to learn in the UD scheme than in the proposed transformed scheme. On the contrary, the choice of the `cop` and `name` structure in the UD results in large losses for many languages. For the other variations considered, the learnability of the scheme highly depends on the language. Table 3 shows the configurations with the largest positive and negative differences in scores.

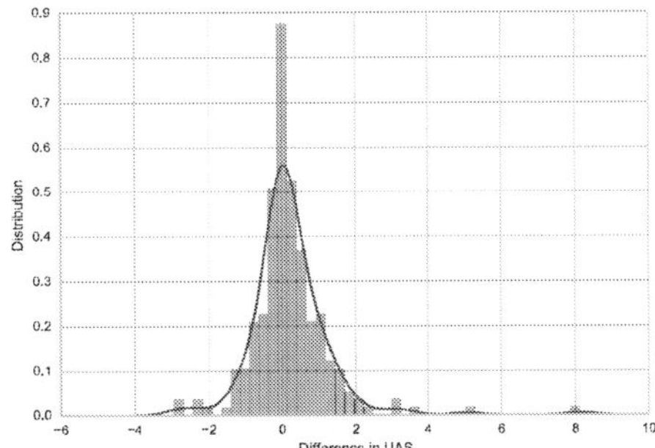

Figure 4: Distribution of differences between the UAS achieved on the UD and transformed corpora for the different languages and transformations considered. Positive differences indicates better results with UD annotations.

case	44.74%	mark	58.33%	det	80.56%
cc	89.47%	mwe	50.00%	name	45.83%
cop	25.00%				

Table 2: Number of times, for each transformation, a parser trained and evaluated on UD data outperforms a parser trained and evaluated on transformed data.

Lang.	Transfo.	UAS(trans.)	UAS(UD)
la	conjunction	52.57%	**60.69%**
gl	case	72.17%	**77.21%**
ar	conjunction	72.35%	**75.83%**
kk	case	56.62%	**59.67%**
zh	mark	66.67%	**69.65%**
nl	copule	**69.82%**	67.73%
fi	copule	**66.59%**	64.30%
et	copule	**70.38%**	67.95%
la	copule	**59.34%**	56.47%
sl	copule	**79.69%**	76.75%

Table 3: Languages and transformations with the highest UAS difference.

Analysis To understand the empirical preferences of annotation schemes we consider several measures of the 'learnability' and 'complexity' of a treebank:

metric	
distance	43.6%
predictability	64.8%
derivation complexity	62.6%
derivation perplexity	61.2%

Table 4: Number of times a given learnability measure is able to predict which annotation scheme will result in the best parsing performance.

- the average absolute *distance* (in words) between a dependent and its head; because transition-based dependency parsers are known to favor short dependencies over long ones (McDonald and Nivre, 2007);

- the *predictability* of the scheme introduced by (Schwartz et al., 2012) defined as the entropy of the conditional distribution of the PoS of the dependent knowing the PoS of its head;

- the *derivation perplexity* introduced by (Søgaard and Haulrich, 2010) defined as the perplexity of 3-gram language model estimated on a corpus in which words of a sentence appear in the order in which they are attached to their head;[6]

- the *derivation complexity* defined as the sum of the number of distinct substrings in the gold derivations of the corpora references.

The first three metrics have been used in several studies on the learnability of dependencies annotations. We introduce the last one as a new way to characterize the difficulty of predicting a sequence of actions, building on the intuition that the more diverse a derivation, the harder its prediction. For this metric, the gold derivation is the concatenation of arc-eager actions representing the sequence of actions generating a reference tree. In case of ambiguity in the generation of the reference tree, we always select the actions in the following order: SHIFT, REDUCE, LEFT, RIGHT. Using a generalized suffix tree it is then possible to count the number of different substrings in the derivations with a complexity in $\mathcal{O}(n)$ (Gusfield, 1997).

---

[6]Similarly to (Søgaard and Haulrich, 2010) we consider a trigram language model but use a Witten-Bell smoothing as many corpora were too small to use a Knesser-Ney smoothing. As for the derivation complexity, the words are ordered according to an oracle prediction of the reference structure.

A metric is said *coherent* if it scores the syntactic structure that achieves the best parsing performance higher than its variation. Table 4 reports the numbers of times, averaged over languages and transformations, that each metric is coherent.

Contrarily to what has been previously reported, the considered metrics are hardly able to predict which annotation scheme will result in the best parsing performance. Several reasons can explain this result. First, it is the first time, to the best of our knowledge that these metrics are compared on such a wide array of languages. It is possible that these metrics are not as language-independent as can be expected. Second, as our transformations are directly applied on the dependency structures rather than when converting the dependency structure from a constituency structure, it is possible that some of their transformations are erroneous and the resulting complexity metric biased.

6 Conclusion

Comparing the performance of parsers trained and evaluated on UD data and transformed data, it appears that the UD scheme leads mainly to better scores and that measures of learnability and complexity are not sufficient to explain the annotation preferences of dependency parsers.

7 Acknowledgement

Ophélie Lacroix is funded by the ERC Starting Grant LOWLANDS No. 313695.

References

Lauriane Aufrant and Guillaume Wisniewski. 2016. PanParser: a Modular Implementation for Efficient Transition-Based Dependency Parsing. Technical report, LIMSI-CNRS, March.

Miryam de Lhoneux and Joakim Nivre. 2016. Should have, would have, could have. investigating verb group representations for parsing with universal dependencies. In *Proceedings of the Workshop on Multilingual and Cross-lingual Methods in NLP*, pages 10–19, San Diego, California, June. Association for Computational Linguistics.

Marie-Catherine De Marneffe and Christopher D Manning. 2008. The stanford typed dependencies representation. In *Proceedings of the workshop on Cross-Framework and Cross-Domain Parser Evaluation*, pages 1–8. Association for Computational Linguistics.

Jakob Elming, Anders Johannsen, Sigrid Klerke, Emanuele Lapponi, Hector Martinez Alonso, and

Anders Søgaard. 2013. Down-stream effects of tree-to-dependency conversions. In *Proceedings of the 2013 Conference of the North American Chapter of the Association for Computational Linguistics: Human Language Technologies*, pages 617–626, Atlanta, Georgia, June. Association for Computational Linguistics.

Dan Gusfield. 1997. *Algorithms on Strings, Trees, and Sequences: Computer Science and Computational Biology*. Cambridge University Press, New York, NY, USA.

Ryosuke Kohita, Hiroshi Noji, and Yuji Matsumoto. 2017. Multilingual back-and-forth conversion between content and function head for easy dependency parsing. In *Proceedings of the 15th Conference of the European Chapter of the Association for Computational Linguistics: Volume 2, Short Papers*, pages 1–7, Valencia, Spain, April. Association for Computational Linguistics.

Ryan McDonald and Joakim Nivre. 2007. Characterizing the errors of data-driven dependency parsing models. In *Proceedings of the 2007 Joint Conference on Empirical Methods in Natural Language Processing and Computational Natural Language Learning (EMNLP-CoNLL)*, pages 122–131, Prague, Czech Republic, June. Association for Computational Linguistics.

Ryan McDonald, Joakim Nivre, Yvonne Quirmbach-Brundage, Yoav Goldberg, Dipanjan Das, Kuzman Ganchev, Keith Hall, Slav Petrov, Hao Zhang, Oscar Täckström, Claudia Bedini, Núria Bertomeu Castelló, and Jungmee Lee. 2013. Universal Dependency Annotation for Multilingual Parsing. In *Proceedings of ACL 2013, the 51st Annual Meeting of the Association for Computational Linguistics (Volume 2: Short Papers)*, pages 92–97, Sofia, Bulgaria, August.

Jens Nilsson, Joakim Nivre, and Johan Hall. 2006. Graph transformations in data-driven dependency parsing. In *Proceedings of the 21st International Conference on Computational Linguistics and 44th Annual Meeting of the Association for Computational Linguistics*, pages 257–264, Sydney, Australia, July. Association for Computational Linguistics.

Joakim Nivre, Željko Agić, Lars Ahrenberg, Maria Jesus Aranzabe, Masayuki Asahara, Aitziber Atutxa, Miguel Ballesteros, John Bauer, Kepa Bengoetxea, Yevgeni Berzak, Riyaz Ahmad Bhat, Cristina Bosco, Gosse Bouma, Sam Bowman, Gülşen Cebirolu Eryiit, Giuseppe G. A. Celano, Çar Çöltekin, Miriam Connor, Marie-Catherine de Marneffe, Arantza Diaz de Ilarraza, Kaja Dobrovoljc, Timothy Dozat, Kira Droganova, Tomaž Erjavec, Richárd Farkas, Jennifer Foster, Daniel Galbraith, Sebastian Garza, Filip Ginter, Iakes Goenaga, Koldo Gojenola, Memduh Gokirmak, Yoav Goldberg, Xavier Gómez Guinovart, Berta Gonzáles Saavedra, Normunds Grūzītis, Bruno Guillaume, Jan Hajič, Dag Haug, Barbora Hladká, Radu Ion, Elena Irimia, Anders Johannsen, Hüner Kaşkara, Hiroshi Kanayama, Jenna Kanerva, Boris Katz, Jessica Kenney, Simon Krek, Veronika Laippala, Lucia Lam, Alessandro Lenci, Nikola Ljubešić, Olga Lyashevskaya, Teresa Lynn, Aibek Makazhanov, Christopher Manning, Cătălina Mărănduc, David Mareček, Héctor Martínez Alonso, Jan Mašek, Yuji Matsumoto, Ryan McDonald, Anna Missilä, Verginica Mititelu, Yusuke Miyao, Simonetta Montemagni, Keiko Sophie Mori, Shunsuke Mori, Kadri Muischnek, Nina Mustafina, Kaili Müürisep, Vitaly Nikolaev, Hanna Nurmi, Petya Osenova, Lilja Øvrelid, Elena Pascual, Marco Passarotti, Cenel-Augusto Perez, Slav Petrov, Jussi Piitulainen, Barbara Plank, Martin Popel, Lauma Pretkalnia, Prokopis Prokopidis, Tiina Puolakainen, Sampo Pyysalo, Loganathan Ramasamy, Laura Rituma, Rudolf Rosa, Shadi Saleh, Baiba Saulīte, Sebastian Schuster, Wolfgang Seeker, Mojgan Seraji, Lena Shakurova, Mo Shen, Natalia Silveira, Maria Simi, Radu Simionescu, Katalin Simkó, Kiril Simov, Aaron Smith, Carolyn Spadine, Alane Suhr, Umut Sulubacak, Zsolt Szántó, Takaaki Tanaka, Reut Tsarfaty, Francis Tyers, Sumire Uematsu, Larraitz Uria, Gertjan van Noord, Viktor Varga, Veronika Vincze, Jing Xian Wang, Jonathan North Washington, Zdeněk Žabokrtský, Daniel Zeman, and Hanzhi Zhu. 2016. Universal dependencies 1.3. LINDAT/CLARIN digital library at Institute of Formal and Applied Linguistics, Charles University in Prague.

Joakim Nivre. 2003. An Efficient Algorithm for Projective Dependency Parsing. In *Proceedings of IWPT 2003, the 8th International Workshop on Parsing Technologies*, Nancy, France.

Rudolf Rosa, 2015. *Proceedings of the Third International Conference on Dependency Linguistics (Depling 2015)*, chapter Multi-source Cross-lingual Delexicalized Parser Transfer: Prague or Stanford?, pages 281–290. Uppsala University, Uppsala, Sweden.

Roy Schwartz, Omri Abend, and Ari Rappoport. 2012. Learnability-based syntactic annotation design. In *Proceedings of COLING 2012*, pages 2405–2422, Mumbai, India, December. The COLING 2012 Organizing Committee.

Natalia Silveira and Christopher Manning. 2015. Does universal dependencies need a parsing representation? an investigation of english. *Depling 2015*, 310.

Anders Søgaard and Martin Haulrich. 2010. On the derivation perplexity of treebanks. In *Proceedings of Treebanks and Linguistic Theories 9*.

Daniel Zeman, Ondřej Dušek, David Mareček, Martin Popel, Loganathan Ramasamy, Jan Štěpánek, Zdeněk Žabokrtskỳ, and Jan Hajič. 2014. Hamledt: Harmonized multi-language dependency treebank. *Language Resources and Evaluation*, 48(4):601–637.

Yue Zhang and Joakim Nivre. 2011. Transition-based Dependency Parsing with Rich Non-local Features. In *Proceedings of ACL 2011, the 49th Annual Meeting of the Association for Computational Linguistics: Human Language Technologies*, pages 188–193, Portland, Oregon, USA, June. Association for Computational Linguistics.

Author Index

Association for Computational Linguistics
209 N. Eighth Street
Stroudsburg, Pennsylvania 18360

ISBN 978-1-5108-4169-7